2013
青岛统计年鉴

QINGDAO STATISTICAL YEARBOOK

（总 第34期 VOL.34）

青 岛 市 统 计 局
国家统计局青岛调查队 编
QINGDAO MUNICIPAL STATISTICS BUREAU
NBS SURVEY OFFICE IN QINGDAO

中国统计出版社
China Statistics Press

（京）新登字041号

图书在版编目(CIP)数据

青岛统计年鉴. 2013 /青岛市统计局, 国家统计局青岛调查队编. -- 北京 : 中国统计出版社, 2013.7
ISBN 978-7-5037-6862-0

Ⅰ. ①青… Ⅱ. ①青… ②国… Ⅲ. ①统计资料－青岛市－2013－年鉴 Ⅳ. ①C832.523-54

中国版本图书馆CIP数据核字(2013)第154177号

青岛统计年鉴-2013

作　　者/ 青岛市统计局 国家统计局青岛调查队
责任编辑/ 陈越月
封面设计/ 青岛天之韵广告文化传播有限公司
出版发行/ 中国统计出版社
通信地址/ 北京市西城区月坛南街57号
邮政编码/ 100826
办公地址/ 北京市丰台区西三环南路甲6号
邮政编码/ 100073
电　　话/ 邮购（010）63376909　书店（010）68783171
网　　址/ http://csp.stats.gov.cn
印　　刷/ 青岛星球印刷有限公司
经　　销/ 新华书店
开　　本/ 880x1230毫米 1/16
字　　数/ 1113千字
印　　张/ 25.5
版　　别/ 2013年7月第 1 版
版　　次/ 2013年7月第 1 次印刷
定　　价/ 280.00元

如有印装差错，由本社发行部调换。

全市生产总值构成（%）

Composition Of Gross Domestic Product（%）

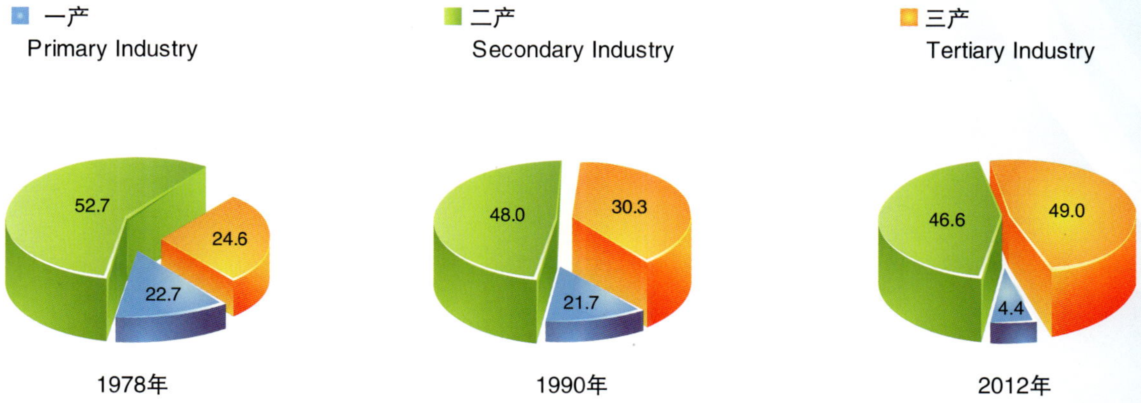

全市生产总值（亿元）

Gross Domestic Product (100 million yuan)

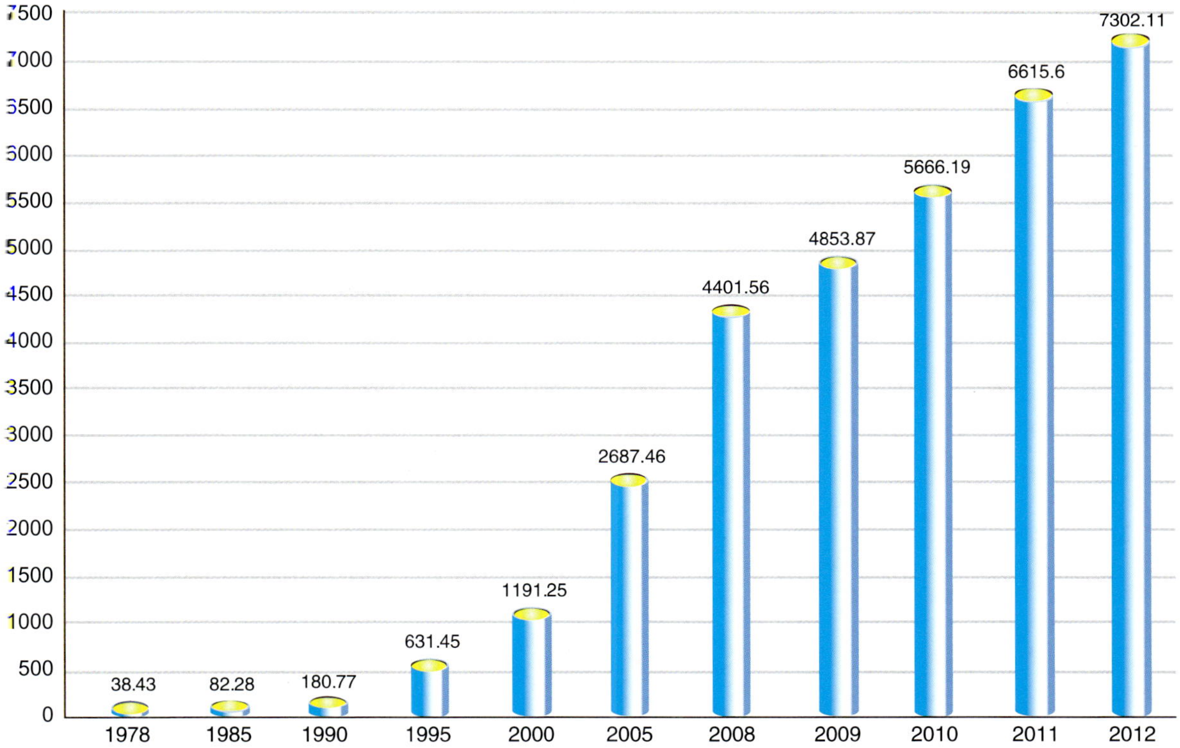

农林牧渔业总产值（亿元）
Gross Output Value Of Agriculture (100 million yuan)

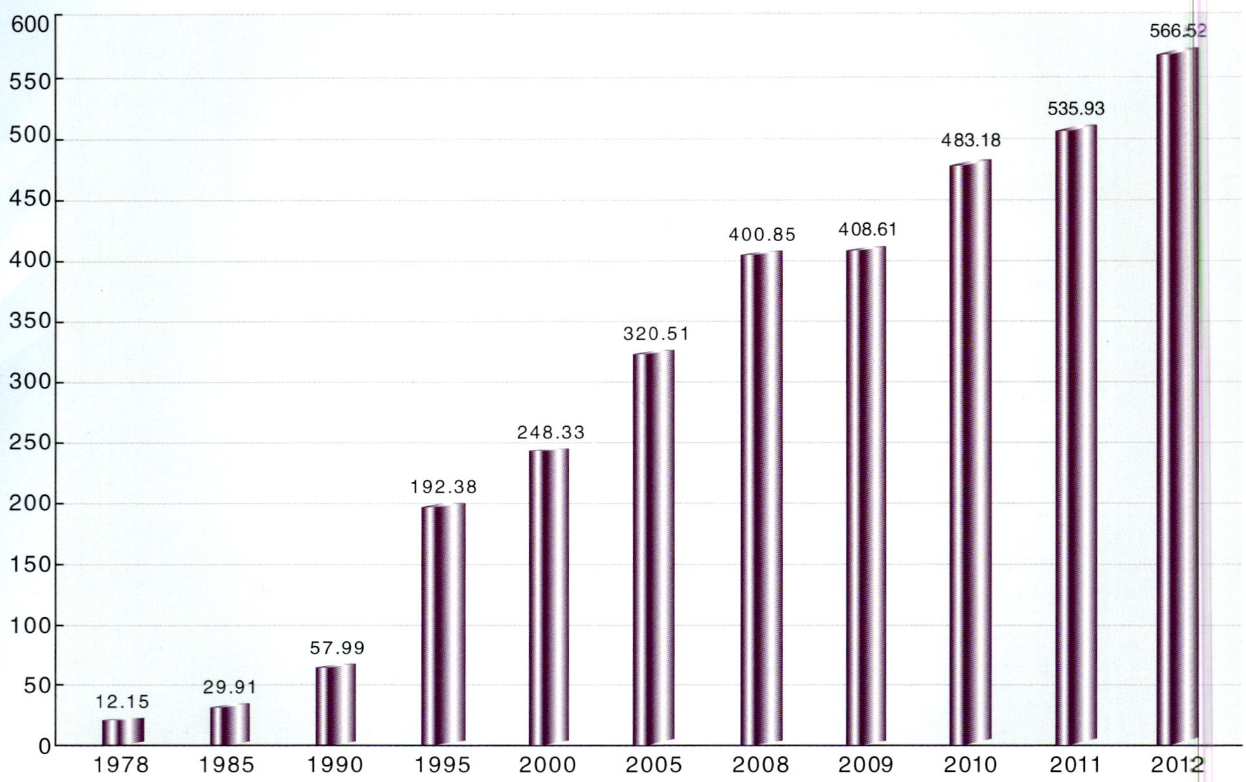

主要农产品产量（万吨）
Output Of Farm Products (10000 tons)

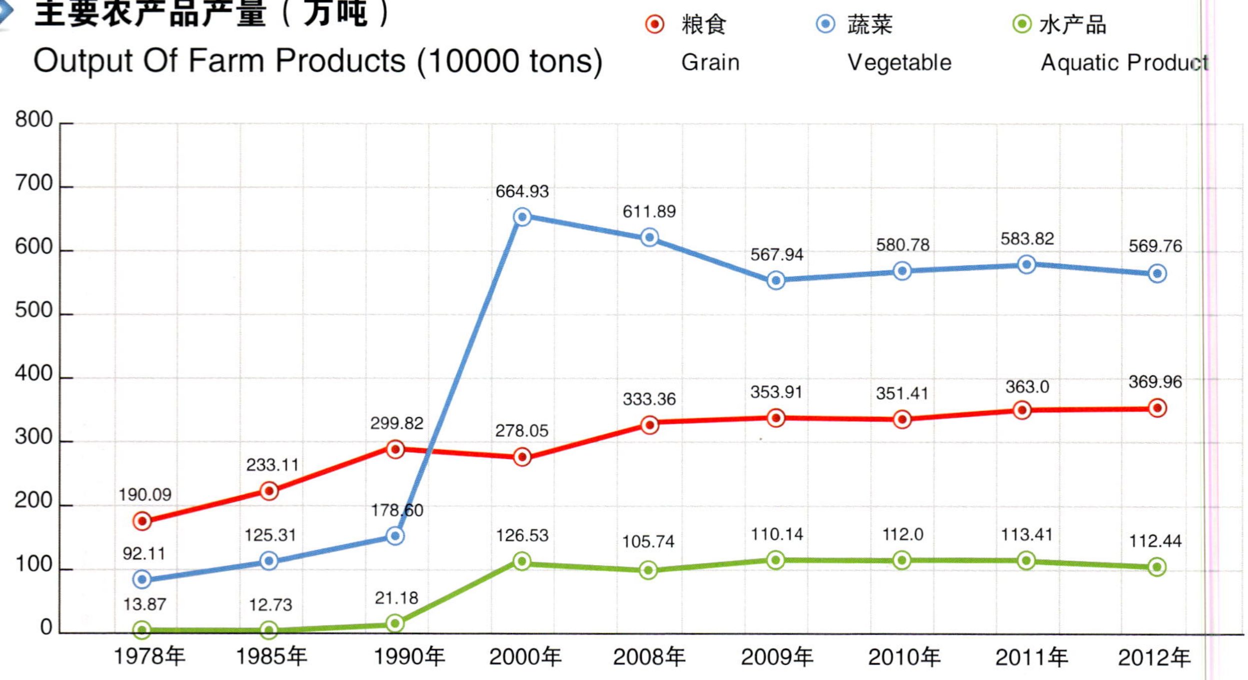

工业总产值（亿元）

Gross Industrial Output Value (100 million yuan)

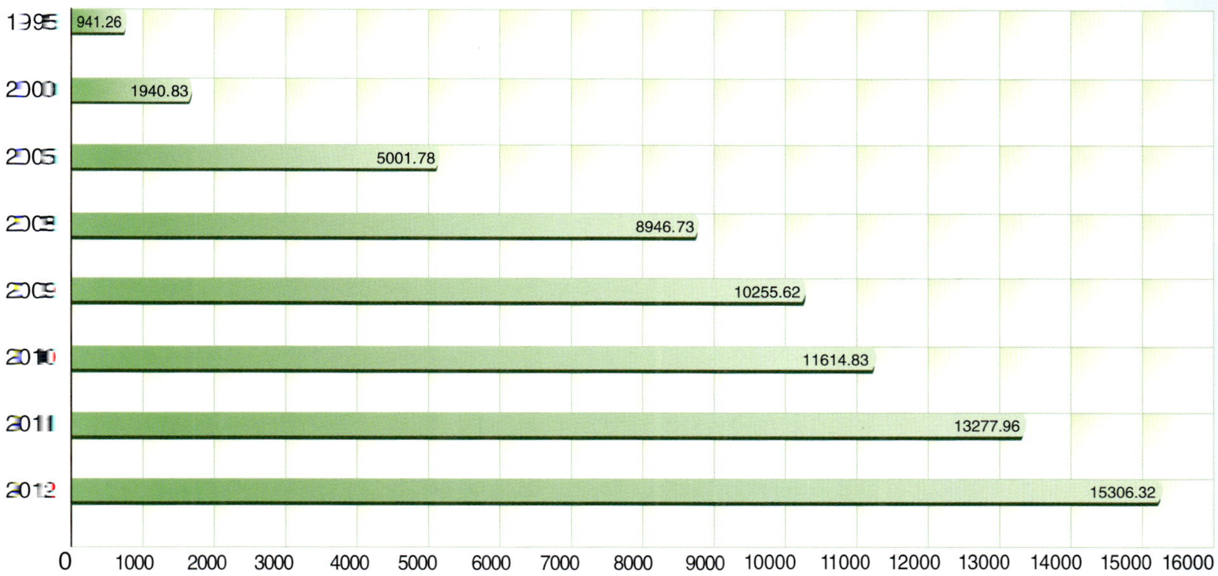

规模以上工业实现利税总额（亿元）

Total Profits And Taxes Of Industry Above Designated Size (100 million yuan)

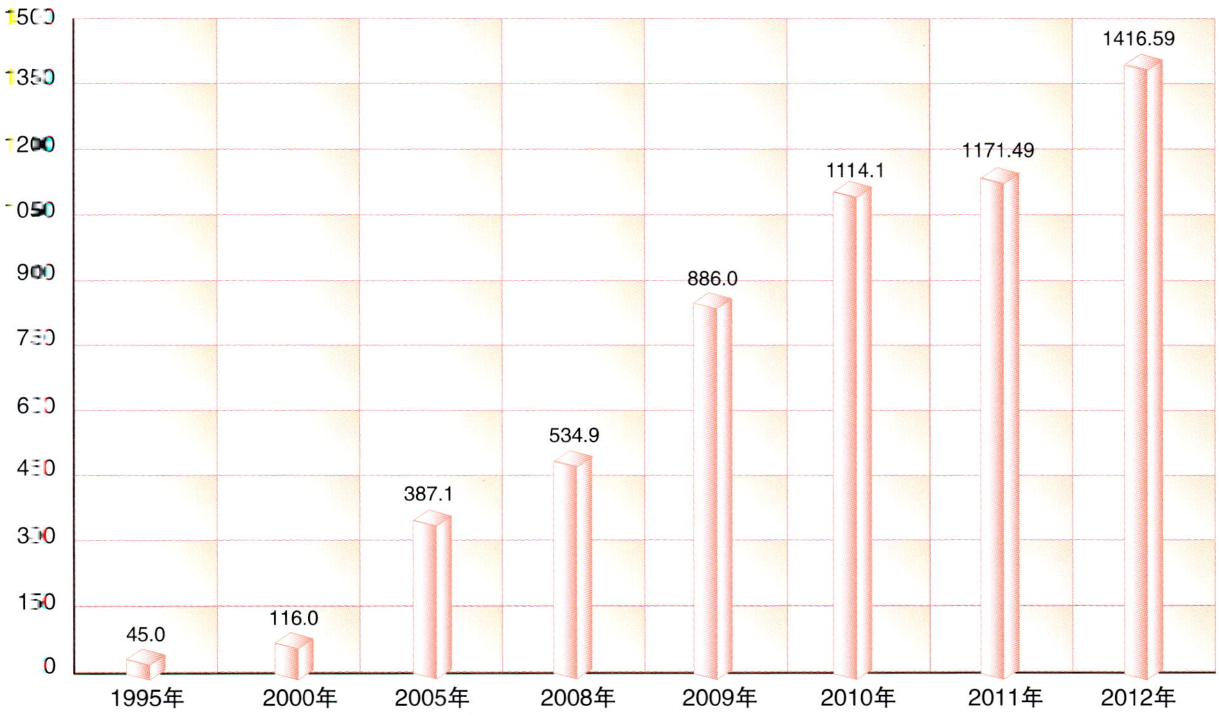

投 资
INVESTMENT

规模以上固定资产投资（亿元）
Investment In Fixed Assets Above Designated Size (100 million yuan)

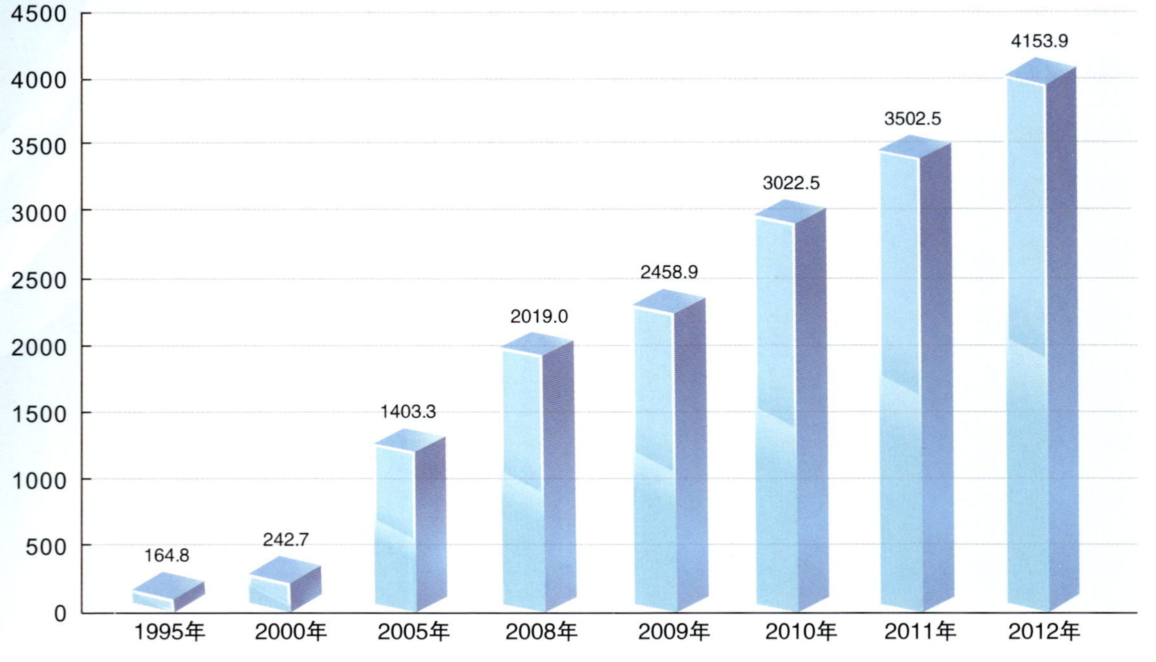

房屋竣工面积、住宅竣工面积（万平方米）
Floor Space Of Buildings Completed， Floor Space Of Residential Buildings Completed(10000 sq.m)

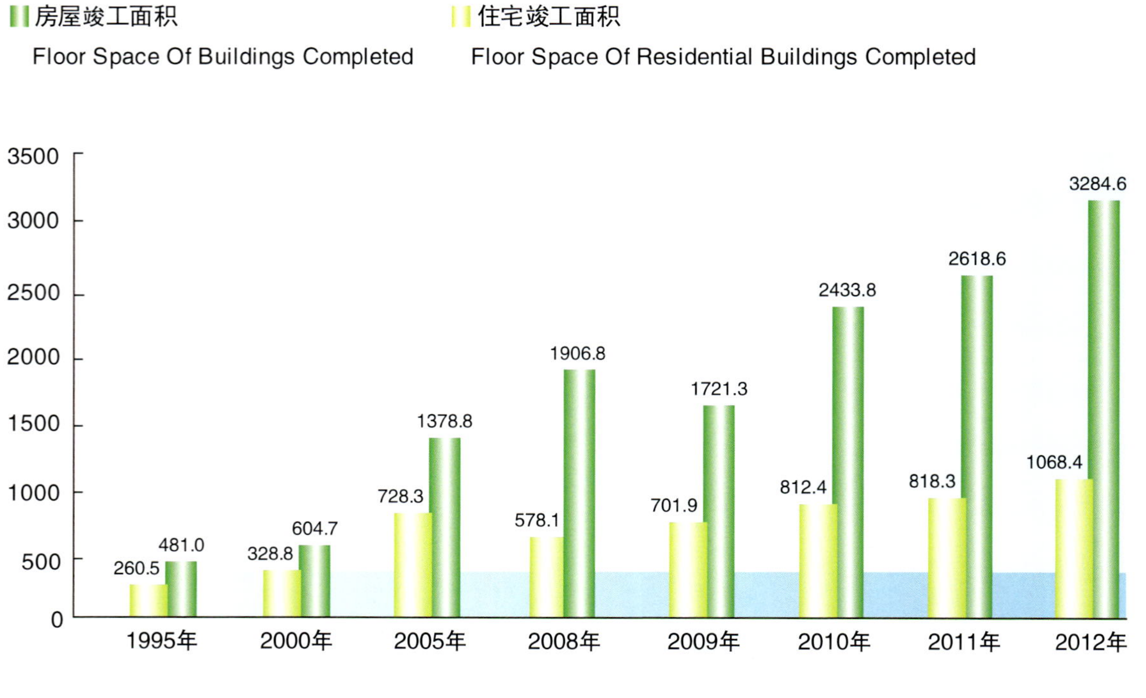

消费构成（%）(2012年)

2012 Composition Of Consumption (%)

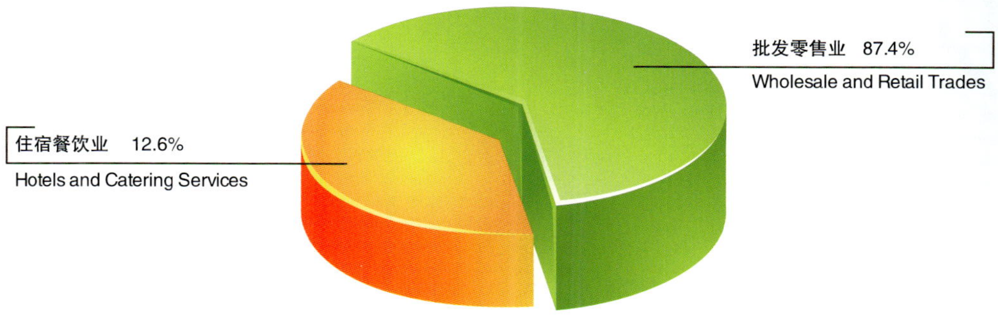

社会消费品零售总额（亿元）

Total Retail Sales Of Consumer Goods(100 million yuan)

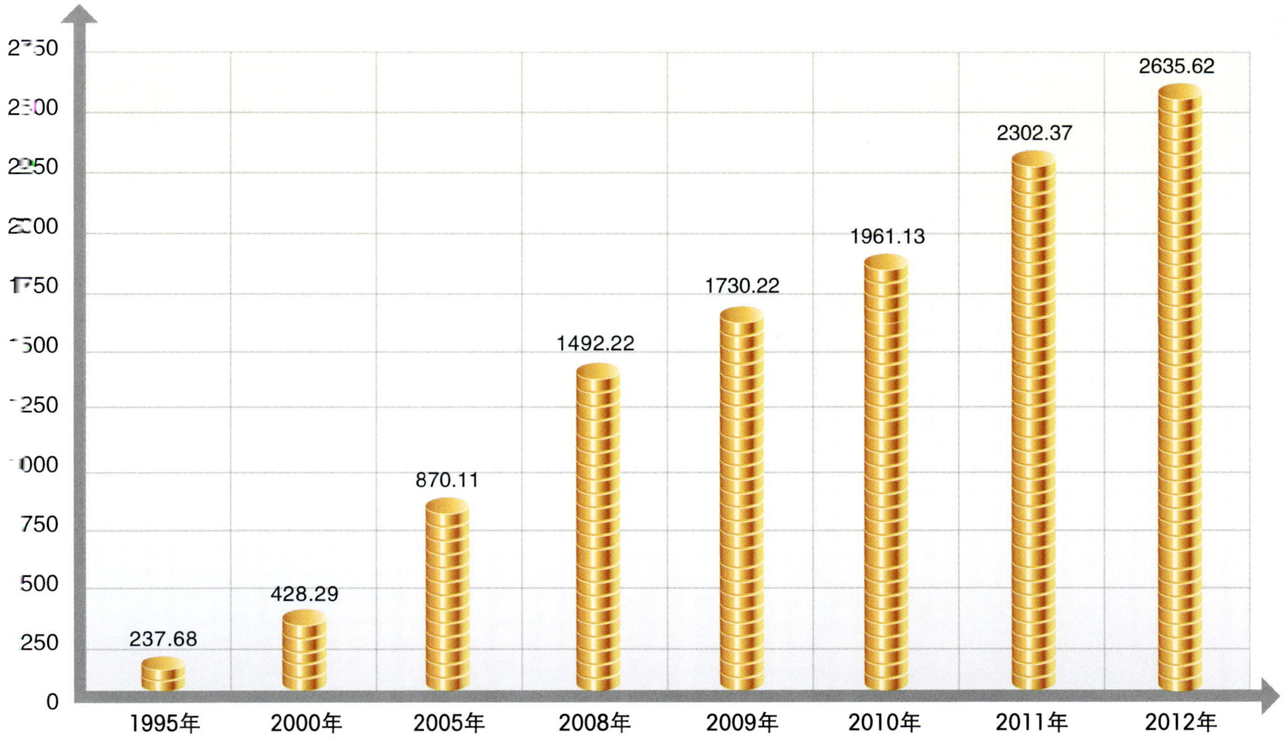

进出口总额（亿美元）
Total Imports And Exports (100 million USD)

旅游总人数（万人次）
Number Of Tourists (10000 person–times)

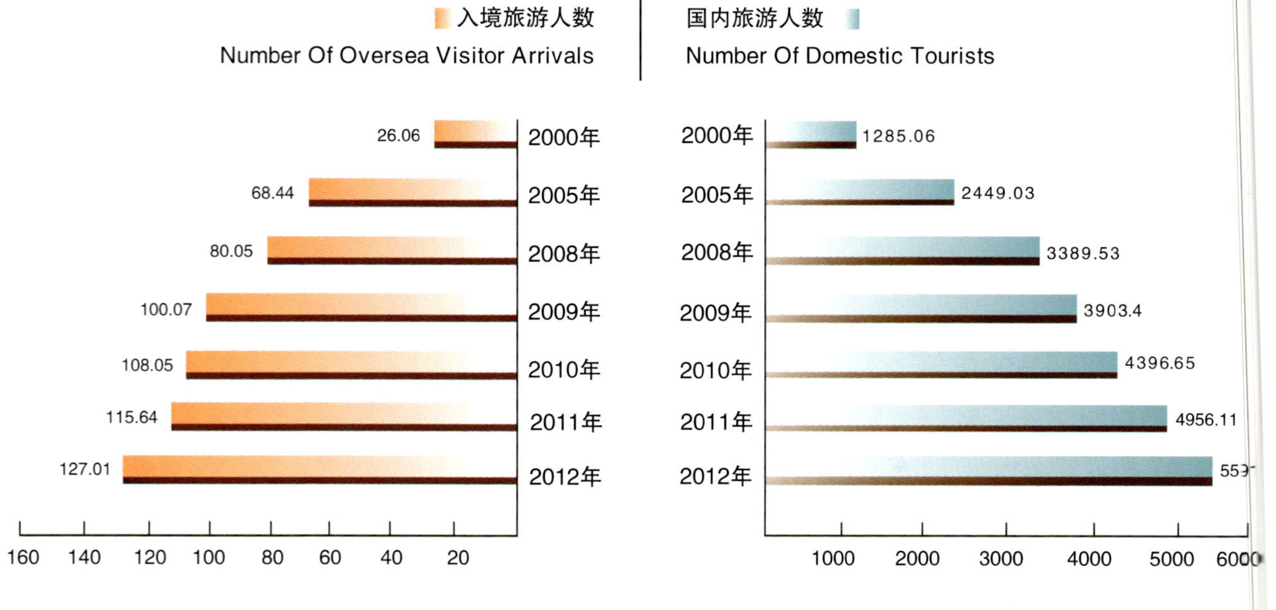

地方财政收入（亿元）
Revenue Of Local Government Finance (100 million yuan)

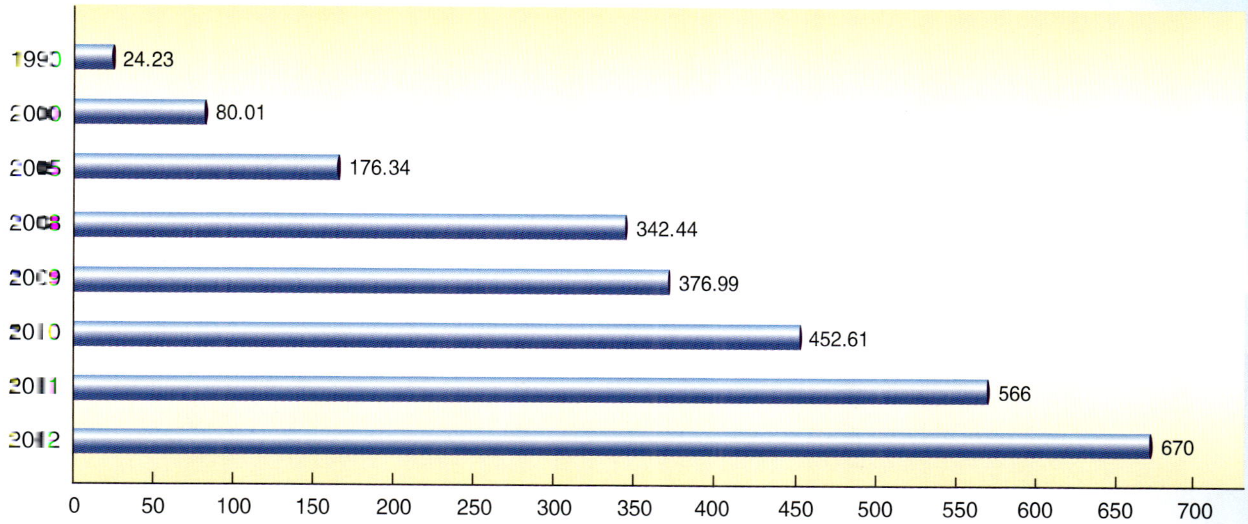

注：2002年以后财政收入为一般预算收入数。

Note:Since 2002,revenue of government finance refers to general budgetary revenue.

金融机构年末人民币存贷款余额（亿元）
Year-end Savings Deposits And Loans Of Financial Institution(RMB) (100 million yuan)

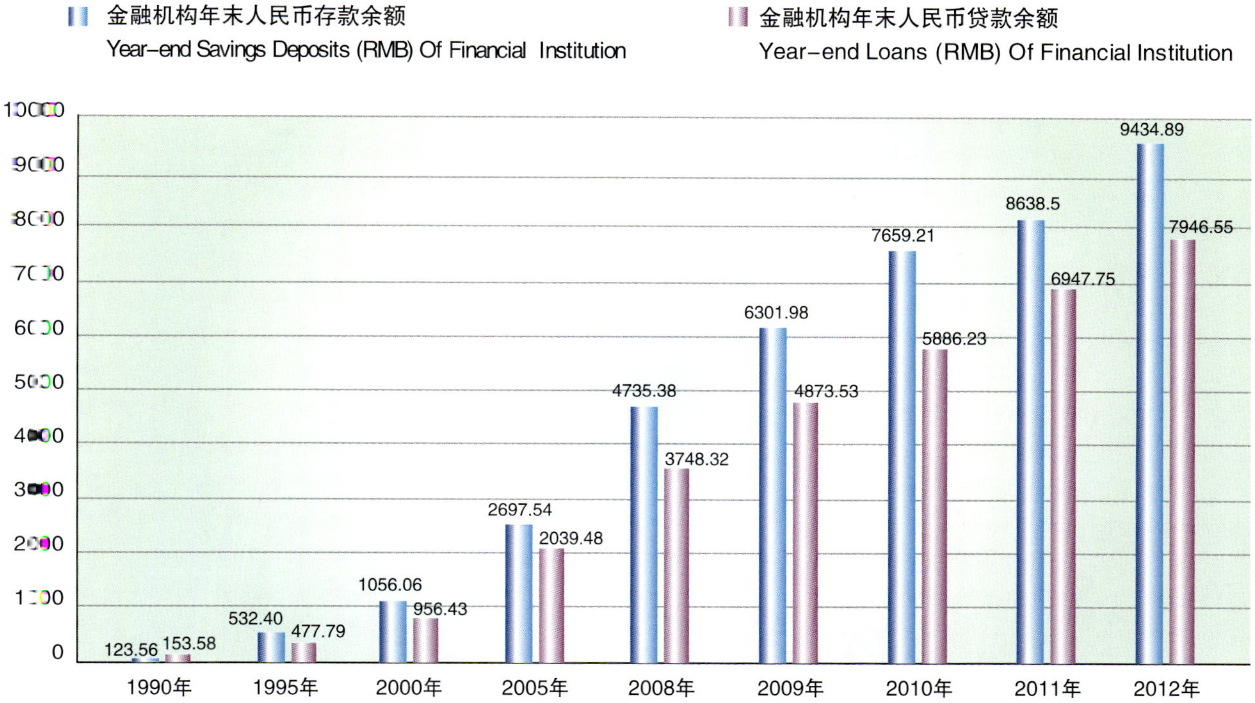

社会从业人数(万人)

Social Employment(100 million persons)

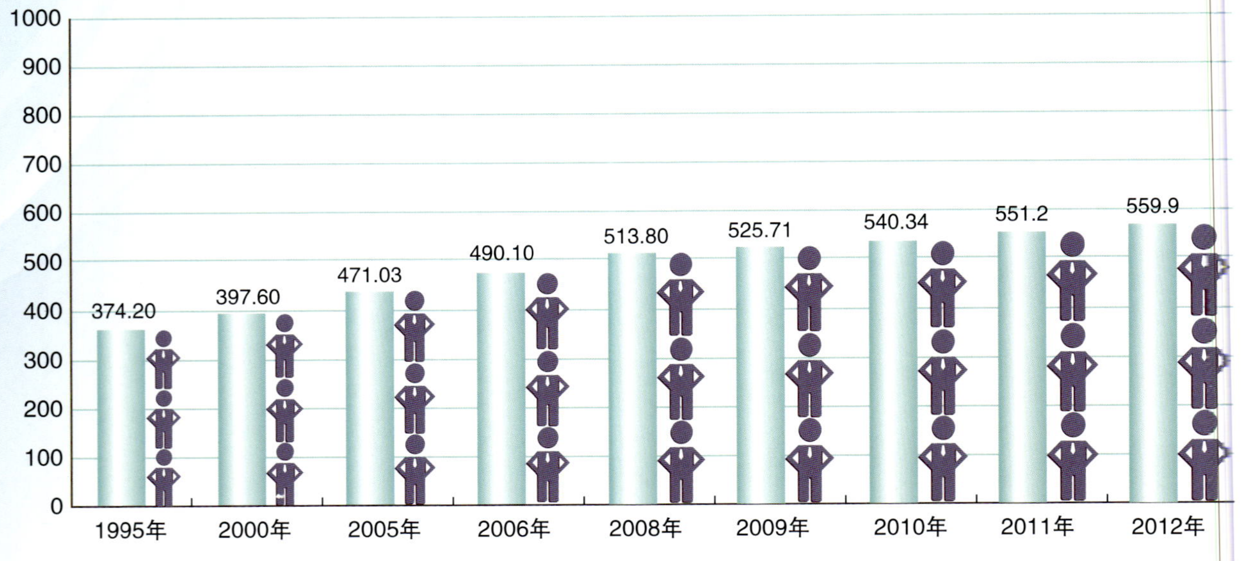

在岗职工平均工资(元)

Average Wage Of Employed Staff And Workers(yuan)

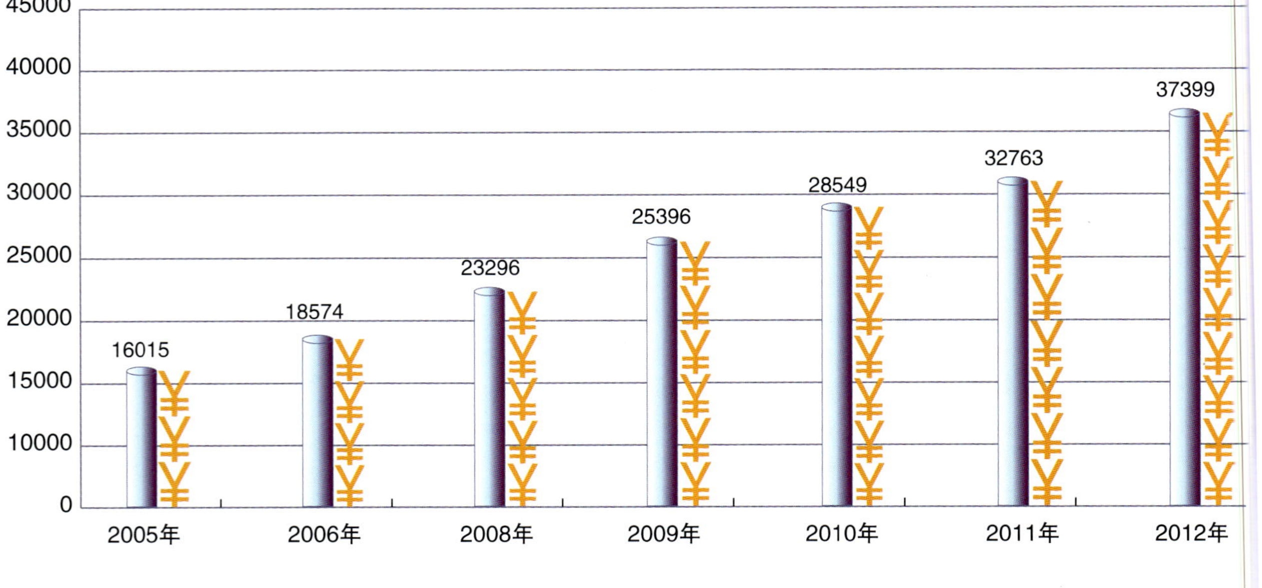

城乡居民收入（元）
Income Of Urban And Rural Households (yuan)

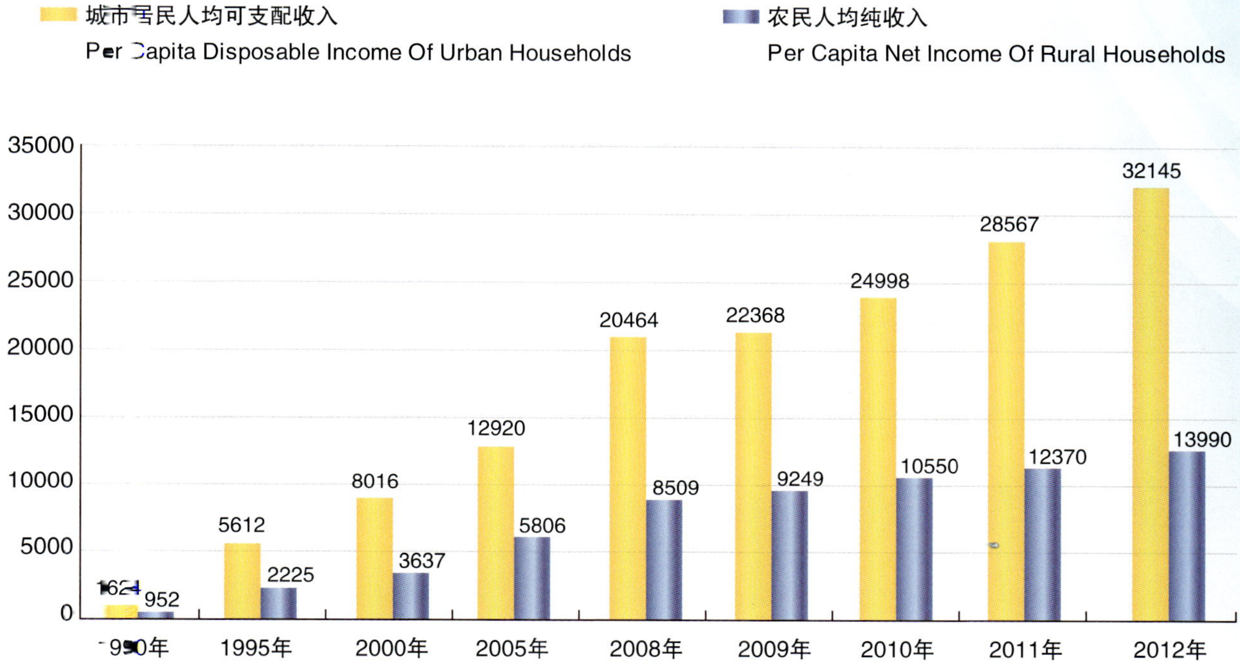

城乡居民人民币储蓄存款余额（亿元）
Savings Deposit Of Urban And Rural Households (RMB)(100 million yuan)

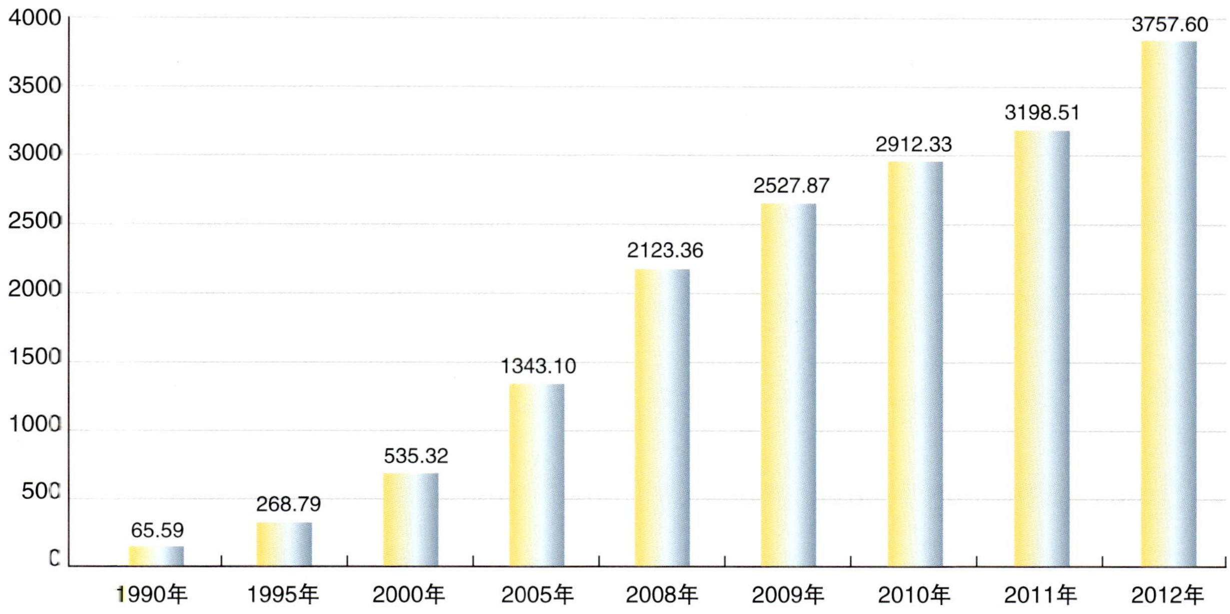

居民消费价格指数(上年=100)
Consumer Price Indices(preceding year=100)

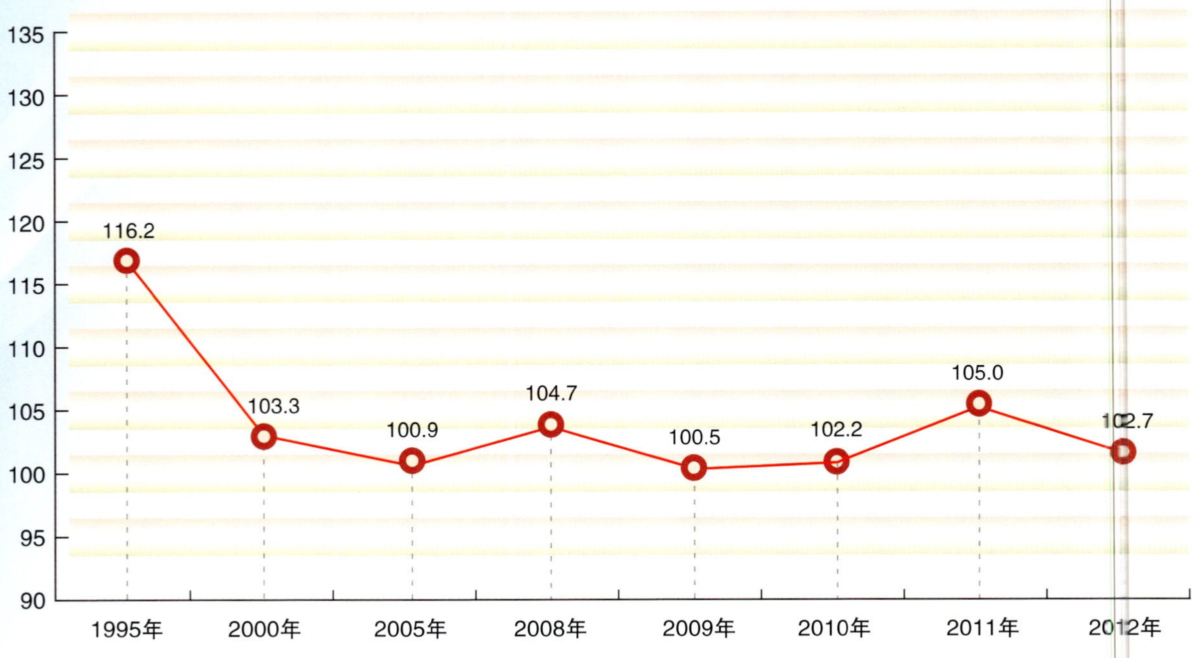

商品零售价格指数(上年=100)
Retail Price Indices(preceding year=100)

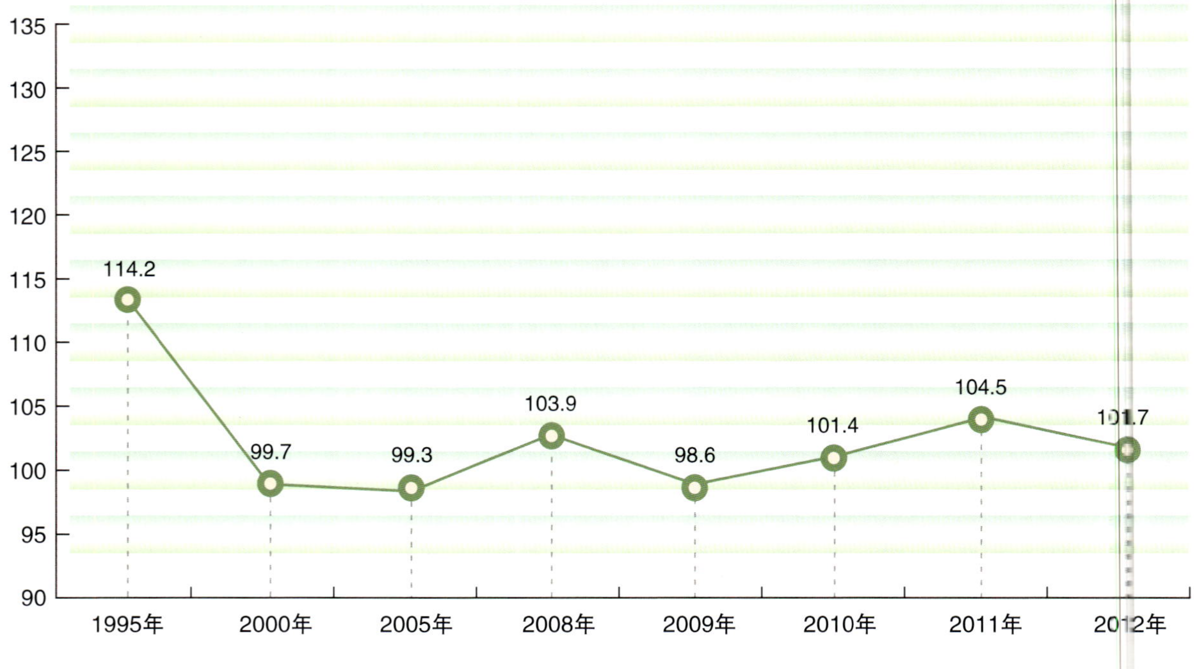

城市建成区面积、铺装道路面积

Developed Area Of the City And Area Of Roads

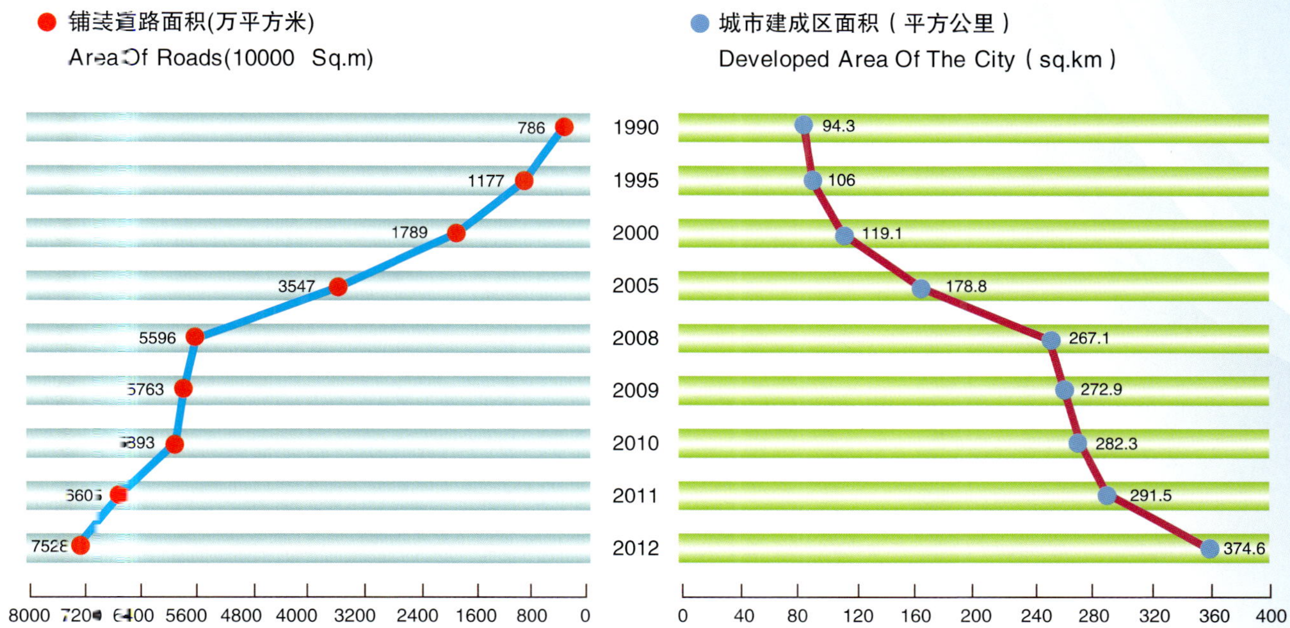

建成区绿化覆盖率（%）

Green Coverage Rate Of Developed Area(%)

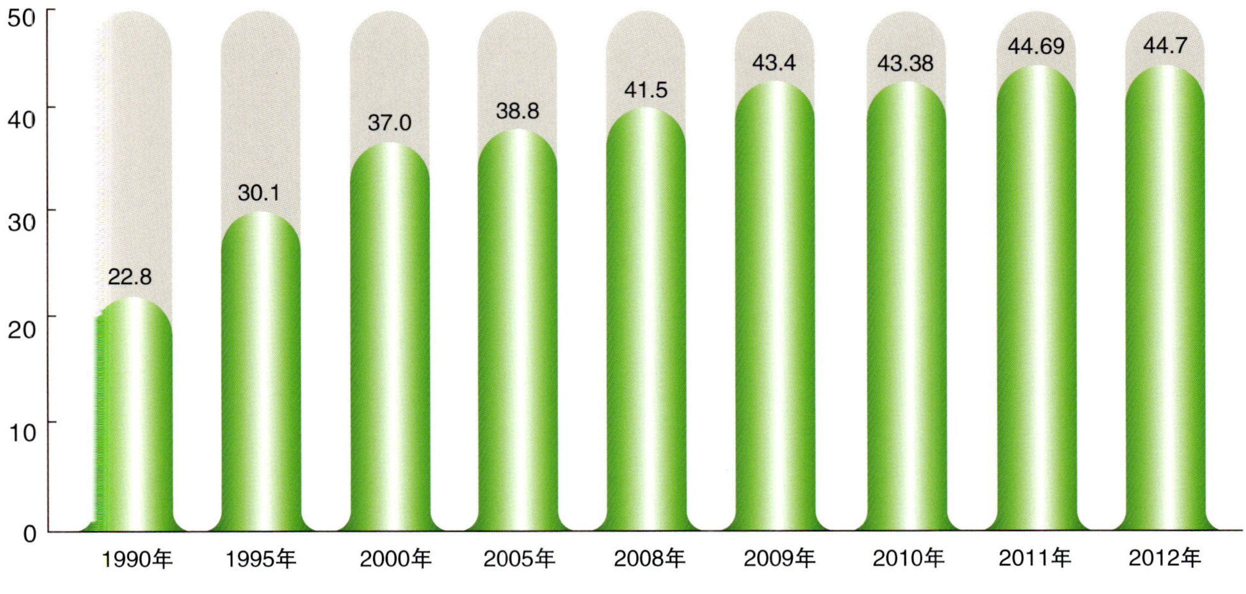

授权专利（件） Patents Granted (piece)

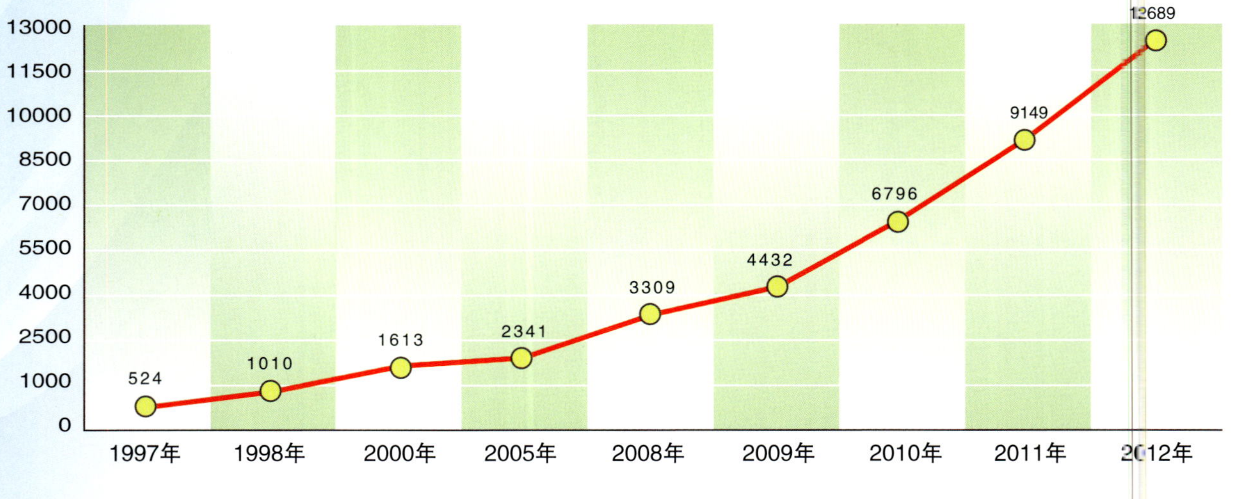

医疗卫生机构（个）Health Care Institutions(unit)

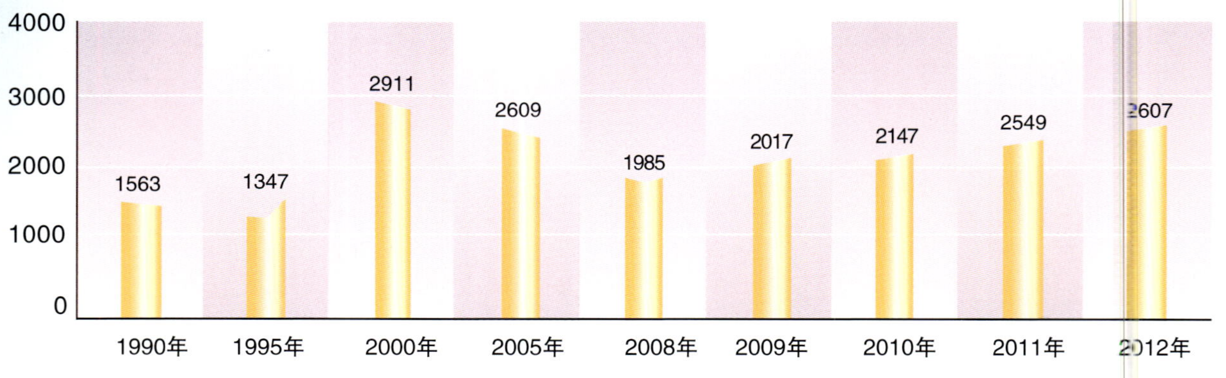

普通高校在校人数（万人）

Students Enrollment Of Regular Institutions Of Higher Education(10000 persons)

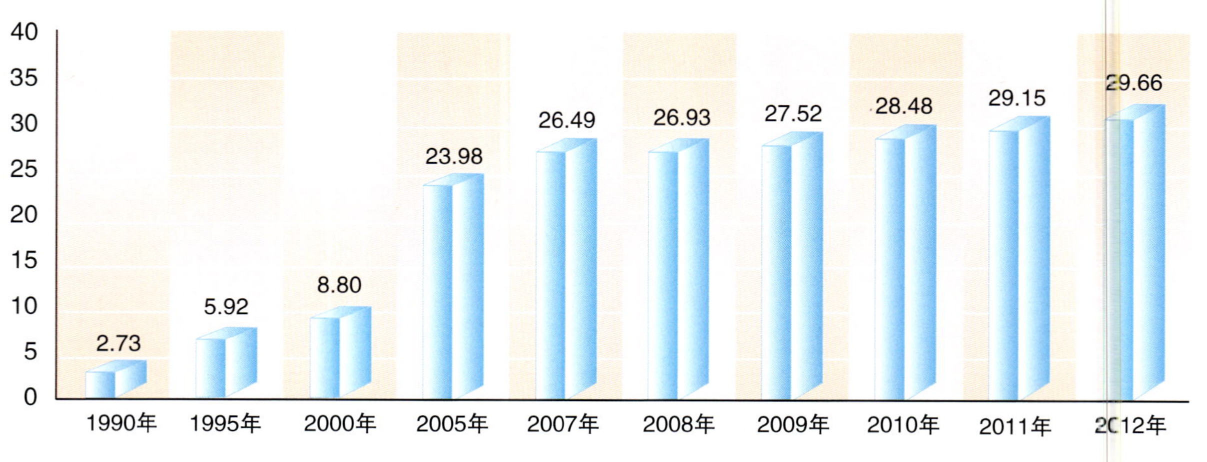

编辑委员会

EDITORIAL BOARD

编者说明

一、《青岛统计年鉴 –2013》是一部全面反映青岛市国民经济和社会发展情况、信息高度密集的资料工具书。

二、《青岛统计年鉴 –2013》共包括发展成果图、统计公报、统计表、附录四大部分。

统计表部分收录了 2012 年青岛市经济和社会等各方面的统计数据，以及建国以来重要年份和改革开放以来的主要统计数据，包括：综合，人口，从业人员及职工工资，固定资产投资，对外经济贸易，能源消耗，财政金融和保险业，物价，人民生活，城市建设、环境保护，农业，工业，建筑业，运输、邮电，批发和零售业，住宿、餐饮业和旅游，教育、科技和文化，体育、卫生和民政、司法。

为方便读者正确地使用年鉴资料，各篇章前设有《简要说明》，概括介绍各篇主要内容和资料来源；篇末还附有《主要统计指标解释》。

三、本《年鉴》部分历史数据已根据经济普查数据进行了调整，在此之前公布的数据凡与本年鉴数字不符的一律以本年鉴为准。

四、本年鉴中的符号说明：年鉴各表中的“空格”表示该项统计指标数据不足本表最小单位数、数据不详或无该项数据；"#" 表示其中的主要项。

五、《青岛统计年鉴》自公开出版以来，受到社会各界的关心和支持，对于年鉴的内容和编辑工作提出了许多宝贵的意见，对此我们深表谢意。限于我们的水平，欢迎读者继续对年鉴的不足之处给予批评和指正，帮助我们进一步改进年鉴编辑工作，以期更好地为广大读者服务。

《青岛统计年鉴》编委会

2013年7月

Editor's Note

Ⅰ. *Qingdao Statistical Yearbook 2013* is a very important reference book, which reflects various aspects of Qingdao's social and economic development and contains High-density information.

Ⅱ. The yearbook contains the following four parts: achievement graphs, statistic gazette, statistics and appendixes.

Statistics contains all kinds of data on Qingdao's social and economic development in 2012, and data in significant year or data since the beginning of reform and opening up, including: General Survey; Population; Employment and Wages; Investment in Fixed Assets; Foreign Trade; Consumption of Energy; Government Finance ,Financial Intermediation and Insurance; Price; People's Living Conditions; City Construction and Environment Protection; Agriculture; Industry; Construction; Transport, Postal and Telecommunication Services; Wholesale and Retail Trades; Hotels, Catering Services and Tourism; Education, Science and Culture; Sports, Public Health and Civil Affairs, Judicial Affairs.

In brief introduction at the beginning of each chapter, main coverage, data sources and statistical coverage are concerned. Meanwhile explanatory notes on major statistical indicators have been attached for readers to use the data correctly.

Ⅲ. Some of the data in the book have been adjusted on the basis of statistics of economic census. In any case the data of this book shall be deemed as the authentic ones.

Ⅳ. Marks in this book:

"(blank)" indicates that the figure is not large enough to be measured with the smallest unit in the table, the data is not available, or the data is not available;

"#" indicates the major items of the total.

Ⅴ. Previous editions of *Qingdao Statistical Yearbook* have won wide acclaim among the readers. In order to excel, we welcome all candid comments and criticism from our readers.

Editorial Board

July, 2013

目　　录
CONTENTS

二、人　　口

Chapter 2. POPULATION

三、从业人员及职工工资

Chapter 3. EMPLOYMENT AND WAGES

四、固定资产投资

Chapter 4 INVESTMENT IN FIXED ASSETS

五、对外经济贸易

Chapter 5. FOREIGN TRADE

六、能源消耗
Chapter 6. CONSUMPTION OF ENERGY

七、财政、金融和保险业
Chapter 7. GOVERNMENT FINANCE, FINANCIAL INTERMEDIATION AND INSURANCE

八、物 价

Chapter 8. PRICE

九、人民生活

Chapter 9. PEOPLE'S LIVING CONDITIONS

十、城市建设、环境保护

Chapter 10. CITY CONSTRUCTION AND ENVIRONMENT PROTECTION

十一、农　业

Chapter 11. AGRICULTURE

十二、工　业

Chapter 12. INDUSTRY

十三、建 筑 业

Chapter 13. CONSTRUCTION

十四、运输、邮电

Chapter 14. TRANSPORT, POSTAL AND TELECOMMUNICATION SERVICES

十五、批发和零售业

Chapter 15. WHOLESALE AND RETAIL TRADES

十六、住宿、餐饮业和旅游
Chapter 16. HOTELS, CATERING SERVICES AND TOURISM

十七、教育、科技和文化
Chapter 17. EDUCATION, SCIENCE & TECHNOLOGY AND CULTURE

十八、体育、卫生和民政、司法
Chapter 18. SPORTS,PUBLIC HEALTH AND CIVIL AFFAIRS,JUDICIAL AFFAIRS

附　录
APPENDIX

2012年
青岛市国民经济和社会发展统计公报

青岛市统计局

国家统计局青岛调查队

(2013年3月7日)

2012年，面对复杂严峻的国内外经济形势，全市深入贯彻科学发展观，全面落实中央各项宏观调控政策，积极推进改革开放，加快创新转型步伐，经济运行稳中有进，社会事业继续进步，民生状况持续改善。

一、综 合

初步核算，全市实现生产总值(GDP)7302.11亿元，按可比价格计算，增长10.6%。其中，第一产业增加值324.41亿元，增长3.2%；第二产业增加值3402.23亿元，增长11.5%；第三产业增加值3575.47亿元，增长10.5%。三次产业比例为4.4:46.6:49.0。

表1 全市季度GDP

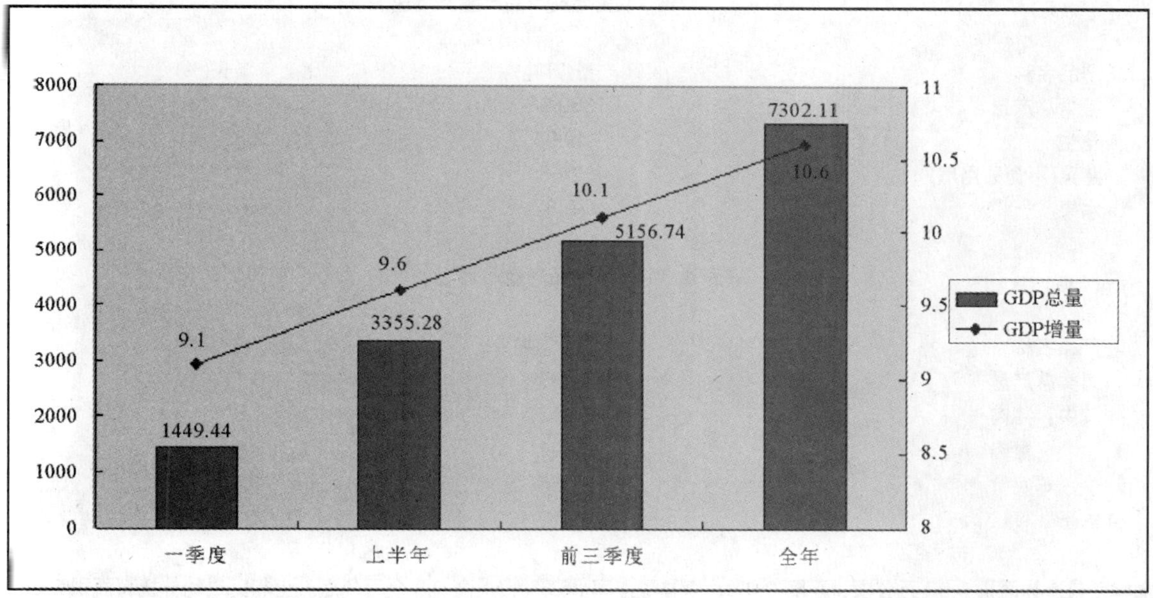

全年财政总收入实现2449.69亿元，增长1.7%；公共财政预算收入670.18亿元，增长18.4%；公共财政预算支出765.98亿元，增长16.3%。全年国税系统组织税收收入(含海关代征)1326.13亿元，增长8.5%；其中，国内税收581.95亿元，增长11.6%。地税税收收入462.8亿元，增长17.9%。

全年居民消费价格平均比上年上涨2.7%,其中，12月份同比上涨1.8%。全年工业生产者出厂价格下降1.39%，工业生产者购进价格下降3%。12月份市区新建住宅价格同比下降3.4%；二手住宅价格同比下降1.2%。

表 2　居民消费价格比上年涨跌幅度

指标名称	比上年涨跌(%)
居民消费价格	2.7
非食品价格	2.0
服务项目价格	2.1
消费品价格	2.9
1.食品	4.3
#粮食	2.3
猪肉	-10.0
鲜蛋	-5.2
鲜菜	12.1
2.烟酒	1.3
3.衣着	6.3
4.家庭设备用品及维修服务	1.9
5.医疗保健和个人用品	1.9
6.交通和通信	-0.9
7.娱乐教育文化用品及服务	
8.居住	

二、农 业

全市粮食播种面积 54.08 万公顷，下降 0.9%，粮食总产量达到 369.96 万吨，增长 1.9%。

表 3　主要农产品产量及增速

产品名称	产量(万吨)	比上年增长(%)
粮食总产量	369.96	1.9
花生	49.95	3.5
蔬菜(不含果用瓜)	534.65	-2.2
水果	79.87	-0.8

表 4　主要畜产品产量及增速

产品名称	产量(万吨)	比上年增长(%)
肉类总产量	61.37	3.1
其中：猪肉	27.12	1.8
禽肉	32.91	4.6
牛、羊奶	37.64	1.3
禽蛋	19.12	-0.1

全年完成造林面积 0.92 万公顷，下降 0.9%；森林覆盖率 38.6%，提高 0.8 个百分点。全年完成幼林抚育面积 2.2 万公顷，提高 2.1%。

水产品总产量 112.44 万吨，下降 0.9%，其中，捕捞产量 27.21 万吨，增长 1.9%；养殖产量 85.23 万吨，下降 1.7%。海、淡水养殖面积 5.23 万公顷，下降 4.7%。

年末全市拥有农业机械总动力 797.71 万千瓦，增长 1.7%。农用拖拉机 20.63 万台，增长 2.1%。农田有效灌溉面积 333.63 万公顷，增长 0.6%，其中，节水灌溉面积 174.88 万公顷，增长 5.2%。

三、工业与建筑业

全市规模以上工业企业(年主营业务收入 2000 万元及以上的工业法人企业)4783 家，完成增加值增长 11.6%。其中，国有及国有控股企业增长 3.7%；集体企业增长 2.5%；股份制企业增长 13.6%；外商及港澳台投资企业增长 9.9%。按轻重工业分，重工业增长 12.0%，轻工业增长 11.2%。

全年规模以上工业企业共完成高新技术产业产值5199.79亿元，增长14.0%，占规模以上工业总产值的39.8%，比重较年初提高1.0个百分点；十条工业千亿级产业链产值10903.41亿元，占规模以上工业比重75.6%；规模以上工业中战略性新兴产业产值3424.65亿元，增长17.6%。

表5　规模以上工业战略性新兴产业发展情况

产业名称	企业户数(户)	总产值(亿元)	增速(%)	主营业务收入(亿元)	增速(%)
战略性新兴产业	1000	3424.65	17.6	3316.95	15.6
节能环保产业	26	45.29	59.4	39.57	37.8
新一代信息技术产业	170	983.09	14.5	1030.83	10.8
生物产业	44	91.73	18.8	83.51	16.2
高端装备制造产业	461	1518.55	12.3	1437.02	14.2
新能源产业	34	75.11	28.9	69.48	45.1
新材料产业	265	710.88	32.0	656.54	23.3

表6　规模以上工业主要产品产量及增速

产品名称	产量(单位)	比上年增长(%)
彩色电视机	1439.98万台	24.8
家用电冰箱	575.01万台	−20.0
家用洗衣机	583.6万台	−3.5
房间空气调节器	465.61万台	13.1
卷烟	530.13亿支	1.5
啤酒	162.01万千升	4.8
纱	1.94万吨	4.6
布	4.9亿米	−1.3
碳酸钠(纯碱)	63.35万吨	−12.1
农用氮、磷、钾化学肥料总计(折纯)	6.98万吨	−24.6
橡胶轮胎外胎	5646.08万条	27.1
水泥	556.57万吨	−5.4
平板玻璃	494.54万重量箱	−3.0
粗钢	252.78万吨	−20.6
汽车	57.47万辆	17.7
发电量	174.72亿千瓦小时	0.6

规模以上工业实现利税总额1255.28亿元，增长11.8%；利润670.7亿元，增长9.7%。主营业务收入13751.98亿元，增长12.6%。资本保值增值率107.49%，产品销售率98.65%。

表7　规模以上工业分经济类型利润情况

指标名称	利润总额(亿元)	增速(%)
总计	670.73	9.7
其中：国有及国有控股经济	92.78	10.3
集体经济	53.91	8.9
股份制经济	297.13	11.5
外商及港澳台投资经济	193.92	−0.1

全年建筑业实现增加值360.92亿元，增长8.5%。实现利税总额59亿元，增长8%；其中，国有及国有控股企业实现利税14亿元，增长12%。

四、固定资产投资

全市固定资产投资(包括城镇、农村500万元以上投资项目)4153.9亿元，增长22.3%。其中，第一产业投资68.5亿元，增长62.2%，第二产业投资1998.6亿元，增长35.7%，第三产业投资2086.8亿元，增长10.9%。

全年固定资产投资施工项目4198个，新开工项目3344个，竣工项目2496个；在建项目计划总投资规模10684.8亿元，增长10.1%。全年新增固定资产2376.5亿元，项目建成投产率59.5%，固定资产交付使用率57.2%。

全年房地产开发完成投资930.1亿元，增长18.8%。商品房竣工1211.6万平方米，增长33.7%；全市销售房屋面积950.9万平方米，下降7.5%。保障性安居工程施工面积613.1万平方米，竣工面积116.8万平方米。

五、国内贸易

全年实现社会消费品零售额 2564.5 亿元，增长 14.9%。分地域看，城市市场实现零售额 2133.25 亿元，增长 15.2%；农村市场实现零售额 431.25 亿元，增长 13.0%。分行业看，批发和零售业实现零售额 2242.11 亿元，增长 14.7%；住宿和餐饮业实现零售额 322.39 亿元，增长 15.8%。

全年限额以上企业(单位)消费品零售额 1051.82 亿元，增长 17.9%。限额以上单位实现汽车类零售额 294.13 亿元，增长 7.4%；石油及其制品类零售额 153.47 亿元，增长 30.1%；粮油、食品、饮料、烟酒类零售额 119.22 亿元，增长 17.4%；日用品类零售额 29.89 亿元，增长 16.4%；体育及娱乐用品类零售额 5.88 亿元，下降 7.1%；化妆品类零售额 19.66 亿元，增长 22.1%；金银珠宝类零售额 23.71 亿元，增长 12.1%。

六、对外经济

全市实现外贸进出口总额 732.08 亿美元，增长 4.2%。其中，出口额 408.2 亿美元，增长 3.6%，进口额 323.83 亿美元，增长 5.0%。

表 8　全市主要商品出口情况

种类	金额(万美元)	比上年增长(%)
纺织服装	740114	-2.5
农产品	488853	-0.3
机电产品	1490495	-0.1
高新技术产品	263509	-6.9

表 9　全市主要商品进口情况

种类	金额(万美元)	比上年增长(%)
纺织服装	84243	-7.7
农产品	492248	3.0
机电产品	613269	-11.2
高新技术产品	290186	26.1

据青岛海关统计，青岛口岸对外贸易进出口总额 1489.2 亿美元，下降 1.3%，其中，出口额 712.2 亿美元，进口额 777.0 亿美元，分别下降 2.4%和 0.4%。

实际使用外资 46 亿美元，增长 27.8%。

全年完成对外承包工程新签合同金额 14.2 亿美元，增长 7.4%；营业额 33.2 亿美元，增长 130.2%；对外劳务合作派出各类劳务人员 7629 人次，增长 31.1%。

七、交通运输、邮电和旅游业

全年港口吞吐量 41464.82 万吨，增长 9.2%；外贸吞吐量 28936.1 万吨，增长 8.3%；集装箱吞吐量 1450 万标准箱，增长 11.4%。

表 10　各种运输方式完成的运输量及增速

运输方式	运输量(单位)	比上年增长(%)
客运周转量	197.21 亿人公里	6.9
铁路	57.37 亿人公里	11.1
公路	139.2 亿人公里	5.6
水运	0.64 亿人公里	-41.4
货运周转量	2064.88 亿吨公里	21.7
铁路	186.24 亿吨公里	7.5
公路	452.61 亿吨公里	10.7
水运	1426.03 亿吨公里	28

年末拥有国内航线 95 条，国际航线 11 条，港澳地区航线 3 条，全年航空旅客吞吐量达到 1260.12 万人次，增长 7.6%；航空行货邮吞吐量 17.19 万吨，增长 3.2%。

全年完成邮电业务总量 208.68 亿元，增长 5.7%。其中，邮政业务总量 6.02 亿元，增长 14%；电信业务总量 202.65 亿元，增长 5.5%。信函 8498 万件，下降 8.4%。2012 年互联网用户累计达 218.2 万户，增长 17.5%，使用时长达 1980.22 亿分钟，增长 16.8%。年末固定电话用户达到 253.15 万户；全市移动电话发展到 1178.95 万户，其中，年内新增 117.92 万户。

全年全市旅游总收入 807.58 亿元，增长 18.5%。其中国内旅游收入 755.51 亿元，增长 18.5%；入境旅游(外汇)收入 8.25 亿美元，增长 19.6%。全年共接待国内外游客 5717.5 万人次，增长 12.6%；其中国内游客 5590.5 万人次，增长 12.8%；入境游客 127 万人次，增长 9.8%。年末 A 级旅游景区 76 处，其中，5A 级旅游景区 1 处，4A 级旅游景区 21 处；星级饭店 157 家，其中，5 星级饭店 9 家，4 星级饭店 32 家。

八、金融业

年末金融机构本外币存款余额 9818.33 亿元，比年初增加 917.05 亿元；人民币存款余额 9434.89 亿元，比年初增加 796.39 亿元，其中，储蓄存款 3757.6 亿元，比年初增加 559.09 亿元。本外币贷款余额 8632.84 亿元，比年初增加 1134.89 亿元；人民币贷款余额 7946.55 亿元，比年初增加 996.1 亿元。

全年全市承保金额 4.47 万亿元，增长 17.5%，实现保费收入 160.29 亿元，增长 10%。其中：财产保费收入 66.34 亿元，增长 16.1%；人身险保费收入 93.95 亿元，增长 6.1%。赔款支出金额 51.5 亿元，增长 11.1%；其中财产险赔付金额 33.58 亿元，人身险赔付金额 17.92 亿元。

九、科学技术和教育

初步统计，全年全市共取得重要科技成果 304 项。获得国家级科技奖励 9 项，其中，技术发明奖 2 项，科技进步奖 7 项；获得省级科技奖励 105 项，其中，自然科学奖 7 项，技术发明奖 5 项，科技进步奖 93 项。

全年共成交技术合同项目 2721 项，成交额 25.37 亿元。全年专利申请量 27009 件，授权专利 12689 件。

年末全市共有各类大专院校(含民办高校)24 所，其中普通高校 22 所，在校学生 29.7 万人，增长 1.9%。普通中学 292 所，在校学生 37 万人，下降 0.98%；中等专业学校和技工学校 88 所，在校学生 13.7 万人，下降 6.9%。接受中等职业教育的学生占高中阶段在校生约 52.5%。共有小学 840 所，在校学生 48.5 万人，增长 1.1%。学龄儿童入学率 100%，初中入学率达 99%以上。

十、文化、卫生和体育

全市共有各类文化机构 475 处。其中，影剧院 40 处，文化馆(站)185 处，博物馆 10 处，公共图书馆 13 处，艺术表演团体 7 个，广播电台 1 座、12 套节目，电视台 1 座、15 套节目，全市有线电视用户达到 243.5 万户，数字电视用户达到 225.8 万户。全市出版各类杂志 2866 万册，出版报纸 108616 万份。全市共有档案馆 14 处。

年末全市共有卫生机构(含诊所)2606 处，其中，医院、卫生院 288 处，疾病预防控制中心 28 处，妇幼保健机构 13 处，门诊部(所)、卫生保健所、医务室 1950 处。年末各类卫生技术人员 5.5 万人，其中，医生 2.2 万人。全市拥有医疗床位 4.7 万张，其中，医院、卫生院床位 4.1 万张。

全市运动员在各项比赛中共获得金牌 319 枚，银牌 227 枚，铜牌 200 枚。共打破全国纪录 1 项。全市共有体育专业队 1 个，队员 84 人。重点体校 2 所，学员 984 人，业余体校 12 所，学员 1624 人。群众体育运动蓬勃开展。

十一、城市建设

建成区面积 374.64 平方公里，增长 7.8%。城市平均每天供水量 117 万吨，增长 4.5%。城市全年实际用水量 3.7 亿吨，增长 5.1%，其中生产用水和生活用水分别为 1.49 亿吨和 2.13 亿吨。

城市使用液化气、煤制气、天然气的总户数达到 136.93 万户，全年供应液化气总量 5.97 万吨，供应煤制气总量 7999 万立方米，供应天然气总量 68922 万立方米。城市气化率达到 100%。

全年新增供热面积 1060 万平方米，年末供热面积达到 10503 万平方米，增长 11.2%。

年末市区公共汽、电车线路 263 条，增长 15.9%。共有营运的公交汽、电车 5397 辆。年末全市共有出租汽车 9693 辆，增长 0.1%。

年末城市道路总长度 4311 公里，扩建、翻建道路 120 条，城市下水道总长度 6182 公里。

据抽样调查，年末城市人均现住房建筑面积 27.86 平方米，农民人均拥有住房面积 33.2 平方米。

十二、能源、环境和安全生产

初步统计，全年全市规模以上工业综合能源消费量 1689 万吨标准煤，比上年增长 2.2%。其中，原煤消费量下降 3.5%，原油消费量增长 9.4%，天然气消费量增长 71.7%。全社会用电量 318 亿千瓦时，增长 1.6%。其中，工业用电 200 亿千瓦时，城乡居民生活用电 52 亿千瓦时，分别增长 2%和 3%。风力发电装机容量累计 40 万千瓦，增长 2.1 倍，风力发电 4.5 亿千瓦时，增长 4.8 倍。

全年空气质量按功能区达标率为 100%；市区空气质量优良天数达到 340 天，优良率 92.9%，比上年提高 1.4 个百分点。市区区域环境噪声平均值 53.7 分贝，市区交通干线噪声平均值 68.4 分贝。市区共植树 1390 万株。建成区绿化覆盖率达到 44.78%。市区园林绿地面积达 21121.44 公顷，增长 4.4%；新增公共绿地面积 147.63 公顷，人均拥有公共绿地面积 14.58 平方米。全市现有公园、动物园 80 个。

各类生产安全事故 2355 起，死亡人数 388 人，分别下降 8.9%和 9.1%。亿元 GDP 生产安全事故死亡 0.053 人，下降 18.5%。道路交通事故万车死亡 1.9 人，下降 9.5%。未发生重特大事故。

十三、蓝色经济和重大项目建设

全年实现蓝色经济增加值 1210.54 亿元，增长 17.2%(现价)，其中，第一产业增加值 83.30 亿元，增长 11.4%；第二产业增加值 582.72 亿元，增长 20.7%；第三产业增加值 544.51 亿元，增长 14.6%。

全年实现海洋经济增加值 1114.4 亿元，增长 19.9%(现价),占 GDP 比重为 15.3%，较上年提高 1.2 个百分点。

全年全市计划总投资 1 亿元及以上的新开工项目(含房地产项目,下同)421 个，增加 77 个；完成投资 912 亿元，增长 24.5%。从区域分布看，原七区新开工项目 173 个，占全市新开工的 41.1%；实际完成投资 485.6 亿元，增长 18.6%，占全部新开工项目投资的 53.2%。原五市新开工 228 个，占 54.2%；完成投资 389.1 亿元，增长 50.8%，占 42.7%。

世园会建设中园区基础设施、世园大道工程、青岛世界园艺博览会世园村接待中心、世园大厦、青岛世界园艺博览会世园村参展服务中心、世园度假酒店等项目计划总投资 124.7 亿元，全年完成投资 49.95 亿元。

地铁(三号线)计划总投资 175.4 亿元，全年完成投资 24.1 亿元。

十四、人口、人民生活和社会保障

年末全市户籍总人口为 769.56 万人，增长 0.42%，其中，市区(含原胶南市)363.9 万人，增长 0.74%；四市(县级)405.66 万人，增长 0.13%。全年新出生人口 74910 人，出生率为 9.75‰；死亡人口 62830 人，死亡率为 8.18‰；人口自然增长率为 1.57‰。

城市居民人均可支配收入 32145 元，增长 12.5%；城市居民人均消费性支出 20391 元，增长 5.7%。全年城市居民人均可支配收入中位数 28924 元，增长 14.3%。按城市居民五等份收入分组，低收入组人均可支配收入 15753 元，中等偏下收入组人均可支配收入 22558 元，中等收入组人均可支配收入 28974 元，中等偏上收入组人均可支配收入 35490 元，高收入组人均可支配收入 61840 元。城市居民家庭食品消费支出占家庭消费性支出的 36.5%。全市单位在岗职工平均工资 37399 元，增长 14.2%；其中，城镇非私营单位在岗职工平均工资 49052 元，增长 13.9%。

表 11　城市居民每百户家庭主要耐用消费品拥有量

消费品名称	单位	数量
钢琴	架	9
微波炉	台	82
电冰箱	台	108
淋浴热水器	台	93
洗衣机	台	98
彩色电视机	台	115
计算机	台	101
摄像机	架	24
照相机	架	79
空调器	台	104
固定电话	部	63
移动电话	部	231
健身器材	套	11
家用汽车	辆	29
摩托车	辆	8
助力车	辆	6

农民人均纯收入 13990 元，增长 13.1%；农民人均生活消费支出 8653 元，增长 12.9%。农村居民人均纯收入中位数 12587 元，增长 12.4%。按农村居民五等份收入分组，低收入组人均纯收入 5528 元，中等偏下收入组人均纯收入 9511 元，中等收入组人均纯收入 12426 元，中等偏上收入组人均纯收入 16705 元，高收入组人均纯收入 28895 元。农村居民家庭食品消费支出占家庭消费总支出的 36.2%。

表 12　农村居民每百户家庭主要耐用消费品拥有量

消费品名称	单位	数量
微波炉	台	32
电冰箱	台	102
淋浴热水器	台	85
洗衣机	台	91
彩色电视机	台	114
家用电脑	台	55
摄像机	架	1
照相机	架	21
空调器	台	37
固定电话	部	62
移动电话	部	216
家用汽车	辆	16
摩托车	辆	68
电动自行车	辆	62

年末全市单位从业人员 283.2 万人，增长 2.7%。年末全市城镇登记失业率为 2.93%，减少 0.02 个百分点。

年末全市城镇职工基本养老保险参保缴费人数为 220.24 万人，参加失业保险人数为 164.15 万人，全年累计领取失业保险金的人数为 6.27 万人。全市新型农村合作医疗参合率达到 100%。

全市各类社会福利院床位达 31503 张，收养 18102 人。

注：

1、公报中统计数据均为初步统计数。

2、公报中全市生产总值、各产业增加值绝对数按现价计算，增长速度按可比价计算。

3、规模以上工业统计的起点标准为年主营业务收入 2000 万元，固定资产投资项目统计的起点标准为计划总投资额 500 万元。

4、战略性新兴产业根据国家规划，现阶段主要包括节能环保、新一代信息技术、生物、高端装备制造、新能源、新材料、新能源汽车等七个产业领域。我市目前战略性新兴产业统计监测所涉及的行业主要包括节能环保、生物、高端装备制造、新能源、新材料、新一代信息技术等 6 个产业。

5、在岗职工指在本单位工作并由单位支付工资的人员，以及有工作岗位，但由于学习、病伤产假等原因暂未工作，仍由单位支付工资的人员。

职工工资指各单位在一定时期内直接支付给本单位职工的劳动报酬总额。各单位支付给职工的劳动报酬以及其他根据有关规定支付的工资，不论是计入成本的还是不计入成本的，不论是按国家规定列入计征奖金税项目的，还是未列入计征奖金税项目的，不论是以货币形式支付的还是以实物形式支付的，均包括在工资总额内。

全市单位包括国有单位、集体单位、联营经济、股份制经济、外商投资经济、港澳台投资经济、私营经济等单位。城镇非私营单位，包括国有单位、集体单位、联营经济、股份制经济、外商投资经济、港澳台投资经济等单位。

6、城乡居民人均收入中位数是指将所有调查户按人均收入水平从低到高顺序排列，处于最中间位置的调查户的人均收入。城乡居民收入五等份分组是指将所有调查户按人均收入水平从低到高顺序排列，平均分为五个等份，处于最高 20%的收入群体为高收入组，依此类推依次为中等偏上收入组、中等收入组、中等偏下收入组、低收入组。

7、建成区面积、供水、供热、供气、植树、绿化、道路、公园、动物园等数据系市城乡建设委提供，统计范围为区划调整后的六区，原胶南市仅含珠海、珠山、滨海、铁山、灵山、隐珠六个街道办事处。

STATISTICS COMMUNIQUÉ QINGDAO'S ECONOMIC AND SOCIAL DEVELOPMENT DURING 2012

Qingdao Municipal Statistics Bureau

NBS Survey Office in Qingdao

March 7, 2013

In 2012, Qingdao saw steady economic growth under difficult domestic and international economic conditions. It has been resolutely implementing the central government's macroeconomic regulations and control policies while continuing to adhere to the Concept of Scientific Development, pushing for more reform and opening up, and accelerating the pace of innovation and transformation of its growth model. The city also witnessed overall progress in social programs and further improvement in personal incomes.

I. General

Preliminary statistics showed a gross domestic product (GDP) of RMB 730.211 billion, up 10.6% over the previous year. Of the total, primary industries contributed RMB 32.441billion in added value, up 3.2%, secondary industries contributed RMB 340.223billion, up 11.5%, and tertiary industries contributed RMB 357.547 billion, up 10.5%. The ratio of primary, secondary and tertiary industries was 4.4, 46.6 and 49.0.

Table 1: Quarterly GDP of Qingdao

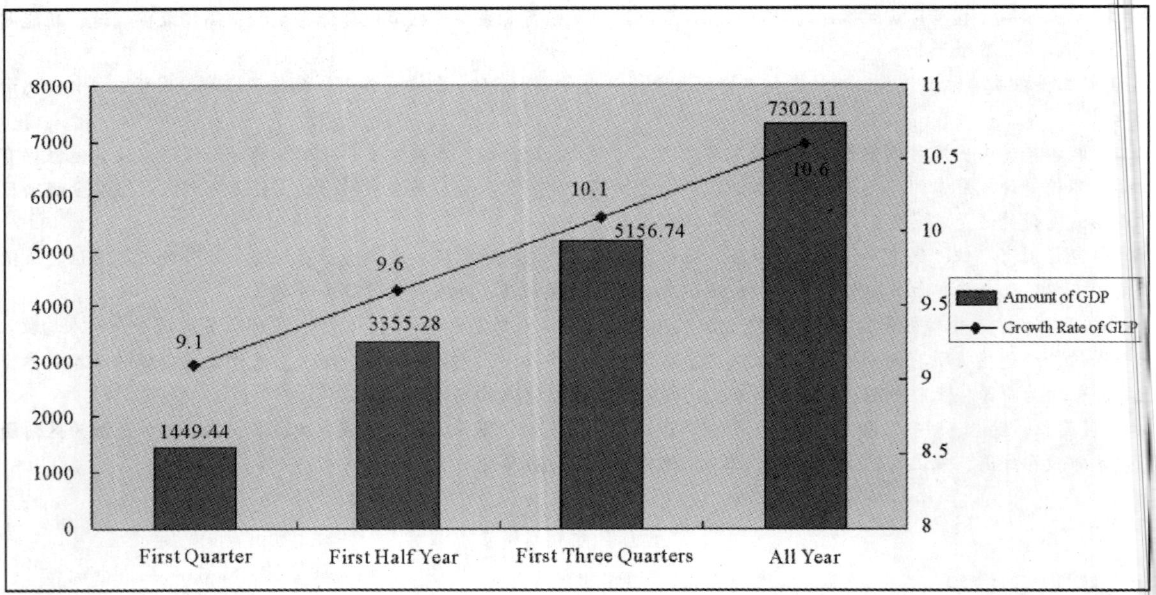

Qingdao realized RMB 244.969 billion in the local government's general revenue, up 1.7%, RMB 67.018 billion in the public budget revenue, up 18.4% and RMB 76.598 billion in the public budget expenditure, up 16.3%. The national tax revenue (including those collected by customs) rose by 8.5% to RMB 132.613 billion. Internal revenue increased 11.6% to RMB 58.195 billion and local tax revenue increased 17.9% to RMB 46.28 billion.

The total consumer price index increased 2.7%. In December, the index increased 1.8% from the same period a year ago. The factory price index for main industrial products decreased 1.39% year-on-year. The purchase price index decreased 3% year-on-year. In December, urban newly-built residential housing prices decreased 3.4% while second-hand residential housing prices decreased 1.2% year-on-year.

Table 2: Movements of Consumer Price Index in 2012 over the previous year

Description	+/-% over the previous year
Consumer Price Index	2.7
Non-food	2.0
Services	2.1
Consumption goods	2.9
1. Food	4.3
Grain	2.3
Pork	-10.0
Eggs	-5.2
Fresh vegetables	12.1
2. Tobacco and wine	1.3
3. Clothes	6.3
4. Household appliances and repair services	1.9
5. Medical care and personal articles	1.9
6. Transportation and communications	-0.9
7. Entertainment, educational and cultural products and services	0.5
8. Housing	2.2

II. Agriculture

The sown area for crops totaled 540,800 hectares, down 0.9%. The total grain output reached 3, 699,600 tons, up 1.9%.

Table 3: Output of major farm products and growth rate

Description	Output (ton)	+/-% over the previous year
Grains	3,699,600	1.9
Peanuts	499,500	3.5
Vegetables (excluding melons used as fruits)	5,346,500	-2.2
Fruits	798,700	-0.8

Table 4: Output of major livestock products and growth rate

Description	Output (ton)	+/-% over the previous year
Meets	613,700	3.1
Pork	271,200	1.8
Poultry meet	329,100	4.6
Cow and goat's milk	376,400	1.3
Fowl eggs	191,200	-0.1

9,200 hectares of trees were planted in the year, down 0.9%. Forest coverage reached 38.6%, up 0.8 percent. 22,000 hectares of young growth were cultivated, up 2.1%.

The total output of aquatic products reached 1,124,400 tons, down 0.9%. Of the total, 272,100 tons were from fishing, up 1.9% and 852,300 tons were from farmed fish, a decrease of 1.7%. The combined seawater and freshwater farming area was 52,300 hectares, down 4.7%.

By the end of 2012, power from farming machines totaled 7,977,100 KW, up 1.7%. Farming tractors totaled 206,300 units, up 2.1%. Effective irrigation area was 333,630 hectares, up 0.6%, including 174,880 hectares of water-saving irrigation area, up 5.2%.

III. Industry and Construction

In 2012, the Industrial Enterprises above Designated Size (Industrial Corporate Enterprises with an annual operating income of RMB 20,000,000 or more) numbered 4,783. Their industrial added value grew 11.6%; the state-owned and controlled enterprises grew 3.7%; collective enterprises increased 2.5%; shareholder enterprises rose 13.6%; enterprises invested by foreign companies and by compatriots from Hong Kong, Macao and Taiwan, increased 9.9%. By industry, light industry increased 11.2% while heavy industry rose 12.0%.

The Industrial Enterprises above Designated Size finished a total output of RMB 519.979 billion in Hi-tech Industries, up 14.0% year-on-year, or 39.8% of the total industrial output value finished by Industrial Enterprises above Designated Size, an increase of 1.0 percentage from the beginning of the year. The production value of ten 100-billion-level industry chains amounts to RMB 1,090.341 billion, accounting for 75.6% of that of the Industrial Enterprises above the Designated Size. The production value of strategic emerging industries above the designated size amounts to RMB 342.465 billion, up 17.6%.

Table 5: Developments of strategic emerging industries above the designated size

Description	Number of Enterprises	Total Production Value (billion RMB)	Growth Rate (%)	Operating Revenue (billion RMB)	Growth Rate (%)
Strategic emerging industries	1,000	342.465	17.6	331.695	15.5
Energy-saving and environmental protection industry	26	4.529	59.4	3.957	37.8
New generation information technology industry	170	98.309	14.5	103.083	10.5
Biological industry	44	9.173	18.8	8.351	16.2
High-end equipment manufacturing industry	461	151.855	12.3	143.702	14.2
New energy industry	34	7.511	28.9	6.948	45.1
New material industry	265	71.088	32.0	65.654	23.3

Table 6: The output and growth rate of the main products of industries above designated size

Description	Output	+/-% over the previous year
Color TV sets	14,399,800 sets	24.8
Household refrigerators	5,750,100 sets	-20.0
Household washing machine	5,836.000 sets	-3.5
Room air conditioners	4,656,100 sets	13.1
Cigarettes	53.013 billion pieces	1.5
Beer	1,620,100 kilolitres	4.8
Yarn	19,400 tons	4.6
Cloth	0.49 billion meters	-1.3
Sodium carbonate(soda ash)	633,500 tons	-12.1
Total of agricultural nitrogen, phosphorus, potassium fertilizer(100 percent equivalent)	69,800 tons	-24.6
Tire casings	56,460,800 pieces	27.1
Cement	5,565,700 tons	-5.4
Sheet glass	4,945,400 weight cases	-3.0
Raw steel	2,527,800 tons	-20.6
Motor vehicles	574,700 units	17.7
Power output	17.472 billion KWh	0.6

Industrial enterprises above the designated size realized the total pre-tax profits of RMB 125.528 billion, up 11.8%, with after-tax profits of RMB 67.07 billion, up 9.7%. Operating incomes totaled RMB 1,375.198 billion, up 12.6%. The capital maintenance and appreciation ratio was 107.49 %. The sales ratio was 98.65%.

Table 7: Profits of industrial enterprises above the designated size by business type

Description of indicators	Total profits (billion RMB)	Growth rate (%)
Total	67.073	9.7
State-owned and state-controlled businesses	9.278	10.3
Collective businesses	5.391	8.9
Shareholder businesses	29.713	11.5
Businesses invested by foreign business people and by compatriots from Hong Kong, Macao and Taiwan	19.392	-0.1

The construction industries generated RMB 36.092 billion in added value, up 8.5% and RMB 5.9 billion in pre-tax profit, up 8%, of which RMB 1.4 billion was finished by the state-owned and controlled enterprises, up 12 %.

IV. Fixed Assets Investment

The fixed asset investment (including the projects with investment over RMB 5,000,000 in townships and rural areas) totaled RMB 415.39 billion, up 22.3%. Of that figure, RMB 6.85 billion was invested in primary industries, up 62.2%, RMB 199.86 billion in secondary industries, up 35.7% and RMB 208.68 billion in tertiary industries, up 10.9%.

The fixed assets investment construction projects numbered 4,198. New start-up projects numbered 3,344 and completed projects numbered 2,496. The amount of investment in projects in progress was RMB 1,068.48 billion, up 10.1%. Another RMB 237.65 billion was invested in fixed assets for the whole year. The project completion ratio was 59.5% and the fixed asset delivery ratio was 57.2%.

Finished investment in real estate development for the whole year reached RMB 93.01 billion, up 18.8%. Completed commercial housing totaled 12,116,000 square meters, up 33.7%; sold housing floor area was 9,509,000 square meters, down 7.5%. The construction area of affordable housing totaled 6,131,000 square meters, of which, 1,168,000 square meters were completed.

V. Domestic Trade

In 2012, total retail sales of consumer goods increased by 14.9% to RMB 256.45 billion. Geographically, RMB 213.325 billion was generated by the urban market, up 15.2% and RMB 43.125 billion by the rural market, up 13.0%. By industry, wholesale and retail industries realized sales of RMB 224.211 billion, up 14.7%, while the lodging and catering industries generated RMB 32.239 billion, up 15.8%.

In 2012, the retail sales of consumer goods of enterprises (units) above the designated size amounted to RMB 105.182 billion, up 17.9%. The retail sales of motor vehicles above the limited value reached RMB 29.413 billion, up 7.4%; that of petroleum and petroleum products totaled RMB 15.347 billion, up 30.1%; that of grain and oil, food, beverages, cigarettes and alcohols amounted to RMB 11.922 billion, up 17.4%; that of daily necessities added up to RMB 2.959 billion, up 16.4%; that of sports and entertainment products amounted to RMB 0.588 billion, down 7.1%; that of cosmetics totaled RMB 1.966 billion, up 22.1%; and that of gold, silver and jewelry was RMB 2.371billion, up 12.1%.

VI. Foreign Trade

Qingdao's import and export volume was USD 73.208 billion, up 4.2%, with exports amounting to USD 40.82 billion, up 3.6% and imports amounting to USD 32.388 billion, up 5.0%.

Table 8: The exports of main commodities from Qingdao

Category	Amount (USD)	+/-% over the previous year
Textiles and garments	7,401,140,000	-2.5
Agricultural products	4,888,530,000	-0.3
Electrical and mechanical products	14,904,950,000	-0.1
High-tech products	2,635,090,000	-6.9

Table 9: The imports of main commodities to Qingdao

Category	Amount (USD)	+/-% over the previous year
Textiles and garments	842,430,000	-7.7
Agricultural products	4,922,480,000	3.0
Electrical and mechanical products	6,132,690,000	-11.2
High-tech products	2,901,860,000	26.1

According to Qingdao Customs' statistics, imports and exports registered at Qingdao ports totaled USD 148.92 billion, down 1.3%. Of the total, USD 71.22 billion were exports, down 2.4% and USD 77.70 billion were imports, down 0.4%.

In 2012, direct foreign investment reached USD 4.6 billion, up 27.8%.

Total contracted value of overseas contractor projects and services was USD 1.42 billion, up 7.4%. Turnover amounted to USD 3.32 billion, up 130.2%; the number of personnel sent overseas reached 7,629, up 31.1%.

VII. Transportation, Post, Telecommunications and Tourism

Port throughput totaled 414,648,200 tons for the whole year, up 9.2%, with 289,361,000 tons handled for foreign trade, up 8.3%. Container throughput reached 14,500,000 TEUs, up 11.4%.

Table 10: Volume completed by various transportation means and increase/decrease

Transportation means	Volume	+/-% over the previous year
Passenger volume	19.721 billion person-km	6.9
Railways	5.737 billion person-km	11.1
Highways	13.92 billion person-km	5.6
Waterways	0.064 billion person-km	-41.4
Cargo volumes	206.488 billion ton-km	21.7
Railways	18.624 billion ton-km	7.5
Highways	45.261 billion ton-km	10.7
Waterways	142.603 billion ton-km	28

By the end of the year, there were 95 domestic airlines, 11 international airlines and 3 airlines to/from Hong Kong and Macao. The airport passenger throughput for the whole year reached 12,601,200 person-times, up 7.6% and air cargo and mail throughput was 171,900 tons, up 3.2%.

Postal and telecommunication service business transactions in 2012 totaled RMB 20.868 billion, up 5.7%. Of the total, RMB 0.602 billion was from the postal service, up 14%, and RMB 20.265 billion from the telecommunication service, up 5.5%. The total number of letters handled was 84,980,000, down 8.4%. Internet users numbered 2,182,000 in 2012, up 17.5% and time online reached 198.022 billion minutes, up 16.8%. At the end of the year, fixed-line telephone users numbered 2,531,500. Mobile phone users numbered 11,789,500, of which 1,179,200 were new users.

Tourism income for the year totaled RMB 80.758 billion, up 18.5%. Of the total, RMB 75.551 billion was from domestic tourism, up 18.5% and USD 0.825 billion from international tourism, up 19.6%. Tourists to Qingdao during the year totaled 57,175,000 person-times, up 12.6%. Of the total, 55,905,000 were domestic tourists, up 12.8% and

1,270,000 overseas tourists, up 9.8%. By the end of the year, there were 76 A-rated tourist attractions, of which one is 5A-rated and 21 are 4A rated, and 157 star hotels, of which 9 are 5 star-rated and 32 are 4 star-rated.

VIII. Finance

At year-end, the balance of local and foreign currencies on the deposit accounts with financial institutions in Qingdao stood at RMB 981.833 billion, an increase of RMB 91.705 billion from the beginning of this year. The balance of deposits in local currency (RMB) was RMB 943.489 billion, an increase of RMB 79.639 billion from the beginning of the year. Of the total, the balance of savings was RMB 375.76 billion, an increase of RMB55.909 billion from the beginning of the year. The loan balance in local and foreign currencies reached RMB 863.284 billion, an increase of RMB 113.489 billion from the beginning of this year. The loan balance in local currency (RMB) was RMB794.655 billion, an increase of RMB 99.61 billion from the beginning of the year.

The insured amount was RMB 4,470 billion, up 17.5%. The insurance premium totaled RMB 16.029 billion, up 10%. Of the total, RMB 6.634 billion was for property insurance, up 16.1%; and RMB 9.395 billion for personal insurance, up 6.1%. Expenses for claims amounted to RMB 5.15 billion, up 11.1%. Of this figure, RMB 3.358 billion was for property claims and RMB 1.792 billion for personal claims.

IX. Science, Technology and Education

Preliminary statistics show that Qingdao achieved 304 key scientific and research results in 2012 and received national 9 scientific and technological prizes. Of the total, 2 were for technological invention and 7 were for scientific and technological progress; it also received 105 provincial-level scientific and technological prizes. Of them, 7 were for natural science, 5 were for technological inventions, 93 were for scientific and technological progress.

In 2012 there were a total of 2,721 technology transfer contracts completed with a value of RMB 2.537 billion; 27,009 patents were pending and 12,689 more were granted with patent certificates.

By the end of 2012, there were 24 higher education schools (including private schools) including 22 ordinary colleges and universities. There were 297,000 students enrolled, up 1.9%. 292 were ordinary middle schools, enrolling 370,000 students, down 0.98%; technical secondary schools and vocational schools numbered 88, enrolling 137,000, down 5.9%. The number of students in vocational secondary schools accounted for 52.5% of the number of senior middle school students. There were 840 primary schools enrolling 485,000 pupils, up 1.1% and 100% of pre-school aged children were schooled. The schooling of youngsters for junior middle school was over 99%.

X. Culture, Public Health Services and Sports

There were a total of 475 cultural institutions in Qingdao, including 40 cinemas and theatres, 185 cultural centers (stations), 10 museums, 13 public libraries, 7 performing arts troupes, one radio and broadcasting station with 12 programs and one TV station with 15 programs. Cable TV users numbered 2,435,000. Digitalization TV users numbered 2,258,000. 28,660,000 magazines and 1,086,160,000 issues of newspapers were published. There were 14 archives in Qingdao.

At the end of the year, there were 2,606 public health institutions (including clinics). Of the total, there were 288 hospitals, 28 epidemic prevention institutions, 13 children and women's health care centers and 1,950 clinical and medical health locations. There were 55,000 medical professionals, including 22,000 doctors. Medical beds numbered 47,000, with 41,000 beds in hospitals and clinics.

Qingdao athletes won 319 gold medals, 227 silver medals and 200 bronze medals in various games, creating 1 new national record. There were 1 professional sport teams totaling 84 members. Key sports schools numbered 2, enrolling 984 students. Part-time sports schools numbered 12, enrolling 1,624 students. Mass sports and fitness exercise programs were very popular and enjoyed all over Qingdao.

XI. Urban Construction

Built-up area reached 374.64 square kilometers, up 7.8%. Urban water supply averaged 1,170,000 tons per day, up 4.5%. The actual water consumption for the year totaled 0.37 billion tons, up 5.1%, including 0.149 billion tons for production use and 0.213 billion tons for residential use.

Liquefied petroleum fuel, coal gas and natural gas users numbered 1,369,300. The total supply for liquefied petroleum fuel for the year was 59,700 tons, for coal gas was 79,990,000 cubic meters, and for natural gas was 689,220,000 cubic meters. The urban gas coverage was 100%.

Total heating space increased by 10,600,000 square meters to 105,030,000 square meters by the end of the year, up 11.2%.

At the end of the year, there were 263 public bus and trolley lines operating in urban areas, up 15.9%. 5,397 public buses and trolleys were in operation. Taxicabs numbered 9,693, up 0.1%.

Distance covered by roads in urban areas totaled 4,311 km, and 120 roads were expanded and rebuilt. The total length of underground sewers was 6,182 km.

A survey showed that the per capita average floor space in urban areas was 27.86 square meters at the end of the year, and the per capita average floor space for rural residents was 33.2 square meters.

XII. Energy, Environment and Work Safety

Preliminary statistics showed that the total energy consumption of industrial enterprises above the designated size in Qingdao in 2012 was 16,890,000 tons of standard coal, up 2.2% over the previous year. Consumption of raw coal decreased by 3.5%; consumption of crude oil increased by 9.4%; and consumption of natural gas rose 71.7%. The total power consumption was 31.8 billion kilowatt-hours, up 1.6%. Industrial power consumption was 20 billion kilowatt-hours; rural and urban residents' power consumption was 5.2 billion kilowatt-hours, up 2% and 3% respectively. The total installed capacity of wind power was 400,000 KW, increased by 2.1 folds; the wind power generation output was 0.45 billion kilowatt-hour, up 4.8 folds.

The air quality of functional regions all reached the desired standards. Acceptable air quality percentages in urban areas reached 340 days, accounting for 92.9% of the whole year, an increase of 1.4 percentage points over the previous year. Environmental noise pollution in urban areas averaged 53.7 dB. Noise pollution at traffic trunk lines in urban areas averaged 68.4 dB. A total of 13,900,000 trees were planted in the urban area. "Green area" coverage reached 44.78%. The "green area" of parks and gardens totaled 21,121.44 hectares, up 4.4%. The increase in public "green area" was 147.63 hectares. Per capita "green area" was 14.58 square meters. There are 80 parks and zoos in the City of Qingdao.

There were 2,355 accidents happened at work, down 8.9%, with 388 people died, down 9.1%. The death toll from work accidents for every RMB 100 million of GDP was 0.053 persons, a decline of 18.5%. The road traffic death toll per 10 thousand vehicles was 1.9 persons, a decrease of 9.5%. No extraordinarily large accidents happened.

XIII. The Blue Economy and the construction of major projects

The Blue Economy created RMB 121.054 billion in added value, up 17.2%, calculated at current prices; of which, the primary industry contributed RMB 8.330 billion, up 11.4%; the secondary industry contributed RMB 58.272 billion, up 20.7%; and the tertiary industry contributed RMB 54.451 billion, up 14.6%.

The marine economy finished RMB 111.44 billion in added value, up 19.9%, measured at current prices, accounting for 15.3% of the GDP, 1.2 per cent points higher than that of the year earlier.

The new projects including real estate projects whose construction was started in 2012, each with a planned investment of RMB 100,000,000 or more, numbered 421, 77 more than that of the previous year; RMB 91.2 billion has been invested in the projects, up 24.5%. Breaking it down geographically, the original 7 districts has started 173 new projects, accounting for 41.1% of the city's total, which have used investments of RMB 48.56 billion, up 18.6%, accounting for 53.2% of the total investment amount of the newly started projects. The original 5 districts had started 228 new projects, accounting for 54.2% of the total, which have used investments of RMB 38.91 billion, up 50.8%, accounting for 42.7% of the total.

The total planned investment for the construction of the infrastructure of the park for the Qingdao International Horticultural Exposition including the main road, reception center, main building, exhibition service center, resort hotel and other projects is RMB 12.47 billion. RMB 4.995 billion of the investment was used in 2012.

The total planned investment for the subway line No.3 is RMB 17.54 billion. RMB 2.41 billion of the investment was used in 2012.

XIV. Population, Living Conditions and Social Security

At the end of the year, Qingdao's total registered population was 7,695,600, up 0.42%. Of the total, 3,639,000 represent the population of the City of Qingdao (including the former city of Jiaonan), up 0.74%; 4,056,600 represent the population of the Greater Qingdao regions, up 0.13%. New births in 2012 totaled 74,910, a birth rate of 9.75‰. The number of deceased persons totaled 62,830, a percentage rate of 8.18‰. The population natural growth rate was 1.57‰.

The per capita disposable income of urban residents was RMB 32,145, up 12.5%. The per capita consumption expense of urban residents was RMB 20,391, up 5.7%. The median of the annualized per capita disposable income of urban residents was RMB 28,924, up 14.3%. By dividing urban residents in five equal income groups, the per capita disposable income of the low income group was RMB 15,753; the per capita disposable income of the lower middle income group was RMB 22,558; the per capita disposable income of the middle income group was RMB 28,974; the per capita disposable income of the upper middle income group was RMB 35,490; the per capita disposable income of the high income group was RMB 61,840. The Engel Coefficient for urban areas was 36.5%. The wages of employees in Qingdao averaged RMB 37,399, an increase of 14.2%. The wages of employees employed by non-private organizations in urban areas averaged RMB 49,052, up 13.9%.

Table 11: Amount of major durable consumer goods owned by every 100 urban households

Item	Unit	Quantity
Pianos	set	9
Microwave ovens	set	82
Refrigerators	set	108
Water heaters	set	93
Washing machines	set	98
Color TV sets	set	115
Computers	set	101
Video cameras	set	24
Cameras	set	79
Air-conditioners	set	104
Fixed-line telephones	set	63
Mobile telephones	set	231
Body building equipments	set	11
Household automobiles	unit	29
Motorcycles	unit	8
Motorbikes	unit	6

The average net income among farmers was RMB 13,990, up 13.1%; per capita consumption expense was RMB 8,653, up 12.9%. The median of the per capita net income of rural residents was RMB 12,587, up 12.4%. By dividing rural residents in five equal income groups, the per capita net income of the low income group was RMB 5,528; the per capita net income of the lower middle income group was RMB 9,511; the per capita net income of the middle income group was RMB 12,426; the per capita net income of the upper middle income group was RMB 16,705; the per capita net income of the high income group was RMB 28,895. The Engel Coefficient for rural areas was 36.2%.

Table 12: Amount of major durable consumer goods owned by every 100 rural households

Item	Unit	Quantity
Microwave ovens	set	32
Refrigerators	set	102
Water heaters	set	85
Washing machines	set	91
Color TV sets	set	114
Computers	set	55
Video cameras	set	1
Cameras	set	21
Air-conditioners	set	37
Fixed-line telephones	set	62
Mobile telephones	set	216
Household automobiles	unit	16
Motorcycles	unit	68
Electric bicycles	unit	62

At the end of 2012, the number of people employed in Qingdao was 2,832,000, up 2.7%. At year-end, the registered urban unemployment rate was 2.93%, down 0.02 percentage points.

The number of people covered under the basic pension program was 2,202,400, people who participated in the unemployment insurance program numbered 1,641,500, and people who received payment from the unemployment insurance program numbered 62,100. In 2012, the coverage of the new rural cooperative medical care program in Qingdao reached 100%.

Nursing homes registered 31,503 beds with 18,102 residents.

Note:

1. Figures reported herein are preliminary statistics.

2. The total production value and the absolute added value of the industries in Qingdao were calculated at current prices and growth rates were calculated at comparable prices.

3. The statistics starting point for industries above the designated size is RMB 20,000,000 in terms of annual operating revenue. The statistics starting point for fixed asset investment projects is 5,000,000 in terms of total planned investment amount.

4. According to the national planning, the strategic emerging industries refer to the seven industries or sectors including energy conservation and environmental protection, the new generation of information technology, biology, high-end equipment manufacturing, new energy, new materials and new energy vehicles. At present, the strategic emerging industries being monitored for statistics in Qingdao cover 6 sectors, namely, energy conservation and environmental protection, biology, high-end equipment manufacturing, new energy, new materials and the new generation of information technology.

5. The term of employees means the people who are employed and paid salaries by their employer(s) and those who have a work post or position in the working unit, but are not on job due to training, sick leave, injury leave, maternity leave or other reasons, and are still paid salaries by their employer(s).

Employees' wage means the amount of labor remuneration paid at a certain time to employees by their employers.

Labor remunerations and other pays paid to employees by their employers according to relevant regulations, whether or not included in the cost, whether or not included in the assessment of bonus taxes, and whether paid in cash or in kind, are included in the payroll.

Employers in Qingdao are of such ownership types as the state-owned, collectively-owned, joint operation, shareholding, wholly-foreign-owned, privately-owned and investment by foreign business people and by compatriots from Hong Kong, Macao and Taiwan. Non-private employers in urban areas include those that are state-owned, collectively-owned, joint operation, shareholding, wholly-foreign-owned and investment by foreign business people and by compatriots from Hong Kong, Macao and Taiwan.

6. The median of per capita income of residents in rural and urban areas means the per capita income of the surveyed residents at the middle of the per capita income levels of the surveyed residents which are arranged in the order from low to high. The five equal income groups of rural and urban residents refer to the surveyed residents are arranged with their per capita income levels arranged in the order from low to high, divided into five equal parts; the 20% income group in the highest is the high income group, and following from the top to bottom are the upper middle income group, middle income group, lower middle income group and low income group.

7. The data of the built-up area, water supply, heating, gas supply, tree planting, greening, road, park, zoo, etc. are provided by Qingdao Rural and Urban Construction Commission. The statistics include the data of the newly-divided six districts of Qingdao City with the former Jiaonan city only including 6 sub-districts, namely Zhuhai, Zhushan, Binhai, Tieshan, Lingshan and Yinzhu.

1 综　合

GENERAL SUREY

简 要 说 明

一、本篇资料的主要内容

本篇资料是对我市行政区划、气象情况、分行业法人单位数、各部门机构数和国民经济、社会发展的综合反映，主要包括行政区划、气象情况、分行业法人单位数、各部门机构数、国民经济主要比例关系、国民经济和社会发展主要指标占全国全省比重、国民经济和社会发展主要指标及其增长速度等资料。

二、本篇资料的来源

1、"行政区划"主要包括2012年底各区(市)街道办事处(乡镇)、社区居委会(村民委员会)区划资料，数据来源于市民政局。

2、"气象情况"包括分区市、市区分月气象资料，数据来源于市气象局。

3、"全市生产总值"来源于国民经济核算统计报表，由市统计局国民经济核算处整理提供。

4、国民经济和社会发展综合部分来源于本年鉴各篇章中的资料，由市统计局国民经济综合统计处加工整理。

Brief Introduction

I. Main Content

Data in this chapter cover the main indicators on divisions of administrative areas, meteorology, corporate units, number of grass-roots units and national economy and social development, including divisions of administrative areas, meteorology, number of corporate units, number of grass-roots units, average daily social and economic activities, ratio, and percentage of main indicators of Qingdao to the whole nation and the whole province and growth rate of main indicators.

II. Source of Data

(1) Data on divisions of administrative areas are mainly including the information on sub-district offices (villages and towns) and community neighborhood committees (villagers residents' committees) at the end of 2012.The data are provided by Qingdao Municipal Bureau of Civil Affairs.

(2)Data on meteorology are provided by Qingdao Municipal Meteorological Bureau.

(3)Data on gross national product are prepared according to the data of national accounts and compiled by the Division of National Accounts of Qingdao Municipal Bureau of Statistics.

(4)Data on general survey of economy and society are based on those of different chapters and compiled by the Division of Comprehensive Statistics of Qingdao Municipal Bureau of Statistics.

1-1 行政区划(2012年底)

ADMINISTRATIVE DIVISION(END OF 2012)

单位:个(unit)

市、区名称	Region	街道办事处 Subdistrict Offices 小计 Sub-total	社区居委会 Community Residents' Committees	镇 Town 小计 Sub-total	村民委员会 Villagers' Committees
全　市	**Whole Municipality**	**102**	**1 170**	**43**	**5 447**
市南区	Shinan District	14	65		
市北区	Shibei District	31	173		
李沧区	Licang District	11	121		
崂山区	Laoshan District	4	157		
城阳区	Chengyang District	8	241		1
黄岛区	Huangdao District	12	259	10	965
即墨市	Jimo	8	35	7	1 028
胶州市	Jiaozhou	6	51	6	811
平度市	Pingdu	5	43	12	1 781
莱西市	Laixi	3	25	8	861

注:按新行政区划统计。

Note: The statistics data in this form are according to the new administrative division.

1 -2 气象情况(2012 年)
METEOROLOGY(2012)

市、区名称	Region	平均气温(摄氏度) Average Temperature (℃)	极端气温 Extreme Temperature(℃) 最高(摄氏度) Maximum(℃)	最低(摄氏度) Minimum(℃)	降水量(毫米/年) Precipitation (millimeter/year)	日照时数(小时/年) Sunshine Hours (hour/year)	平均气压(百帕) Average Atmospheric Pressure(100 pa)
市　区	Urban Area	12.7	33.4	-9.8	632.9	2 116.6	1 008.0
崂山区	Laoshan District	13.5	34.3	-10.3	602.6	2 303.5	1 011.9
即墨市	Jimo	13.2	36.1	-11.7	543.4	2 469.9	1 013.4
胶州市	Jiaozhou	12.4	35.3	-12.4	572	2 233.3	1 007.8
原胶南市	Jiaonan	13.0	34.7	-11.1	1 142.6	2 205.3	1 015.6
平度市	Pingdu	12.5	35.9	-13.1	514.9	2 511.7	1 010.8
莱西市	Laixi	11.7	35.8	-14.4	557.4	2 471	1 007.5

1 -3 市区分月气象情况(2012 年)
MONTHLY METEOROLOGY OF URBAN AREA(2012)

月　份	Month	平均气温(摄氏度) Average Temperature (℃)	降水量(毫　米) Precipitation (millimeter)	日照时数(小　时) Sunshine Hours (hour)
一月	Jan.	-0.3	1.8	148.7
二月	Feb.	0.3	2.5	171.2
三月	Mar.	4.7	31.1	177.9
四月	Apr.	11.5	61.7	204.9
五月	May	17.8	2.2	237.3
六月	June	20.6	25.2	131.1
七月	July	24.9	192.9	115.4
八月	Aug.	25.5	165.8	176.4
九月	Sept.	21.8	26.4	201.9
十月	Oct.	17.3	11.0	228.5
十一月	Nov.	7.9	80.8	185.2
十二月	Dec.	0	31.5	138.1
全年	Annual Total	12.7	632.9	2 116.6

1－4 各部门机构数(2012 年底)
GRASS-ROOTS UNITS IN VARIOUS SECTORS(END OF 2012)

项　目	Item	单位	Unit	机构数 Grass-roots Units
农村基层单位	**Rural Grass-roots Units**			
镇政府	Town Governments	个	unit	43
乡村户数	Number of Rural Households	万户	10 000 households	156
工业企业单位	**Industrial Enterprises**	**个**	**unit**	**73 160**
规模以上工业	Above Designated Size	个	unit	4 817
#国有企业	State-owned Enterprises	个	unit	144
集体企业	Collective-owned Enterprises	个	unit	28
外商及港澳台商投资企业	Enterprises with Funds from Hong Kong, Macao, Taiwan and Foreign Countries	个	unit	1 599
规模以下工业	Under Designated Size	个	unit	68 343
#个体	of which: Individual	个	unit	46 224
交通运输业	**Transportation**			
铁路	Railway	个	unit	
公路	Highway	个	unit	76
水运	Waterway	个	unit	18
邮电业	**Postal and Telecommunication Services**			
邮电局所	Post Offices	处	unit	668
建筑业企业	**Construction Enterprises**	**个**	**unit**	**596**
国有企业	State-owned Enterprises	个	unit	31
集体企业	Collective-owned Enterprises	个	unit	23
其他	Others	个	unit	542
批发和零售业、住宿和餐饮业	**Wholesale & Retail Trades, Hotels and Catering Services**			
限额以上批发业	Wholesale Trade above Designated Size	个	unit	927
限额以上零售业	Retail Trade above Designated Size	个	unit	573
限额以上住宿业	Hotel above Designated Size	个	unit	162
限额以上餐饮业	Catering Service above Designated Size	个	unit	200

1-4 续表
continued

项　目	Item	单位	Unit	机构数 Grass-roots Units
教育事业	**Education**			
普通高等学校	Regular Institutions of Higher Education	所	unit	22
中等专业学校	Specialized Secondary Schools	所	unit	8
普通中学	Regular Secondary Schools	所	unit	292
普通小学	Regular Primary Schools	所	unit	840
幼儿园	Kindergartens	所	unit	2 475
科研机构	**Science and Technology Institutions**	**个**	**unit**	**48**
中央属	Central Level	个	unit	11
省属	Provincial Level	个	unit	11
市属	Municipal Level	个	unit	24
县级市属	County Level	个	unit	2
文化及相关产业	**Culture and Related Industry**			
文化事业机构	Cultural Institutions	个	unit	250
公共图书馆	Public Libraries	个	unit	13
影剧院	Cinemas	个	unit	36
广播、电视台	**Radio and Television Broadcasting Stations**			
广播电台	Radio Stations	个	unit	1
电视台	Television Stations	个	unit	1
卫生事业	**Public Health**	**个**	**unit**	**2 6[illegible]7**
#医院	Hospitals	个	unit	2[illegible]8
民政行政单位	**Civil Affairs Departments**			
#社会福利事业机构	Institutions of Social Welfare	个	unit	263

1-5 按行业分法人单位数
NUMBER OF CORPORATE UNITS BY SECTOR

单位：个(unit)

行　业	Sector	2012	2011
总　计	**Total**	**161 158**	**145 788**
农、林、牧、渔业	Agriculture Forestry Animal Husbandry and Fishery	2 852	2 094
采矿业	Mining	297	393
制造业	Manufacturing	40 668	39 670
电力、燃气及水的生产和供应业	Production and Supply of Electricity Gas and Water	292	273
建筑业	Construction	8 490	7 543
批发和零售业	Wholesale and Retail Trades	55 144	46 819
交通运输、仓储和邮政业	Transport Storage and Post	5 411	4 851
住宿和餐饮业	Hotels and Catering Services	2 321	2 214
信息传输、软件和信息技术服务业	Information Transmission Computer Services and Software	2 711	3 326
金融业	Financial Intermediation	604	350
房地产业	Real Estate	4 300	4 099
租赁和商务服务业	Leasing and Business Services	13 275	12 079
科学研究和技术服务业	Scientific Research and Technical Services	3 082	2 669
水利、环境和公共设施管理业	Management of Water Conservancy Environment and Public Facilities	850	781
居民服务、修理和其他服务业	Services to Households and Other Services	4 314	3 518
教　育	Education	2 603	2 591
卫生和社会工作	Health Social Security and Social Welfare	1 324	1 302
文化、体育和娱乐业	Culture Sports and Entertainment	2 396	966
公共管理、社会保障和社会组织	Public Management and Social Organizations	10 224	10 250
国际组织	International Organization		

注：本表数据来源于基本单位统计年报。

Note: Data in this form are based on the annual report of basic units.

1－6 国民经济主要平均指标
AVERAGE INDICATORS ON NATIONAL ECONOMY

指　　标	Indicator	单 位	Unit	1990	1995
人口密度	Density of Population	人/平方公里	person/sq. km	626	643
每户年平均人口	Average Household Size	人	person	3.57	3.29
在岗职工年平均工资	Annual Average Wage of Employed Staff and Workers	元	yuan	2 400	6 164
城市居民人均年可支配收入	Annual Per Capita Disposable Income of Urban Households	元	yuan	1 624	5 612
农民人均年纯收入	Annual Per Capita Net Income of Rural Households	元	yuan	952	2 225
每一播亩平均粮食产量	Output of Grain Per Mu of Sowing Area	千克	kg	351	409
每亩蔬菜平均产量	Average Output of Vegetables Per Mu	千克	kg	3 017	3 274
每亩茶叶平均产量	Average Output of Tea Per Mu	千克	kg	35.0	8.0
每亩花生平均产量	Average Output of Peanut Per Mu	千克	kg	244	311
每亩棉花平均产量	Average Output of Cotton Per Mu	千克	kg	55	39
每台拖拉机负担耕地面积	Cultivated Area Ploughed by Per Tractor	亩/台	mu/unit	135	129
每亩耕地施用化肥量（折纯）	Chemical Fertilizer Consumption Per Mu(convert to pure amount)	千克	kg	27	43
每人平均消费品零售额	Per Capita Retail Sales of Consumer Goods	元	yuan	995	3 487
城市每天平均生活用水量	Daily Residential Consumption of Water	万吨	10 000 tons	11.70	22.50
城市每人平均公园绿地面积	Per Capita Public Green Areas	平方米	sq. m	3.70	5.40
每万人拥有医疗床位	Number of Hospital Beds per 10000 Population	张	bed	35.3	36.9
每万人拥有医生数	Number of Doctors per 10000 Population	人	person	20.6	20.2
每万人中高等学校学生数	Students Enrollment of Institutions of Higher Education per 10 000 Population	人	person	23	36
每万人中中等学校学生数	Students Enrollment of Secondary Schools per 10 000 Population	人	person	527	658
每万人中小学学生数	Students Enrollment of Primary Schools per 10000 Population	人	person	948	870

注：1990 年、1995 年在岗职工年平均工资统计范围为城镇单位全部职工。

Note: Annual average wage of employed staff and workers in 1990 and 1995 refers to average wage of units in urban area.

2000	2005	2006	2007	2008	2009	2010	2011	2012
564	695	703	711	715	676	677	679	682
3.14	3.12	3.13	3.14	3.13	3.12	3.1	3.09	3.09
10 07[illegible]	20 022	23 457	27 083	30 233	33 258	37 805	43 077	49 052
8 015	12 920	15 328	17 856	20 464	22 368	24 998	28 567	32 145
[illegible]	5 806	6 546	7 477	8 509	9 249	10 550	12 370	13 990
4[illegible]1	421	407	422	436	446	437	444	456
2 7[illegible]5	2 985	3 078	3 166	3 511	3 562	3 606	3 759	3 755.7
8.1	16.5	18.0	21.0	28.0	28.0	30.0	30.4	33.1
298	327	309	312	315	312	303	313	321.4
83	74	76	75	78	79	78	87	104.6
56	39	36	36	36	35	32	31.2	
45	52	52	55	50	48	47	46.6	
6 07[illegible]	11 822	13 640	16 137	19 640	22 699	25 694	30 043	34 248
[illegible]	34.35	29.27	31.25	30.96	33.56	34.31	27.53	33.21
[illegible]	11.82	11.80	13.30	14.53	14.50	14.58	14.58	14.6
34.5	41.3	38.3	39.7	42.5	43.0	47.2	52.2	61.4
21.0	20.3	20.6	19.8	21.4	21.9	23.2	23.9	28.1
[illegible]55	324	347	349	354	361	373	380	386
[illegible]04	768	740	737	765	740	701	659	635
[illegible]57	648	646	640	627	610	606	626	630

1 -7 主要年份社会经济主要指标
MAJOR YEAR'S INDICATORS ON SOCIETY AND ECONOMY

指　标	Indicator	单 位	Unit	1990	1995
人口	**Population**				
总人口(年末)	Population at Year-end	万人	10 000 persons	666.65	684.63
男性人口	Male	万人	10 000 persons	339.23	347.63
女性人口	Female	万人	10 000 persons	327.42	337.00
市区人口	Urban Area	万人	10 000 persons	205.78	213.38
就业	**Employment**				
社会从业人员	Employment	万人	10 000 persons	352.8	374.2
#单位从业人员	Employed Persons in Units	万人	10 000 persons	103.2	111.6
经济总量	**Gross Economic Amount**				
全市生产总值(当年价)	GDP(at current price)	亿元	100 million yuan	180.77	631.45
第一产业增加值	Primary Industry	亿元	100 million yuan	39.26	112.53
第二产业增加值	Secondary Industry	亿元	100 million yuan	86.76	294.43
第三产业增加值	Tertiary Industry	亿元	100 million yuan	54.75	224.49
人均生产总值	Per Capita GDP	元	yuan	2 714	9 089
农林牧渔业总产值(当年价)	Gross Output Value of Farming, Forestry, Animal Husbandry and Fishery (at current price)	亿元	100 million yuan	57.99	192.38
工业总产值(当年价)	Gross Industrial Output Value (at current price)	亿元	100 million yuan	357.18	941.26

注:1. 单位从业人员 2004 年以前为职工人数(不含私营企业)。
2. 规模以上固定资产投资数据 2003 年以前为城镇以上统计范围。
3. 2002 年以前地方财政一般预算收支数据为地方财政收支口径。

Note: 1. Before 2004, the data of employed persons in units refers to the number of staff and workers (excluding private enterprises).
2. Before 2003, the data of investment in fixed assets above designated size refers to urban investment.
3. Before 2002, the data of general budgetaty revenue and expenditure of local government finance refers to revenue and expenditure of local government finance.

2000	2005	2006	2007	2008	2009	2010	2011	2012
706.6[illegible]	740.91	749.38	757.99	761.56	762.92	763.64	766.36	769.56
357.[illegible]	374.03	377.99	381.66	382.46	382.35	381.92	382.69	383.82
348.[illegible]1	366.87	371.39	376.33	379.10	380.56	381.72	383.67	385.74
2[illegible]4.[illegible]0	265.43	270.99	275.55	276.25	275.47	275.50	277.09	279.57
397.6	471.0	490.1	505.8	513.8	525.7	540.3	551.2	559.9
11[illegible].3	224.3	243.2	249.8	254.1	260.5	269.4	275.9	283.2
1 [illegible]91.2[illegible]	2 687.46	3 183.18	3 750.16	4 401.56	4 853.87	5 666.19	6 615.60	7 302.11
140.8[illegible]	178.33	183.95	203.59	223.40	230.25	276.99	306.38	324.41
55[illegible].2	1 392.02	1 666.96	1 934.52	2 234.83	2 420.14	2 758.62	3 150.72	3 402.23
49[illegible].1[illegible]	1 117.10	1 332.28	1 612.05	1 943.33	2 203.48	2 630.58	3 158.50	3 575.47
16 00[illegible]	33 085	38 608	44 964	52 266	57 251	65 827	75 563	82 680
243.[illegible]	320.51	339.61	342.99	400.85	408.61	483.18	535.93	566.52
[illegible] 9[illegible]0.[illegible]3	5 001.78	5 918.81	7 430.64	8 946.73	10 255.62	11 614.83	13 277.96	15 306.32

1-7 续表 1
continued

指　　标	Indicator	单 位	Unit	1990	1995
财政	**Government Finance**				
公共财政预算收入	Budgetaty Revenue of Public Finance	亿元	100 million yuan	24.23	29.48
公共财政预算支出	Budgetaty Expenditure of Public Finance	亿元	100 million yuan	13.39	37.70
规模以上固定资产投资额	**Investment in Fixed Assets above Designated Size**	**亿元**	**100 million yuan**	**28.46**	**164.83**
社会消费品零售额	**Total Retail Sales of Consumer Goods**	**亿元**	**100 million yuan**	**65.83**	**237.68**
港口吞吐量	**Volume of Freight Handled in Ports**	**万吨**	**10 000 tons**	**3 068**	**5 165**
集装箱吞吐量	**Volume of Containers Handled**	**万吨**	**10 000 tons**		
民航货邮吞吐量	**Volume of Freight and Mail Handled in Civil Aviation**	**万吨**	**10 000 tons**	**0.20**	**2.10**
对外贸易	**Foreign Trade**				
外贸进出口总额(不含中央省公司)	Imports and Exports (excluding central and provincial companies)	亿美元	100 million USD	4.16	37.64
#出口总额	Exports	亿美元	100 million USD	3.35	24.51
教育、卫生、文化	**Education Public Health, Culture**				
小学在校学生数	Students Enrollment in Primary Schools	万人	10 000 persons	63.23	59.39
普通中学在校学生	Students Enrollment in Regular Secorndary Schools	万人	10 000 persons	29.62	37.23

	2000	2005	2006	2007	2008	2009	2010	2011	2012
	80.01	176.34	225.77	292.58	342.44	376.99	452.61	566.14	670.18
	87.37	203.06	236.79	321.18	369.41	433.58	532.39	658.06	765.98
	242.68	**1 403.30**	**1 485.69**	**1 635.36**	**2 019.01**	**2 458.89**	**3 022.48**	**3 502.54**	**4 153.91**
	428.29	**870.11**	**1 016.35**	**1 216.22**	**1 492.22**	**1 730.22**	**1 961.13**	**2 302.37**	**2 635.62**
	8 561	**18 727**	**22 438**	**26 507**	**30 029**	**31 668**	**35 012**	**37 971**	**41 465**
	212.0	**630.7**	**770.0**	**946.6**	**1 037.7**	**1 027.7**	**1 201.0**	**1 302.0**	**1 450**
	4.84	**8.91**	**10.10**	**11.57**	**13.05**	**13.54**	**16.37**	**16.65**	**17.19**
	108.31	304.55	365.57	436.05	521.59	439.86	561.49	712.63	732.08
	51.14	175.88	216.45	267.76	314.62	269.22	333.51	400.56	408.20
	53.49	47.98	48.39	48.48	47.72	46.50	46.27	47.95	49.50
	39.85	39.11	36.52	36.04	37.39	37.74	38.00	37.32	36.96

1 –7 续表 2
continued

指　　标	Indicator	单　位	Unit	1990	1995
高等学校在校学生	Students Enrollment in Institutions of Higher Education	万人	10 000 persons	1.54	2.49
小学专任教师	Full-time Teachers in Primary Schools	万人	10 000 persons	3.15	3.00
普通中学专任教师	Full-time Teachers in Regular Secorndary Schools	万人	10 000 persons	2.04	2.26
影剧院	Cinemas	个	unit	106	61
医生总数	Doctors	万人	10 000 persons	1.38	1.38
医院床位数	Hospital Beds	万张	10 000 beds	1.66	1.81
人民生活	**People's Living Conditions**				
在岗职工工资总额	Total Wage Bill of Employed Staff and Workers	亿元	100 million yuan	24.39	68.30
城市居民人均可支配收入	Per Capita Disposable Income of Urban Households	元	yuan	1 624	5 612
农民人均纯收入	Per Capita Net Income of Rural Households	元	yuan	952	2 225
城乡人民币储蓄存款余额	Savings Deposit of Urban and Rural Households	亿元	100 million yuan	65.59	268.79
物价指数	**Price Indexes**				
商品零售价格指数(以1950年价格为100)	Retail Price Index(1950 = 100)	%	%	269.7	536.2
居民消费价格指数(以1950年价格为100)	Consumer Price Index(1950 = 100)	%	%	269.7	587.3
#食品价格指数(以1950年价格为100)	Food Price Index(1950 = 100)	%	%	333.3	792.5

注:在岗职工工资总额2005年前统计范围为全部职工不含私营企业。

Note: Before 2005, the statistics range of total wage bill of employed staff and workers is all the staff and workers except those in private enterprises.

2000	2005	2006	2007	2008	2009	2010	2011	2012
4.61	23.98	26.03	26.49	26.93	27.52	28.49	29.15	29.66
3.17	3.17	3.22	3.26	3.24	3.22	3.2	3.16	3.17
2.63	2.97	2.92	2.96	2.99	3.06	3.08	3.14	3.2
45	39	40	40	40	40	40	40	36
1.49	1.50	1.55	1.50	1.63	1.67	1.77	1.83	2.16
2.01	2.86	2.67	2.81	2.99	3.05	3.34	3.56	4.12
12[illegible].[illegible]	359.5	445.6	518.1	578.7	638.1	738	877.5	1 044.3
3 0 6	12 920	15 328	17 856	20 464	22 368	24 998	28 567	32 145
3 637	5 806	6 546	7 477	8 509	9 249	10 550	12 370	13 990
535.32	1 343.10	1 567.62	1 702.04	2 123.36	2 527.88	2 912.33	3 198.51	3 757.60
520.5	495.0	493.5	506.8	526.6	519.2	526.5	550.2	559.6
711.9	753.1	759.9	794.1	831.4	835.6	854.0	896.7	920.9
800.1	871.8	886.6	989.5	1 105.3	1 123.0	1 194.9	1 327.5	1 384.6

1－8 国民经济主要结构指标
COMPOSITION INDICATORS ON NATIONAL ECONOMY

指　　标	Indicator	1990	1995	2000
社会从业人员	**Employment**			
产业结构	Industrial Composition			
第一产业	Primary Industry	44.4	41.5	36.4
第二产业	Secondary Industry	34.9	35.4	33.9
第三产业	Tertiary Industry	20.7	23.1	29.7
全市生产总值	**GDP**			
产业结构	Industrial Composition			
第一产业	Primary Industry	21.7	17.8	11.8
第二产业	Secondary Industry	48.0	46.6	46.6
第三产业	Tertiary Industry	30.3	35.6	41.6
农业	**Agriculture**			
农林牧渔业产值结构	Composition of Farming, Forestry, Animal Husbandry and Fishery			
#农业	Farming	65.8	53.1	45.[illegible]
林业	Forestry	2.4	1.4	0.8
牧业	Animal Husbandry	20.6	26.2	27.9
渔业	Fishery	11.3	19.3	26.4
工业	**Industy**			
轻重工业产值结构	Composition of Output Value of Light and Heavy Industry			
轻工业	Light Industry	57.6	59.3	64.1
重工业	Heavy Industry	42.4	40.7	35.9
固定资产投资	**Investment in Fixed Assets**			
投资结构	Composition of Investment			
生产性	Productive	74.0	56.1	54.0
非生产性	Non-productive	26.0	43.9	46.0

单位:%

2005	2006	2007	2008	2009	2010	2011	2012
22.2	21.0	20.2	19.9	20.1	19.5	19.2	18.8
41.8	42.8	43.1	43.0	41.9	41.4	41.2	41.0
36.0	36.2	36.7	37.1	38.0	39.1	39.6	40.2
5.[illegible]	5.8	5.4	5.1	4.7	4.9	4.6	4.4
51.[illegible]	52.4	51.6	50.8	49.9	48.7	47.6	46.6
[illegible]1.5	41.8	43.0	44.1	45.4	46.4	47.8	49.0
39.5	40.1	43.3	44.4	45.4	48.4	44.1	44.0
0.8	0.7	0.6	0.6	0.5	0.4	0.4	0.4
3[illegible].4	31.7	28.4	30.3	28.4	26.2	29.1	27.9
2[illegible].3	25.2	24.2	21.4	22.0	21.8	23.0	24.2
[illegible]9.4	48.5	45.0	42.3	41.7	38.7	38.3	39.5
[illegible]0.6	51.5	55.0	57.7	58.3	61.3	61.7	60.5
65.4	62.0	62.6	61.6	56.3	53.6	53.2	58.4
34.6	38.0	37.4	38.4	43.7	46.4	46.8	41.6

1 -9 平均每天主要社会经济活动
SELECTED INDICATORS ON AVERAGE DAILY SOCIAL AND ECONOMIC ACTIVITIES

指　　标	Indicator	单位	Unit	1990	1995
全市生产总值	GDP	万元	10 000 yuan	4 952	17 300
工业总产值	Gross Industrial Output Value	万元	10 000 yuan	9 786	25 788
农林牧渔业总产值	Gross Output Value of Farming, Forestry, Animal Husbandry and Fishery	万元	10 000 yuan	1 589	5 271
主要工业产品产量	Output of Major Industrial Products				
发电量	Electricity	万千瓦时	10 000 kW · h	1 102	1 772
钢材	Rolled-steel	吨	ton	1 042	1 359
纱	Yarn	吨	ton	275	218
布	Cloth	万米	10 000 m	93	113
家用电冰箱	Refrigerator	台	unit	751	2 956
彩色电视机	Color TV set	台	unit	507	1 658
社会消费品零售总额	Total Retail Sales of Consumer Goods	万元	10 000 yuan	1 803	6 512
固定资产投资	Investment in Fixed Assets above Designated Size	万元	10 000 yuan	780	4 516
外贸进出口总额	Imports and Exports	万美元	10 000 USD		2 352
港口吞吐量	Volume of Freight Handled in Ports	万吨	10 000 tons	8.41	14.15

注:固定资产投资包括城镇、农村500万元以上投资项目。
Note: Investment in fixed assets includes construction projects involving an urban or rural investment of 5,000,000 yuan and over.

2000	2005	2006	2007	2008	2009	2010	2011	2012
32 637	73 629	87 210	102 744	120 591	132 983	155 238	181 249	200 058
53 174	137 035	162 159	203 579	245 116	280 976	318 215	363 780	419 351
6 803	8 781	9 304	9 397	10 982	11 195	13 238	14 683	15 521
2 489	2 701	3 412	4 255	4 509	4 730	4 984	4 759	4 787
2 558	9 049	10 288	10 015	9 593	9 579	9 136	9 101	7 525
191	198	154	131	118	106	97	53	53
114	141	151	121	133	85	48	120	134
8 523	24 899	35 342	22 173	19 813	22 663	21 951	19 686	15 754
10 395	36 282	33 030	23 989	22 922	29 170	30 444	31 622	39 452
11 734	23 839	27 845	33 321	40 883	47 403	53 730	63 079	72 209
6 6[illegible]9	38 446	40 704	44 804	55 315	67 367	82 808	95 960	113 806
3 7[illegible]7	9 047	12 527	12 527	14 695	12 288	15 633	19 768	20 057
23.[illegible]3	51.31	61.47	72.62	82.27	86.76	95.92	104.03	114

1－10 主要指标占全国全省比重(2012 年)

PERCENTAGE OF MAIN INDICATORS TO CHINA AND SHANDONG(2012)

指　标	Indicator	单位	Unit
一、生产总值	GDP	亿元	100 million yuan
第一产业	Primary Industry	亿元	100 million yuan
第二产业	Secondary Industry	亿元	100 million yuan
第三产业	Tertiary Industry	亿元	100 million yuan
二、年末总人口(常住人口)			
三、主要工业产品产量	Output of Major Industrial Products		
纱	Yarn	万吨	10 000 tons
布	Cloth	亿米	100 million m
家用电冰箱	Refrigerator	万台	10 000 units
彩色电视机	Color TV Set	万部	10 000 units
发电量	Electricity	亿千瓦时	100 million kW · h
钢材	Rolled-steel	万吨	10 000 tons
水泥	Cement	万吨	10 000 tons
四、主要农产品产量	Output of Major Farm Products		
粮食	Grain	万吨	10 000 tons
油料	Oil Plants	万吨	10 000 tons
棉花	Cotton	万吨	10 000 tons
肉类产量	Meat	万吨	10 000 tons
水产品	Aquatic Products	万吨	10 000 tons
五、固定资产投资额	Investment in Fixed Assets	亿元	100 million yuan
六、社会消费品零售总额	Total Retail Sales of Consumer Goods	亿元	100 million yuan
七、高等学校在校学生	Students Enrollment of Institutions of Higher Education	万人	10 000 persons

注:1. 本表全国、全省均为公报数。
　2. 青岛市主要工业产品产量数据为本地口径。

Note:1. The number of the country and the province in the table are obtained from the statistical report.
　2. The output of main industrial products of qingdao are at local calibre.

全国 China	全省 Shandong	青岛市 Qingdao	青岛市占全国 比重(%) Qingdao/China	青岛市占全省 比重(%) Qingdao/Shandong
519 32[illegible]	50 013	7 302.11	1.41	14.60
52 37[illegible]	4 282	324.41	0.62	7.58
23[illegible] 31[illegible]	25 736	3 402.23	1.45	13.22
231 62[illegible]	19 996	3 575.47	1.54	17.88
13[illegible] 404	9 685	886.90	0.66	9.16
[illegible] 9[illegible]4	832.5	1.94	0.07	0.23
[illegible]40[illegible] 8	143.4	4.9	0.58	3.42
8 4[illegible]7	575.01	575.01	6.82	100.00
12 [illegible]23	1 505	1 439.98	11.23	95.71
[illegible]9 [illegible]78	3 195	174.72	0.35	5.47
[illegible]5 [illegible]18	7 818	274.67	0.29	3.51
2[illegible]1 [illegible]00	15 386	556.57	0.25	3.62
[illegible]8 [illegible]57	4511.4	369.96	0.63	8.20
3 [illegible]76	351	45.9	1.32	13.08
[illegible]84	69.8	0.43	0.06	0.62
8 [illegible]84	752.5	61.37	0.73	8.16
5 [illegible]906	841.9	112.44	1.90	13.36
[illegible]74 676	31 256	4 153.9	1.11	13.29
[illegible]10 307	19 175	2 635.62	1.25	13.74
[illegible] 391	165.8	29.7	1.24	17.91

1-11 主要年份全市生产总值(按当年价格计算)

MAJOR YEAR'S GROSS DOMESTIC PRODUCT(AT CURRENT PRICE)

单位:亿元（100 million yuan)

年份 Year	全市生产总值 GDP	第一产业 Primary Industry	第二产业 Secondary Industry	#工业 Industry	第三产业 Tertiary Industry	人均生产总值(元) Per Capita GDP (yuan)
1949	2.87	1.19	1.10	-	0.58	71
1952	6.74	1.76	3.25	2.95	1.73	163
1957	10.82	2.00	5.76	5.39	3.06	239
1962	9.69	1.11	4.68	4.27	3.90	205
1965	15.50	1.80	8.96	8.48	4.74	325
1970	23.23	3.15	14.46	13.86	5.62	451
1975	29.07	6.93	15.39	14.67	6.75	522
1978	38.43	8.73	20.25	19.15	9.45	663
1980	48.65	10.19	26.27	24.28	12.19	819
1985	82.28	21.29	37.55	34.03	23.44	1 311
1988	142.87	32.72	70.32	63.42	39.83	2 199
1989	159.68	30.79	82.03	74.33	46.86	2 426
1990	180.77	39.26	86.76	78.94	54.75	2 714
1991	205.65	43.04	98.94	89.64	63.67	3 053
1992	261.35	43.92	130.27	117.61	87.16	3 856
1993	371.90	62.20	183.35	164.35	126.35	5 455
1994	510.81	85.12	244.30	218.87	181.39	7 436
1995	631.45	112.53	294.43	263.98	224.49	9 089
1996	713.60	133.27	322.33	289.87	258.00	10 130
1997	802.59	117.47	378.25	342.80	306.87	11 235
1998	901.19	140.66	409.60	369.89	350.93	12 443
1999	1 018.97	138.19	468.67	424.15	412.11	13 884
2000	1 191.25	140.85	555.21	504.44	495.19	15 009
2001	1 368.55	144.35	643.44	582.99	580.76	1[illegible] 128
2002	1 583.51	147.21	758.33	686.55	677.97	20 655
2003	1 869.44	148.92	923.76	832.31	796.76	23 986
2004	2 270.16	163.49	1 149.94	1 032.50	956.73	28 540
2005	2 687.46	178.33	1 392.02	1 259.06	1 117.10	33 085
2006	3 183.18	183.95	1 666.96	1 517.28	1 332.28	38 608
2007	3 750.16	203.59	1 934.52	1 766.28	1 612.05	44 964
2008	4 401.56	223.40	2 234.83	2 034.25	1 943.33	52 266
2009	4 853.87	230.25	2 420.14	2 174.43	2 203.48	57 251
2010	5 666.19	276.99	2 758.62	2 454.19	2 630.58	65 827
2011	6 615.60	306.38	3 150.72	2 794.56	3 158.50	75 563
2012	7 302.11	324.41	3 402.23	3 041.31	3 575.47	82 680

注:1. 人均生产总值按常住人口计算 。

2. 自 2005 年起三次产业分类采用《国民经济行业分类》(GB/T4754-2002)标准。

3. 本表数据为第二次经济普查修订后数据。

Note:1. Per capita GDP are calculated at permanent population.

2. Three Industries are grouped by "Classification and Code of the Sectors of the National Economy"(GB / T4754-2002) since 2005

3. Data in this form have been amended according to the results of the Second China Economic Census.

1－12 主要年份全市生产总值构成(以全市生产总值为100)

COMPOSITION OF MAJOR YEAR'S GROSS DOMESTIC PRODUCT(GROSS DOMESTIC PRODUCT＝100)

单位:%

年份 Year	全市生产总值 GDP	第一产业 Primary Industry	第二产业 Secondary Industry	#工业 Industry	第三产业 Tertiary Industry
1952	100	26.1	48.2	43.8	25.7
1957	100	18.5	53.3	49.8	28.2
1962	100	11.4	48.3	44.1	40.3
1965	100	11.6	57.8	54.7	30.6
1970	100	13.6	62.2	59.7	24.2
1975	100	23.9	52.9	50.5	23.2
1978	100	22.7	52.7	49.8	24.6
1980	100	21.0	54.0	49.9	25.1
1985	100	25.9	45.6	41.4	28.5
1988	100	22.9	49.2	44.4	27.9
1989	100	19.3	51.4	46.6	29.3
1990	100	21.7	48.0	43.7	30.3
1991	100	20.9	48.1	43.6	31.0
1992	100	16.8	49.8	45.0	33.4
1993	100	16.7	49.3	44.2	34.0
1994	100	16.7	47.8	42.8	35.5
1995	100	17.8	46.6	41.8	35.6
1996	100	18.7	45.2	40.6	36.2
1997	100	14.6	47.1	42.7	38.2
1998	100	15.6	45.5	41.0	38.9
1999	100	13.6	46.0	41.6	40.4
2000	100	11.8	46.6	42.3	41.6
2001	100	10.5	47.0	42.6	42.4
2002	100	9.3	47.9	43.4	42.8
2003	100	8.0	49.4	44.5	42.6
2004	100	7.2	50.7	45.5	42.1
2005	100	6.6	51.8	46.8	41.6
2006	100	5.8	52.4	47.7	41.8
2007	100	5.4	51.6	47.1	43.0
2008	100	5.1	50.8	46.2	44.1
2009	100	4.7	49.9	44.8	45.4
2010	100	4.9	48.7	43.3	46.4
2011	100	4.6	47.6	41.5	47.8
2012	100	4.4	46.6	41.6	49.0

1－13 主要年份全市生产总值增长速度(以上年为100)

GROWTH RATE OF MAJOR YEAR'S GROSS DOMESTIC PRODUCT(PRECEDING YEAR＝100)

单位:%

年份 Year	全市生产总值 GDP	第一产业 Primary Industry	第二产业 Secondary Industry	第三产业 Tertiary Industry	人均生产总值 Per Capita GDP
1979	12.0	10.6	12.9	11.4	10.4
1980	10.4	4.3	13.1	10.3	9.4
1981	-2.0	-9.1	-2.4	4.7	-3.2
1982	4.1	5.5	-0.2	11.9	2.6
1983	16.9	42.8	9.3	12.7	15.3
1984	13.0	18.9	11.5	10.3	12.0
1985	9.9	5.4	5.8	21.3	9.3
1986	9.2	2.6	12.1	10.0	8.3
1987	12.0	3.6	16.0	12.0	10.6
1988	13.8	-0.3	21.5	11.2	12.1
1989	5.1	-0.8	4.6	9.9	3.8
1990	9.3	9.8	7.3	12.2	8.0
1991	10.6	9.9	11.0	10.5	9.4
1992	18.1	2.7	23.5	20.7	17.4
1993	22.4	20.5	21.1	25.6	21.7
1994	14.4	3.6	14.7	20.2	13.5
1995	12.0	10.9	12.1	12.4	10.8
1996	7.2	7.7	7.6	6.4	5.7
1997	11.5	-10.6	16.8	14.6	9.9
1998	12.9	17.6	11.3	13.4	11.3
1999	13.9	4.1	15.5	15.3	12.4
2000	15.2	6.5	16.4	16.4	13.6
2001	13.7	2.3	16.3	14.2	12.1
2002	14.5	3.2	16.9	14.6	12.7
2003	16.3	2.5	20.1	14.9	14.4
2004	16.7	2.7	20.3	15.2	14.3
2005	16.6	0.4	19.6	15.7	14.1
2006	15.3	0.9	16.8	15.8	13.6
2007	15.5	-2.6	15.3	18.3	14.2
2008	13.2	1.4	11.1	17.1	12.1
2009	12.2	3.0	12.8	12.5	11.4
2010	12.9	1.4	12.6	14.4	11.2
2011	11.7	5.0	11.6	12.4	9.8
2012	10.6	3.2	11.5	10.5	9.7
1978－2010 平均每年增长 1978－2010 Average Increase Rate	12.4	5.3	13.1	13.9	11.0
1991－2010 平均每年增长 1991－2010 Average Increase Rate	14.2	4.2	15.5	15.3	12.8
1996－2010 平均每年增长 1996－2010 Average Increase Rate	13.8	2.5	15.2	14.5	13.0
2001－2010 平均每年增长 2001－2010 Average Increase Rate	14.7	1.5	16.1	15.2	13.0
2006－2010 平均每年增长 2006－2010 Average Increase Rate	13.8	0.8	13.7	15.6	12.5

1-14 分市、区生产总值(2012 年)
GROSS DOMESTIC PRODUCT BY REGION(2012)

单位:亿元(100 million yuan)

市、区名称	Region	地区生产总值 GDP	第一产业 Primary Industry	第二产业 Secondary Industry	#工业 Industry	第三产业 Tertiary Industry
市南区	Shinan District	710.11		63.15	32.56	646.96
原市北区	Original Shibei District	330.45		56.19	32.19	274.26
原四方区	Original Sifang District	198.00		80.50	66.42	117.50
李沧区	Licang District	272.69		133.83	124.02	138.86
崂山区	Laoshan District	403.35	5.42	222.56	190.00	175.37
原黄岛区	Original Huangdao District	1365.01	4.56	857.88	797.79	502.57
城阳区	Chengyang District	726.58	3.04	435.32	421.39	288.22
即墨市	Jimo	787.97	56.80	417.65	375.64	313.52
胶州市	Jiaozhou	754.28	47.68	418.85	377.70	287.75
原胶南市	Original Jiaonan	725.71	52.31	422.65	384.55	250.75
平度市	Pingdu	704.47	89.05	353.45	326.96	261.97
莱西市	Laixi	529.88	52.50	259.43	232.52	217.95

注:1. 本表按当年价格计算。

2. 三次产业分类采用《国民经济行业分类》(GB/T4754-2002)标准 。

Note:1 The data are calculated at current price.

2 Three Industries are grouped by "Classification and Code of the Sectors of the National Economy" (GB/T4754-2002).

1－15 按支出法计算的全市生产总值(2012 年)

GROSS DOMESTIC PRODUCT BY EXPENDITURE APPROACH(2012)

单位:亿元(100 million yuan)

项　目	Item	2012	2011	2012 年为 2011 年% 2012/2011(%)
支出法计算的全市生产总值	**Gross Domestic Product by Expenditure Approach**	**7 302.11**	**6 615.60**	**110.6**
(一)最终消费	Final Consumption Expenditures	2 433.84	2 228.55	107.0
1. 居民消费	Household Consumption Expenditures	1 824.53	1 676.91	106.5
农村居民	Rural Household	295.06	273.23	105.4
城镇居民	Urban Household	1 529.48	1 403.68	106.5
2. 政府消费	Government Consumption Expenditures	609.31	551.64	108.6
(二)资本形成总额	Gross Capital Formation	4 159.37	3 590.37	114.3
1. 固定资本形成总额	Gross Fixed Capital Formation	4 024.09	3 469.72	114.4
2. 存货增加	Change in Inventories	135.28	120.65	111.0
(三)货物和服务净流出	Net Exports of Goods and Services	708.90	796.68	105.2

注:绝对额按当年价格计算,速度按可比价格计算。

Note:The absolute numbers are calculated at current price, their growth are calculated at constant price.

1-16 全市生产总值构成(2012年)
COMPOSITION OF GROSS DOMESTIC PRODUCT(2012)

指　标	Indicator	增加值(亿元) Added Value (100 million yuan)	2012年为2011年% 2012/2011(%)
全市生产总值	**GDP**	**7 302.11**	**110.6**
第一产业	Primary Industry	324.41	103.2
农、林、牧、渔业	Farming, Forestry, Animal Husbandry and Fishery	324.41	103.2
第二产业	Secondary Industry	3 402.23	111.5
工业	Industry	3 041.31	111.9
建筑业	Construction	360.92	108.5
第三产业	Tertiary Industry	3 575.47	110.5
交通运输、仓储和邮政业	Transport, Storage and Post	549.24	111.9
信息传输、计算机服务和软件业	Information Transmission, Computer Services and Software	134.16	99.5
批发和零售业	Wholesale and Retail Trade	842.00	105.6
住宿和餐饮业	Hotels and Catering Services	146.58	84.5
金融业	Financial Intermediation	397.62	119.0
房地产业	Real Estate	362.43	138.1
租赁和商务服务业	Leasing and Business Services	265.00	137.1
科学研究、技术服务和地质勘查业	Scientific Research, Technical Services and Geologic Prospecting	104.15	113.7
水利、环境和公共设施管理业	Management of Water Conservancy, Environment and Public Facilities	39.40	113.0
居民服务和其他服务业	Services to Households and Other Services	96.87	68.8
教育	Education	221.25	112.3
卫生、社会保障和社会福利业	Health, Social Security and Social Welfare	118.70	121.3
文化、体育和娱乐业	Culture, Sports and Entertainment	51.93	114.8
公共管理和社会组织	Public Management and Social Organization	246.14	101.2

注:表中绝对数按现行价格计算;相对数按可比价格计算。

Note: The absolute numbers are calculated at current price, the relative numbers are calculated at constant price.

主要统计指标解释

国内生产总值(GDP)　指按市场价格计算的一个国家(或地区)所有常住单位在一定时期内生产活动的最终成果。国内生产总值有三种表现形态,即价值形态、收入形态和产品形态。从价值形态看,它是所有常住单位在一定时期内生产的全部货物和服务价值超过同期中间投入的全部非固定资产货物和服务价值的差额,即所有常住单位的增加值之和;从收入形态看,它是所有常住单位在一定时期内创造并分配给常住单位和非常住单位的初次收入分配之和;从产品形态看,它是所有常住单位在一定时期内最终使用的货物和服务价值与货物和服务净出口价值之和。在实际核算中,国内生产总值有三种计算方法,即生产法、收入法和支出法。三种方法分别从不同的方面反映国内生产总值及其构成。对于一个地区来说,称为地区生产总值或地区 GDP。

人均 GDP　人均 GDP 是一定时期内 GDP 与同期人口平均数的比值。按照国际标准,人口平均数应该是同期平均常住人口。我国在核算制度中也规定,无论是国家还是地区,人口数都采用常住人口。国家统计局规定从 2004 年开始,过去采用户籍人口计算人均 GDP 的地区,作为过渡性措施,可在两年内同时计算两种口径的人均 GDP(数据后面必须注明是什么口径),两年后取消按户籍人口计算的人均 GDP。我市采用常住人口计算人均 GDP。

三次产业　是根据社会生产活动历史发展的顺序对产业结构的划分,产品直接取自自然界的部门称为第一产业,对初级产品进行再加工的部门称为第二产业,为生产和消费提供各种服务的部门称为第三产业。它是世界上通用的产业结构分类,但各国的划分不尽一致。我国的三次产业划分是:

第一产业:是指农业、林业、畜牧业、渔业和农林牧渔服务业。

第二产业:是指采矿业,制造业,电力、燃气及水的生产和供应业;建筑业。

第三产业:除第一、第二产业以外的其他行业。

支出法国内生产总值　是从最终使用角度反映一个国家(或地区)一定时期内生产活动最终成果的一种方法,包括最终消费支出,资本形成总额及货物和服务净出口三部分。对于地区,名称为“支出法地区生产总值”。

最终消费　指常住单位为满足物质、文化和精神生活的需要,从本国经济领土和国外购买的货物和服务的支出; 不包括非常住单位在本国经济领土内的消费支出。最终消费分为居民消费和政府消费。

居民消费　指常住住户在一定时期内对货物和服务的全部最终消费支出。居民消费支出除了直接以货币形式购买货物和服务的消费之外,还包括以其他方式获得的货物和服务的消费支出,即所谓的虚拟消费支出。居民虚拟消费支出包括以下几种类型: 单位以实物报酬及实物转移的形式提供给劳动者的货物和服务; 住户生产并由本住户消费了的货物和服务,其中的服务仅指住户的自有住房服务和付酬的家庭雇员提供的家庭和个人服务; 金融机构提供的金融媒介服务。

政府消费　指政府部门为全社会提供公共服务的消费支出和免费或以较低价格向居民住户提供的货物和服务的净支出。前者等于政府服务的产出价值减去政府单位所获得的经营收入的价值; 后者等于政府部门免费或以较低价格向居民住户提供的货物和服务的市场价值减去向住户收取的价值。

资本形成总额　指常住单位在一定时期内获得的减去处置的固定资产和存货的净额,包括固定资本形成总额和存货增加。

固定资本形成总额　指常住单位在一定时期内获得的固定资产减处置的固定资产的价值总额。固定资产是通过生产活动生产出来的,且使用年限在一年以上、单位价值在规定标准以上的资产,不包括自然资产。分有形固定资产形成总额和无形固定资产形成总额。有形固定资产形成总额包括一定时期内完成的建筑工程、安装工程和设备工器具购置(减处置)价值,以及土地改良、新增役、种、奶、毛、娱乐用牲畜和新增经济林木价值。无形固定资产形成总额包括矿藏的勘探、计算机软件等获得减处置。

存货增加　指常住单位在一定时期内存货实物量变动的市场价值,即期末价值减期初价值的差额,再扣除当期由于价格变动而产生的持有收益。存货增加可以是正值,也可以是负值; 正值表示存货上升,负值表示存货下降。它包括生产单位购进的原材料、燃料和储备物资等存货,以及生产单位生产的产成品、在制品和半成品等存货。

货物和服务净出口 指货物和服务出口减货物和服务进口的差额。出口包括常住单位向非常住单位出售或无偿转让的各种货物和服务的价值；进口包括常住单位从非常住单位购买或无偿得到的各种货物和服务的价值。由于服务活动的提供与使用同时发生，一般把常住单位从国外得到的服务作为进口，非常住单位从本国得到的服务作为出口。货物的出口和进口都按离岸价格计算。

气候 指地球与大气之间长期能量交换与质量交换所形成的一种自然环境状态，它是多种因素综合作用的结果。气候既是人类生活和生产的环境要素之一，又是供给人类生活和生产的重要资源。气温、降水、湿度等气象要素的多年平均值是用来描述一个地区气候状况的主要参数，而各种气象要素某年、某月的平均值（或总量）则可以反映出该时期天气气候状况的重要特征。

气温 指空气的温度，我国一般以摄氏度（℃）为单位表示。气象观测的温度表是放在离地面约 1.5 米处通风良好的百叶箱里测量的，因此，通常说的气温指的是离地面 1.5 米处百叶箱中的温度。其统计计算方法为：月平均气温是将全月各日的平均气温累加，除以该月的天数而得。

年平均气温是将 12 个月的月平均气温累加后除以 12 而得。

降水量 指从天空降落到地面的液态或固态（经融化后）水，未经蒸发、渗透、流失而在地面上积聚的深度。其统计计算方法为：月降水量是将全月各日的降水量累加而得。年降水量是将 12 个月的月降水量累加而得。

Explanatory Notes on Main Statistical Indicators

Gross Domestic Product(GDP) refers to the final products at market prices producted by all resident units in a country(or a region) during a certain period of time. Gross domestic product is expressed in three different persperctives, namely value, income, and products respectively. GDP in its value perspective refers to the total value of all goods and services produced by all resident units during a certain period of time, minus the total value of input of goods and services of the nature of non-fixed assets; in other words, it is the sum of the value-added of all resident units. GDP from the perspective of products refers to the value of all goods and services for final consumption by all resident units minus the net exports of goods and services during a given period of time. In the practice of national accounting, gross domestic product is calculated from three approaches, namely production approach, income approach and expenditure approach, which reflect gross domestic product and its composition from different angles. For a certain region, it refers region gross product or region GDP.

Per Capita GDP refers to the ratio of GDP in a certain term and average population in the same term. According to the international standard, average population should be average permanent population in the same term. In the account regulation, population of both the country and the region should be permanent population. In the after two yers since 2004, per capita GDP can be calculated at two coverage. i. e. at permanent population and household registered population(the note of coverage should follow the data.) The per capita GDP calculated with household registered population will be abolished after two years. Per capita GDP of Qingdao is calculated at permanent population.

Three Strata of Industries has been classfied according to the historical sequence of development. Primary industry refers to extraction of natural resources; secondary industry involves processing of primary products; and tertiary industry provides services of various kinds for production and consumption. The above classification is universal although it varies to some extent form country to country. In China economic activities are categorized into the following three strata of industry:

Primary industry refers to farming, forestry, animal husbandryand fishery and services in support of these industries.

Secondary industry refers to mining and quarrying, manufacturing, production and supply of electricity, water and gas, and construction.

Tertiary industry refers to all other economic activities not included in primary or secondary industries.

GDP by Expenditure Approach refers to the method of measuring the final results of production activities of a country (region) during a given period from the perspective of final use. It includes final consumption, total capital formation and net export of goods and services. It reflects use and composition of gross domestic product. For a certain region, it refers region gross product by expenditure approach.

Final Consumption refers to the total expenditure of resident units for purchases of goods and services from both the domestic economic territory and abroad to meet the needs of material, cultural and spiritual life. It does not include the expenditure of non-resident units on consumption in the economic territory of the country. The final consumption is broken down into household consumption and government consumption.

Household Consumption refers to the total expenditure of resident households on the final consumption of goods and services. In addition to the consumption of goods and services bought by the households directly with money, the household consumption also includes expenditure on goods and services obtained by the households in other ways, i. e. the so-called imputed consumption, which includes the following: (a) the goods and services provided to households by employers in the form of payment in kind and transfer in kind; (b) goods and services produced and consumed by the households themselves, in which the services refer to the owner-occupied housing and services offered by payed family employees; (c) financial intermediate services provided by financial institution.

Government Consumption refers to the consumption expenditure spent for the provision of public services provided by the government to the whole country and the net expenditure on the goods and services provided by the government to households free of charge or at reduced prices. The former equals to the output value of the government services minus the value of operating income obtained by the government departments. The latter equals to the market value of the goods and services provided by the government free of charge or at reduced prices to the households minus the value received by the government from the households.

Gross Capital Formation refers to the fixed assets acquired less disposal and the net value of inventory, thus including the gross fixed capital formation and charges in inventories.

Gross Fixed Capital Formation refers to the value of acquisitions less those disposals of fixed assets during a given period. Fixed assets are the assets produced through production activities with unit value above a specified amount and which could be used for over one year. Natural assets are not included. Gross fixed capital formation can be categorized into total tangible fixed capital formation and total intangible fixed capital formation. Total tangible fixed capital formation includes the value of the construction projects and installation projects completed and the equipment, apparatus and instruments purchased (less those disposed) as well as the value of land improved, the value of draught animals, breeding stock and animals for milk, for wool and for recreational purposes and the newly increased forest with economic value. Total intangible fixed capital formation includes the prospecting of minerals and the acquisition of computer software minus the disposal of them.

Charges in Inventories refers to the market value of the change in the physical volume of inventory of resident units during a given period, i. e. the difference between the values at the beginning and at the end of the period minus the gains due to the change in prices. The changes in inventories can have a positive or a negative value. A positive value indicates an increase in inventory while a negative value indicates a decrease in inventory. The inventory includes raw materials, fuels and reserve materials purchased by the production units as well as the inventory of finished products, semi-finished products and work-in-progress.

Net Export of Goods and Services refers to the exports of goods and services subtracting the imports of goods and services. Exports include the value of various goods and services sold or gratuitously transferred by resident units to non-resident units. Imports include the value of various goods and services purchased or gratuitously acquired resident units from non-resident units. Because the provision of services and the use of them happen simultaneously, the acquisition of services by resident units from abroad is usually treated as import while the acquisition of services by non-resident units in this country is usually treated as export. The exports and imports of goods are calculated at FOB.

Climate refers to the natural environmental status formed by the long-term exchange of energy and mass between the earth and the air, and is the results of interaction of many factors. Climate is both one of the environment factors and the important resources for the living and production activities of the human being. The average values across several years of meteorological factors such as temperature, rainfall and humidity are used as important parameters to describe the climate of a region, while the average values (or total values) of a given year or month of meteorological factors reflect the key characteristics of climate for that period of time.

Temperature refers to the air temperature. China uses centigrade as the unit. The thermometry used for weather observation is put in a breezy shutter, which is 1.5 meters high from the ground. Therefore, the commonly used temperature refers to the temperature in the breezy shutter 1.5 meters away from the ground. The calculation method is as follows:

Monthly average temperature is the summation of average daily temperature of one month divided by the actual days of that particular month.

Annual average temperature is the summation of monthly average of a year divided by 12 months.

Volume of Precipitation refers to the deepness of liquid state or solid state (thawed) water falling from the sky to the ground that has not been evaporated, infiltrated or run off. The calculation method is as follows:

Monthly precipitation is the summation of daily precipitation of a month.

Annual precipitation is the summation of 12 months precipitation of a year.

2 人　口
POPULATION

简要说明

一、本篇资料的主要内容

本篇资料主要反映了全市人口方面的基本情况，包括全市主要年份和12区（市）的户数、人口数、人口密度、土地面积数据、人口出生率、死亡率、自然增长率、计划生育等数据。另外还对建国以来开展的六次人口普查主要数据进行了比较。

二、本篇资料的来源

本篇资料分别来源于国家开展的人口普查、人口抽样调查和市公安局的户籍登记资料，由市统计局人口和社会科技统计处整理提供。

Brief Introduction

I. Main Content

Data in this chapter show the basic condition of population, such as the basic condition of 12 districts and county-level cities, household, population, density of population, birth rate, death rate, natural growth rate and family planning situation. Furthermore, relevant figures obtained from the six national population censuses have been compared.

II. Source of Data

Data in this chapter are from national population censuses, national sample survey. Some are derived from household registration provided by Qingdao Municipal Bureau of Public Security. The data are compiled by the Division of Population and Science & Technology of Qingdao Municipal Bureau of Statistics.

2 -1 主要年份全市总人口数
MAJOR YEAR'S TOTAL POPULATION

单位:人(person)

年份 Year	总人口 Total Population	按性别分 Grouped by Sex 男 Male	 女 Female	平均人口 Average Population
1949	4 056 550	1 997 293	2 059 257	4 054 431
1952	4 233 586	2 125 392	2 108 194	4 203 428
1957	4 822 756	2 424 729	2 398 027	4 773 862
1962	4 627 432	2 319 658	2 307 774	4 578 313
1965	4 901 670	2 461 629	2 440 041	4 859 712
1970	5 391 852	2 720 633	2 671 219	5 337 282
1975	5 742 206	2 904 347	2 837 859	5 717 456
1978	5 853 321	2 959 800	2 893 521	5 841 638
1980	5 961 129	3 015 357	2 945 772	5 937 187
1985	6 267 223	3 185 409	3 081 814	6 253 157
1988	6 516 920	3 319 534	3 197 386	6 474 541
1989	6 571 597	3 348 454	3 223 143	6 544 259
1990	6 666 482	3 392 253	3 274 229	6 619 040
1991	6 709 277	3 411 776	3 297 501	6 687 880
1992	6 731 072	3 420 886	3 310 186	6 720 175
1993	6 753 497	3 431 149	3 322 348	6 742 285
1994	6 785 291	3 446 019	3 339 272	6 769 394
1995	6 846 346	3 476 300	3 370 046	6 815 819
1996	6 902 677	3 502 600	3 400 077	6 874 512
1997	6 954 391	3 527 588	3 426 803	6 928 534
1998	6 995 666	3 545 403	3 450 263	6 975 029
1999	7 029 707	3 561 061	3 468 646	7 012 687
2000	7 066 481	3 577 367	3 489 114	7 048 094
2001	7 104 875	3 595 652	3 509 223	7 085 678
2002	7 156 537	3 619 778	3 536 759	7 130 706
2003	7 206 806	3 644 032	3 562 774	7 181 672
2004	7 311 228	3 692 991	3 618 237	7 259 017
2005	7 409 052	3 740 309	3 668 743	7 360 140
2006	7 493 812	3 779 891	3 713 921	7 451 432
2007	7 579 910	3 816 620	3 763 290	7 536 861
2008	7 615 647	3 824 665	3 790 982	7 597 779
2009	7 629 161	3 823 534	3 805 627	7 622 404
2010	7 636 392	3 819 240	3 817 152	7 632 777
2011	7 663 612	3 826 931	3 836 681	7 650 002
2012	7 695 585	3 838 205	3 857 380	7 679 599

2-2 主要年份全市户数、人口数、人口密度
MAJOR YEAR'S HOUSEHOLDS, POPULATION AND DENSITY OF POPULATION

年份 Year	总户数(万户) Total Households (10000 households)		总人口(万人) Total Population (10000 persons)		平均每户人口(人) Average Persons Per Household(person)		人口密度(人/平方公里) Density of Population (person/sq. km)	
	全市 Whole Municipality	市区 Urban Area	全市 Whole Municipality	市区 Urban Area	全市 Whole Municipality	市区 Urban Area	全市 Whole Municipality	市区 Urban Area
1949	90.64	21.68	405.66	103.69	4.48	4.78	381	941
1952	93.96	22.70	423.36	107.62	4.51	4.74	397	977
1957	102.56	27.41	482.28	134.76	4.70	4.92	453	1 223
1962	106.11	29.29	462.74	137.86	4.36	4.71	434	1 251
1965	105.31	29.64	490.17	146.74	4.65	4.95	460	1 332
1970	113.07	32.14	539.19	150.81	4.77	4.69	506	1 369
1975	123.18	36.56	574.22	161.13	4.66	4.41	539	1 462
1978	131.27	40.08	585.33	168.00	4.46	4.19	549	1 525
1980	138.44	43.03	596.11	175.27	4.31	4.07	560	1 591
1985	157.06	53.43	626.72	190.87	3.99	3.57	588	1 732
1988	169.72	58.95	651.69	201.38	3.84	3.42	612	1 827
1989	177.47	61.57	657.16	203.63	3.70	3.31	617	1 848
1990	186.79	63.94	666.65	205.78	3.57	3.22	626	1 867
1991	192.46	67.15	670.93	207.22	3.49	3.09	630	1 880
1992	199.08	68.94	673.11	209.28	3.38	3.04	632	1 899
1993	201.36	70.13	675.35	212.06	3.35	3.02	634	1 924
1994	204.05	71.24	678.53	214.97	3.33	3.02	637	1 951
1995	208.13	72.53	684.63	218.38	3.29	3.01	643	1 982
1996	212.40	75.11	690.27	223.86	3.25	2.98	648	2 032
1997	215.12	76.39	695.44	227.22	3.23	2.97	653	2 062
1998	218.59	77.90	699.57	229.58	3.20	2.95	657	2 084
1999	222.61	79.27	702.97	231.94	3.16	2.93	660	2 105
2000	224.73	80.46	706.65	234.60	3.14	2.92	664	2 129
2001	227.43	81.41	710.49	237.60	3.12	2.92	667	2 156
2002	229.67	82.85	715.65	241.74	3.12	2.92	672	2 194
2003	232.26	84.15	720.68	246.77	3.10	2.93	677	2 240
2004	235.29	86.93	731.12	258.40	3.11	2.97	686	2 229
2005	237.35	87.99	740.91	265.43	3.12	3.02	695	2 290
2006	239.33	89.12	749.38	271.00	3.13	3.04	703	2 338
2007	241.55	90.21	757.99	275.55	3.14	3.05	711	2 377
2008	243.18	91.22	761.56	276.25	3.13	3.03	715	2 384
2009	244.74	92.15	762.92	275.47	3.12	2.99	676	1 873
2010	246.11	93.30	763.64	275.50	3.10	2.95	677	1 873
2011	247.94	94.69	766.36	277.09	3.09	2.93	679	1 884
2012	249.27	95.87	769.56	279.57	3.09	2.92	682	1 901

2-3 第一、二、三、四、五、六次人口普查主要数据
MAIN DATA FROM THE SIX NATIONAL POPULATION CENSUSES

项　目	Item	第一次人口普查 1st National Population Census	第二次人口普查 2nd National Population Census	第三次人口普查 3rd National Population Census	第四次人口普查 4th National Population Census	第五次人口普查 5th National Population Census	第六次人口普查 6th National Population Census
一、总人口（万人）	**Total Population (10000 persons)**	**91.68**	**138.34**	**422.76**	**666.40**	**749.42**	**871.51**
按性别分	By Sex						
男（万人）	Male(10000 persons)	48.44	69.64	214.09	338.86	375.74	439.18
女（万人）	Female(10000 persons)	43.24	68.71	208.67	327.54	373.68	432.33
二、总户数（万户）	**Total Household (10000 households)**	**19.27**	**28.01**	**101.41**	**186.61**	**241.62**	**296.64**
家庭户（万户）	Family Household (10000 households)			101.09	185.56	232.70	282.43
平均家庭户规模（人）	Average Family Household Size(person)			4.07	3.49	2.97	2.79
三、民　族	**Ethnicity**						
民族个数（个）	Number of Ethnic Groups (unit)	14	16	25	41	51	53
汉族人口（万人）	Population of Han (10000 persons)	91.33	137.76	422.09	665.58	746.12	863.84
少数民族人口（万人）	Populaiton of Ethnic Minorities(10000 persons)	0.36	0.58	0.67	0.82	3.3	7.67
四、各种文化程度人口	**Popution with Various Education Attainments**						
大学（万人）	College(10000 persons)		1.51	3.62	12.39	41.64	129.54
高中（万人）	Senior Secondary School (10000 persons)		4.86	34.82	68.42	111.40	150.82
初中（万人）	Junior Secondary School (10000 persons)		13.72	102.28	195.10	281.91	334.22
小学（万人）	Primary School (10000 persons)		51.25	144.52	236.34	206.91	170.77

2-4 分市、区户数与人口数(2012年底)

TOTAL HOUSEHOLDS AND POPULATION BY REGION(END OF 2012)

市、区名称	Region	户数(户) Households (household)	人口(人) Population (person)	按性别分 Grouped by Sex 男 Male	女 Female	平均人口(人) Average Population (person)
总　计	**Total**	**2 492 679**	**7 695 585**	**3 838 205**	**3 857 380**	**7 679 599**
市　区	Urban Area	958 716	2 795 694	1 380 330	1 415 364	2 783 312
市南区	Shinan District	172 751	548 604	267 926	280 678	548 536
原市北区	Original Shibei District	187 920	499 027	245 609	253 418	496 936
原四方区	Original Sifang District	136 665	372 225	187 038	185 187	372 148
李沧区	Licang District	117 507	315 196	156 536	158 660	312 470
崂山区	Laoshan District	79 466	258 125	127 793	130 332	253 628
原黄岛区	Original Huangdao District	90 313	316 923	160 974	155 949	315 793
城阳区	Chengyang District	174 094	485 594	234 454	251 140	433 803
即墨市	Jimo	341 380	1 133 970	565 960	568 010	1 132 882
胶州市	Jiaozhou	251 200	809 435	403 659	405 776	808 288
原胶南市	Original Jiaonan	267 181	843 276	423 595	419 681	842 249
平度市	Pingdu	423 253	1 377 850	695 445	682 405	1 377 027
莱西市	Laixi	250 949	735 360	369 216	366 144	735 [illegible]42

2-5 分市、区土地面积、人口和人口密度(2012年底)

LAND AREA, POPULATION AND DENSITY OF POPULATION BY REGION(END OF 2012)

市、区名称	Region	土地面积 Land Area 面积(平方公里) Area(sq. km)	比重(%) Percentage(%)	年末人口 Year-end Population 人口(人) Population(person)	比重(%) Percentage(%)	人口密度(人/平方公里) Density of Population (person/sq. km)
总　计	**Total**	**11 282**	**100.00**	**7 695 585**	**100.00**	**682**
市　区	Urban Area	1 471	13.03	2 795 694	36.33	1 901
即墨市	Jimo	1 921	17.03	1 133 970	14.73	590
胶州市	Jiaozhou	1 324	11.74	809 435	10.52	611
原胶南市	Original Jiaonan	1 822	16.15	843 276	10.96	463
平度市	Pingdu	3 176	28.15	1 377 850	17.90	434
莱西市	Laixi	1 568	13.90	735 360	9.56	469

注:土地面积为第二次全国土地调查数据。

Note: Data on land area are based on the data of the Second China Land Census.

2-6 主要年份人口自然变动
MAJOR YEAR'S NATURAL CHANGE OF POPULATION

年份 Year	出生 Birth			死亡 Death			自然增长 Natural Growth		
	人数(万人) Population (10 000 persons)	出生率(‰) Birth Rate (‰)	#市区 Urban Area	人数(万人) Population (10 000 persons)	死亡率(‰) Death Rate (‰)	#市区 Urban Area	人数(万人) Population (10 000 persons)	增长率(‰) Natural Growth Rate(‰)	#市区 Urban Area
1949	11.62	28.66	31.86	6.10	15.03	11.25	5.52	13.62	20.61
1952	15.51	36.91	39.60	4.97	11.83	9.18	10.54	25.08	30.42
1957	17.82	37.34	42.40	6.38	13.37	8.82	11.44	23.97	33.58
1962	17.29	37.77	35.75	5.82	12.70	8.08	11.47	25.07	27.67
1965	17.63	36.28	27.18	4.66	9.59	5.61	12.97	26.69	21.57
1970	17.65	33.06	23.79	3.79	7.11	5.55	13.86	25.95	18.24
1975	10.55	18.45	17.52	3.95	6.90	5.67	6.60	11.55	11.85
1978	8.55	14.64	11.64	3.65	6.24	5.53	4.90	8.40	6.11
1980	8.00	13.48	11.28	3.77	6.35	5.73	4.23	7.13	5.55
1985	5.82	9.31	10.37	3.88	6.21	5.64	1.94	3.10	4.73
1988	10.22	15.79	15.39	4.17	6.44	5.29	6.05	9.35	10.10
1989	10.37	15.85	14.13	3.88	5.93	5.48	6.49	9.92	8.65
1990	11.44	17.28	11.68	4.35	6.58	5.78	7.09	10.70	5.90
1991	7.98	11.93	8.17	4.15	6.21	5.56	3.83	5.72	2.61
1992	6.17	9.18	8.65	4.54	6.75	6.14	1.63	2.43	2.51
1993	5.95	8.82	8.49	4.44	6.59	6.01	1.51	2.23	2.48
1994	6.92	10.22	8.66	4.71	6.96	6.40	2.21	3.26	2.26
1995	8.15	11.96	9.03	4.52	6.62	6.08	3.63	5.34	2.95
1996	8.40	12.21	8.98	4.83	7.03	6.38	3.57	5.18	2.60
1997	7.80	11.26	8.76	4.80	6.93	6.33	3.00	4.33	2.43
1998	7.51	10.77	8.62	4.68	6.71	6.12	2.83	4.06	2.50
1999	6.48	9.24	8.05	4.56	6.50	6.05	1.92	2.74	2.00
2000	7.31	10.38	9.25	4.95	7.02	6.33	2.37	3.36	2.92
2001	6.74	9.51	8.37	4.64	6.54	6.17	2.10	2.97	2.20
2002	7.54	10.57	9.24	4.74	6.65	6.12	2.80	3.92	3.12
2003	5.11	7.11	5.89	4.81	6.70	6.12	0.30	0.41	-0.23
2004	7.93	10.93	8.93	4.92	6.78	6.03	3.01	4.15	2.90
2005	7.55	10.26	7.84	4.81	6.54	6.10	2.74	3.72	1.74
2006	7.01	9.40	7.47	5.16	6.93	5.77	1.85	2.47	1.70
2007	7.65	10.15	9.38	4.76	6.32	5.84	2.89	3.83	3.54
2008	6.89	9.06	8.86	5.57	7.33	5.98	1.32	1.73	2.88
2009	6.30	8.27	8.40	5.14	6.75	5.82	1.16	1.52	2.58
2010	6.85	8.98	9.61	6.33	8.29	6.25	0.52	0.69	3.36
2011	6.58	8.60	9.31	5.55	7.26	6.05	1.03	1.34	3.26
2012	7.49	9.75	10.94	6.28	8.18	6.53	1.21	1.57	4.41

2-7 分市、区人口出生率、死亡率、自然增长率(2012 年底)

RATE OF BIRTH, DEATH AND NATURAL GROWTH IN POPULATION BY REGION (END OF 2012)

市、区名称	Region	出生 Birth		死亡 Death		自然增长 Natural Growth	
		人数(人) Population (person)	出生率(‰) Birth Rate (‰)	人数(人) Population (person)	死亡率(‰) Death Rate (‰)	人数(人) Population (person)	增长率(‰) Natural Growth Rate (‰)
总 计	**Total**	**74 910**	**9.75**	**62 830**	**8.18**	**12 080**	**1.57**
市 区	Urban Area	30 461	10.94	18 177	6.53	12 284	4.41
市南区	Shinan District	5 445	9.93	2 960	5.40	2 485	4.53
原市北区	Original Shibei District	5 069	10.20	3 728	7.50	1 341	2.70
原四方区	Original Sifang District	3 783	10.17	2 963	7.96	820	2.21
李沧区	Licang District	3 878	12.41	2 105	6.74	1 773	5.67
崂山区	Laoshan District	2 954	11.65	1 364	5.38	1 590	6.27
原黄岛区	Original Huangdao District	4 018	12.72	1 674	5.30	2 344	7.42
城阳区	Chengyang District	5 314	10.98	3 383	6.99	1 931	3.99
即墨市	Jimo	9 418	8.31	9 265	8.18	153	0.13
胶州市	Jiaozhou	7 789	9.64	8 069	9.98	-280	-0.34
原胶南市	Original Jiaonan	7 879	9.35	7 435	8.83	444	0.52
平度市	Pingdu	13 469	9.78	12 306	8.94	1 163	0.84
莱西市	Laixi	5 894	8.01	7 578	10.30	-1 684	-2.29

2-8 分市、区人口机械变动(2012 年底)

MECHANICAL CHANGE OF POPULATION BY REGION (END OF 2012)

市、区名称	Region	迁入人数(人) Inflows (person)	迁出人数(人) Outflows (person)	增(+)、减(-) Increase(+), Decrease(-)
总 计	**Total**	**59 265**	**39 453**	**19 812**
市 区	Urban Area	37 633	25 102	12 531
市南区	Shinan District	9 503	8 619	884
原市北区	Original Shibei District	4 030	1 740	2 290
原四方区	Original Sifang District	4 122	3 802	320
李沧区	Licang District	2 736	750	1 986
崂山区	Laoshan District	6 859	1 581	5 278
原黄岛区	Original Huangdao District	6 441	6 043	398
城阳区	Chengyang District	3 942	2 567	1 375
即墨市	Jimo	4 634	2 646	1 988
胶州市	Jiaozhou	4 871	2 311	2 560
原胶南市	Original Jiaonan	4 648	3 070	1 578
平度市	Pingdu	4 474	4 009	465
莱西市	Laixi	3 005	2 315	690

2-9 计划生育情况(1978-2012年)
FAMILY PLANNING SITUATION(1978-2012)

年份 Year	已婚有生育能力的人数(人) Married and Fertile Persons(person)	节育人数(人) Persons under Birth Control(person)	节育率(%) Contraceptive Prevalence Rate(%)	四项手术人数(人) Persons Performed Four-operation(person)	#放环人数 Persons Set Rings
1978	694 292	571 077	82.25	125 913	68 475
1980	763 226	673 069	88.19	180 979	70 927
1985	1 017 649	929 284	91.32	146 742	67 234
1990	1 258 232	1 165 216	92.61	149 327	70 964
1991	1 319 722	1 219 795	92.43	153 970	77 406
1992	1 348 503	1 256 271	93.16	90 107	56 226
1993	1 380 717	1 271 884	92.12	76 783	45 492
1994	1 400 425	1 268 378	90.57	73 169	41 482
1995	1 427 442	1 285 264	90.04	84 099	52 716
1996	1 459 465	1 316 516	90.21	84 370	57 648
1997	1 482 204	1 340 399	90.43	76 579	55 285
1998	1 505 499	1 367 648	90.84	74 199	50 526
1999	1 523 471	1 378 131	90.46	73 663	44 976
2000	1 521 331	1 371 447	90.15	74 285	45 999
2001	1 514 274	1 360 543	89.85	70 205	43 601
2002	1 541 855	1 400 145	90.81	50 575	45 453
2003	1 518 448	1 354 917	89.23	57 458	47 953
2004	1 540 706	1 357 703	88.04	52 934	42 859
2005	1 590 476	1 417 755	89.14	58 097	49 716
2006	1 604 665	1 427 785	88.98	51 864	42 457
2007	1 595 390	1 426 787	89.43	50 074	41 198
2008	1 587 344	1 410 426	88.85	120 539	93 291
2009	1 623 969	1 418 178	87.33	111 084	100 193
2010	1 591 103	1 377 726	86.59	78 721	51 794
2011	1 581 231	1 355 808	85.74	70 823	48 210
2012	1 575 996	1 349 572	85.63	62 880	43 021

2 -10 分市、区计划生育情况(2012 年)
FAMILY PLANNING SITUATION BY REGION(2012)

市、区名称	Region	计划生育率(%) Fertility Rate(%)	计划内出生(人) Birth within the Plan(person)		计划外出生(人) Birth without the Plan(person)		多胎(人) Third Birth and Above (person)
			一胎 First Birth	二胎 Second Birth	一胎 First Birth	二胎 Second Birth	
总　计	**Total**	**96.90**	**62 620**	**15 984**	**181**	**1 958**	**376**
市　区	Urban Area	97.49	28 234	3 248	33	727	52
市 南 区	Shinan District	97.00	6 422	383	8	157	11
原市北区	Original Shibei District	97.72	4 783	306	7	108	5
原四方区	Original Sifang District	97.67	3 546	191	7	78	4
李 沧 区	Licang District	97.15	3 254	191	1	96	4
崂 山 区	Laoshan District	97.56	2 365	395	2	65	2
黄 岛 区	Huangdao District	96.70	3 931	580	4	136	14
城 阳 区	Chengyang District	98.05	3 933	1 202	4	87	12
即 墨 市	Jimo	96.99	7 409	3 277	27	241	64
胶 州 市	Jiaozhou	96.93	5 775	2 076	19	188	42
原胶南市	Original Jiaonan	96.73	5 910	1 976	27	206	34
平 度 市	Pingdu	95.44	9 951	3 684	40	452	160
莱 西 市	Laixi	97.21	5 341	1 723	35	144	24

主要统计指标解释

人口数　指一定时点、一定地区范围内有生命的个人总和。

出生率（又称粗出生率）　指在一定时期内（通常为一年）一定地区的出生人数与同期内平均人数（或期中人数）之比，用千分率表示。本资料中的出生率指年出生率，其计算公式为：

$$出生率=\frac{年出生人数}{年平均人数}\times 1000‰$$

式中：出生人数指活产婴儿，即胎儿脱离母体时（不管怀孕月数），有过呼吸或其他生命现象。

死亡率（又称粗死亡率）　指在一定时期内（通常为一年）一定地区的死亡人数与同期内平均人数（或期中人数）之比，用千分率表示。本资料中的死亡率指年死亡率，其计算公式为：

$$死亡率=\frac{年死亡人数}{年平均人数}\times 1000‰$$

人口自然增长率　指在一定时期内（通常为一年）人口自然增加数（出生人数减死亡人数）与该时期内平均人数（或期中人数）之比，用千分率表示。计算公式为：

$$人口自然增长率=\frac{本年出生人数-本年死亡人数}{年平均人数}\times 1000‰$$
$$=人口出生率-人口死亡率$$

Explanatory Notes on Main Statistical Indicators

Total Population　refers to the total number of people alive at a certain point of time within a given area.

Birth Rate (or Crude Birth Rate)　refers to the ratio of the number of births to the average population (or mid-period population) during a certain period of time (usually a year), expressed in ‰. Birth rate in the chapter refers to annual birth rate. The following formula is used:

Birth Rate = (Number of Births/Average Number of Population) × 1000‰

Number of births in the formula refers to live births, i. e. when a baby has breathed or showed any vital phenomena regardless of the length of pregnancy.

Annual average number of population is the average of the number of population at the beginning of the year and that at the end of the year. Sometimes it is substituted by the mid-year population.

Death Rate (or Crude Death Rate)　refers to the ratio of the number of deaths to the average population (or mid-period population) during a certain period of time (usually a year), expressed in ‰. Death rate in the chapter refers to annual death rate. The following formula is used:

Death Rate = (Number of Deaths/Annual Average Number of Population) × 1000‰

Natural Growth Rate of Population　refers to the ratio of natural increase in population (number of births minus number of deaths) in a certain period of time (usually a year) to the average population (or mid-period population) of the same period, expressed in ‰. The following formula is applied:

Natural Growth Rate of Population = [(Number of Births-Number of Deaths)/Average Number of Population] × 1000‰

Natural Growth Rate of Population = Birth Rate-Death Rate

3 从业人员及职工工资
EMPLOYMENT AND WAGES

简要说明

一、本篇资料的主要内容

本篇资料主要反映了全市从业人员和职工工资方面的基本情况，主要包括全市社会从业人数及各区（市）单位从业人数、在岗职工工资总额和平均工资等方面的资料。

二、本篇资料的来源

单位从业人员和职工工资来源于劳动统计年报，全市从业人员根据劳动统计年报、农村年报和市工商行政管理局、市人力资源和社会保障局、市交通委相关资料测算。由市统计局人口和社会科技统计处整理提供。

Brief Introduction

I. Main Content

Data in this chapter show the basic conditions of Qingdao's employment and wages, including the main data on labor statistics of employment, number of employment of the whole city and 12 district and county-level cities, total wage bill and average wage of staff and workers, etc.

II. Source of Data

Data on employment and wages are prepared according to the annual reports of labor statistics.Data on social employment are measured according to the annual reports of labor statistics,countryside statistics and related information from Industry & Commerce Administration Bureau,Human Resources & Social Security Bureau and Transportation Commision.

Data in this chapter are compiled by the Division of Population and Science & Technology of Qingdao Municipal Bureau of Statistics.

3－1 社会从业人数(1978－2012年)
SOCIAL EMPLOYMENT(1978－2012)

单位:万人(10 000 persons)

年 份 Year	合 计 Total	第一产业 Primary Industry	第二产业 Secondary Industry	第三产业 Tertiary Industry
1978	256.70	157.40	65.60	33.70
1979	265.60	156.10	72.20	37.30
1980	270.10	153.60	82.10	43.20
1981	278.90	153.60	82.10	43.20
1982	282.70	151.10	86.20	45.40
1983	289.60	156.40	85.00	48.10
1984	304.20	149.20	97.70	57.40
1985	315.30	149.20	104.50	61.70
1986	326.40	149.90	112.10	64.60
1987	334.80	149.90	120.20	64.70
1988	336.50	147.60	123.20	65.70
1989	344.20	152.50	122.10	69.60
1990	352.80	156.50	123.30	73.10
1991	361.20	161.90	124.30	74.90
1992	370.30	161.70	127.80	80.80
1993	365.70	160.50	128.80	76.40
1994	367.60	157.10	129.40	81.20
1995	374.20	155.40	132.40	86.40
1996	381.50	152.20	137.10	92.20
1997	388.70	155.20	138.10	95.30
1998	393.10	154.80	138.60	99.70
1999	396.10	150.30	142.00	103.80
2000	397.60	144.70	134.91	117.99
2001	400.50	133.90	142.30	124.30
2002	413.31	121.38	153.85	138.08
2003	438.96	119.91	163.93	155.12
2004	458.81	113.98	180.63	164.20
2005	471.03	104.48	196.80	169.75
2006	490.10	102.97	209.83	177.30
2007	505.80	102.30	217.80	185.70
2008	513.80	102.40	220.80	190.60
2009	525.71	105.65	220.33	199.73
2010	540.34	105.16	223.85	211.33
2011	551.18	106.02	227.08	218.08
2012	559.88	104.95	229.79	225.14

3-2 主要年份全市单位从业人员人数

MAJOR YEAR'S NUMBER OF EMPLOYED PERSONS IN ALL UNITS OF THE CITY

单位：万人（10 000 persons）

年 份 Year	合 计 Total	#市 区 Urban Area	国有单位 State-owned Units	集体单位 Collective-owned Units	其他所有制单位 Other Ownership Units
1949	14.8	13.4	9.3	5.5	
1952	23.4	20.1	18.3	5.1	
1957	29.7	24.5	24.1	5.6	
1962	32.3	26.8	24.5	7.8	
1965	36.7	30.6	26.8	9.9	
1970	45.6	37.4	32.2	13.4	
1975	53.4	43.5	38.0	15.4	
1978	70.7	54.5	49.2	21.5	
1980	79.2	61.5	55.0	24.2	
1985	88.8	66.7	59.8	28.9	0.1
1988	98.2	70.0	66.7	31.2	0.3
1989	99.2	70.4	67.7	31.0	0.5
1990	103.2	70.6	69.5	32.9	0.3
1991	105.4	78.4	71.5	32.5	1.4
1992	108.2	80.4	73.6	32.8	1.8
1993	109.4	80.8	75.3	29.5	4.5
1994	110.1	80.2	72.4	28.3	9.4
1995	111.6	80.2	72.4	27.5	11.7
1996	118.4	81.1	71.6	26.0	20.8
1997	117.1	78.1	69.0	22.6	25.5
1998	116.2	75.6	64.2	19.0	33.0
1999	119.0	78.3	60.4	16.6	42.0
2000	118.3	76.6	57.6	14.2	46.5
2001	117.5	75.1	53.2	12.2	52.1
2002	119.1	75.2	49.5	10.3	59.3
2003	118.0	74.3	47.2	8.9	61.9
2004	207.1	111.1	43.7	18.0	145.4
2005	224.3	122.3	43.9	18.2	162.2
2006	243.2	133.7	41.7	16.2	185.3
2007	249.8	137.3	45.1	17.9	186.8
2008	254.1	140.9	44.4	15.4	194.3
2009	260.5	145.6	44.4	14.6	201.5
2010	269.4	151.1	44.6	15.1	209.7
2011	275.9	156.5	44.3	14.7	216.9
2012	283.2	162.1	44.0	13.8	225.4

注：2004 年以前为城镇单位职工人数.

Note: Before 2004, the data refer to number of staff and workers in urban units.

3-3 全市单位国民经济各行业从业人员人数(2012年)

NUMBER OF EMPLOYED PERSONS IN ALL UNITS OF THE CITY BY SECTOR(2012)

单位:万人(10 000 persons)

		2012		2011	
		合计 Total	女性 Female	合计 Total	女性 Female
总计	**Total**	**283.2**	**121.7**	**275.9**	**118.4**
1. 农、林、牧、渔业	Farming, Forestry, Animal Husbandry and Fishery	0.9	0.3	1.0	0.4
2. 采矿业	Mining	2.1	0.4	2.1	0.4
3. 制造业	Manufacturing	145.0	66.6	143.7	66.1
4. 电力、煤气及水的生产供应业	Production and Supply of Electricty, Gas and Water	2.8	0.6	2.7	0.7
5. 建筑业	Construction	18.3	3.7	17.3	3.5
6. 批发和零售业	Wholesale and Retail Trade	29.8	14.1	28.0	12.5
7. 交通运输、仓储及邮政业	Transport, Storage and Post	12.7	3.5	12.1	3.5
8. 住宿和餐饮业	Hotels and Catering Services	8.7	4.7	8.3	4.6
9. 信息传输、计算机服务和软件业	Information Transmission, Computer Services and Software	1.8	0.8	1.6	0.6
10. 金融业	Financial Intermediation	5.4	3.0	5.1	2.8
11. 房地产业	Real Estate	6.2	2.1	5.9	2.0
12. 租赁和商务服务业	Leasing and Business Services	11.1	4.8	10.4	4.5
13. 科学研究、技术服务和地质勘察业	Scientific Research, Technical Services and Geologic Prospecting	3.2	1.3	3.0	1.3
14. 水利、环境和公共设施管理业	Management of Water Conservancy, Environment and Public Facilities	2.5	0.8	2.5	0.8
15. 居民服务和其他服务业	Services to Households and Other Services	3.2	1.1	3.0	1.1
16. 教育	Education	13.9	7.5	13.7	7.4
17. 卫生、社会保障和社会福利业	Health, Social Security and Social Welfare	5.3	3.5	5.2	3.4
18. 文化、体育和娱乐业	Culture, Sports and Entertainment	2.3	0.7	2.3	0.7
19. 公共管理和社会组织	Public Management and Social Organization	8.0	2.2	8.0	2.1
20. 国际组织	International Organization				

3 -4 全市单位分市、区国民经济各部门从业人员人数(2012 年)
NUMBER OF EMPLOYED PERSONS IN ALL UNITS OF THE CITY BY REGION AND SECTOR (2012)

市、区名称	Region	合计 Total	农林牧渔业 Farming, Forestry, Animal Husbandry and Fishery	采矿业 Mining	制造业 Manufacturing	电力燃气和水生产供应业 Production and Supply of Electricty, Gas and Water	建筑业 Construction
总　计	**Total**	**283.2**	**0.9**	**2.1**	**145.0**	**2.8**	**18.3**
#崂山区	Laoshan District	16.8			6.9	0.1	0.7
原黄岛区	Original Huangdao District	24.6			14.1	0.2	2.7
城阳区	Chengyang District	37.1	0.1	0.1	27.9	0.1	1.6
即墨市	Jimo	32.1	0.2		23.4	0.1	2.3
胶州市	Jiaozhou	29.9	0.2		20.6	0.1	3.7
原胶南市	Original Jiaonan	21.7		0.3	15.7	0.2	1.0
平度市	Pingdu	18.3	0.2	1.1	11.9	0.2	0.9
莱西市	Laixi	19.1	0.1	0.3	12.9	0.2	1.4

3 -4 续表
Continued

市、区名称	Region	金融业 Financial Intermediation	房地产业 Real Estate	租赁和商务服务业 Leasing and Business Services	科学研究技术服务和地质勘察业 Scientific Research, Technical Services and Geologic Prospecting	水利环境和公共设施管理业 Management of Water Conservancy, Environment and Public Facilities
总　计	**Total**	**5.4**	**6.2**	**11.1**	**3.2**	**2.5**
#崂山区	Laoshan District	0.1	0.8	0.6	0.4	0.2
原黄岛区	Original Huangdao District	0.1	0.4	0.7	0.4	0.1
城阳区	Chengyang District	0.1	0.8	0.8	0.3	0.2
即墨市	Jimo	0.3	0.4	0.3		0.1
胶州市	Jiaozhou	0.3	0.4	0.3	0.1	0.2
原胶南市	Original Jiaonan	0.2	0.3	0.1	0.2	0.1
平度市	Pingdu	0.2	0.3			0.1
莱西市	Laixi	0.1	0.1	0.1	0.1	0.1

单位：万人(10 000 persons)

批发和零售业 Wholesale and Retail Trade	交通运输仓储及邮政业 Transport, Storage and Post	住宿和餐饮业 Hotels and Catering Services	信息传输计算机服务软件业 Information Transmission, Computer Services and Software
29.8	**12.7**	**8.7**	**1.8**
3.5	0.5	1.2	0.3
1.9	1.0	0.6	0.2
1.4	1.0	0.5	0.2
1.4	0.2	0.4	0.1
1.1	0.2	0.4	
1.0	0.2	0.4	
0.5	0.1	0.1	0.1
1.1	0.1	0.4	0.1

单位：万人(10 000 persons)

居民服务和其他服务业 Services to Households and Other Services	教育 Education	卫生社会保障和社会福利业 Health, Social Security and Social Welfare	文化体育和娱乐业 Culture, Sports and Entertainment	公共管理和社会组织 Public Management and Social Organization	国际组织 International Organization
[illegible]	**13.9**	**5.3**	**2.3**	**8.0**	
0.2	0.6	0.1	0.1	0.5	
0.1	1.3	0.2	0.1	0.5	
0.3	1.0	0.2		0.5	
	1.4	0.4	0.1	1.0	
0.1	1.2	0.4		0.6	
	1.1	0.3		0.6	
	1.4	0.4	0.1	0.7	
	0.9	0.4		0.7	

3－5 全市单位分市、区全部从业人员人数(2012 年底)

NUMBER OF EMPLOYED PERSONS IN ALL UNITS OF THE CITY BY REGION(END OF 2012)

单位:万人(10 000 persons)

市、区名称	Region	年末人数 Year-end Population	国有单位 State-owned Units	集体单位 Collective-owned Units	其他经济类型单位 Others
总　计	**Total**	**283.2**	**44.0**	**13.8**	**225.4**
市　区	Urban Area	162.1	28.3	5.8	128.0
#崂山区	Laoshan District	16.8	1.8	1.6	13.4
原黄岛区	Original Huangdao District	24.6	2.3	0.4	21.9
城阳区	Chengyang District	37.1	2.4	2.6	32.1
即墨市	Jimo	32.1	3.1	1.9	27.1
胶州市	Jiaozhou	29.9	4.7	2.1	23.1
原胶南市	Original Jiaonan	21.7	2.6	1.4	17.7
平度市	Pingdu	18.3	2.8	1.2	14.3
莱西市	Laixi	19.1	2.5	1.4	15.2

3-6 全市在岗职工工资总额、平均工资(1978-2012年)
TOTAL WAGE BILL AND AVERAGE WAGE OF EMPLOYED STAFF AND WORKERS(1978-2012)

年份 Year	工资总额(亿元) Total Wage Bill(100 million yuan)		平均工资(元) Average Wage(yuan)	
	全社会单位 All Units	其中:非私营单位 of which:Non-private Units	全社会单位 All Units	其中:非私营单位 of which:Non-private Units
1978		4.0		584
1979		4.8		662
1980		6.0		782
1981		6.3		778
1982		6.6		785
1983		6.9		809
1984		9.0		1 041
1985		9.6		1 103
1986		11.8		1 311
1987		14.2		1 519
1988		18.0		1 862
1989		20.7		2 120
1990		24.4		2 400
1991		26.4		2 553
1992		31.8		2 970
1993		40.4		3 694
1994		59.5		5 455
1995		68.3		6 164
1996		78.2		6 640
1997		82.5		7 030
1998		87.2		7 518
1999		100.1		8 405
2000		120.4		10 072
2001		135.8		11 426
2002		153.8		12 839
2003	225.6	160.3	12 597	15 335
2004	280.5	193.4	13 932	17 190
2005	359.5	242.8	16 015	20 022
2006	445.6	292.0	18 574	23 457
2007	518.1	338.6	21 419	27 083
2008	578.7	371.9	23 296	30 233
2009	638.1	393.2	25 396	33 258
2010	738.0	446.8	28 549	37 805
2011	877.5	522.0	32 763	43 077
2012	1 044.3	613.1	37 399	49 052

注:2003年以前为职工工资总额、平均工资。

Note: The data before 2003 refer to the total wage bill and average wage of staff and workers.

3-7 全市在岗职工工资总额、平均工资指数(1978-2012 年)

INDEXES OF TOTAL WAGE BILL AND AVERAGE WAGE OF EMPLOYED STAFF AND WORKERS(1978-2012)

年份 Year	工资总额指数 Total Wage Bill Indexes 全社会单位 All Units	工资总额指数 Total Wage Bill Indexes 其中:非私营单位 of which:Non-private Units	平均工资指数 Average Wage Indexes 全社会单位 All Units	平均工资指数 Average Wage Indexes 其中:非私营单位 of which:Non-private Units
1978		120.80		104.66
1979		119.53		113.36
1980		123.95		118.[illegible]3
1981		106.71		99.49
1982		103.80		100.90
1983		104.14		103.06
1984		130.64		128.68
1985		107.11		105.95
1986		123.22		118.86
1987		120.10		115.87
1988		126.48		122.58
1989		115.29		113.85
1990		117.66		113.21
1991		108.28		106.38
1992		120.26		116.33
1993		127.09		124.38
1994		147.46		147.67
1995		114.76		113.00
1996		114.54		107.72
1997		105.50		105.87
1998		105.64		106.94
1999		114.81		111.80
2000		120.29		119.83
2001		112.77		113.44
2002		113.31		112.37
2003		108.84		110.30
2004	124.34	120.65	110.60	112.10
2005	128.16	125.54	114.95	116.47
2006	123.95	120.26	115.98	117.16
2007	116.27	115.96	115.32	115.46
2008	111.70	109.83	108.76	111.63
2009	110.26	105.73	109.01	110.01
2010	115.66	113.63	112.42	113.67
2011	118.90	116.83	114.76	113.95
2012	119.01	117.45	114.15	113.87

注:2004 年以前为职工工资总额、平均工资指数。

Note:The data before 2004 refer to the indexes of total wage bill and average wage of staff and workers.

3-8 分行业在岗职工平均工资(2012 年)
AVERAGE WAGE OF EMPLOYED STAFF AND WORKERS BY SECTOR(2012)

行 业	Sector	非私营单位 (元) Non-private Units (yuan)	私营单位 (元) Private Units (yuan)
总 计	**Total**	**49 052**	**27 715**
农、林、牧、渔业	Farming, Forestry, Animal Husbandry and Fishery	34 498	25 744
采矿业	Mining	32 192	27 799
制造业	Manufacturing	38 760	27 950
电力、煤气及水的生产供应业	Production and Supply of Electricty, Gas and Water	63 855	29 866
建筑业	Construction	47 814	29 434
批发和零售业	Wholesale and Retail Trade	41 308	26 598
交通运输、仓储及邮政业	Transport, Storage and Post	55 711	26 233
住宿和餐饮业	Hotels and Catering Services	35 592	27 168
信息传输、计算机服务和软件业	Information Transmission, Computer Services and Software	91 669	31 726
金融业	Financial Intermediation	143 929	28 787
房地产业	Real Estate	51 009	30 881
租赁和商务服务业	Leasing and Business Services	47 681	28 858
科学研究、技术服务和地质勘察业	Scientific Research, Technical Services and Geologic Prospecting	68 630	32 231
水利、环境和公共设施管理业	Management of Water Conservancy, Environment and Public Facilities	41 678	28 322
居民服务和其他服务业	Services to Households and Other Services	41 143	24 602
教育	Education	65 128	26 678
卫生、社会保障和社会福利业	Health, Social Security and Social Welfare	59 828	26 260
文化、体育和娱乐业	Culture, Sports and Entertainment	58 137	26 939
公共管理和社会组织	Public Management and Social Organization	73 609	

3-9 分市、区在岗职工工资总额(2012 年)

TOTAL WAGE BILL OF EMPLOYED STAFF AND WORKERS BY REGION(2012)

单位:亿元(100 million yuan)

市、区名称	Region	合计 Total	国有单位 State-owned Units	集体单位 Collective-owned Units	其他所有制单位 Other Ownership Units
总　计	**Total**	**1 044.3**	**252.1**	**43.3**	**748.9**
#崂山区	Laoshan District	69.1	14.0	4.1	51.0
原黄岛区	Original Huangdao District	105.4	16.3	1.6	87.5
城阳区	Chengyang District	122.5	15.4	7.4	99.7
即墨市	Jimo	100.4	16.7	5.4	78.3
胶州市	Jiaozhou	93.7	18.2	5.6	69.9
原胶南市	Original Jiaonan	68.3	16.6	3.6	48.1
平度市	Pingdu	61.1	15.8	2.9	42.4
莱西市	Laixi	65.4	11.6	3.1	50.7

3-10 分市、区在岗职工平均工资(2012 年)

AVERAGE WAGE OF EMPLOYED STAFF AND WORKERS BY REGION(2012)

单位:元/年(yuan/year)

市、区名称	Region	合计 Total	国有单位 State-owned Units	集体单位 Collective-owned Units	其他所有制单位 Other Ownership Units
总　计	**Total**	**37 399**	**67 339**	**31 520**	**32 861**
#崂山区	Laoshan District	40 623	76 313	37 082	34 208
原黄岛区	Original Huangdao District	42 324	73 878	34 996	36 985
城阳区	Chengyang District	34 716	72 056	28 618	32 665
即墨市	Jimo	35 572	55 050	32 864	32 557
胶州市	Jiaozhou	33 871	59 527	33 378	28 449
原胶南市	Original Jiaonan	31 881	63 260	28 074	26 546
平度市	Pingdu	28 107	54 471	25 735	24 542
莱西市	Laixi	29 739	50 006	29 632	27 139

主要统计指标解释

社会从业人员 指从事一定社会劳动并取得劳动报酬或经营收入的全部劳动力。这一指标反映了一定时期内全部劳动力资源的实际利用情况,是研究我国基本国情国力的重要指标。各单位的从业人员是指在各级国家机关、政党机关、社会团体及企业、事业单位中工作,并取得劳动报酬的全部人员。包括在岗职工、再就业的离退休人员、民办教师以及在各单位工作的外方人员和港、澳、台方人员等。

职工 指在内资(国有、集体、股份合作、联营、有限责任公司、股份有限公司)单位、港澳台商投资单位和外商投资单位及其附属机构工作,并由其支付工资的在岗人员以及不在岗但劳动关系仍在本单位的离岗人员。

在岗职工 指在本单位工作并由单位支付工资的人员,以及有工作岗位,但由于学习、病伤产假等原因暂未工作,仍由单位支付工资的人员。

职工工资总额 指各单位在一定时期内直接支付给本单位全部职工的劳动报酬总额,即在岗职工工资总额和离岗职工生活费两部分。工资总额的计算原则应以直接支付给职工的全部劳动报酬为根据。各单位支付给职工的劳动报酬以及其他根据有关规定支付的工资,不论是计入成本的还是不计入成本的,不论是按国家规定列入计征奖金税项目的,还是未列入计征奖金税项目的,不论是以货币形式支付的还是以实物形式支付的,均包括在工资总额内。

职工平均工资 指各单位一定时期内平均每人所得的工资。它表明一定时期职工工资收入的高低程度,是反映职工工资水平的主要指标。

全社会单位 包括:国有经济、集体经济、联营经济、股份制经济、外商和港、澳、台投资经济、私营经济、其他内资。

非私营单位 包括:国有经济、集体经济、联营经济、股份制经济、外商和港、澳、台投资经济。

Explanatory Notes on Main Statistical Indicators

Social Employment refers to the persons who are engaged in social working and receive remuneration payment or earn business income. This indicator reflects the actual utilization of total labour force during a certain period of time and is often used for the research on China's economic situation and national power. Persons Employed in Various Units refers to all the persons working in government agencies of various levels, political and party organizations, social organizations, enterprises and institutions, and receiving wages or other forms of payment. They include fully-employed staff and workers, re-employed retirees, teachers in schools run by the local people, foreigners and Chinese compatriots from Hong Kong, Macao, and Taiwan working in various units.

Staff and Workers refer to persons working in, and receive payment from units of state ownership, collective ownership, joint ownership, share holding ownership, foreign ownership, and ownership by entrepreneurs from Hong Kong, Macao, and Taiwan, and other types of ownership and their affiliated units.

Employed Staff and Workers refers to persons who work in, and receive wages from their working units, as well as persons who have their work posts, but are temporarily absent from work for reasons of study or on sick, injury or maternal leave and still receive wages from their working units.

Total Wage Bill refer to the total remuneration payment to staff and workers in various units during a certain period of time. The calculation of total wages is based on the total remuneration payment to the staff and workers. Therefore, all the wages and salaries and other payments to staff and workers are included in the total wages regardless of their sources, category, and forms (in kind or cash). (Total wages of staff and workers in this yearbook include only total wages of fully employed staff and workers, excluding the living allowances distributed to those who have left their working units while keeping their labour contract/employment relation unchanged).

Average Wage refers to the average wage in money terms per person during a certain period of time for staff and workers in enterprises, institutions, and government agencies, which reflects the general level of wage income during a certain period of time.

All Units include state ownership, collective ownership, joint ownership, share holding ownership, foreign ownership, ownership by entrepreneurs from Hong Kong, Macao and Taiwan, private ownership, and domestic ownership.

Non-private Units include state ownership, collective ownership, joint ownership, share holding ownership, foreign ownership, and ownership by entrepreneurs from Hong Kong, Macao and Taiwan.

4 固定资产投资

INVESTMENT IN FIXED ASSETS

简要说明

一、本篇资料的主要内容

本篇资料主要反映了全市固定资产投资及房地产开发方面的情况，主要包括固定资产投资的规模、结构、资金来源和房地产开发投资、施竣工及销售情况等方面的资料。

二、本篇资料的来源

本篇资料来源于固定资产投资及房地产开发投资统计年报，由市统计局固定资产投资统计处整理提供。

Brief Introduction

I. Main Content

Data in this chapter show the basic conditions of investment in fixed assets and real estate development of the whole city, mainly including the total investment in fixed assets, the structure of investment, the resources of investment and investment in real estate development, construction, completion, sales, etc.

II. Source of Data

Data in this chapter are based on the annual report on investment in fixed assets and real estate development, and provided by the Division of Investment and Construction Statistics of Qingdao Municipal Bureau of Statistics.

4-1 主要年份固定资产投资

MAJOR YEAR'S INVESTMENT IN FIXED ASSETS

单位:万元(10 000 yuan)

年份 Year	规模以上固定资产投资总额 Investment in Fixed Assets above Designated Size	按用途分 Grouped by Use		
		生产性投资 Productive Investment	非生产性投资 Non- Productive Investment	#住宅投资 Investment in Residential Buildings
1949	16	12	4	3
1952	3 097	1 368	1 729	1 007
1957	5 923	3 947	1 976	1 151
1962	2 747	2 049	698	192
1965	5 481	4 155	1 326	375
1970	6 100	5 813	287	154
1975	15 839	13 548	2 381	1 064
1978	29 660	23 499	6 161	3 203
1980	47 499	33 865	13 634	9 335
1985	107 421	60 643	73 424	19 058
1989	262 214	190 950	71 264	26 592
1990	284 576	210 453	74 123	38 898
1991	349 031	256 633	92 398	51 898
1992	583 068	420 748	162 320	83 844
1993	953 274	511 684	441 590	162 419
1994	1 329 716	728 532	601 184	324 094
1995	1 648 281	925 194	723 087	390 206
1996	1 610 562	972 398	638 164	285 412
1997	1 611 902	932 207	679 695	278 951
1998	1 909 711	1 125 821	783 890	316 999
1999	2 205 891	1 246 328	959 563	421 151
2000	2 426 820	1 311 538	1 115 282	470 963
2001	2 934 728	1 487 762	1 446 966	729 181
2002	3 683 623	1 962 588	1 721 035	765 030
2003	5 475 526	3 023 930	2 451 596	1 038 304
2004	9 845 646	6 336 279	3 509 367	1 608 738
2005	14 032 960	9 172 206	4 860 754	1 841 644
2006	14 856 894	9 214 578	5 642 316	2 222 733
2007	16 353 636	10 231 673	6 121 963	2 720 970
2008	20 190 098	12 443 179	7 746 919	3 315 538
2009	24 588 889	13 852 653	10 736 236	3 831 976
2010	30 224 785	16 207 885	14 016 900	5 609 189
2011	35 025 382	18 622 819	16 402 563	5 707 625
2012	41 539 146	24 246 803	17 292 343	6 689 114

注:1. 规模以上固定资产投资数据2003年以前为城镇以上统计范围。

2. 自2004年以来数据有调整,故表中数据不可比。

Note:1. The data of investment above designated size refer to investment above city and town level before 2003.

2. The data since 2004 are not comparable with other data because of the adjustment.

4-1 续表
continued

单位:万元(10 000 yuan)

年 份 Year	按构成分 Grouped by Composition of Funds			按资金来源分 Grouped by Sources of Funds			
	建筑安装工程 Construction and Installation	设备工器具购置 Purchase of Equipment and Instruments	其他费用 Others	国家投资 State Investment	国内贷款 Domestic Loans	利用外资 Foreign Investment	自筹及其他 Self-raising Fund and Others
1949	11	3	2	16			
1952	2 146	870	81	1 512			1 585
1957	2 853	2 773	297	3 816			2 107
1962	1 631	984	132	2 205			542
1965	3 346	1 859	276	4 451			1 030
1970	3 136	2 835	129	2 721			3 379
1975	7 489	8 133	217	9 378	1 362		5 099
1978	19 968	9 124	568	16 828	1 601		11 231
1980	30 993	15 541	965	10 371	12 925	1 420	22 783
1985	64 665	35 100	7 656	17 377	35 888	1 136	53 020
1989	141 821	95 333	17 269	38 747	79 999	25 081	114 939
1990	167 731	91 305	25 540	24 687	91 895	23 688	144 306
1991	196 212	108 929	43 890	22 615	131 676	38 325	156 415
1992	304 060	208 384	70 624	22 660	213 217	89 130	258 061
1993	600 011	225 555	127 708	23 736	208 672	94 469	526 397
1994	842 809	272 126	214 781	26 062	318 334	221 265	764 055
1995	1 020 484	385 934	241 863	25 683	379 198	328 124	915 276
1996	929 735	458 284	222 543	35 639	444 443	310 722	819 758
1997	875 057	485 122	251 723	27 928	297 089	363 789	923 096
1998	1 034 500	574 852	300 359	67 762	491 812	170 709	1 179 428
1999	1 456 473	459 596	289 822	128 603	584 120	145 589	1 347 579
2000	1 476 397	652 640	297 783	75 978	489 697	164 175	1 806 238
2001	1 781 235	744 549	408 944	93 491	620 562	217 526	2 157 787
2002	2 328 492	796 685	558 446	78 775	719 677	411 704	2 831 288
2003	3 544 790	1 133 333	797 403	127 861	989 178	722 644	4 237 643
2004	6 413 046	2 312 139	1 120 461	85 549	1 100 297	1 016 145	8 245 272
2005	8 949 231	3 141 732	1 941 997	136 632	1 250 343	1 850 921	11 540 604
2006	8 818 614	3 668 191	2 370 089	391 315	2 126 523	1 662 897	11 855 506
2007	9 981 666	4 171 878	2 200 092	215 649	2 427 031	1 788 056	13 109 824
2008	11 795 435	5 907 195	2 487 468	322 484	3 309 471	1 951 468	15 855 082
2009	14 911 874	5 869 214	3 807 801	778 090	4 217 265	1 593 287	21 555 685
2010	18 725 922	6 362 880	5 135 983	1 305 737	5 881 886	2 135 736	27 893 294
2011	22 865 421	7 521 441	4 638 520	1 640 702	5 871 709	1 766 278	33 579 182
2012	26 080 239	8 601 282	6 857 625	1 324 159	5 484 459	1 561 597	37 356 847

4 -2 主要年份固定资产投资构成(以投资总额为100)

COMPOSITION OF MAJOR YEAR'S INVESTMENT IN FIXED ASSETS(TOTAL INVESTMENT = 100)

年份 Year	按用途分 Grouped by Use		
	生产性投资 Productive Investment	非生产性投资 Non-Productive Investment	#住宅投资占非生产性比重 Percentage of Investment in Residential Buildings to Non-Productive Investment
1949	75.00	25.00	75.00
1952	44.17	55.83	58.24
1957	66.64	33.36	58.25
1962	74.59	25.41	27.51
1965	75.81	24.19	28.28
1970	95.30	4.70	53.66
1975	84.97	15.03	44.69
1978	79.23	20.77	51.99
1980	71.30	28.70	68.47
1985	56.45	43.55	40.74
1989	72.82	27.18	37.30
1990	73.95	26.05	52.50
1991	73.53	26.47	56.17
1992	72.16	27.84	51.65
1993	53.68	46.32	36.78
1994	54.79	45.21	53.91
1995	56.10	43.90	54.00
1996	60.40	39.60	44.70
1997	57.80	42.20	41.00
1998	59.00	41.00	16.60
1999	56.50	43.50	19.10
2000	54.00	46.00	19.40
2001	50.70	49.30	50.40
2002	53.30	46.70	44.50
2003	55.20	44.80	42.40
2004	64.40	35.60	45.80
2005	65.40	34.60	37.90
2006	62.00	38.00	39.40
2007	62.60	37.40	44.40
2008	61.60	38.40	42.80
2009	56.30	43.70	35.70
2010	53.62	46.38	40.02
2011	53.17	46.83	34.80
2012	58.37	41.63	38.68

4-2 续表
continued

年份 Year	按构成分 Grouped by Composition of Funds			按资金来源分 Grouped by Sources of Funds			
	建筑安装工程 Construction and Installation	设备工器具购置 Purchase of Equipment and Instruction	其他费用 Others	国家投资 State Investment	国内贷款 Domestic Loans	利用外资 Foreign Investment	自筹及其他 Self-raising Fund and Others
1949	68.75	18.75	12.5	100			
1952	69.29	28.09	2.62	48.82			51.18
1957	48.17	46.82	5.01	64.43			35.57
1962	59.37	35.82	4.81	80.27			19.73
1965	61.05	33.92	5.03	81.21			18.79
1970	51.41	46.48	2.11	44.61			55.39
1975	47.28	51.35	1.37	59.21	8.60		32.19
1978	67.32	30.76	1.92	56.74	5.40		37.86
1980	65.25	32.72	2.03	21.83	27.21	2.99	47.97
1985	60.20	32.68	7.12	16.18	33.41	1.06	49.35
1989	54.08	36.36	6.59	14.78	30.51	9.56	45.15
1990	58.94	32.08	8.98	8.68	32.29	8.32	50.71
1991	56.22	31.21	12.57	6.48	37.73	10.98	44.81
1992	52.15	35.74	12.11	3.89	36.56	15.29	44.26
1993	62.94	23.66	13.40	2.49	21.89	9.91	65.71
1994	63.38	20.46	16.16	1.96	23.94	16.64	57.46
1995	61.9	23.4	14.7	1.6	23.0	19.9	55.5
1996	57.7	28.5	13.8	2.2	27.6	19.3	50.9
1997	54.3	30.1	15.6	1.7	18.4	22.6	57.3
1998	54.2	20.8	15.7	3.5	25.8	8.9	61.8
1999	66.0	20.8	13.2	5.8	26.5	6.6	61.1
2000	60.8	26.9	12.3	3.1	20.2	6.8	74.4
2001	60.7	25.4	13.9	3.0	20.1	7.0	69.9
2002	63.2	21.6	15.2	1.9	17.8	10.2	70.1
2003	64.7	20.7	14.6	2.1	16.3	11.9	69.7
2004	65.1	23.5	11.4	0.8	10.6	9.7	78.9
2005	63.8	22.4	13.8	0.9	8.5	12.5	78.1
2006	59.4	24.7	15.9	2.4	13.3	10.4	73.9
2007	61.0	25.5	13.5	1.2	13.8	10.2	74.8
2008	58.4	29.3	12.3	1.5	15.4	9.1	74.0
2009	60.6	23.9	15.5	2.8	15.0	5.6	76.6
2010	62.0	21.0	17.0	3.5	15.8	5.7	75.0
2011	65.3	21.5	13.2	3.8	13.7	4.1	78.4
2012	62.8	20.7	16.5	2.9	12.0	3.4	81.7

4-3 按三次产业分规模以上固定资产投资(2012年)

INVESTMENT IN FIXED ASSETS ABOVE DESIGNATED SIZE BY THREE STRATA OF INDUSTRY(2012)

单位:万元(10 000 yuan)

指标	Indicator	2012年
总计	**Total**	**41 539 146**
第一产业	Primary Industry	685 290
第二产业	Secondary Industry	19 893 735
#工业	Industry	18 488 651
第三产业	Tertiary Industry	20 960 121

4-4 分市、区固定资产投资额(2012年)

INVESTMENT IN FIXED ASSETS BY REGION(2012)

单位:万元(10 000 yuan)

市、区名称	Region	规模以上固定资产投资额 Investment in Fixed Assets above Designated Size	#房地产开发 Investment in Real Estate Development
总计	**Total**	**41 539 146**	**9 301 099**
市区	Urban Area	18 043 060	7 448 036
#崂山区	Laoshan District	1 557 361	1 092 202
原黄岛区	Original Huangdao District	5 436 813	1 096 902
城阳区	Chengyang District	4 634 920	927 952
即墨市	Jimo	5 153 457	417 818
胶州市	Jiaozhou	5 273 453	613 928
原胶南市	Original Jiaonan	5 069 951	515 388
平度市	Pingdu	4 279 357	230 156
莱西市	Laixi	3 719 868	75 773

4-5 规模以上固定资产投资(2012 年)
INVESTMENT IN FIXED ASSETS ABOVE DESIGNATED SIZE(2012)

单位:万元(10 000 yuan)

项　　目	Item	合计 Total	#房地产开发 Investment in Real Estate Development
一、本年施工项目(个)	**Projects Under Construction This Year(unit)**	**4 198**	
#本年新开工(个)	of which:Newly Started(unit)	3 344	
二、本年建成投产项目(个)	**Projects Completed and Put into Use This Year(unit)**	**2 771**	
三、本年完成投资	**Investment Completed This Year**	**41 539 146**	**9 301 099**
1.按构成分	Grouped by Composition		
#建筑工程	Construction Projects	23 718 433	4 683 804
安装工程	Installation Projects	2 361 806	975 370
设备工器具购置	Purchase of Equipment and Instruments	8 601 282	124 108
#用于更新的设备	Equipment Used in Updates	2 023 753	
2.按建设性质分	Grouped by Type of Construction		
#新　建	New Construction	21 412 273	
扩　建	Expansion	4 829 571	
改　建	Reconstruction	3 964 818	
3.按隶属关系分	Grouped by Subordination Relation		
中央单位	Central Units	1 308 656	795 790
地方单位	Local Units	40 230 490	8 505 309
4.按国民经济行业分	Grouped by Economic Sector		
(1)农、林、牧、渔业	Farming,Forestry,Animal Husbandry and Fishery	685 290	
农　业	Farming	248 738	
林　业	Forestry	50 387	
畜牧业	Animal Husbandry	86 292	
渔　业	Fishery	199 422	
农、林、牧、渔服务业	Farming,Forestry,Animal Husbandry and Fishery Services	100 451	
(2)采矿业	Mining	146 944	
煤炭开采和洗选业	Mining and Washing of Coal		
石油和天然气开采业	Extraction of Petroleum and Natural Gas		
黑色金属矿采选业	Mining of Ferrous Metal Ores	53 291	
有色金属矿采选业	Mining of Non-ferrous Metal Ores	42 187	
非金属矿采选业	Mining and Processing of Nonmetal Ores	41 616	
开采辅助活动	Auxiliary Activities of Mining	9 850	
其他采矿业	Mining of Other Ores		

4-5 续表 1
continued

单位:万元(10 000 yuan)

项　目	Item	合计 Total	#房地产开发 Investment in Real Estate Development
(3)制造业	Manufacturing	17 820 228	
农副食品加工业	Processing of Food from Agricultural Products	1 428 528	
食品制造业	Manufacture of Foods	488 270	
酒、饮料和精制茶制造业	Manufacture of Liquor, Beverage and Refind Tea	162 789	
烟草制品业	Manufacture of Tobacco		
纺织业	Manufacture of Textile	431 547	
纺织服装、服饰业	Manufacture of Textile Wearing Apparel	866 298	
皮革、毛皮、羽毛及其制品和制鞋业	Manufacture of Leather, Fur, Feather & Its Products Footwear	369 036	
木材加工和木、竹、藤、棕、草制品业	Processing of Timbers, Manufacture of Wood, Bamboo, Rattan, Palm and Straw Products	275 513	
家具制造业	Manufacture of Furniture	296 847	
造纸和纸制品业	Manufacture of Paper and Paper Products	272 820	
印刷和记录媒介复制业	Printing, Reproduction of Recording Media	252 768	
文教、工美、体育和娱乐用品制造业	Manufacture of Articles for Culture, Arts & Crafts, Sports and Entertainment	548 978	
石油加工、炼焦和核燃料加工业	Processing of Petroleum, Coking, Processing of Nucleus Fuel	379 510	
化学原料和化学制品制造业	Manufacture of Chemical Raw Material and Chemical Products	661 149	
医药制造业	Manufacture of Medicines	193 106	
化学纤维制造业	Manufacture of Chemical Fiber	25 160	
橡胶和塑料制品业	Manufacture of Rubber and Plastic	987 617	
非金属矿物制品业	Manufacture of Non-metallic Mineral Products	1 037 152	
黑色金属冶炼和压延加工业	Smelting and Pressing of Ferrous Metals	152 412	
有色金属冶炼和压延加工业	Smelting and Pressing of Non-ferrous Metals	263 971	
金属制品业	Manufacture of Metal Products	1 192 344	
通用设备制造业	Manufacture of General Purpose Machinery	1 824 424	
专用设备制造业	Manufacture of Special Purpose Machinery	1 832 127	
汽车制造业	Manufacture of Vehicle	988 629	
铁路、船舶、航空航天和其他运输设备制造业	Manufacture of Transport Equipment for Railway, Shipping, Aerospace and other uses	1 157 754	
电气机械和器材制造业	Manufacture of Electrical Machinery & Equipment	838 971	
计算机、通信和其他电子设备制造业	Manufacture of Computer, Communication Equipment and Other Electronic Equipment	498 976	
仪器仪表制造业	Manufacture of Measuring Instrument	198 574	
其他制造业	Manufacture of Other Products	54 689	
废弃资源综合利用业	Recycling and Disposal of Waste Resources	78 758	
金属制品、机械和设备修理业	Maintenance of Metal Products, Machinery and Equipment	61 511	

4-5 续表2
continued

单位:万元(10 000 yuan)

项　目	Item	合计 Total	房地产开发 Investment in Real Estate Development
(4)电力、燃气及水的生产和供应业	Production and Supply of Electricity Gas and Water	521 479	
电力、热力的生产和供应业	Production and Supply of Electric Power and Heat Power	408 701	
燃气生产和供应业	Production and Supply of Gas	44 604	
水的生产和供应业	Production and Supply of Water	68 174	
(5)建筑业	Construction	1 405 084	
(6)交通运输、仓储及邮政业	Transport Storage and Post	2 364 232	
铁路运输业	Railway Transport	271 495	
道路运输业	Road Transport	934 091	
水上运输业	Water Transport	466 160	
航空运输业	Air Transport	4 151	
管道运输业	Pipeline Transport	128 425	
装卸搬运和运输代理业	Handing, Corrying and Transportation Agent	88 530	
仓储业	Ware houses and Storage	471 380	
邮政业	Post		
(7)信息传输、软件和信息技术服务业	Information Transmission Computer Services and Software	228 045	
(8)批发和零售业	Wholesale and Retail Trade	1 224 492	
(9)住宿和餐饮业	Hotels and Catering Services	841 590	
(10)金融业	Financial Intermediation	57 282	
(11)房地产业	Financial Intermediation	11 362 177	9 301 099

4-5 续表3
continued

单位:万元(10 000 yuan)

项　目	Item	合计 Total	#房地产开发 Investment in Real Estate Development
(12)租赁和商务服务业	Leasing and Business Services	963 538	
(13)科学研究、技术服务和地质勘察业	Scientific Research, Technical Service and Geologic Prospecting	183 227	
(14)水利、环境和公共设施管理业	Management of Water Conservancy, Environment and Public Facilities	2 325 010	
水利管理业	Management of Water Conservancy	55 434	
环境管理业	Environmental Management	81 850	
公共设施管理业	Management of Public Facilities	2 187 726	
(15)居民服务和其他服务业	Services to Households and Other Services	100 537	
居民服务业	Services to Households	46 613	
机动车、电子产品和日用产品修理业	Maintenance of Vehicle, Electronic Products and Daily Articles	45 324	
其他服务业	Other Services	8 600	
(16)教育	Education	391 630	
(17)卫生和社会工作	Health and Social Work	186 391	
卫生	Health	88 347	
(18)文化、体育和娱乐业	Culture, Sports and Entertainment	250 703	
新闻出版业	Journalism and Publishing Activities	2 210	
广播、电视、体育和音像业	Broadcasting, Movies, Televisions and Audiovisual Activities	9 365	
文化艺术业	Cultural and Art Activities	42 069	
体育	Sports Activities	13 763	
娱乐业	Entertainment	183 296	
(19)公共管理、社会保障和社会组织	Public Management, Social Security and Social Organization	481 267	
中国共产党机关	Communist Party of China	7 742	
国家机构	Government Agencies	155 514	
人民政协、民主党派	People's Political Consultatioe Conference, Democratic Party		
社会保障	Social Security		
群众团体、社会团体和其他成员组织	Non-Governmental Institutions, Social Organizations and Other Organizations	12 921	
基层群众自治组织	Local People Self-government Organization	305 090	
(20)国际组织	International Organization		

4-5 续表4
continued

单位:万元(10 000 yuan)

项目	Item	合计 Total	#房地产开发 Investment in Real Estate Development
四、本年新增固定资产	**Newly Increased Fixed Assets This Year**		
(1)农、林、牧、渔业	Farming, Forestry, Animal Husbandry and Fishery	513 578	
(2)采矿业	Mining	54 621	
(3)制造业	Manufacturing	13 656 405	
(4)电力、燃气及水的生产和供应业	Construction	303 806	
(5)建筑业	Production and Supply of Electricty, Gas and Water	1 097 103	
(6)交通运输、仓储和邮政业	Transport, Storage and Post	1 188 263	
(7)信息传输、计算机服务和软件业	Information Transmission, Computer Services and Software	99 010	
(8)批发和零售业	Wholesale and Retail Trade	861 221	
(9)住宿和餐饮业	Hotels and Catering Services	247 009	
(10)金融业	Financial Intermediation	58 582	
(11)房地产业	Real Estate	4 854 227	[illegible] 002 975
(12)租赁和商务服务业	Leasing and Business Services	172 170	
(13)科学研究、技术服务和地质勘察业	Scientific Research, Technical Services and Geologic Prospecting	114 911	
(14)水利、环境和公共设施管理业	Management of Water Conservancy, Environment and Public Facilities	779 635	
(15)居民服务和其他服务业	Services to Households and Other Services	92 910	
(16)教育	Education	227 835	
(17)卫生、社会保障和社会福利业	Health, Social Security and Social Welfare	141 334	
(18)文化、体育和娱乐业	Culture, Sports and Entertainment	82 167	
(19)公共管理和社会组织	Public Management and Social Organization	235 588	
(20)国际组织	International Organization		
五、本年资金来源合计	**Total Funds This Year**	**52 753 366**	**17 685 546**
上年末结余资金	Balance of Last Year	7 016 324	5 396 419
本年资金来源小计	Sub-total Funds This Year	45 727 062	12 289 127
国家预算内资金	State Budget	1 324 159	
国内贷款	Domestic Loans	5 484 459	2 443 230
债券	State Treasury Bond		
利用外资	Foreign Investment	1 561 597	14 649
自筹资金	Self-raising Funds	31 244 445	4 299 284
其他资金来源	Others	6 112 402	5 531 964

4-6 主要年份房地产开发投资
MAJOR YEAR'S INVESTMENT IN REAL ESTATE DEVELOPMENT

单位:万元、万平方米(10 000 yuan,10 000 sq. m)

年份 Year	房地产开发投资额 Investment in Real Estate Development	房屋施工面积 Floor Space Under Construction	房屋竣工面积 Floor Space Completed	房屋实际销售面积 Floor Space of Buildings Sold	房屋实际销售额 Sale of Buildings
1995	562 861	1 008	240	103	185 384
1996	455 765	748	203	80	125 150
1997	426 570	675	237	113	216 311
1998	438 059	742	259	178	351 805
1999	629 717	900	474	240	430 123
2000	675 142	1 047	352	301	550 401
2001	925 153	1 374	532	406	802 364
2002	1 036 476	1 417	537	427	933 031
2003	1 277 969	1 765	552	469	1 121 885
2004	1 626 965	2 101	635	516	1 530 964
2005	2 238 370	2 363	811	740	2 666 738
2006	2 683 631	2 751	654	719	3 054 907
2007	3 223 547	3 224	641	833	4 333 566
2008	3 805 652	3 773	672	770	3 924 175
2009	4 594 829	4 310	814	1 262	7 036 744
2010	6 024 387	5 058	1 020	1 360	8 952 942
2011	7 827 193	5 693	925	1 026	7 702 379
2012	9 301 099	6 474	1 212	951	7 660 684

4-7 房地产开发投资情况(2012 年)
INVESTMENT IN REAL ESTATE DEVELOPMENT(2012)

单位:万元(10 000 yuan)

指标名称	Indicator	合计 Total	按经济类型分 Grouped by Economic Types		
			国有经济 State-owned	集体经济 Collective-owned	其他经济 Others
本年完成投资额	**Investment Completed This Year**	**9 301 099**	**1 347 101**	**190 839**	**7 763 159**
#土地开发投资额	Investment in Land Development				
1. 住宅	Residential Buildings	5 935 524	585 231	107 958	5 242 335
2. 办公楼	Office Buildings	682 232	248 567	2 656	431 009
3. 商业营业用房	Houses for Business Use	1 402 393	288 911	69 593	1 043 889
4. 其他	Others	1 280 950	224 410	10 632	1 045 908

4-7 续表
continued

单位:万元(10 000 yuan)

指标名称	Indicator	按资质等级分 Grouped by Qualification Criteria					
		一级 First Grade	二级 Second Grade	三级 Third Grade	四级 Fourth Grade	暂定 Provisional	其他 Others
本年完成投资额	**Investment Completed This Year**	**239 272**	**584 772**	**841 346**	**213 898**	**6 715 309**	**706 502**
#土地开发投资额	Investment in Land Development						
1. 住宅	Residential Buildings	135 954	423 863	554 644	158 419	4 165 029	497 615
2. 办公楼	Office Buildings	45 143	4 516	26 369	6 638	568 352	31 214
3. 商业营业用房	Houses for Business Use	15 126	79 374	96 501	22 254	1 086 010	103 128
4. 其他	Others	43 049	77 019	163 832	26 587	895 918	74 545

4-8 房地产施工、竣工面积及竣工价值(2012 年)
FLOOR SPACE UNDER CONSTRUCTION AND COMPLETED AND COMPLETED VALUE OF REAL ESTATE(2012)

单位:万平方米(10 000 sq. m)

施工、竣工房屋面积及竣工价值	Indicator	施工面积 Floor Space Under Construction	#新开工 Newly Started	竣工面积 Floor Space Completed	竣工房屋价值(万元) Completed Value (10 000 yuan)
房屋建筑面积总计	**Floor Space of Buildings**	**6 473.7**	**1 763.2**	**1 211.6**	**3 185 557**
住　宅	Residential Buildings	4 467.7	1 234.2	928.9	2 375 743
其中:经济适用房	of which: Economically Affordable Housing	107.1	26.2	23.9	
办公楼	Office Buildings	283.9	88.1	32.2	174 577
商业营业用房	Houses for Business Use	807.4	191.8	105.2	277 472
其　他	Others	914.8	249.1	145.3	357 765

4-9 商品房屋销售情况(2012 年)
BASIC STATISTICS ON SALES OF COMMERCIALIZED BUILDINGS(2012)

单位:万平方米(10 000 sq. m)

商品房屋销售情况	Sales and Rental of Commercialized Buildings	实际销售 Actual Sales	实际销售额(万元) Actual Sales Volume (10 000 yuan)	待售面积 Area for Sale
房屋面积总计	**Floor Space of Buildings**	**950.9**	**7 660 684**	**365.2**
住　宅	Residential Buildings	842.5	6 388 962	229.2
其中:经济适用房	of which: Economically Affordable Housing			
办公楼	Office Buildings	42.2	494 049	27.8
商业营业用房	Houses for Business Use	50.6	717 442	70.6
其　他	Others	15.6	60 231	37.6

主要统计指标解释

固定资产投资 是以货币形式表现的在一定时期内全社会建造和购置固定资产的工作量以及与此有关的费用的总称。该指标是反映固定资产投资规模、结构和发展速度的综合性指标,又是观察工程进度和考核投资效果的重要依据。全社会固定资产投资按登记注册类型可分为国有、集体、个体、联营、股份制、外商、港澳台商、其他等。

城镇固定资产投资 是指城镇各种登记注册类型的企业、事业、行政单位及个体户进行的计划总投资(或实际需要总投资)500万元及500万元以上的建设项目投资、房地产开发投资、城镇和工矿区私人建房投资。县城及以上区域内发生的投资,县及县以上各级政府及主管部门直接领导、管理的建设项目和企业事业单位的投资均为城镇固定资产投资。

固定资产投资 包括城镇、农村500万元以上投资项目。

房地产开发投资 指各种登记注册类型的房地产开发公司、商品房建设公司及其他房地产开发法人单位和附属于其他法人单位实际从事房地产开发或经营活动的单位统一开发的包括统代建、拆迁还建的住宅、厂房、仓库、饭店、宾馆、度假村、写字楼、办公楼等房屋建筑物和配套的服务设施,土地开发工程(如道路、给水、排水、供电、供热、通讯、平整场地等基础设施工程)的投资;不包括单纯的土地交易活动。

固定资产投资的资金来源 根据固定资产投资的资金来源不同,分为国家预算内资金、国内贷款、利用外资、自筹资金和其他资金。

固定资产投资按国民经济行业分 根据建设项目建成投产后的主要产品或主要用途及社会经济活动性质来确定国民经济行业。一般情况下,一个建设项目或一个企业、事业单位只能属于一种国民经济行业。

固定资产投资按建设性质分 建设项目的性质一般分为新建、扩建、改建和技术改造、迁建、恢复。

固定资产投资按构成分 固定资产投资活动按其工作内容和实现方式分为建筑安装工程,设备、工具、器具购置,其他费用三个部分。

施工项目 指报告期内进行过建筑或安装施工活动的项目。凡是报告期内施过工的建设项目,不论施工时间长短,均作为施工项目统计。

新增生产能力(或工程效益) 指通过固定资产投资活动而增加的设计能力(或工程效益),它是以实物形态表现的固定资产投资成果。

新增生产能力(或工程效益)一般有以下几种表现形式:

(1)以建设项目或单项工程建成后的年产能力表示,如煤炭开采,石油开采等。

(2) 以建设项目或单项工程建成后处理原料的能力表示,如选矿工程的年处理矿石能力,城市污水处理能力等。

(3)以新增加的主要设备的数量或容量表示,如新增棉布织机、电机组容量等。

(4)用建筑物容积、容量、面积、长度表示,如新建公路、水库容量、学校学生席位等。

房屋施工面积 是指报告期内施工的全部房屋建筑面积。包括本期新开工的面积和上期开工跨入本期继续施工的房屋面积,以及上期已停缓建在本期恢复施工的房屋面积。本期竣工和本期施工后又停缓建的房屋,其建筑面积仍计入本期房屋施工面积中。

房屋竣工面积 是指在报告期内房屋建筑按照设计要求全部完工,达到住人和使用条件,经验收鉴定合格(或达到竣工验收标准),正式移交使用单位的各栋房屋建筑面积的总和。

新增固定资产 又称交付使用的固定资产,是指已经完成建造和购置过程,并已交付生产或使用单位的固定资产价值。新增固定资产是表示固定资产投资成果的价值量指标,也是反映建设进度、计算固定资产投资效果的必要数据。

固定资产交付使用率 指一定时期新增固定资产与同期完成投资额的比率。该指标是反映固定资产动用速度,衡量建设过程中宏观投资效果的综合指标。由于新增固定资产是较长时期内形成的结果，而投资额则是当年完成的，因此，该指标一般适宜于反映较长时期内固定资产的动用情况。

Explanatory Notes on Main Statistical Indicators

Investment in Fixed Assets referss to the volume of activities in construction and purchases of fixed assets and related fees, expressed in monetary terms. It is a comprehensive indicator which shows the size, structure and growth of the investment in fixed assets, providing basis for observing the progress of construction projects and evaluating results of investment. Total investment in fixed assets in the whole country includes, by type of ownership, the investment by the state-owned units, collective units, individuals, joint ownership units, share-holding units, as well as investment by businessmen from foreign countries and from Hong Kong, Macau and Taiwan, and by other units.

Urban Investment in Fixed Assets refers to construction projects involving a total planned (or required) investment of 5,000,000 yuan and over by urban enterprises and institutions of various types of ownership, by administrative units and by individuals, investment in real estate development, and housing investment by individuals in urban areas and in industrial and mining areas. In other words, all investments that take place in county towns and urban areas, investment in construction projects under the direct leadership and management of government agencies at and above county levels and investments by enterprises and institutions at and above county levels are covered in urban investment in fixed assets.

Investment in Fixed Assets includes construction projects involving an urban or rural investment of 5,000,000 yuan and over.

Investment in Real Estate Development refers to the investment by the real estate development companies, commercial buildings construction companies and other real estate development units of various types of ownership in the construction of house buildings, such as residential buildings, factory buildings, warehouses, hotels, guesthouses, holiday villages, office buildings, and the complementary service facilities and land development projects, such as roads, water supply, water drainage, power supply, heating, telecommunications, land leveling and other projects of infrastructure. It excludes the activities in pure land transactions.

Sources of Funds for Investment in Fixed Assets include fund from state budget, domestic loans, foreign investment, self-raised funds, and others depending on the source of investment.

Investment in Fixed Assets by Sector The classification of construction projects by sector is determined by the major products or the purpose of the projects when they are put into production or use, and by the nature of their social economic activities. In general, one project or one enterprise or institution can only be classified into one sector.

Investment in Fixed Assets by Type of Construction The construction projects in general can be classified, by the type of construction, into new construction, expansion, reconstruction and technical transformation, moving and restoration. However, investment by type of construction is not applied to investment by real-estate development units, investment in rural areas and investment in housing by urban individuals.

Investment in Fixed Assets by Structure By their contents, investment activities are classified into 3 categories, i. e. construction and installation, purchase of equipment and instrument, and other expenses.

Projects under Construction refer to projects with construction and installation activities undertaken in the reference period. All projects that have construction activities undertaken during the reference period are reported as projects under construction irrespective of the length of construction work.

Newly Increased Production Capacity (or Project Efficiency) refers to the increase of designed capacity (or project efficiency) through investment in fixed assets, which reflects the accomplishment of investment in fixed assets in kind.

The newly increased production capacity (project efficiency) are usually expressed in one of the following forms:

(1) output of products, i. e. the output that the project can produce during a given period (usually a year). For instance, the capacity in coal mining is expressed in 10,000 tons/year, the capacity in producing chemical pesticides expressed in ton/year, the capacity in producing tractors in tractor/year, etc. For some chemical products where the effective contents differ significantly, the production capacity is expressed as the designed effective content equivalent, such as in the case of sulphuric acid, soda ash, caustic soda, etc;

(2) raw materials processing capacity, i. e. the volume of raw materials that could be processed by the project per day (or per hour), such as tons of materials processed per day by a sugar refining project or edible vegetable oil project, or tons of urban sewage processed per day;

(3) number or capacity of major equipment increased, such as number of cotton or silk looms increased, wool spindles increased, or capacity (in kilowatts) of power generators increased; and

(4) physical measures (volume, capacity, area, and length) of construction, which is typical for non-industrial projects, for instance, the length of railways put into operation, the length of highways, the capacity of reservoirs, the capacity of warehouses, the floor space of housing projects, capacity for new students in schools or beds in hospitals, areas under new irrigation project, etc.

Floor Space of Buildings under Construction refers to total floor space of all buildings under construction during the reference period, including floor space of newly started buildings during the reference period, floor space of construction extended from the previous period to the current period, and floor space of construction suspended during the previous period and resumed in the current period. Floor space of construction completed in the current period, and floor space of construction started and then suspended in the current period are also included in the floor space under construction of the current year.

Floor Space of Buildings Completed refers to the floor space of all buildings completed in the reference period, which have been appraised and accepted (or come up to the designed standards) and have been transferred to the owners for use.

Newly Increased Fixed Assets refer to the newly increased value of fixed assets, constructed or purchased, that have been transferred to the investors. This is an indicator that demonstrates the results of investment in fixed assets in monetary terms, and an important indicator to reflect the speed of construction and to calculate the efficiency of investment.

Rate of Projects of Fixed Assets Completed and Put into Operation refers to the ratio of the newly increased fixed assets to the total investment made in the same period. This is a comprehensive indicator reflecting the speed of the employment of fixed assets and the investment efficiency at the macro-level. As the newly increase fixed assets is the result of a long period while the investment is completed in the current year, this indicator is expected to be used to reflect the employment of fixed assets over a long period of time.

5 对外经济贸易
FOREIGN TRADE

简要说明

一、本篇资料的主要内容

本篇资料主要反映了全市外经外贸和外资企业的基本情况，主要包括外贸进出口、利用外资、外商投资企业生产经营状况等方面的资料。

二、本篇资料的来源

1、口岸进出口数据来源于市口岸办。

2、进出口、利用外资等资料来源于市商务局。

3、外商投资企业经营情况数据来源于全国外商投资企业联合年检。

本篇资料由市统计局外经贸易统计处整理提供。

Brief Introduction

I. Main Content

Data in this chapter show the basic conditions of foreign trade and foreign-funded enterprises, mainly including imports and exports, utilization of foreign capitals, production and operation condition of foreign-funded enterprises, etc.

II. Source of Data

(1)Data on imports and exports of Qingdao port are provided by Office of Qingdao Port Administration.

(2)Data on imports & exports and utilization of foreign capitals are provided by Qingdao Municipal Commerce Bureau.

(3)Data on production and operation condition of foreign-funded enterprises are based on the National Union Annual Inspection of foreign-funded enterprises.

Data in this chapter are prepared and compiled by the Division of Trade and External Economic Relations Statistics of Qingdao Municipal Bureau of Statistics.

5-1 青岛口岸进出口总额(1985-2012年)
TOTAL VALUE OF IMPORTS AND EXPORTS OF QINGDAO PORT(1985-2012)

单位:万美元(10000 USD)

年份 Year	青岛口岸进出口总额 Total Value of Imports and Exports of Qingdao Port	#出口 Exports	进口 Imports
1985	414 448	234 652	179 796
1986	382 840	191 926	190 914
1987	445 090	259 458	185 632
1988	474 516	259 176	215 340
1989	506 152	268 397	237 755
1990	477 117	304 011	173 106
1991	519 273	332 949	186 324
1992	581 495	350 163	231 332
1993	678 013	360 297	317 716
1994	888 574	510 760	377 814
1995	1 307 508	705 245	602 263
1996	1 391 323	760 566	629 757
1997	1 542 284	936 142	609 142
1998	1 463 718	933 392	530 326
1999	1 696 514	1 063 768	632 746
2000	2 520 420	1 423 266	1 097 154
2001	2 797 085	1 636 888	1 160 197
2002	3 128 048	1 889 612	1 238 436
2003	4 088 096	2 366 046	1 722 050
2004	5 677 570	3 197 697	2 479 873
2005	6 932 944	3 959 947	2 972 997
2006	8 019 198	4 495 731	3 523 467
2007	9 257 099	5 263 539	3 993 560
2008	11 558 079	5 953 501	5 604 578
2009	9 049 699	4 694 832	4 354 867
2010	11 912 702	5 988 254	5 924 448
2011	15 095 088	7 294 226	7 800 862
2012	14 888 716	7 120 813	7 767 903

5-2 进出口总额(1988-2012 年)
TOTAL VALUE OF IMPORTS AND EXPORTS(1988-2012)

单位:万美元(10000 USD)

年份 Year	进出口总额(含中央、省驻青公司) Total Value of Imports and Exports (including central and provincial companies)	#出口 Exports	进口 Imports	进出口总额(不含中央、省驻青公司) Total Value of Imports and Exports (excluding central and provincial companies)	#出口 Exports	进口 Imports
1988				28 097	21 731	6 366
1989				39 327	27 797	11 530
1990				41 649	33 529	8 120
1991				54 624	44 746	9 878
1992				88 600	66 291	22 309
1993	517 643	346 288	171 355	139 048	100 201	38 847
1994	633 213	434 102	199 111	234 978	164 135	70 843
1995	858 560	536 386	322 174	376 372	245 072	131 300
1996	863 521	516 317	347 204	461 950	287 123	174 827
1997	916 269	579 261	377 008	521 967	338 535	183 432
1998	882 042	573 020	309 022	595 826	382 657	213 169
1999	1 009 885	631 072	378 813	775 565	446 260	329 305
2000	1 353 222	826 891	526 331	1 083 133	611 426	471 707
2001	1 541 564	950 160	591 404	1 235 781	712 024	523 757
2002	1 692 567	1 057 141	635 426	1 409 598	850 420	559 178
2003	2 065 912	1 239 199	826 713	1 784 556	1 035 528	749 028
2004	2 698 781	1 578 167	1 120 614	2 433 188	1 391 171	1 042 017
2005	3 302 230	1 942 242	1 359 988	3 045 542	1 758 834	1 286 708
2006	3 911 543	2 346 552	1 564 991	3 655 737	2 164 541	1 491 196
2007	4 572 534	2 831 004	1 741 530	4 360 499	2 677 596	1 682 903
2008	5 363 659	3 262 476	2 101 183	5 215 886	3 146 246	2 069 540
2009	4 485 115	2 729 865	1 755 250	4 398 639	2 692 197	1 706 442
2010	5 705 963	3 391 560	2 314 403	5 614 928	3 335 141	2 279 787
2011	7 215 217	4 061 309	3 153 908	7 126 310	4 005 572	3 120 738
2012				7 320 781	4 081 968	3 238 313

注:2012 年起,取消含中央、省驻青公司统计口径。

Note: Since 2012, the statistical calibre including central and provincial companies has been cancled.

5-3 分国别外贸出口总额(不含中央、省驻青公司)

TOTAL VALUE OF EXPORTS BY COUNTRIES OR REGIONS (EXCLUDING CENTRAL AND PROVINCIAL COMPANIES)

单位:万美元(10000 USD)

国别(地区)	Country(Region)	2012	2011	2012年比2011年±% 2012/2011(±%)
总计	**Total**	**4 081 968**	**3 940 124**	**3.6**
亚洲	Asia	1 773 983	1 704 114	4.1
香港	Hong Kong	111 738	132 863	-15.9
日本	Japan	629 998	617 645	2.0
韩国	Korea	401 533	400 732	0.2
台湾	Taiwan	46 909	58 563	-19.9
非洲	Africa	224 226	187 794	19.4
南非	South Africa	32 175	30 382	5.9
欧洲	Europe	873 495	885 898	-1.4
欧盟	EU	777 398	813 178	-4.4
南美洲	South America	290 713	286 699	1.4
北美洲	North America	811 514	793 269	2.3
美国	United States	718 460	724 985	-0.9
大洋洲	Oceanica	107 472	82 480	30.3
澳大利亚	Australia	92 818	71 896	29.1

5-4 外贸出口商品分类(不含中央、省驻青公司)

EXPORT COMMODITIES BY CATEGORY(EXCLUDING CENTRAL AND PROVINCIAL COMPANIES)

单位:万美元(10000 USD)

项　目	Item	2012	2011	2012 年比 2011 年 ±% 2012/2011(±%)
合　计	**Total**	**4 081 968**	**3 940 124**	**3.6**
按企业性质划分	By Enterprises Nature			
国有企业	State-owned Enterprises	420 155	431 371	-2.6
外商投资企业	Foreign Funded Enterprises	1 788 166	1 904 330	-6.1
其他企业	Other Enterprises	1 873 647	1 605 524	16.7
按贸易方式划分	By Customs Regime			
一般贸易	Ordinary Trade	2 236 630	1 970 599	13.5
加工贸易	Processing Trade	1 650 053	1 779 992	-7.3
其他贸易	Others	195 285	190 336	2.6
按大类商品划分	By Category of Commodities			
纺织服装	Textile Garments	740 114	759 091	-2.5
农产品	Agricultural Products	488 853	490 324	-0.3
机电产品	Mechanical and Electrical Products	1 490 495	1 491 987	-0.1
高新技术产品	High-tech Products	263 509	283 039	-6.9

5-5 主要出口商品总值(不含中央、省驻青公司)

TOTAL VALUE OF MAJOR EXPORT COMMODITIES(EXCLUDING CENTRAL AND PROVINCIAL COMPANIES)

单位:万美元(10000 USD)

商品名称	Name	2012	2011	2012年比2011年±% 2012/2011(±%)
服装	Garments	500 333	504 877	-0.9
机械设备	Machinery and Equipment	471 967	430 627	9.6
电器及电子类产品	Electric Appliance and Electronic Products	371 564	360 392	3.1
运输工具	Transport Tools	333 795	434 629	-23.2
纺织品	Textile Products	239 797	253 753	-5.5
金属制品	Metal Products	226 734	179 378	26.4
计算机与通信技术	Computer and Communication Technology	208 971	230 398	-9.3
轮胎	Tyre	182 879	165 801	10.3
水海产品	Aquatic and Seawater Products	144 777	150 496	-3.8
鞋类	Shoes	106 727	100 025	6.7
钢材	Rolled Steel	90 114	67 704	33.1
家具及其零件	Furniture	88 643	65 371	35.6
箱包	Luggage and Bags	83 733	65 828	27.2
蔬菜	Vegetables	74 961	92 544	-19.0
塑料制品	Plastic Articles	67 027	39 037	71.7
汽车零件	Parts of Motor Vehicles	47 646	49 683	-4.1
电话机	Telephone Sets	36 657	66 168	-44.6
空调	Air Conditioner	20 515	20 701	-0.9
铁合金	Ferroalloy	614	8 187	-92.5
游戏机	Game Console	243	27 000	-99.1

5-6 利用外资情况(1990-2012 年)
UTILIZATION OF FOREIGN CAPITAL(1990-2012)

项　目	Item	单位	Unit	1990	1995
批准企业(项目)个数	**Number of Enterprises (Projects) Approved**	**个**	**unit**	**167**	**1 148**
一、外商直接投资	Foreign Direct Investments	个	unit	64	718
中外合资企业	Sino-foreign Joint Ventures	个	unit	40	260
中外合作企业	Sino-foreign Cooperative Enterprises	个	unit	7	45
外商独资企业	Foreign-owned Enterprises	个	unit	17	412
其它	Others	个	unit		1
二、外商其他投资	Other Foreign Investments	个	unit	103	430
合同外资金额	**Total Amount of Contracted Foreign Investment**	**万美元**	**10000 USD**	**8 137**	**155 402**
一、外商直接投资	Foreign Direct Investments	万美元	10000 USD	6 900	1 467 343
中外合资企业	Sino-foreign Joint Ventures	万美元	10000 USD	3 265	52 118
中外合作企业	Sino-foreign Cooperative Enterprises	万美元	10000 USD	346	14 774
外商独资企业	Foreign-owned Enterprises	万美元	10000 USD	3 289	79 342
其它	Others	万美元	10000 USD		
二、外商其他投资	Other Foreign Investments	万美元	10000 USD	1 237	18 668
实际利用外资金额	**Total Amount of Foreign Investment Actually Utilized**	**万美元**	**10000 USD**	**7 770**	**86 573**
一、外商直接投资	Foreign Direct Investments	万美元	10000 USD	4 839	70 310
中外合资企业	Sino-foreign Joint Ventures	万美元	10000 USD	4 161	22 640
中外合作企业	Sino-foreign Cooperative Enterprises	万美元	10000 USD	19	2 571
外商独资企业	Foreign-owned Enterprises	万美元	10000 USD	659	44 999
其它	Others	万美元	10000 USD		
二、外商其他投资	Other Foreign Investments	万美元	10000 USD	2 931	16 263

单位:万美元(10000 USD)

2000	2005	2006	2007	2008	2009	2010	2011	2012
1 132	**2 530**	**1 397**	**1 068**	**640**	**647**	**731**	**707**	**553**
1 128	2 530	1 397	1 068	640	647	731	707	553
303	274	267	165	99	99	153	158	113
57	18	13	11	4	2	4	4	2
76	2 236	1 117	892	537	545	574	544	438
1	2				1		1	
4								
269 081	**954 486**	**311 697**	**382 500**	**304 505**	**271 504**	**475 723**	**528 501**	**600 231**
266 221	954 486	311 697	382 500	304 505	271 504	475 723	528 501	600 231
69 889	112 777	31 368	51 821	81 796	61 734	124 148	142 535	102 252
26 835	17 588	6 883	13 878	367	4 531	9 179	15 173	122
169 37[illegible]	813 485	273 446	316 187	221 759	204 187	341 977	369 425	490 764
127	10 636		614	583	1 052	419	1 368	7 093
2 860								
128 1[illegible]1	**365 625**	**365 815**	**380 652**	**264 295**	**186 397**	**284 281**	**363 350**	**460 027**
125 1[illegible]2	365 625	365 815	380 652	264 295	186 397	284 281	363 350	460 027
39 224	77 636	49 240	46 370	43 810	46 856	84 920	100 699	169 469
3 886	5 654	7 123	15 490	2 945	3 971	3 567	2 759	6 262
82 [illegible]92	280 130	309 452	318 578	217 540	135 026	194 500	255 763	275 579
30	2 205		214		544	1 294	4 129	8 717
2 [illegible]3[illegible]								

5-7 当年外商直接投资项目数和投资额(2012 年)

NUMBER OF PROJECTS AND TOTAL AMOUNT OF FOREIGN DIRECT INVESTMENT(2012)

项　目	Item	批准企业项目数（个）Number of Projects Approved (unit)	合同外资金额（万美元）Total Amount of Contracted Foreign Investment(10000 USD)	实际利用外资金额(万美元) Total Amount of Foreign Investment Actually Utilized(10000 USD)
外商直接投资	**Foreign Direct Investments**	**553**	**600 231**	**460 027**
一、按投资方式分	**Grouped by Investment Form**			
中外合资企业	Sino-foreign Joint Ventures	113	102 252	169 469
中外合作企业	Sino-foreign Cooperative Enterprises	2	122	6 262
外商独资企业	Foreign-owned Enterprises	438	490 764	275 579
二、按主要行业分	**Grouped by Sector**			
#农、林、牧、渔业	Farming, Forestry, Animal Husbandry and Fishery	29	15 999	11 959
制造业	Manufacturing	202	290 787	223 216
电力、燃气及水的生产和供应业	Production and Supply of Electricity, Gas and Water	4	19 321	3 628
建筑业	Construction	5	2 690	2 685
交通运输、仓储和邮政业	Transport, Storage and Post	9	33 392	24 713
批发和零售业	Wholesale and Retail Trades	191	73 999	53 423
住宿和餐饮业	Hotels and Catering Services	11	-3 489	3 472
房地产业	Real Estate	13	81 358	87 162
租赁和商务服务业	Leasing and Business Services	42	37 652	21 676
三、按主要国别(地区)分	**Grouped by Countries(Regions)**			
#韩国	Korea	188	124 402	55 374
香港	Hong Kong	152	234 579	202 763
日本	Japan	51	50 971	50 [illegible]48
美国	United States	24	29 299	30 398
台湾省	Taiwan	37	21 324	16 031
英属维尔京群岛	Virgin Islands	10	29 380	21 762
新加坡	Singapore	14	27 278	21 025

注:从 2011 年开始,数据来源于当年外商投资企业联合年检。

Note: Since 2011, the data have been derived from annual joint examination of enterprises with foreign investment in the corresponding year.

5-8 外商投资企业生产经营状况(2012年)
PRODUCTION AND OPERATION CONDITION OF FOREIGN-FUNDED ENTERPRISES(2012)

项目	Item	单位	Unit	总计 Total	中外合资企业 Sino-foreign Joint Ventures	中外合作企业 Sino-foreign Cooperative Enterprises	外商独资企业 Foreign-owned Enterprises
实有企业数	Number of Enterprises	个	unit	6 761	1 062	79	4 055
#亏损企业	of which: Loss-making Enterprises	个	unit	3 965	522	40	2 551
主营业务收入	Revenue from Principal Business	万元	10000 yuan	33 746 839	9 283 223	311 048	12 543 346
从业人员	Employment	人	person	615 014	123 965	8 630	349 964
#外籍人员	of which: Foreign Employees	人	person	8 489	632	40	6 973
企业资产总计	Total Assets	万元	10000 yuan	43 312 578	12 261 984	741 905	11 538 140
#流动资产合计	of which: Total Current Assets	万元	10000 yuan	26 316 994	7 037 903	504 370	6 608 461
#固定资产合计	Total Fixed Assets	万元	10000 yuan	7 748 271	2 219 056	110 575	3 151 558
负债合计	Total Liabilities	万元	10000 yuan	25 595 357	7 833 128	492 950	6 018 384
所有者权益	Owners' Equity	万元	10000 yuan	17 717 221	4 428 857	248 955	5 519 753
费用总额	Total Expenses	万元	10000 yuan	3 780 688	855 373	53 261	1 431 044
利润总额	Total Profits	万元	10000 yuan	1 337 367	676 860	20 352	235 055
税金总额	Total Taxes	万元	10000 yuan	1 924 460	626 086	22 048	580 295
R&D研发经费支出	Expenditure for R&D	万元	10000 yuan	219 138	25 092	6 923	160 009

5-8 续表
continued

项　目	Item	单位	Unit
实有企业数	Number of Enterprises	个	unit
#亏损企业	of which: Loss-making Enterprises	个	unit
主营业务收入	Revenue from Principal Business	万元	10000 yuan
从业人员	Employment	人	person
#外籍人员	of which: Foreign Employees	人	person
企业资产总计	Total Assets	万元	10000 yuan
#流动资产合计	of which: Total Current Assets	万元	10000 yuan
#固定资产合计	Total Fixed Assets	万元	10000 yuan
负债合计	Total Liabilities	万元	10000 yuan
所有者权益	Owners' Equity	万元	10000 yuan
费用总额	Total Expenses	万元	10000 yuan
利润总额	Total Profits	万元	10000 yuan
税金总额	Total Taxes	万元	10000 yuan
R&D 研发经费支出	Expenditure for R&D	万元	10000 yuan

港澳台与大陆合资经营企业 Hong Kong, Macao and Taiwan and Mainland Joint Ventures	港澳台与大陆合作经营企业 Hong Kong, Macao and Taiwan and Mainland Cooperative Enterprises	港澳台独资企业 Hong Kong, Macao and Taiwan Funded Enterprises	中外股份制 Sino-foreign Stock Enterprises
594	47	911	13
305	19	526	2
4 387 643	1 695 400	3 789 971	1 736 208
57 100	4 888	60 463	10 004
141	14	666	23
9 372 398	1 127 144	6 229 500	2 041 508
6 927 053	441 990	3 957 460	839 757
799 153	212 963	1 083 653	171 314
6 546 282	783 287	3 246 861	674 465
2 826 117	343 856	2 982 639	1 367 044
566 896	56 716	485 932	331 467
186 520	8 102	17 260	193 217
280 145	67 113	176 163	172 611
14 172		11 845	1 097

5-9 分行业外商投资企业生产经营状况(2012年)
PRODUCTION AND OPERATION CONDITION OF FOREIGN-FUNDED ENTERPRISES BY SECTOR(2012)

行　业	Sector
农、林、牧、渔业	Farming, Forestry, Animal Husbandry and Fishery
其中:农业	of which: Farming
采矿业	Mining
制造业	Manufacturing
其中:农副食品加工业	Processing of Food from Agricultural Products
食品制造业	Manufacture of Foods
饮料制造业	Manufacture of Beverage
纺织业	Manufacture of Textile
纺织服装、鞋、帽制造业	Manufacture of Textile Wearing Apparel, Footware, and Caps
皮革、皮衣、羽毛(绒)及其制造品业	Manufacture of Leather, Fur, Feather & Its Products
家具制造业	Manufacture of Furniture
造纸及纸制品业	Manufacture of Paper and Paper Products
文教体育用品制造业	Manufacture of Articles for Culture, Education and Sport Activity
化学原料及化学制品制造业	Manufacture of Chemical Raw Material and Chemical Products
医药制造业	Manufacture of Medicines
橡胶制品业	Manufacture of Rubber
塑料制品业	Manufacture of Plastic
黑色金属冶炼及压延加工业	Smelting and Pressing of Ferrous Metals
有色金属冶炼及压延加工业	Smelting and Pressing of Non-ferrous Metals
金属制品业	Manufacture of Metal Products
通用设备制造业	Manufacture of General Purpose Machinery
专业设备制造业	Manufacture of Special Purpose Machinery
交通运输设备制造业	Manufacture of Transport Equipment
电气机械及器材制造业	Manufacture of Electrical Machinery & Equipment
通信设备、计算机及其他电子设备	Manufacture of Communication Equipment, Computer and Other Electronic Equipment
工艺品及其他制造业	Manufacture of Artwork and Other Manufacture
电力、燃气及水的生产和供应业	Production and Supply of Electricity, Gas and Water
建筑业	Construction
交通运输、仓储和邮政业	Transport, Storage and Post
信息传输、计算服务和软件业	Information Transmission, Computer Services and Software
批发与零售业	Wholesale and Retail Trades
其中:批发业	Wholesale Trade
零售业	Retail Trade
住宿和餐饮业	Hotels and Catering Services
其中:住宿业	Hotels
餐饮业	Catering Service
房地产业	Real Estate
租赁和商务服务	Leasing and Business Services
科学研究、技术服务与地质勘查业	Scientific Research, Technical Service and Geologic Prospecting
水利、环境和公共设施管理业	Management of Water Conservancy, Environment and Public Facilities
居民服务和其他服务业	Services to Households and Other Services
教育	Education
卫生、社会保障和社会福利业	Health, Social Security and Social Welfare
文化、体育和娱乐业	Culture, Sports and Entertainment

主营业务收入(万元) Revenue from Principal Business (10000 yuan)	税金总额 (万元) Total Taxes (10000 yuan)	利润总额 (万元) Total Profits (10000 yuan)	从业人员 (人) Employment (person)
72 181	822	9 293	2 072
17 807	255	-717	1 143
16 815	2 809	2 838	433
23 158 373	1 491 987	1 123 226	538 546
2 287 194	43 182	21 376	36 835
1 056 188	63 552	78 955	18 861
1 447 181	170 191	152 371	5 806
1 134 426	32 994	9 673	28 272
1 507 652	42 920	16 625	110 158
413 003	12 336	-5 853	30 780
209 000	4 503	-3 137	9 533
271 561	9 839	-2 036	4 807
400 072	11 268	-4 086	20 909
2 710 026	264 626	147 578	13 877
138 414	9 726	6 649	3 042
599 641	32 033	15 561	11 362
822 046	27 339	10 208	16 377
1 023 709	21 112	-650	2 652
1 094 181	19 882	-1 058	2 137
2 334 017	74 537	130 706	33 703
1 785 492	128 308	109 402	23 541
908 828	69 177	26 980	15 131
1 648 972	155 209	197 820	24 631
1 665 924	93 631	108 273	17 863
2 702 509	108 027	41 559	53 390
981 479	29 904	8 185	35 372
183 816	10 719	24 554	2 112
25 040	2 586	5 361	518
1 039 409	61 405	160 138	11 247
23 796	2 434	3 635	1 555
2 793 360	96 198	13 880	22 641
2 129 020	56 813	7 938	11 766
664 340	39 384	5 942	10 875
324 224	39 375	13 526	23 328
76 028	18 081	-9 859	4 465
248 196	21 294	23 385	18 863
572 752	197 167	-9 995	4 296
380 430	5 631	-22 510	1 872
34 605	2 750	-385	1 111
10 907	311	-9	361
85 028	6 729	2 481	4 316
4 174	157	-184	177
163	6	3	6
1 573	268	-986	328

5－10 分国别(地区)外商投资企业生产经营状况(2012 年)

PRODUCTION AND OPERATION CONDITION OF FOREIGN-FUNDED ENTERPRISES BY COUNTRIES(REGIONS)(2012)

国别(地区)	Country(Region)	主营业务收入(万元) Revenue from Principal Business (10000 yuan)	税金总额(万元) Total Taxes (10000 yuan)	利润总额(万元) Total Profits (10000 yuan)	从业人员(人) Employment (person)
按投资国别、地区分组	**Grouped by Countries and Regions**				
1、亚洲	Asia	25 435 019	1 399 938	585 590	467 983
#香港	Hong Kong	10 659 196	645 685	369 643	114 220
澳门	Macao	8 654	7 704	－2 441	299
台湾	Taiwan	582 098	26 791	－437	13 832
印度尼西亚	Indonesia	24 614	279	－425	217
日本	Japan	3 581 855	163 718	100 619	89 065
马来西亚	Malaysia	137 731	736	109	1 167
菲律宾	Philippines	18 686	355	1 349	297
新加坡	Singapore	2 777 584	246 329	100 124	7 558
韩国	Korea	6 178 234	262 452	－57 758	228 825
泰国	Thailand	142 410	1 316	814	1 047
2、非洲	Africa	756 756	92 401	266 667	9 040
3、欧洲	Europe	2 713 120	181 090	203 278	54 668
#比利时	Belgium	398	15	－60	80
丹麦	Denmark	103 140	16 219	20 746	1 410
英国	United Kingdom	351 781	15 828	19 059	8 329
德国	Germany	457 555	38 755	52 084	6 149
法国	France	300 541	13 989	24 468	3 468
爱尔兰	Ireland	71	2	－23	12
意大利	Italy	280 348	8 807	8 793	5 019
卢森堡	Luxemburg	77 911	5 867	8 564	2 157
荷兰	Netherlands	441 632	42 298	41 059	18 708
希腊	Greece	278	0	－11	8
葡萄牙	Portugal	29 171	3 189	28	160
西班牙	Spain	21 541	1 186	－1 943	431
芬兰	Finland	0	0	－1	1
瑞士	Switzerland	213 073	15 969	14 296	1 888
4、拉丁美洲	Latin America	2 191 350	116 742	105 561	26 289
#英属维尔京群岛	Virgin Islands(E)	1 981 686	95 400	73 980	23 526
5、北美洲	North America	2 018 218	99 853	105 242	47 825
#加拿大	Canada	173 069	5 143	－1 474	5 489
美国	United States	1 598 600	91 097	107 306	35 976
6、大洋洲	Oceanica	437 639	23 647	58 733	8 002
#澳大利亚	Australia	231 871	11 858	6 248	3 526
新西兰	New Zealand	18 849	1 441	44 267	656

5－11 分市、区外商投资企业生产经营状况(2012 年)

PRODUCTION AND OPERATION CONDITION OF FOREIGN-FUNDED ENTERPRISES BY REGION(2012)

单位:万元(10 000 yuan)

市、区名称	Region	资产总计 Total Assets	#流动资产合计 Total Current Assets	固定资产合计 Total Fixed Assets
合　计	**Total**	**43 312 578**	**26 316 994**	**7 748 271**
市　区	Urban Area	30 642 028	18 539 442	5 086 365
#崂山区	Laoshan District	5 476 702	4 092 859	479 480
原黄岛区	Original Huangdao District	9 678 727	4 186 692	2 231 476
城阳区	Chengyang District	6 571 926	4 667 671	1 284 575
即墨市	Jimo	3 329 942	1 985 720	610 405
胶州市	Jiaozhou	3 243 994	2 075 791	616 591
原胶南市	Original Jiaonan	2 436 567	1 602 808	478 733
平度市	Pingdu	1 693 392	902 016	440 605
莱西市	Laixi	1 412 282	801 785	456 070
高新区	High-tech Zone	554 373	409 432	59 502

5－11 续表 1

continued

单位:万元(10 000 yuan)

市、区名称	Region	负债合计 Total Liabilities	#流动负债合计 Total Current Liabilities	长期负债合计 Total Long-term Liabilities	所有者权益合计 Total Owners' Equity
合　计	**Total**	**25 595 357**	**22 220 663**	**3 374 695**	**17 717 221**
市　区	Urban Area	18 456 221	15 753 914	2 702 307	12 185 806
#崂山区	Laoshan District	3 822 520	3 324 902	497 618	1 654 180
原黄岛区	Original Huangdao District	5 181 055	4 226 870	954 185	4 497 672
城阳区	Chengyang District	4 054 041	3 750 262	303 779	2 517 885
即墨市	Jimo	1 793 161	1 669 686	123 475	1 536 781
胶州市	Jiaozhou	1 912 150	1 762 979	149 171	1 331 845
原胶南市	Original Jiaonan	1 370 588	1 196 295	174 293	1 065 979
平度市	Pingdu	848 613	792 727	55 887	844 778
莱西市	Laixi	829 224	711 144	118 079	583 059
高新区	High-tech Zone	385 400	333 917	51 483	168 973

5 -11 续表 2
continued

单位:万元(10 000 yuan)

市、区名称	Region	主营业务收入 Revenue from Principal Business	主营业务成本 Cost of Principal Business	费用总额 Total Expenses	利润总额 Total Profits
合　　计	**Total**	**33 746 839**	**28 404 451**	**3 780 688**	**1 337 367**
市　　区	Urban Area	23 716 187	19 718 824	2 697 848	1 110 764
#崂山区	Laoshan District	3 462 453	2 714 815	491 481	164 780
原黄岛区	Original Huangdao District	8 722 089	7 460 000	701 082	521 051
城阳区	Chengyang District	5 705 293	4 740 604	618 145	174 842
即墨市	Jimo	2 613 126	2 244 985	258 473	72 076
胶州市	Jiaozhou	2 976 678	2 604 463	286 587	85 353
原胶南市	Original Jiaonan	1 443 508	1 199 742	179 505	51 280
平度市	Pingdu	1 340 785	1 191 466	163 657	6 584
莱西市	Laixi	1 355 471	1 197 008	144 341	7 356
高新区	High-tech Zone	301 084	247 963	50 278	3 955

5 -11 续表 3
continued

单位:万元(10 000 yuan)

市、区名称	Region	税金总额 Total Taxes	从业人员(人) Employment(person)	研发经费 Expenditure for R&D	单位数量(个) Number of Company (unit)
合　　计	**Total**	**1 924 460**	**615 014**	**219 138**	**6761**
市　　区	Urban Area	1 488 286	322 381	194 046	4 044
#崂山区	Laoshan District	270 215	28 664	43 813	382
原黄岛区	Original Huangdao District	560 272	80 187	49 367	851
城阳区	Chengyang District	275 676	144 164	96 396	1319
即墨市	Jimo	103 760	92 046	3 182	757
胶州市	Jiaozhou	137 417	81 017	15 153	715
原胶南市	Original Jiaonan	72 631	39 048	5 768	398
平度市	Pingdu	66 857	40 336	467	514
莱西市	Laixi	46 497	39 150	1	319
高新区	High-tech Zone	9 012	1 036	522	14

主要统计指标解释

批准企业(项目)个数 是指外商直接投资中批准设立的外商投资企业个数、批准的合作开发项目个数。

合同外资金额 是指批准外商投资企业的合同、章程中规定的外国投资者认缴的出资额和企业投资总额内的应由外方投资者以自己的境外自有资金直接向企业提供的贷款。包括新批准企业合同外资和原有企业的增资减资,增资减资不对企业(项目)个数进行调整。

实际使用外资金额 是指合同外资金额的实际执行金额。

外商直接投资 是指外国企业和经济组织或个人(包括华侨、港澳台胞以及我国在境外注册的企业)按我国有关政策、法规,用现汇、实物、技术等在我国境内开办外商独资企业、与我国境内的企业或经济组织共同举办中外合资经营企业、合作经营企业或合作开发资源的投资(包括外商投资收益的再投资)以及经政府有关部门批准的项目投资总额内,企业从境外借入的资金。

外商其它投资 是指除外商直接投资以外其他方式吸收的外资。

进出口总额 指实际进出我国国境的货物总金额。包括对外贸易实际进出口货物,来料加工装配进出口货物,国家间、联合国及国际组织无偿援助物资和赠送品,华侨、港澳台同胞和外籍华人捐赠品,租赁期满归承租人所有的租赁货物,进料加工进出口货物,边境地方贸易及边境地区小额贸易进出口货物(边民互市贸易除外),中外合资企业、中外合作经营企业、外商独资经营企业进出口货物和公用物品,到、离岸价格在规定限额以上的进出口货样和广告品(无商业价值、无使用价值和免费提供出口的除外),从保税仓库提取在中国境内销售的进口货物,以及其他进出口货物。

Explanatory Notes on Main Statistical Indicators

Enterprises(Projects) Permitted refers to number of foreign invested enterprises and developed projects under cooperation through the permission.

Contracted Foreign Investment refers to expenditure promised by the foreign investor and loan stemed from broad innate fund of the foreign investor,according to the contract and regulation approved of enterprise invested by foreigner.

Actual Utilization of Foreign Investment refers to actual usage of contracted foreign investment,including cash,investment in kind and incorporeal agreed by the both sides as part of the investment,such as services and technology.

Foreign Direct Investment refers to the investments by foreign enterprises and economic organizations or individuals(including overseas Chinese,compatriots from Hong dong,Macao and Taiwan,and Chinese enterprises registered abroad),following the relevant policies and laws of China,for the establishment of ventures and cooperative enterprises or cooperative exploration of resources with enterprises or economic organizations in China,lt includes the reinvestment of the foreign entrepreneurs with the profits gained from the investment and the funds that enterprises borrow from aboard in the total investment of projects which are approved by the relevant department of the government.

Other Investment by Foreign Entrepreneurs refers to all forms of utilization of foreign capitals other than foreign direct investment.

Total Imports and Exports refers to the real value of commodities imported into and exported from the boundary of China. They include the actual imports and exports through foreign trade, imported and exported goods under the processing and assembling trades and materials, supplies and gifts as aid given gratis between governments and by the United Nations and other international organizations, and contributions donated by overseas Chinese, compatriots in Hong Kong and Macao and Chinese with foreign citizenship, leasing commodities owned by tenant at the expiration of leasing period, the imported and exported commodities processed with imported materials, commodities trading in border areas (excluding mutual exchange goods), the imported and exported commodities and articles for public use of the Sino-foreign joint ventures, cooperative enterprises and ventures exclusively with foreign own investment. Also included are import or export of samples and advertising goods for whose CIF or FOB value are beyond the permitted ceiling (excluding goods of no trading or use value and free commodities for export), imported goods sold in China from bonded warehouses and other imported or exported goods.

6 能 源 消 耗
CONSUMPTION OF ENERGY

简 要 说 明

一、本篇资料的主要内容

本篇资料主要反映了全市规模以上工业主要能源消费与库存情况，主要包括规模以上工业主要能源消费与库存、规模以上工业主要能源分行业消费量、重点耗能工业企业能源加工转换、规模以上工业主要能源工业消费量等方面的资料。

二、本篇资料的来源

本篇资料来源于规模以上工业能源统计年报，由市统计局能源统计处整理提供。

Brief Introduction

I. Main Content

Data in this chapter show the consumption and stock of major energy of industry above designated size, including consumption and stock of major energy of industry above designated size, major energy consumption of industry above designated size grouped by sector, energy conversion of major energy-consuming industrial enterprises and major energy consumption of industry above designated size, etc.

II. Source of Data

Data in this chapter are based on the annual report of energy consumed by industrial enterprises above designated size. The data are provided by the Division of Energy Statistics of Qingdao Municipal Bureau of Statistics.

6-1 规模以上工业主要能源消费与库存(2012年)

CONSUMPTION AND STOCK OF MAJOR ENERGY OF INDUSTRY ABOVE DESIGNATED SIZE(2012)

名称	Name	计算单位	Unit	年初库存 Stock at Year-beginning	本年消费 Consumption in the Year	#工业 Industry	#非工业 Non-industry	年末库存 Stock at Year-end
原煤	Raw Coal	吨	ton	2 012 111.89	16 017 632.24	15 966 680.71	50 951.56	1 950 266.18
焦炭	Coke	吨	ton	66 310.91	1 175 506.03	1 175 502.03	4.00	30 941.97
焦炉煤气	Coking Gas	万立方米	10 000 cu.m		5 998.59	5 990.42	8.15	
高炉煤气	Blast Furnace Gas	万立方米	10 000 cu.m		15 260.35	15 186.35	74.00	
原油	Crude Oil	吨	ton	450 367.29	14 112 814.08	14 112 814.08	0.00	512 073.62
汽油	Petrol	吨	ton	598.33	166 522.44	141 933.48	24 589.01	429.70
煤油	Kerosene	吨	ton	4.00	2 518.78	2 474.31	44.48	
柴油	Diesel Oil	吨	ton	2 082.38	160 113.39	140 655.67	19 457.74	1 708.10
燃料油	Fuel Oil	吨	ton	27 959.76	657 782.23	657 136.47	645.76	21 658.53
液化石油气	Liquefied Petroleum Gas	吨	ton	509.50	159 200.19	158 758.72	441.47	413.00
炼厂干气	Refinery Dry Gas	吨	ton		428 986.66	428 986.66		
热力	Heat	百万千焦	million kJ		32 298 979.58	31 534 776.45	764 203.13	
电力	Electricity	万千瓦时	10 000 kW·h		2 311 663.78	2 275 781.25	35 882.67	

补充资料:2012年综合能源消费量1689.1万吨标准煤。

Note: In 2012, comprehensive energy consumption is 16.891 million tons SCE.

6 -2 规模以上工业主要能源分行业消费量(2012 年)

MAJOR ENERGY CONSUMPTION OF INDUSTRY ABOVE DESIGNATED SIZE BY SECTOR (2012)

名称	Name	原煤(吨) Raw Coal (ton)	焦炭(吨) Coke (ton)	焦炉煤气(万立方米) Coking Gas (10 000 cu. m)	原油(吨) Crude Oil (ton)	汽油(吨) Petrol (ton)
总　计	**Total**	**16 017 632.24**	**1 175 506.03**	**5 998.59**	**14 112 814.08**	**166 522.44**
采掘业	Mining	13 267.69				2 612.75
制造业	Manufacturing	4 791 863.92	1 175 506.03	5 998.59	14 112 814.08	160 865.11
电力煤气及水生产供应业	Production and Supply of Electricity, Gas and Water	11 212 500.63				3 044.58

6 -2 续表

continued

名称	Name	煤油(吨) Kerosene (ton)	柴油(吨) Diesel Oil (ton)	燃料油(吨) Fuel Oil (ton)	液化石油气(吨) Liquefied Petroleum Gas (ton)	热　力(百万千焦) Heat (million kJ)	电　力(万千瓦时) Electricity (10 000 kW · h)
总　计	**Total**	**2 518.78**	**160 113.39**	**657 782.23**	**159 200.19**	**32 298 979.58**	**2 311 663.78**
采掘业	Mining		2 627.43				16 101.29
制造业	Manufacturing	2 518.78	154 316.52	655 732.42	159 197.82	30 415 528.88	1 945 039.36
电力煤气及水生产供应业	Production and Supply of Electricity, Gas and Water		3 169.44	2 049.81	2.37	1 883 450.70	350 523.13

6-3 重点耗能工业企业能源加工转换(2012年)

ENERGY CONVERSION OF MAJOR ENERGY-CONSUMING INDUSTRIAL ENTERPRISES(2012)

名称	Name	单位	Unit	能源消费合计 Total Energy Consumption	#加工转换投入 Conversion Input	火电 Thermal Power	供热 Heating	炼油 Petrolume Refining	制气 Gas Production	能源加工转换产出 Conversion Output of Energy
原煤	Raw Coal	吨	ton	12 750 565.64	12 218 669.24	7 673 953.96	4 544 715.28			
洗精煤	Dressing Coal	吨	ton	1 060 122.55	1 060 122.55				527 066.55	
煤制品	Coal Products	吨	ton							
焦炭	Coke	吨	ton	1 111 347.00						795 215.21
其他焦化产品	Other Coking Products	吨	ton	92 241.72						24 823.73
焦炉煤气	Coking Gas	万立方米	10 000 cu. m							8 147.55
高炉煤气	Blast Furnace Gas	万立方米	10 000 cu. m	15 176.35	15 176.35		15 176.35			
原油	Raw Oil	吨	ton	14 112 550.35	14 104 573.94			14 104 573.94		
汽油	Petrol	吨	ton	500.72						3 756 090.75
煤油	Kerosene	吨	ton							667 734.19
柴油	Diesel Oil	吨	ton	6 229.30						5 177 937.68
燃料油	Fuel Oil	吨	ton	628 716.04	627 893.63	1 376.00	179.00	626 338.63		335 606.79
液化石油气	Liquefied Petroleum Gas	吨	ton	318.98						1 031 352.78
炼厂干气	Refinery Dry Gas	吨	ton	428 986.66	5 001.17	500.12	4 501.06			428 986.66
其他石油制品	Other Petroleum Products	吨	ton	603 724.26	49 110.79			49 110.79		1 399 109.37
热力	Heat	百万千焦	million kJ	16 412 759.54						81 271 686.78
电力	Electricity	万千瓦时	10 000 kW·h	488 194.10						1 849 940.43
其他燃料	Other Fuel	吨标准煤	ton SCE							
能源合计	**Total**	**吨标准煤**	**ton SCE**	**35 184 071.02**	**31 055 710.42**	**5 467 425.23**	**3 511 243.12**	**21 113 336.81**	**474 359.90**	**26 729 239.60**

6-4 规模以上工业主要能源工业消费量(2012年)

MAJOR ENERGY CONSUMPTION OF INDUSTRY ABOVE DESIGNATED SIZE(2012)

行业	Sector
总　计	**Total**
煤炭开采和洗选业	Mining and Washing of Coal
石油和天然气开采业	Extraction of Petroleum and Natural Gas
黑色金属矿采选业	Mining of Ferrous Metal Ores
有色金属矿采选业	Mining of Non-ferrous Metal Ores
非金属矿采选业	Mining and Processing of Nonmetal Ores
开采辅助活动	Auxiliary Activities of Mining
其他采矿业	Mining of Other Ores
农副食品加工业	Processing of Food from Agricultural Products
食品制造业	Manufacture of Foods
酒、饮料和精制茶制造业	Manufacture of Liquor, Beverage and Refind Tea
烟草制品业	Manufacture of Tobacco
纺织业	Manufacture of Textile
纺织服装、服饰业	Manufacture of Textile Wearing Apparel
皮革、毛皮、羽毛及其制品和制鞋业	Manufacture of Leather, Fur, Feather & Its Products Footwear
木材加工和木、竹、藤、棕、草制品业	Processing of Timbers, Manufacture of Wood, Bamboo, Rattan, Palm and Straw Products
家具制造业	Manufacture of Furniture
造纸和纸制品业	Manufacture of Paper and Paper Products
印刷和记录媒介复制业	Printing, Reproduction of Recording Media
文教、工美、体育和娱乐用品制造业	Manufacture of Articles for Culture, Arts & Crafts, Sports and Entertainment
石油加工、炼焦和核燃料加工业	Processing of Petroleum, Coking, Processing of Nucleus Fuel
化学原料和化学制品制造业	Manufacture of Chemical Raw Material and Chemical Products
医药制造业	Manufacture of Medicines
化学纤维制造业	Manufacture of Chemical Fiber
橡胶和塑料制品业	Manufacture of Rubber and Plastic
非金属矿物制品业	Manufacture of Non-metallic Mineral Products
黑色金属冶炼和压延加工业	Smelting and Pressing of Ferrous Metals
有色金属冶炼和压延加工业	Smelting and Pressing of Non-ferrous Metals
金属制品业	Manufacture of Metal Products
通用设备制造业	Manufacture of General Purpose Machinery
专用设备制造业	Manufacture of Special Purpose Machinery
汽车制造业	Manufacture of Vehicle
铁路、船舶、航空航天和其他运输设备制造业	Manufacture of Transport Equipment for Railway, Shipping, Aerospace and other uses
电气机械和器材制造业	Manufacture of Electrical Machinery & Equipment
计算机、通信和其他电子设备制造业	Manufacture of Computer, Communication Equipment and Other Electronic Equipment
仪器仪表制造业	Manufacture of Measuring Instrument
其他制造业	Manufacture of Other Products
废弃资源综合利用业	Recycling and Disposal of Waste Resources
金属制品、机械和设备修理业	Maintenance of Metal Products, Machinery and Equipment
电力、热力的生产和供应业	Production and Supply of Electric Power and Heat Power
燃气生产和供应业	Production and Supply of Gas
水的生产和供应业	Production and Supply of Water

[illegible]煤 (吨) Raw Coal (ton)	洗精煤 (吨) Dressing Coal (ton)	其他洗煤 (吨) Other Dressing Coal (ton)	煤制品 (吨) Coal Products (ton)	焦炭 (吨) Coke (ton)
16 0[illegible]7 [illegible]32.24	**1 219 285.55**	**378.06**	**8 910.43**	**1 175 506.03**
4 123.60				
9 144.09				
18[illegible] 918.39	13 111.00		703.91	386.24
5[illegible] 332.81	300.00	371.26		
7[illegible] 555.38				
16[illegible] 709.77			1 475.89	
185 781.65			7.00	710.00
9[illegible] 059.84				
4 583.75				
[illegible]0 347.10				20.00
1[illegible]0 015.62			963.00	
[illegible]2 575.46				
[illegible]02 249.94				110.90
19 087.50				
1 [illegible]35 472.40	145 735.00		587.60	
9 648.80			1 330.25	
5 129.00				
[illegible]14 470.98	17.00	6.80		966.00
[illegible]69 301.32			184.58	14.50
[illegible]536 358.07	533 056.00			1 116 786.00
17 224.66				
306 624.63				30 980.57
145 661.40			960.00	8 481.36
114 291.77			1 382.00	9 365.06
37 278.11				6 457.00
86 044.19			1 281.00	1 224.40
290 196.19				
26 908.66			35.20	4.00
13 326.00				
2 863.08				
850.00				
3 997.45				
1 034 488.63				
177 969.00	527 066.55			
43.00				

6-4 续表1
continued

行业	Sector
总　计	**Total**
煤炭开采和洗选业	Mining and Washing of Coal
石油和天然气开采业	Extraction of Petroleum and Natural Gas
黑色金属矿采选业	Mining of Ferrous Metal Ores
有色金属矿采选业	Mining of Non-ferrous Metal Ores
非金属矿采选业	Mining and Processing of Nonmetal Ores
开采辅助活动	Auxiliary Activities of Mining
其他采矿业	Mining of Other Ores
农副食品加工业	Processing of Food from Agricultural Products
食品制造业	Manufacture of Foods
酒、饮料和精制茶制造业	Manufacture of Liquor, Beverage and Refind Tea
烟草制品业	Manufacture of Tobacco
纺织业	Manufacture of Textile
纺织服装、服饰业	Manufacture of Textile Wearing Apparel
皮革、毛皮、羽毛及其制品和制鞋业	Manufacture of Leather, Fur, Feather & Its Products Footwear
木材加工和木、竹、藤、棕、草制品业	Processing of Timbers, Manufacture of Wood, Bamboo, Rattan, Palm and Straw Products
家具制造业	Manufacture of Furniture
造纸和纸制品业	Manufacture of Paper and Paper Products
印刷和记录媒介复制业	Printing, Reproduction of Recording Media
文教、工美、体育和娱乐用品制造业	Manufacture of Articles for Culture, Arts & Crafts, Sports and Entertainment
石油加工、炼焦和核燃料加工业	Processing of Petroleum, Coking, Processing of Nucleus Fuel
化学原料和化学制品制造业	Manufacture of Chemical Raw Material and Chemical Products
医药制造业	Manufacture of Medicines
化学纤维制造业	Manufacture of Chemical Fiber
橡胶和塑料制品业	Manufacture of Rubber and Plastic
非金属矿物制品业	Manufacture of Non-metallic Mineral Products
黑色金属冶炼和压延加工业	Smelting and Pressing of Ferrous Metals
有色金属冶炼和压延加工业	Smelting and Pressing of Non-ferrous Metals
金属制品业	Manufacture of Metal Products
通用设备制造业	Manufacture of General Purpose Machinery
专用设备制造业	Manufacture of Special Purpose Machinery
汽车制造业	Manufacture of Vehicle
铁路、船舶、航空航天和其他运输设备制造业	Manufacture of Transport Equipment for Railway, Shipping, Aerospace and other uses
电气机械和器材制造业	Manufacture of Electrical Machinery & Equipment
计算机、通信和其他电子设备制造业	Manufacture of Computer, Communication Equipment and Other Electronic Equipment
仪器仪表制造业	Manufacture of Measuring Instrument
其他制造业	Manufacture of Other Products
废弃资源综合利用业	Recycling and Disposal of Waste Resources
金属制品、机械和设备修理业	Maintenance of Metal Products, Machinery and Equipment
电力、热力的生产和供应业	Production and Supply of Electric Power and Heat Power
燃气生产和供应业	Production and Supply of Gas
水的生产和供应业	Production and Supply of Water

焦炉煤气（万立方米）Coking Gas (10 000 cu. m)	高炉煤气（万立方米）Blast Furnace Gas (10 000 cu. m)	原油（吨）Crude Oil (ton)	汽油（吨）Petrol (ton)	煤油（吨）Kerosene (ton)
5 998.59	**15 260.35**	**14 112 814.08**	**166 522.44**	**2 518.78**
			1 968.64	
			644.11	
	84.00		15 471.83	3.78
28.26			3 555.13	
			1 363.68	2.55
			167.94	
39.35			5 414.73	1.28
		62.70	10 759.19	420.70
			6 587.20	45.40
			1 080.32	174.00
			3 249.40	
			3 472.98	245.10
			3 036.58	2.95
		3.03	9 706.02	15.60
		14 112 550.35	313.19	14.76
4 377.35			6 313.97	
			1 535.02	
			61.89	
			13 517.81	105.00
749.35			14 806.40	19.60
	15 176.35		1 479.85	67.00
			656.33	
			15 072.57	13.97
			11 081.50	95.95
		198.00	10 779.47	3.27
804.28			5 449.40	0.40
			3 838.17	4.24
			8 019.29	40.62
			2 409.55	1 242.61
			1 129.53	
			333.98	
			159.72	
			42.47	
			1 974.32	
			613.88	
			456.38	

6-4 续表2
continued

行业	Sector
总　计	**Total**
煤炭开采和洗选业	Mining and Washing of Coal
石油和天然气开采业	Extraction of Petroleum and Natural Gas
黑色金属矿采选业	Mining of Ferrous Metal Ores
有色金属矿采选业	Mining of Non-ferrous Metal Ores
非金属矿采选业	Mining and Processing of Nonmetal Ores
开采辅助活动	Auxiliary Activities of Mining
其他采矿业	Mining of Other Ores
农副食品加工业	Processing of Food from Agricultural Products
食品制造业	Manufacture of Foods
酒、饮料和精制茶制造业	Manufacture of Liquor, Beverage and Refind Tea
烟草制品业	Manufacture of Tobacco
纺织业	Manufacture of Textile
纺织服装、服饰业	Manufacture of Textile Wearing Apparel
皮革、毛皮、羽毛及其制品和制鞋业	Manufacture of Leather, Fur, Feather & Its Products Footwear
木材加工和木、竹、藤、棕、草制品业	Processing of Timbers, Manufacture of Wood, Bamboo, Rattan, Palm and Straw Products
家具制造业	Manufacture of Furniture
造纸和纸制品业	Manufacture of Paper and Paper Products
印刷和记录媒介复制业	Printing, Reproduction of Recording Media
文教、工美、体育和娱乐用品制造业	Manufacture of Articles for Culture, Arts & Crafts, Sports and Entertainment
石油加工、炼焦和核燃料加工业	Processing of Petroleum, Coking, Processing of Nucleus Fuel
化学原料和化学制品制造业	Manufacture of Chemical Raw Material and Chemical Products
医药制造业	Manufacture of Medicines
化学纤维制造业	Manufacture of Chemical Fiber
橡胶和塑料制品业	Manufacture of Rubber and Plastic
非金属矿物制品业	Manufacture of Non-metallic Mineral Products
黑色金属冶炼和压延加工业	Smelting and Pressing of Ferrous Metals
有色金属冶炼和压延加工业	Smelting and Pressing of Non-ferrous Metals
金属制品业	Manufacture of Metal Products
通用设备制造业	Manufacture of General Purpose Machinery
专用设备制造业	Manufacture of Special Purpose Machinery
汽车制造业	Manufacture of Vehicle
铁路、船舶、航空航天和其他运输设备制造业	Manufacture of Transport Equipment for Railway, Shipping, Aerospace and other uses
电气机械和器材制造业	Manufacture of Electrical Machinery & Equipment
计算机、通信和其他电子设备制造业	Manufacture of Computer, Communication Equipment and Other Electronic Equipment
仪器仪表制造业	Manufacture of Measuring Instrument
其他制造业	Manufacture of Other Products
废弃资源综合利用业	Recycling and Disposal of Waste Resources
金属制品、机械和设备修理业	Maintenance of Metal Products, Machinery and Equipment
电力、热力的生产和供应业	Production and Supply of Electric Power and Heat Power
燃气生产和供应业	Production and Supply of Gas
水的生产和供应业	Production and Supply of Water

柴油 (吨) Diesel Oil (ton)	燃料油 (吨) Fuel Oil (ton)	液化石油气 (吨)Liquefied Petroleum Gas(ton)	炼厂干气 (吨) Refinery Dry Gas(ton)
16[illegible] 113.39	**657 782.23**	**159 200.19**	**428 986.66**
[illegible]1 412.13			
[illegible] 215.30			
13 983.94	23.80	132.93	
4 245.24	1 480.24	377.20	
1 287.45		302.00	
17.34			
4 363.46	7 025.56	263.49	
7 318.49	388.62	5.00	
3 541.69	3 925.00	9.00	
1 207.03			
3 419.42			
2 926.48	108.00		
2 614.30	45.00		
4 120.78	1 617.78	12.86	
206.54	627 015.73		428 986.66
8 677.28	1 475.00	149 231.00	
3 952.81	410.00		
51.75	7.42		
8 211.97	3 582.00		
27 795.55	7 672.40		
4 891.42	99.55	496.20	
596.52	514.00	25.00	
10 155.96	30.48	3 085.66	
10 682.25		1.52	
6 728.88			
3 582.65		820.15	
9 563.09	256.94	1 446.20	
6 121.63	24.50	2 433.72	
2 448.84	30.40	555.89	
1 214.05			
148.75			
148.52			
92.44			
2 367.53	2 049.81	2.37	
522.45			
279.46			

6-4 续表3
continued

行业	Sector
总　计	**Total**
煤炭开采和洗选业	Mining and Washing of Coal
石油和天然气开采业	Extraction of Petroleum and Natural Gas
黑色金属矿采选业	Mining of Ferrous Metal Ores
有色金属矿采选业	Mining of Non-ferrous Metal Ores
非金属矿采选业	Mining and Processing of Nonmetal Ores
开采辅助活动	Auxiliary Activities of Mining
其他采矿业	Mining of Other Ores
农副食品加工业	Processing of Food from Agricultural Products
食品制造业	Manufacture of Foods
酒、饮料和精制茶制造业	Manufacture of Liquor, Beverage and Refind Tea
烟草制品业	Manufacture of Tobacco
纺织业	Manufacture of Textile
纺织服装、服饰业	Manufacture of Textile Wearing Apparel
皮革、毛皮、羽毛及其制品和制鞋业	Manufacture of Leather, Fur, Feather & Its Products Footwear
木材加工和木、竹、藤、棕、草制品业	Processing of Timbers, Manufacture of Wood, Bamboo, Rattan, Palm and Straw Products
家具制造业	Manufacture of Furniture
造纸和纸制品业	Manufacture of Paper and Paper Products
印刷和记录媒介复制业	Printing, Reproduction of Recording Media
文教、工美、体育和娱乐用品制造业	Manufacture of Articles for Culture, Arts & Crafts, Sports and Entertainment
石油加工、炼焦和核燃料加工业	Processing of Petroleum, Coking, Processing of Nucleus Fuel
化学原料和化学制品制造业	Manufacture of Chemical Raw Material and Chemical Products
医药制造业	Manufacture of Medicines
化学纤维制造业	Manufacture of Chemical Fiber
橡胶和塑料制品业	Manufacture of Rubber and Plastic
非金属矿物制品业	Manufacture of Non-metallic Mineral Products
黑色金属冶炼和压延加工业	Smelting and Pressing of Ferrous Metals
有色金属冶炼和压延加工业	Smelting and Pressing of Non-ferrous Metals
金属制品业	Manufacture of Metal Products
通用设备制造业	Manufacture of General Purpose Machinery
专用设备制造业	Manufacture of Special Purpose Machinery
汽车制造业	Manufacture of Vehicle
铁路、船舶、航空航天和其他运输设备制造业	Manufacture of Transport Equipment for Railway, Shipping, Aerospace and other uses
电气机械和器材制造业	Manufacture of Electrical Machinery & Equipment
计算机、通信和其他电子设备制造业	Manufacture of Computer, Communication Equipment and Other Electronic Equipment
仪器仪表制造业	Manufacture of Measuring Instrument
其他制造业	Manufacture of Other Products
废弃资源综合利用业	Recycling and Disposal of Waste Resources
金属制品、机械和设备修理业	Maintenance of Metal Products, Machinery and Equipment
电力、热力的生产和供应业	Production and Supply of Electric Power and Heat Power
燃气生产和供应业	Production and Supply of Gas
水的生产和供应业	Production and Supply of Water

其他油制品 (吨) Other Petroleum Products(ton)	热　力 (百万千焦) Heat (million kJ)	电　力 (万千瓦时) Electricity (10 000 kW·h)	其他燃料 (吨标准煤) Other Fuel (ton SCE)
60[illegible] 077.61	**32 298 979.58**	**2 311 663.78**	**726.87**
		6 895.36	
		9 205.93	
50.00	849 669.17	131 230.90	
	294 500.00	31 850.50	109.00
	1 899 342.71	22 258.39	
	252 468.00	4 318.08	
6.53	1 602 068.76	60 125.72	18.00
	2 682 615.85	77 314.87	375.00
	376 547.22	37 768.62	
		6 262.77	
	2 606.00	16 938.44	
	1 286 085.53	33 620.43	
	35 489.70	16 641.49	
	18 430.00	42 736.46	
6[illegible]0 666.71	5 879 691.11	112 495.67	
5 776.93	11 528 813.93	177 314.70	
	549 826.00	10 702.08	
	28 371.31	11 316.10	
	270 719.75	178 657.08	
	136 480.00	125 635.42	
	98 558.10	193 103.16	
	40 126.34	30 534.02	
10.53	484 905.10	139 257.15	
24.28	153 287.99	95 832.48	
41.00	41 110.14	61 195.16	47.81
	483 734.78	77 951.75	163.46
6.01	314 678.85	79 084.37	
	809 622.56	105 216.61	13.60
	220 966.98	53 974.32	
		6 298.57	
	74 813.00	2 931.19	
		264.09	
		2 208.77	
	1 791 309.00	329 090.24	
495.62	92 141.70	6 104.22	
		15 328.67	

主要统计指标解释

工业企业能源消费量 工业企业能源消费包括工业企业在生产过程中作为燃料、动力、原料、辅助材料使用的能源以及工艺用能、非生产用能;作为能源加工转换企业,还要包括能源加工转换的投入量。工业企业能源消费量具体包括:

(1)用于本企业产品生产、工业性作业和其他生产性活动的能源。

(2)用于技术更新改造措施、新技术研究和新产品试制以及科学试验等方面的能源。

(3)用于经营维修、建筑及设备大修理、机电设备和交通运输工具等方面的能源。

(4)用于劳动保护的能源。

(5)其他非生产消费的能源。

不包括:

(1)由仓库发到车间,但在报告期最后一天没有消费的能源。这部分能源应在办理假退料手续后计入库存量。

(2)拨到外单位,委托外单位加工用的能源。

(3)调出本单位或借给外单位的能源。

工业生产能源消费 是指工业企业为进行工业生产活动所使用的能源。主要包括:

1. 用于本企业产品生产、工业性作业的能源,包括用作原料、材料、燃料、动力:作为能源加工转换企业,还包括用作加工转换的能源。

2. 产品生产过程中作为辅助材料使用的能源。

3. 生产工艺过程使用的能源。

4. 新技术研究、新产品试制、科学试验使用的能源。

5. 为了工业生产活动而在进行的各种修理过程中使用的能源。

6. 生产区内的劳动保护用能等。

Explanatory Notes on Main Statistical Indicators

Energy Consumption of Industrial Enterprises include energy in the production process as fuel, power, raw materials, supplementary materials, and for use of technology and non-production. As energy processing and conversion enterprises, also include energy processing and conversion of inputs. These specifically include: (1) Energy for the enterprise product, industrial production operations and other activities. (2) Energy for technical upgrading measures and new technology research and new product production and scientific experiments. (3) Energy for operation maintenance, construction and equipment overhaul, electrical and mechanical equipment and transport, and other aspects. (4) Energy for the protection of labor. (5) Energy for Other non-production and consumption. And these exclude: (1) Energy from the warehouse to the workshop, but out of consumption on the last day of the reporting period. This part of the energy should leave retreat materials handling procedures included stock. (2) Energy transferred to other units, entrusted with the processing. (3) Energy transferred out of the unit or loans to other units.

Energy Consumption for Industrial Production refers to energy for industrial enterprises in industrial production activities. These mainly include: 1. Energy for the enterprise products, industrial operations, including energy as raw materials, materials, fuels, and power. As energy processing and conversion enterprises, also include energy for processing and conversion. 2. Energy as supplementary material in product process. 3. Energy used in production process. 4. Energy for new technologies, new product production, and scientific experiment. 5. Energy in process of repairing for industrial production activities. 6. Energy for labor protection in production areas and so on.

7 财政、金融和保险业
GOVERNMENT FINANCE, FINANCIAL INTERMEDIATION AND INSURANCE

简要说明

一、本篇资料的主要内容

本篇资料主要反映了全市财政收支、金融和保险方面的情况，主要包括财政收入、财政支出、金融机构存贷款、保险业务开展等方面的资料。

二、本篇资料的来源

1、财政部分的资料来源于市财政局。

2、金融方面的资料来源于中国人民银行青岛市中心支行。

3、保险方面的资料来源于中国保险监督管理委员会青岛监管局。

本篇资料由市统计局国民经济核算处整理提供。

Brief Introduction

I. Main Content

Data in this chapter show the conditions of local government budgetary finance, banking and insurance,and securities, including government revenue and expenditure, deposits and loans of financial institutions and statistics on insurance companies.

II. Source of Data

(1)Data on local government finance are provided by Qingdao Municipal Finance Bureau.

(2)Data on banking are provided by Qingdao Branch of the People's Bank of China.

(3)Data on insurance are provide by China Insurance Regulatory Commission of Qingdao Bureau.

Data in this chapter are prepared and compiled by the Division of National Accounts of Qingdao Municipal Bureau of Statistics.

7－1 主要年份地方财政收支

MAJOR YEAR'S REVENUE AND EXPENDITURE OF LOCAL GOVERNMENT FINANCE

单位:万元(10 000 yuan)

年份 Year	财政收入 Revenue of Government Finance	财政支出 Expenditure of Government Finance
1949	1 527	306
1952	19 809	2 226
1957	29 875	3 556
1962	32 869	4 327
1965	47 682	6 280
1970	95 778	7 825
1975	90 220	11 966
1978	130 749	19 427
1980	124 835	20 064
1985	165 155	41 996
1988	201 206	93 931
1989	221 183	113 585
1990	242 303	133 875
1991	259 377	137 716
1992	275 589	155 696
1993	182 348	211 938
1994	227 490	277 331
1995	294 771	376 982
1996	379 674	469 569
1997	476 804	564 787
1998	580 434	678 575
1999	680 089	740 937
2000	800 120	878 702
2001	987 080	1 097 848
2002	1 006 616	1 243 880
2003	1 201 398	1 471 747
2004	1 305 136	1 646 214
2005	1 763 412	2 030 622
2006	2 257 663	2 367 875
2007	2 925 798	3 211 777
2008	3 424 359	3 694 111
2009	3 769 896	4 335 754
2010	4 526 138	5 323 888
2011	5 661 400	6 580 605
2012	6 701 820	7 659 801

注:1. 1993 年以后实行新制度,财政收入数与历年不可比。

2. 2002 年以后,财政收入、支出为一般预算数。

Note:1. Since 1993,new regulations have been adopted in calculating revenue of government finance,the figures are not comparable with those over the years.

2. Since 2002,revenue of government finance and expenditure of government finance refer to general budgetary revenue and expenditure.

7－2 分市、区公共财政预算收入(2012 年)

BUDGETARY REVENUE OF PUBLIC FINANCE BY REGION(2012)

单位:万元(10 000 yuan)

市、区名称	Region	公共财政预算收入 Budgetaty Revenue of Public Finance	#增值税 Value-added Tax	营业税 Business Tax	企业所得税 Enterprise Income Tax
总　计	**Total**	**6 701 820**	**643 264**	**1 721 590**	**795 187**
市　区	Urban Area	4 261 516	478 411	1 358 332	394 829
#崂山区	Laoshan District	767 313	107 511	159 548	120 416
原黄岛区	Original Huangdao District	770 622	131 525	166 147	106 259
城阳区	Chengyang District	572 617	86 254	140 874	75 102
即墨市	Jimo	506 206	46 783	83 992	32 540
胶州市	Jiaozhou	450 617	40 671	93 304	50 829
原胶南市	Original Jiaonan	510 535	33 105	106 526	28 142
平度市	Pingdu	358 383	28 464	47 903	23 210
莱西市	Laixi	289 816	15 836	31 533	10 488
市本级	Municipal Level	324 747	－6	0	55 149

注:由于财政体制调整,市本级部分税种税收收入下放区市,本表数据与上年不可比。

Note: According to the adjustment of financial system, revenue of some tax have been delegated from municipal level to district level. The figures in this form are not comparable with previons year.

7－2 续表

continued

单位:万元(10 000 yuan)

市、区名称	Region	个人所得税 Personal Income Tax	城市维护建设税 Urban Maintenance and Development Tax	基金预算收入 Funds Budgetary Revenue
总　计	**Total**	**223 567**	**353 359**	**4 219 [illegible]20**
市　区	Urban Area	178 013	278 800	1 145 [illegible]57
#崂山区	Laoshan District	33 608	75 208	199 [illegible]94
原黄岛区	Original Huangdao District	20 985	57 780	535 [illegible]90
城阳区	Chengyang District	15 982	35 601	253 [illegible]10
即墨市	Jimo	6 550	19 196	323 [illegible]11
胶州市	Jiaozhou	16 512	20 330	228 [illegible]66
原胶南市	Original Jiaonan	12 660	16 338	344 [illegible]25
平度市	Pingdu	4 271	12 461	5[illegible] [illegible]65
莱西市	Laixi	5 561	6 234	5[illegible] [illegible]90
市本级	Municipal Level	0	0	2 165 [illegible]06

7-3 分市、区公共财政预算支出(2012)

BUDGETARY EXPENDITURE OF PUBLIC FINANCE BY REGION(2012)

单位:万元(10 000 yuan)

市、区名称	Region	公共财政预算支出 Budgetaty Expenditure of Public Finance	#一般公共服务支出 General Public Services	公共安全 Public Security	教育 Education	科学技术 Science and Technology	文化体育与传媒 Culture, Sport and Media
总　计	**Total**	**7 659 801**	**1 143 270**	**439 532**	**1 432 445**	**172 904**	**146 670**
市　区	Urban Area	2 572 554	376 673	86 914	565 581	90 232	28 336
#崂山区	Laoshan District	488 148	57 275	13 216	105 852	12 282	6 813
原黄岛区	Original Huangdao District	647 945	58 070	17 268	105 734	32 110	7 673
城阳区	Chengyang District	343 679	67 310	12 753	95 164	12 010	3 706
即墨市	Jimo	614 223	162 275	18 724	176 952	2 774	10 078
胶州市	Jiaozhou	513 198	95 952	25 994	127 304	10 326	5 759
原胶南市	Original Jiaonan	574 237	101 471	26 069	137 942	2 975	10 040
平度市	Pingdu	522 086	84 033	20 747	157 301	7 922	5 934
莱西市	Laixi	388 983	53 606	13 193	80 181	795	2 476
市本级	Municipal Level	2 474 520	269 260	247 891	187 184	57 880	84 047

7-3 续表

continued

单位:万元(10 000 yuan)

市、区名称	Region	社会保障和就业 Social Security and Employment	医疗卫生 Health Care	节能保护 Environment Protection	城乡社区事务 Urban and Rural Community Affairs	农林水事务 Affairs of Agiculture, Forest and Irrigation	基金预算支出 Funds Budgetary Expenditure
总　计	**Total**	**558 018**	**338 630**	**191 713**	**1 299 839**	**397 414**	**4 305 130**
市　区	Urban Area	136 720	97 453	29 380	591 156	95 745	1 585 677
#崂山区	Laoshan District	15 282	13 798	2 096	111 516	47 126	237 380
原黄岛区	Original Huangdao District	25 948	25 361	18 930	208 033	17 991	512 828
城阳区	Chengyang District	18 999	17 748	2 598	47 812	26 973	271 408
即墨市	Jimo	45 072	36 038	20 256	61 393	42 669	253 727
胶州市	Jiaozhou	33 373	29 216	8 527	51 336	55 131	263 595
原胶南市	Original Jiaonan	47 535	17 888	8 133	80 219	59 773	371 640
平度市	Pingdu	53 762	53 388	5 833	53 834	54 442	16 758
莱西市	Laixi	34 796	29 729	3 427	11 512	33 820	32 442
市本级	Municipal Level	206 760	74 918	116 157	450 389	55 834	1 781 291

7 -4 主要年份金融系统人民币存贷款(年末余额)

MAJOR YEAR'S DEPOSITS AND LOANS OF FINANCIAL INSTITUTIONS(YEAR-END BALANCE)

单位:万元(10 000 yuan)

年份 Year	存款合计 Total Deposits	#企业存款 Deposits by Enterprises	储蓄存款 Savings Deposits	贷款合计 Total Loans
1949	693	239	28	278
1952	9 093	4 308	1 838	3 322
1957	10 372	3 359	4 037	30 690
1962	20 040	8 579	3 279	73 601
1965	27 331	11 830	6 347	64 555
1970	38 264	13 024	7 576	125 382
1975	60 622	22 568	15 637	207 006
1978	66 523	21 004	21 455	297 184
1980	120 644	38 105	38 609	379 666
1985	344 760	99 736	155 604	452 142
1988	754 442	206 541	366 483	955 351
1989	932 430	245 529	481 692	1 174 448
1990	1 235 562	321 542	655 895	1 535 751
1991	1 553 564	411 417	824 428	1 871 462
1992	2 076 667	612 868	1 044 165	2 352 449
1993	2 747 294	835 617	1 372 239	2 940 658
1994	3 769 019	1 399 110	1 918 734	3 610 564
1995	5 324 026	2 030 382	2 687 888	4 777 864
1996	6 991 289	2 630 958	3 499 219	5 941 281
1997	7 385 092	2 885 632	4 060 259	6 508 776
1998	8 183 471	3 018 063	4 591 012	7 239 231
1999	9 160 001	3 454 570	4 978 045	8 945 730
2000	10 560 624	4 386 316	5 353 215	9 564 293
2001	12 323 942	4 955 336	6 187 409	10 798 871
2002	15 225 733	5 819 655	7 449 408	13 044 792
2003	18 920 868	7 027 227	9 084 693	16 783 917
2004	22 462 592	7 924 690	10 894 941	18 472 613
2005	26 975 372	8 226 661	13 431 016	20 394 792
2006	32 453 583	10 144 296	15 676 197	25 779 442
2007	38 915 882	13 213 434	17 020 383	30 970 553
2008	47 353 803	14 641 948	21 233 637	37 483 209
2009	63 019 764	21 001 185	25 278 658	48 735 326
2010	76 592 065	27 271 963	29 123 256	58 862 263
2011	86 384 994	49 189 415	31 985 099	69 477 500
2012	94 348 924	50 978 985	37 576 007	79 465 532

注:自 2011 年起,企业存款指标改为单位存款,口径与以前年度不一致。

Note: Since 2011, "Deposits by Corporate" has been used instead of "Deposits by Enterprises", and the caliber is different from the previous year.

7-5 金融系统人民币存贷款(年末余额)

DEPOSITS AND LOANS OF FINANCIAL INSTITUTIONS(YEAR-END BALANCE)

单位:万元(10 000 yuan)

项目	Item	2012 年	比年初增减数 Incremental/Reductions Compared to the Beginning of the Year
一、存款总计	**Total Deposits**	**94 348 924**	**7 963 930**
单位存款	Deposits by Corporate	50 978 985	1 789 570
储蓄存款	Savings Deposits	37 576 007	5 590 908
二、贷款总计	**Total Loans**	**79 465 532**	**9 961 032**
短期贷款	Short-Term Loans	32 886 412	6 014 041
#个人贷款及透支	Personal Loans and Line	3 633 039	816 747
单位贷款及透支	Business Loans and Line	24 974 573	3 495 914
贸易融资	Trade Financing	4 263 299	1 731 617
中长期贷款	Medium&Long-term Loans	42 663 350	2 586 431
#个人贷款	Personal Loans	13 663 771	1 546 232
单位贷款	Business Loans	22 821 096	241 093
银团贷款	Syndicated Loans	4 591 109	457 077
贸易融资	Trade Financing	1 576 353	331 009
票据融资	Notes Financing	3 781 285	1 279 411

7－6 国内保险业务(1990－2012年)
DOMESTIC INSURANCE BUSINESS(1990－2012)

项目	Item	1990	1995	2000	2005	2006
国内保险总值	**Total domestic insurance Value**	**4 392 323**	**11 256 080**	**38 357 485**	**91 691 581**	**119 396 881**
国内业务收入	Domestic Business Income	17 177	107 159	220 780	495 701	605 143
保费收入	Premium Income	12 085	81 976	218 714	495 701	605 143
财产险	Property Insurance	10 417	51 808	85 161	159 746	199 213
农业险	Agriculture Insurance	145	142	18	12	19
人身险	Personal Insurance	1 523	30 026	133 535	335 943	405 911
国内业务支出	**Domestic Business Expenditure**	**5 449**	**40 115**	**94 877**	**214 148**	**252 477**
1. 赔款支出	Claim Expenditure	4 735	32 105	62 275	111 385	131 321
财产险	Property Insurance	4 145	29 420	58 361	92 700	115 214
农业险	Agriculture Insurance	129	24	5	11	3
人身险	Personal Insurance	461	2 661	3 909	18 674	16 104
2. 给付支出	Mature Payment	509	7 652	27 955	32 739	63 144
3. 退保	Surrender	205	358	4 647	70 024	58 012

注：自2011年起，保险业实施新会计准则，保险统计各项指标口径发生变化，与以往年度不可比。

Note: Since 2011, new accounting standard has been used in insurance, indicators caliber of insurance statistics has been changed, and the data are not comparable with the previous year.

单位:万元(10 000 yuan)

2007	2008	2009	2010	2011	2012
228 7[illegible]4 417	**276 989 344**	**293 519 697**	**309 244 255**	**380 829 634**	**447 476 690**
776 [illegible]31	1 027 258	1 153 101	1 538 526	1 457 269	1 602 881
776 [illegible]31	1 027 258	1 153 101	1 538 526	1 457 269	1 602 881
2[illegible]2 564	280 008	339 314	492 190	556 257	644 269
1 542	3 135	4 066	3 261	3 587	5 046
501 325	744 115	809 721	1 043 075	897 425	953 566
361 183	**423 743**	**476 377**	**497 832**	**463 751**	**747 089**
[illegible]71 613	196 318	219 546	279 019	307 564	515 007
38 739	164 415	188 723	250 966	286 214	328 877
53	907	3 452	2 808	1 087	1 833
3[illegible] 821	30 996	27 371	25 245	20 263	184 297
9[illegible] 282	132 621	123 056	109 318	156 188	154 922
9[illegible] 288	94 804	133 775	109 496	69 275	77 159

主要统计指标解释

财政收入　指国家财政参与社会产品分配所取得的收入,是实现国家职能的财力保证。财政收入所包括的内容几经变化,目前主要包括:

(1)税收收入:包括增值税、营业税、企业所得税、个人所得税、资源税、固定资产投资方向调节税、城市维护建设税、房产税、印花税、城镇土地使用税、土地增值税、车船税、耕地占用税、契税、烟叶税、其他税收收入。

(2)非税收入:包括专项收入、行政事业性收费收入、罚没收入、国有资本经营收入、国有资源有偿使用收入、其他收入。

财政支出　国家财政将筹集起来的资金进行分配使用,以满足经济建设和各项事业的需要,主要包括:

(1)一般公共服务支出:反映政府提供一般公共服务的支出。

(2)公共安全:反映政府维护社会公共安全方面的支出,有关事务包括武装警察、公安、国家安全、检察、法院、司法行政、监狱、劳教、国家保密、缉私警察等。

(3)教育支出:反映政府教育事务支出。有关具体教育事务包括教育行政管理、学前教育、小学教育、初中教育、普通高中教育、普通高等教育、初等职业教育、中专教育、技校教育、职业高中教育、高等职业教育、广播电视教育、留学生教育、特殊教育、干部继续教育、教育机关服务等。

(4)科学技术:反映政府用于科学技术方面的支出。

(5)文化体育与传媒:反映政府在文化、文物、体育、广播电视、新闻出版等方面的支出。

(6)社会保障和就业:反映政府在社会保障与就业方面的支出。有关事项包括社会保障与就业管理事务、民政管理事务、财政对社会保险基金的补助、补充全国社会保障基金、行政事业单位离退休、企业改革补助、就业补助、抚恤、退役安置、社会福利、残疾人事业、城市居民最低生活保障、其他城镇社会救济、农村社会救济、自然灾害生活补助、红十字事务等。

(7)医疗卫生支出:反映政府医疗卫生方面的支出。具体包括医疗卫生管理事务支出、医疗服务支出、医疗保障支出、疾病预防控制支出、卫生监督支出、妇幼保健支出、农村卫生支出等。

(8)环境保护:反映政府环境保护支出。具体包括:环境保护管理事务支出、环境监测与监察支出、污染治理支出、自然生态保护支出、天然林保护工程支出、退耕还林支出、风沙荒漠治理支出、退牧还草支出、已垦草原退耕还草支出。

(9)城乡社区事务:反映政府城乡社区事务支出。具体包括:城乡社区管理事务支出、城乡社区规划与管理支出、城乡社区公共设施支出、城乡社区住宅支出、城乡社区环境卫生支出、建设市场管理与监督支出等。

(10)农林水事务:反映政府农林水事务方面的支出。具体包括农业、林业、水利、扶贫支出、农业综合开发支出等。

存款　指企业、机关、团体或居民根据资金必须收回的原则,把货币资金存入银行或其他信贷机构保管并取得一定利息的一种信用活动形式。根据存款对象或性质的不同可划分为企业存款、财政存款、机关团体存款、基本建设存款、储蓄存款、农村存款、委托存款、其他存款等科目。它是银行信贷资金的主要来源。

贷款　指银行或其他信贷机构根据资金必须归还的原则,按一定利率,为企业、个人等提供资金的一种信用活动形式。我国银行贷款分为短期贷款、中期流动资金贷款、中长期贷款、信托贷款、融资租赁、委托贷款、票据融资、各项垫款等。

承保额　又叫保险金额,指保险人承担赔偿或者给付保险金责任的最高限额。

保费　指投保人为取得保险人在约定范围内所承担赔偿责任而支付给保险人的费用。

Explanatory Notes on Main Statistical Indicators

Government Revenue　refers to the revenue of the government finance by means of participating in the distribution of the social products, which is the financial resources for ensuring the government to function. The contents of government revenue have been changed several times. Now it includes the following main items:

(1) Various tax revenues, including value added tax, business tax, enterprise income tax, personal income tax, resources tax, fixed assets investment direction regulating tax, tax on city maintenance and construction, real estate tax, stamp tax, tax on use of urban land, land value added tax, vehicle and vessel tax, tax on occupancy of cultivated land, property tax, tobacco leaf tax, and other tax revenues.

(2) Non-tax Revenues including special revenues, revenues from Administrative and institutional fees, penalty and confiscatory revenues , revenues from state-owned capital operationg, revenues from paid use of state-owned resources, and other revenues.

Government Expenditure refers to the distribution and use of the funds the government finance has raised, so as to meet the needs of economic construction and various causes. It includes the following main items:

(1) Expenditure for general public services: It reflects the expenditure from the government for general public services.

(2) Expenditure on public security: It reflects the expenditure from the government towards safeguarding the public security, including the related affairs of armed police, public security, state security, procuratorial administration, law court, judicial administration, jail , reeducation through labor, state confidentiality, anti-smuggling Patrol, etc.

(3) Expenditure on education: It reflects the expenditure from the government on education, including the related affairs of educational administration management, preschool education, primary education, junior secondary educate, regular senior secondary educate, regular higher education, primary vocational education, specialized secondary educate, technical educate, vocational senior secondary educate, vocational higher education, radio and television education, foreign student educate, special education, cadre continuing education, education institution services, etc.

(4) Expenditure on science and technology: It reflects the expenditure from the government on science and technology.

(5) Expenditure on culture, sport and media: It reflects the expenditure from the government on culture, cultural relics, sport, radio and television, publication, etc.

(6) Expenditure on social security and employment: It reflects the expenditure from the government on social security and employment, including the related affairs of management of social security and employment, civil administration, subsidies to social insurance funds, supplement to national social security funds, retirees of government agencies and institutions, subsidies to enterprises reform, subsidies to employment, pension, settling down demobilized servicemen, social security, disabled person administration, minimum living allowance in urban area, other social relief in urban area, social relief in rural area, subsidies to natural disaster, Red Cross business, etc.

(7) Expenditure on health care: It reflects the expenditure from the government on health care, including expenditure on management of health care, medical services, medical security, disease control and prevention, public health supervision, rural health care, etc.

(8) Expenditure on environment protection: It reflects the expenditure from the government on environment protection, including expenditure on management of environment protection, environment monitoring and supervisory, pollution government, natural ecological protection, project of natural forest protection, returning farmland to forest, sandstorm and wilderness government, returning grazing land to grassland, returning cultivated grassland to grassland, etc.

(9) Expenditure on urban and rural community affairs: It reflects the expenditure from the government on urban and rural community affairs, including expenditure on management of urban and rural community affairs, plan and management of urban and rural community, public utility of urban and rural community, residential buildings of urban and rural community, environmental sanitation of urban and rural community, management and supervision of markets construction, etc.

(10) Expenditure on agriculture, forest and irrigation: It reflects the expenditure from the government on agriculture, forest and irrigation, including expenditure on agriculture, forest, irrigation, poverty alleviation, comprehensive development of agriculture, etc.

Deposit is a form of credit by which enterprises, institutions, organizations or households can put money into banks and other credit institutions for safekeeping and interest earning under the principle of free withdrawal. According to different depositors, deposits are divided into enterprise deposits, treasury deposits, deposits of government agencies and organizations, capital construction deposits, savings deposits, rural saving deposits, entrusted deposits and other deposits. Deposits are major sources of the credit funds of banks.

Loan is a form of credit by which banks and other credit institutions provide funds at certain interest rate to enterprises and individuals in the light of the principle of unconditional repayment. Loans from Chinese banks include circulating capital loans, fixed assets loans, loans to urban and rural individuals engaged in industrial and commercial business and agricultural loans.

Amount Covered which also is known as amount Insured, refers to the maximum that the insurant will get for the claim of the case insured.

Premium is the fee paid by the insurant to the insurer to obtain the obligation of compensation from the insurance within the agreed terms.

8 物价
PRICE

简 要 说 明

一、本篇资料的主要内容

本篇资料主要包括工业生产者出厂、工业生产者购进、固定资产投资、房地产、居民消费、商品零售等价格指数。

二、本篇资料的来源

1、工业生产者出厂、工业生产者购进、固定资产投资、房地产价格指数分别来源于生产、投资、房地产价格统计调查年报，由国家统计局青岛调查队生产投资价格调查处整理提供。

2、居民消费、商品零售价格指数来源于消费价格统计调查年报，由国家统计局青岛调查队消费价格调查处整理提供。

Brief Introduction

I. Main Content

Data in this chapter mainly include producer price indices for manufactured goods, purchasing price indices for industrial producers, price indices of investment in fixed assets, real estate price indices, consumer price indices and retail price indices.

II. Source of Data

(1)Data on producer price indices for manufactured goods, purchasing price indices for industrial producers, price indices of investment in fixed assets, real estate price indices are based on annual report of price survey on production,investment,real estate,and provided by the Division of Production Price Survey of Survey Office of the National Bureau of Statistics in Qingdao.

(2)Data on consumer price indices and retail price indices are based on annual report of consumer price survey, and provided by the Division of Consumer Price Survey of Survey Office of the National Bureau of Statistics in Qingdao.

8-1 主要年份居民消费和商品零售价格指数
MAJOR YEAR'S CONSUMER AND RETAIL PRICE INDEXES

(上年=100)　　　　(preceding year = 100)

年份 Year	居民消费价格指数 Consumer Price Index	#食品类 Food	衣着类 Clothing	服务项目价格指数 Services Price Index	商品零售价格指数 Retail Price Index
1951	110.5	105.2	112.4		110.5
1952	99.8	99.6	98.7		99.8
1957	101.4	101.3	101.4	99.3	101.4
1962	102.6	102.0	100.2	99.9	102.6
1965	101.2	101.3	98.8	96.9	101.2
1970	98.9	99.7	100.0	99.5	98.9
1975	100.3	100.1	100.0	100.0	100.3
1978	100.5	100.2	99.8	100.0	100.5
1980	105.2	108.5	100.3	100.6	105.5
1985	110.4	115.2	102.3	102.7	110.9
1987	109.4	112.5	106.8	102.5	109.8
1988	120.7	125.2	117.3	118.3	120.9
1989	115.3	109.2	121.1	130.2	114.4
1990	104.5	103.4	103.4	118.8	103.6
1991	107.0	107.0	112.1	109.6	106.8
1992	111.4	115.1	108.6	119.9	110.8
1993	123.9	120.9	119.0	158.5	119.8
1994	126.9	135.2	130.1	117.9	122.8
1995	116.2	118.1	122.8	123.2	114.2
1996	112.6	110.1	104.3	130.4	106.0
1997	104.0	101.2	102.3	120.8	100.2
1998	100.0	93.7	94.5	136.2	94.9
1999	100.2	96.7	97.1	115.6	96.6
2000	103.3	100.0	108.3	112.0	99.7
2001	101.0	100.6	98.0	108.7	98.9
2002	98.9	97.8	100.2	101.0	99.5
2003	101.4	104.3	98.4	101.7	98.3
2004	102.1	104.0	103.6	104.7	99.0
2005	102.3	102.1	108.3	101.4	99.3
2006	100.9	101.7	99.4	100.8	99.7
2007	104.5	111.6	99.4	102.4	102.7
2008	104.7	111.7	103.9	99.8	103.9
2009	100.5	101.6	101.4	100.6	98.6
2010	102.2	106.4	101.0	100.4	101.4
2011	105.0	111.1	108.2	103.1	104.5
2012	102.7	104.3	106.3	102.1	101.7

8－2 主要年份居民消费和商品零售价格指数(以1950年价格为100)

MAJOR YEAR'S CONSUMER AND RETAIL PRICE INDEXES (1950＝100)

年份 Year	居民消费价格指数 Consumer Price Index	#食品类 Food	衣着类 Clothing	服务项目价格指数 Services Price Index	商品零售价格指数 Retail Price Index
1951	110.5	105.2	112.4		110.5
1952	110.3	104.8	110.9		110.3
1957	119.5	120.7	115.3	91.6	119.5
1962	127.4	128.8	115.1	94.2	127.4
1965	133.3	138.7	108.4	81.5	133.3
1970	129.0	137.6	110.3	76.8	129.0
1975	128.8	138.2	110.0	75.7	128.8
1978	129.1	138.7	109.8	75.7	129.1
1980	137.6	154.1	109.3	76.1	138.1
1985	160.8	196.1	103.8	80.5	162.5
1987	185.4	235.8	113.6	85.2	188.2
1988	223.8	295.2	133.2	100.8	227.6
1989	258.1	322.4	161.3	131.3	250.3
1990	269.7	333.3	166.8	155.9	259.7
1991	288.6	356.7	187.0	170.9	268.1
1992	321.5	410.5	203.1	204.9	329.2
1993	398.3	496.3	241.7	324.8	372.4
1994	505.4	671.1	314.4	382.9	459.5
1995	587.3	792.5	386.1	471.8	526.2
1996	661.3	872.6	402.7	615.2	558.4
1997	687.8	883.0	412.0	743.1	559.5
1998	687.8	827.4	389.3	1 012.1	540.5
1999	689.2	800.1	378.0	1 170.0	522.1
2000	711.9	800.1	409.4	1 310.4	520.5
2001	719.0	804.9	401.2	1 424.4	514.8
2002	711.1	787.2	402.0	1 438.7	512.2
2003	721.1	821.0	395.6	1 463.1	503.5
2004	736.2	853.9	409.8	1 531.9	498.5
2005	753.1	871.8	443.8	1 553.4	495.0
2006	759.9	886.6	441.2	1 565.8	493.5
2007	794.1	989.5	438.5	1 603.4	505.8
2008	831.4	1 105.3	455.6	1 600.2	526.6
2009	835.6	1 123.0	462.0	1 609.8	519.2
2010	854.0	1 194.9	466.6	1 616.2	526.5
2011	896.7	1 327.5	504.9	1 666.3	550.2
2012	920.9	1 384.6	536.7	1 701.3	559.6

8-3 主要年份生产投资价格指数

MAJOR YEAR'S PRICE INDEXES FOR PRODUCTION AND INVESTMENT

(上年=100)　　　　(preceding year = 100)

年份 Year	工业生产者出厂价格指数 Producer Price Indexes for Industrial Producers	工业生产者购进价格指数 Purchasing Price Indexes for Industrial Producers	房屋销售价格指数 Sales Price Indexes of Houses	房屋租赁价格指数 Renting Price Indexes of Houses	物业管理价格指数 Property Management Price Indexes	固定资产投资价格指数 Price Indexes for Investment in Fixed Assets
1990	104.33	108.64				
1991	101.68	108.10				
1992	105.46	107.13				
1993	115.49	126.91				
1994	121.62	120.30				
1995	112.70	114.25				
1996	103.81	103.25				
1997	100.22	101.93				
1998	94.96	92.77	100.1	94.0		
1999	96.93	95.88	103.7	104.3		
2000	101.89	106.81	102.3	95.8		
2001	98.00	97.81	104.1	107.0		
2002	97.37	96.78	107.6	94.4		
2003	100.97	106.51	114.6	99.4		
2004	102.92	113.62	115.2	98.6		105.8
2005	101.39	106.52	110.9	103.3	100.2	103.1
2006	101.08	105.80	106.9	110.1	99.8	102.6
2007	101.50	106.69	106.5	108.3	100.4	104.1
2008	105.33	115.91	105.1	106.5	102.1	111.0
2009	95.78	90.35	100.3	103.5	100.4	94.6
2010	103.75	112.21		103.0	100.5	104.9
2011	104.90	109.39				107.0
2012	98.61	97.00				100.0

注：自2011年工业品出厂价格改为工业生产者出厂价格；主要原材料、燃料、动力购进价格改为工业生产者购进价格。

Note: Since 2011, "Producer Price Indexes for Industrial Producers" has been used in stead of "Producer Price Indexes for Manufactured Goods", "Purchasing Price Indexes for Industrial Producers" has been used in stead of "Purchasing Price Indexes for Raw Material, Fuel and Power".

8 -4 工业生产者出厂价格指数

PRODUCER PRICE INDEXES FOR INDUSTRIAL PRODUCERS

(上年 =100)　　　　(preceding year =100)

类　别	Item	1990	1995	2000	2005	2006	2007	2008	2009	2010	2011	2012
总 指 数	**General Index**	**104.33**	**112.70**	**101.89**	**101.39**	**101.08**	**101.50**	**105.33**	**95.78**	**103.75**	**104.90**	**98.61**
其中:轻工业	Light Industry	106.19	115.33	98.50	99.78	99.58	100.97	102.93	97.21	100.80	103.46	99.70
重工业	Heavy Industry	102.06	108.61	105.62	104.32	103.94	102.49	109.17	93.45	107.57	105.89	97.87
其中:生产资料	**Means of Production**	**102.78**	**110.20**	**105.03**	**103.24**	**102.49**	**102.41**	**108.76**	**94.25**	**106.43**	**105.54**	**97.55**
采掘	Excavation	113.17	119.02	95.67	114.74	104.73	99.85	115.24	93.44	130.94	112.07	93.35
原料	Raw Materials	108.80	109.54	113.82	106.91	104.05	104.01	108.81	90.67	115.24	111.52	99.05
加工	Processing	99.71	110.29	97.58	101.45	101.86	101.91	108.59	95.34	103.50	103.49	97.20
生活资料	**Means of Livelihood**	**105.83**	**114.77**	**98.25**	**99.13**	**99.74**	**100.64**	**101.72**	**97.45**	**99.61**	**103.82**	**100.42**
食品	Food	108.04	116.48	96.59	98.80	101.52	106.55	108.42	98.21	105.06	109.71	99.91
衣着	Clothing	109.27	117.60	99.37	101.48	102.16	102.46	103.36	102.03	101.56	107.44	102.03
一般日用品	Articles for Daily Use	104.16	117.65	104.52	101.97	101.82	103.21	103.03	99.39	99.96	108.02	101.64
耐用消费品	Durable Consumer Goods	96.72	103.25	97.70	97.43	97.23	96.10	97.13	94.52	93.23	94.34	98.79

8-5 工业生产者购进价格指数
PURCHASING PRICE INDEXES FOR INDUSTRIAL PRODUCERS

(上年=100) (preceding year=100)

名 称	Item	1990	1995	2000	2005	2006	2007	2008	2009	2010	2011	2012
总指数	**General Index**	**108.64**	**114.25**	**106.81**	**106.52**	**105.8**	**106.69**	**115.91**	**90.35**	**112.21**	**109.39**	**97.00**
燃料、动力类	Fuel and Power	97.94	109.96	113.82	117.34	117.17	103.14	126.19	90.53	115.43	111.29	100.64
黑色金属材料类	Ferrous Metals	113.94	97.00	102.66	107.84	95.83	109.61	122.19	82.38	111.97	113.08	93.20
#钢材	Rolled-steel		98.86	105.44	106.57	96.11	108.14	119.10	85.25	108.67	107.95	92.33
其他	Others		93.76	101.10	112.88	94.91	114.43	132.40	72.73	122.64	129.01	94.64
有色金属材料及电线类	Nonferrous Metals and Electric Wire	97.97	128.79	106.75	108.06	131.58	106.51	93.41	86.24	122.65	108.45	93.64
化工原料类	Raw Chemical Materials	98.35	129.93	106.9	112.47	99.71	111.09	123.00	87.66	111.04	113.79	96.72
木材及纸浆类	Timber and Paper Pulp	98.57	109.68	108.98	103.8	104.29	107.23	103.58	89.16	117.06	103.78	93.12
建筑材料及非金属矿类	Building Materials and Nonmetals	144.52	93.94	99.50	115.54	92.83	95.80	124.52	100.98	107.61	116.71	102.48
其他工业原材料及半成品	Other Industrial Raw Materials and Semi-finished Goods		97.04	105.32	97.87	103.33	104.43	109.65	92.70	106.41	103.31	98.05
农副产品	Agricultural Products	115.72	134.17	92.73	101.55	110.87	112.49	117.68	88.60	121.30	115.04	98.21
纺织原料类	Textile Materials	112.47	99.25	104.03	98.15	100.15	104.01	101.44	98.69	112.90	111.11	95.61

8-6 按工业行业分工业生产者出厂价格指数

PRODUCER PRICE INDEXES FOR INDUSTRIAL PRODUCERS BY SECTOR

(上年=100)

行　业	Sector	2000
工业品出厂价格指数	**Producer Price Indexes for Manufactured Goods**	**101.71**
煤炭开采和洗选业	Mining and Washing of Coal	
石油和天然气开采业	Extraction of Petroleum and Natural Gas	
黑色金属矿采选业	Mining of Ferrous Metal Ores	
有色金属矿采选业	Mining of Non-ferrous Metal Ores	
非金属矿采选业	Mining and Processing of Nonmetal Ores	106.09
其他采矿业	Mining of Other Ores	
农副食品加工业	Processing of Food from Agricultural Products	93.78
食品制造业	Manufacture of Foods	87.30
饮料制造业	Manufacture of Beverage	89.51
烟草制品业	Manufacture of Tobacco	100.00
纺织业	Manufacture of Textile	112.46
纺织服装、鞋、帽制造业	Manufacture of Textile Wearing Apparel, Footware, and Caps	
皮革、毛皮、羽毛(绒)及其制品业	Manufacture of Leather, Fur, Feather & Its Products	
木材加工及木、竹、藤、棕、草制品业	Processing of Timbers, Manufacture of Wood, Bamboo, Rattan, Palm, and Straw Products	
家具制造业	Manufacture of Furniture	100.03
造纸及纸制品业	Manufacture of Paper and Paper Products	101.82
印刷业和记录媒介的复制	Printing, Reproduction of Recording Media	
文教体育用品制造业	Manufacture of Articles for Culture, Education and Sport Activity	
石油加工、炼焦及核燃料加工业	Processing of Petroleum, Coking, Processing of Nucleus Fuel	139.69
化学原料及化学制品制造业	Manufacture of Chemical Raw Material and Chemical Products	116.25
医药制造业	Manufacture of Medicines	90.11
化学纤维制造业	Manufacture of Chemical Fiber	
橡胶制品业	Manufacture of Rubber	99.58
塑料制品业	Manufacture of Plastic	98.15
非金属矿物制品业	Manufacture of Non-metallic Mineral Products	102.93
黑色金属冶炼及压延加工业	Smelting and Pressing of Ferrous Metals	101.20
有色金属冶炼及压延加工业	Smelting and Pressing of Non-ferrous Metals	
金属制品业	Manufacture of Metal Products	
通用设备制造业	Manufacture of General Purpose Machinery	
专用设备制造业	Manufacture of Special Purpose Machinery	87.01
交通运输设备制造业	Manufacture of Transport Equipment	102.71
电气机械及器材制造业	Manufacture of Electrical Machinery & Equipment	103.81
通信设备、计算机及其他电子设备制造业	Manufacture of Communication Equipment, Computer and Other Electronic Equipment	101.91
仪器仪表及文化、办公用机械制造业	Manufacture of Measuring Instrument and Machinery for Cultural Activity & Office Work	107.28
工艺品及其他制造业	Manufacture of Artwork, Other Manufacture	
废弃资源和废旧材料回收加工业	Recycling and Disposal of Waste	
电力、热力的生产和供应业	Production and Supply of Electric Power and Heat Power	
燃气生产和供应业	Production and Supply of Gas	100.01
水的生产和供应业	Production and Supply of Water	94.46

(preceding year = 100)

2005	2006	2007	2008	2009	2010	2011	2012
101.39	**101.08**	**101.50**	**105.33**	**95.78**	**103.75**	**104.90**	**98.61**
100.65	96.10	101.24	99.25	101.67	113.85	104.33	99.93
108.54	107.57	104.55	110.23	123.38	122.69	111.39	102.48
117.32	103.80	98.71	116.71	86.15	132.38	145.13	89.33
97.23	101.38	110.20	111.53	95.8	105.68	111.32	98.69
101.21	99.71	100.86	113.82	98.52	107.13	112.52	103.11
100.80	100.20	101.66	104.21	101.63	100.66	104.14	105.89
100.00	100.00	100.00	100.00	100.00	100.00		
101.64	100.67	100.71	104.01	100.22	105.39	105.09	96.15
102.56	103.20	102.83	102.20	99.51	101.82	105.42	101.52
99.38	101.63	103.44	100.52	100.56	100.70	102.95	102.62
101.46	98.54	102.47	102.03	100.54	101.41	108.13	103.21
104.29	99.84	100.13	106.09	100.47	100.01	101.11	102.00
106.98	98.92	102.91	111.51	91.37	104.01	105.71	95.59
100.60	101.11	106.56	115.27	107.72	94.71	110.06	107.10
100.25	100.60	100.12	103.39	100.3	102.21	99.65	103.56
113.93	112.84	110.56	118.02	83.82	124.23	114.95	104.26
107.20	96.74	102.84	107.31	86.37	113.85	114.60	89.61
102.19	98.65	102.45	103.67	99.71	101.52	107.33	95.05
107.79	98.92	101.82	95.98	78.75	114.01	123.72	92.56
99.82	103.49	104.21	105.44	101.5	101.59	118.21	99.41
103.37	100.33	102.40	103.38	92.05	99.92	108.76	100.73
101.18	100.96	102.80	108.40	98.21	104.13	108.15	98.38
101.93	97.31	111.16	133.12	79.23	115.41	110.90	85.57
100.22	128.45	103.03	91.81	85.30	125.88	108.26	89.14
108.47	93.02	102.83	112.00	100.08	98.83	102.19	98.13
103.58	102.09	102.21	108.50	100.32	98.87	100.79	99.95
103.47	100.15	101.87	102.69	104.70	100.91	101.69	101.26
100.98	99.44	100.50	101.65	98.51	99.63	99.22	99.31
102.28	106.64	101.74	100.34	97.15	100.53	103.10	98.40
84.90	88.78	87.30	93.92	89.41	91.49	84.65	95.43
105.75	100.44	100.78	98.75	101.55	102.46	101.77	98.69
105.95	104.84	105.02	104.07	98.39	98.37	100.94	100.38
104.92	103.25	100.00	103.10	104.95	101.17	101.49	104.36
105.85	104.33	101.61	104.29	91.66	112.18	107.34	103.32
120.28	127.90	100.41	99.90	99.83	100.05	100.15	100.25

8 -7 固定资产投资价格指数

PRICE INDEXES FOR INVESTMENT IN FIXED ASSETS

(上年 = 100)　　(preceding year = 100)

项目名称	Item	2004	2005	2006	2007	2008	2009	2010	2011	2012
总　　计	**Total**	**105.8**	**103.1**	**102.6**	**104.1**	**111.0**	**94.6**	**104.9**	**107.0**	**100.0**
建筑安装、装饰工程	Construction and Installation Project	109.3	103.7	103.5	105.4	115.5	92.1	107.5	110.1	99.8
其中:人工费	of which: Labor Cost	105.1	112.7	110.0	111.0	112.7	104.9	112.0	115.9	110.4
材料费	Materials Expenses	111.5	101.0	100.7	103.9	120.5	87.5	107.0	109.6	96.7
机械使用费	Expenses on Machinery Use	108.5	104.2	109.1	107.2	106.9	100.0	104.3	105.0	102.3
设备、工器具购置	Purchase of Equipment, Tools and Instruments	98.3	99.7	100.6	100.8	102.5	98.0	100.2	101.8	99.2
其他费用	Others	101.8	105.5	100.9	103.9	105.9	98.5	102.2	103.0	102.0

8 -8 住宅销售价格指数(2012 年)

SALES PRICE INDEXES FOR RESIDENCE(2012)

(上年 = 100)　　(preceding year = 100)

项目	Item	2012
新建住宅销售价格指数	**Sales Price Indexes for Newly Constructed Residence**	
一月	January	99.8
二月	February	100.0
三月	March	98.5
四月	April	96.4
五月	May	96.1
六月	June	95.9
七月	July	95.6
八月	August	95.7
九月	September	95.2
十月	October	95.5
十一月	November	95.8
十二月	December	96.6
二手住宅销售价格指数	**Sales Price Indexes for Second-hand Residence**	
一月	January	97.9
二月	February	97.8
三月	March	97.6
四月	April	97.2
五月	May	96.6
六月	June	96.5
七月	July	97.6
八月	August	97.0
九月	September	97.2
十月	October	97.6
十一月	November	98.2
十二月	December	98.8

8-9 居民消费价格分类指数(2012 年)

CONSUMER PRICE INDEXES BY CATEGORY(2012)

(上年=100) (preceding year=100)

项 目	Item	指 数 Indexes
居民消费价格总指数	**Consumer Price Index**	**102.7**
非食品价格指数	Non-food Price Index	102.0
服务项目价格指数	Services Price Index	102.1
扣除鲜菜鲜果总指数	Price Index Without Fresh Vegetables and Fresh Fruits	102.6
消费品价格指数	Consumer Goods Price Index	102.9
一、食品	**Food**	**104.3**
1.粮食	Grain	102.3
2.淀粉及薯类	Starches and Tubers	98.1
3.干豆类及豆制品	Beans and Bean Products	97.4
4.油脂	Oil or Fat	112.7
5.肉禽及其制品	Meat Poultry and Its Products	101.4
6.蛋类	Eggs	95.5
7.水产品	Aquatic Products	108.1
8.菜	Vegetables	110.7
9.调味品	Flavoring	108.1
10.糖	Carbohydrate	105.0
11.茶及饮料	Tea and Beverages	106.8
12.干鲜瓜果类	Dried and Fresh Melons and Fruits	96.4
13.糕点饼干面包	Cake, Biscuit and Bread	103.2
14.液体乳及乳制品	Milk and Its Products	103.3
15.在外用膳食品	Outward Dinner Food	106.7
16.其它食品及食品加工服务	Other Foods and Manufacturing Services	109.5
二、烟酒及用品	**Tobacco, Liquor and Articles**	**101.3**
1.烟草	Tobacco	100.2
2.酒	Liquor	102.2

8 -9 续表
continued

项　目	Item	指　数 Indexes
三、衣着	**Clothing**	**106.3**
1.服装	Garments	106.3
2.衣着材料	Clothing Materials	102.6
3.鞋袜帽	Footgear and Hats	106.3
4.衣着加工服务	Clothing Manufacturing Services	109.3
四、家庭设备用品及维修服务	**Household Facilities, Articles and services**	**101.9**
1.耐用消费品	Durable Consumer Goods	99.7
2.室内装饰品	Interior Decorations	99.0
3.床上用品	Bed Articles	102.8
4.家庭日用杂品	Daily Use Household Articles	102.8
5.家庭服务及加工维修服务	Household Services and Maintenance and Renovation	116.6
五、医疗保健和个人用品	**Health Care and Personal Articles**	**101.9**
1.医疗保健	Health Care	101.9
2.个人用品及服务	Personal Articles and Services	101.8
六、交通和通讯	**Transportation and Communication**	**99.1**
1.交通	Transportation	99.9
2.通讯	Communication	97.7
七、娱乐教育文化用品及服务	**Recreation, Education and Culture Articles and Services**	**100.5**
1.文娱用耐用消费品及服务	Durable Consumer Goods for Cultural and Recreational Use and Services	96.7
2.教育	Education	100.6
3.文化娱乐用品	Cultural and Recreational Articles	100.0
4.旅游及外出	Touring and Outing	104.8
八、居住	**Residence**	**102.2**
1.建房及装修材料	Building and Building Decoration Materials	100.1
2.租房	Renting	103.5
3.自有住房	Private Housing	103.4
4.水、电、燃料	Water, Electricity and Fuels	101.4

8-10 商品零售价格分类指数(2012年)

RETAIL PRICE INDEXES BY CATEGORY(2012)

(上年=100) (preceding year=100)

项 目	Item	指 数 Indexes
商品零售价格总指数	**Retail Price Index**	**101.7**
一、食品	**Food**	**104.4**
1. 粮食	Grain	100.9
2. 淀粉及薯类	Starches and Tubers	98.1
3. 干豆类及豆制品	Beans and Bean Products	98.0
4. 油脂	Oil or Fat	112.2
5. 肉禽及其制品	Meat Poultry and Its Products	102.6
6. 蛋	Eggs	95.7
7. 水产品	Aquatic Products	107.7
8. 菜	Vegetables	110.7
9. 调味品	Flavoring	107.6
10. 糖	Carbohydrate	104.6
11. 干鲜瓜果	Dried and Fresh Melons and Fruits	96.5
12. 糕点饼干面包	Cake, Biscuit and Bread	103.2
13. 液体乳及乳制品	Milk and Its Products	103.5
14. 在外用膳食品	Outward Dinner Food	106.8
15. 其他食品	Other Foods	109.5
二、饮料、烟酒	**Beverages, Tobacco and Liquor**	**102.5**
1. 茶及饮料	Tea and Beverages	106.8
2. 烟草	Tobacco	100.2
3. 酒	Liquor	102.2
三、服装、鞋帽类	**Clothing**	**106.2**
1. 服装	Garments	106.3
2. 鞋袜帽	Footgear and Hats	106.2
3. 其他	Others	100.7
四、纺织品类	**Textiles**	**102.9**
1. 衣着材料	Cotton Cloth	102.6
2. 床上用品	Blend Cloth	102.9
五、家用电器及音像器材	**Household Appliances, Music and Video Equipment**	**97.4**
1. 家庭设备	Household Facilities	99.8
2. 文娱用耐用消费品	Durable Consumer Goods for Cultural and Recreational Use and Services	94.0
3. 音像器材类	Music and Video Equipment	97.5

8-10 续表
continued

项　目	Item	指　数 Indexes
六、文化办公用品	**Culture and office Articles**	**97.4**
七、日用品	**Articles for Daily Use**	**102.8**
1. 日用百货	General Merchandise for Daily Use	102.1
2. 日用杂品	Miscellaneous for Daily Use	100.5
3. 洗涤用品	Cleaning Products	105.8
4. 其他日用品	Other Articles for Daily Use	101.6
八、体育娱乐用品	**Sports and Recreation Articles**	**98.6**
1. 体育用品	Sports Articles	97.7
2. 娱乐用品	Recreation Articles	99.2
九、交通、通信用品	**Transportation and Communication Appliances**	**94.6**
1. 交通运输机械	Transportation Machines	97.6
2. 通讯器材类	Communication Equipment	84.7
十、家具	**Furniture**	**99.0**
十一、化妆品类	**Cosmetics**	**102.1**
十二、金银珠宝类	**Gold, Silver and Jewelry**	**97.3**
十三、中西药品及医疗保健用品	**Traditional Chinese and Western Medicals and Health Care Articles**	**102.4**
1. 医疗器具及用品	Medical Apparatus and Articles	104.3
2. 中药材及中成药	Traditional Chinese Medicinal Materials and Medicines	101.5
3. 西药	Western Medicines	102.0
4. 保健器具及用品	Health Care Articles	103.4
十四、书报杂志及电子出版物	**Books, Newspapers, Magazines and Electronic Publications**	**100.3**
1. 教材及参考书	Teaching Material and Reference Books	101.0
2. 书报杂志	Books, Newspapers and Magazines	100.9
3. 电子音像制品	Electronic Music and Video Products	97.1
十五、燃料类	**Fuels**	**103.6**
1. 煤炭及制品类	Coal and Its Products	94.9
2. 石油及制品类	Petroleum and Its Products	104.5
十六、建筑材料及五金电料类	**Building Materials and Hardware**	**99.8**
1. 建筑装璜材料	Building Decoration Materials	100.7
2. 五金电料类	Hardware	93.3

主要统计指标解释

居民消费价格指数　是反映一定时期内城乡居民所购买的生活消费品价格和服务项目价格变动趋势和程度的相对数，是对城市居民消费价格指数和农村居民消费价格指数进行综合汇总计算的结果。该指数可以观察和分析消费品的零售价格和服务价格变动对城乡居民实际生活费支出的影响程度。

商品零售价格指数　是反映一定时期内城乡商品零售价格变动趋势和程度的相对数。商品零售价格的变动直接影响到城乡居民的生活支出和国家的财政收入，影响居民购买力和市场供需的平衡，影响到消费与积累的比例关系。因此，该指数可以从一个侧面对上述经济活动进行观察和分析。

工业生产者出厂价格指数　是反映一定时期内全部工业产品出厂价格总水平的变动趋势和程度的相对数，包括工业企业售给本企业以外所有单位的各种产品和直接售给居民用于生活消费的产品。该指数可以观察出厂价格变动对工业总产值及增加值的影响。

工业生产者购进价格指数　是反映工业企业作为生产投入，而从物资交易市场和能源、原材料生产企业购买原材料、燃料和动力产品时，所支付的价格水平变动趋势和程度的统计指标，是扣除工业企业物质消耗成本中的价格变动影响的重要依据。

住宅销售价格指数　是反映一定时期内住宅销售价格变动趋势和程度的相对数，包括新建住宅销售价格指数、二手住宅销售价格指数。

Explanatory Notes on Main Statistical Indicators

Consumer Price Indices　reflect the trend and degree of changes in prices of consumer goods and services purchased by urban and rural households during a given period. They are obtained by combining the Urban Consumer Price Indices and the Rural Consumer Price Indices The Indices enable the observation and analysis of the degree of impact of the changes in the prices of retailed goods and services on the actual living expenses of urban and rural residents.

Retail Price Indices　reflect the trend and degree of change in retail prices of commodities during a given period. The change in retail prices of commodities directly affect the living expenditure of urban and rural residents, government revenue, purchasing power of residents and the equilibrium of market supply and demand, and the ratio of consumption to accumulation. Therefore, the retail price indices are useful to analyze the changes of the above economic activities.

Producer Price Indices for Industrial Producers　reflect the trend and degree of changes in general ex-factory prices of all industrial products during a given period, including sales of industrial products by an industrial enterprise to all units outside the enterprise, as well as sales of consumer goods to residents. It can be used to analyze the impact of ex-factory prices on gross output value and value-added of the industrial sector.

Purchasing Price Indices for Industrial Producers　reflect changes in the level and degree of prices paid by industrial enterprises when they purchase production input such as raw materials, fuels and power from the market or from other energy or raw materials producing enterprises. These indices provide important basis for measuring the material consumption of industrial enterprises after removing influence of price changes.

Sales Price Indices for Residence　reflect the trend and degree of changes in prices of residence during a given period, including sales price indices for newly constructed residential buildings and secondhand residential buildings.

9 人民生活

PEOPLE'S LIVING CONDITIONS

简要说明

一、本篇资料的主要内容

本篇资料主要反映了全市城市、农村居民的家庭收支、就业、居住、耐用消费品拥有量、生产和生活等方面的情况。

二、本篇资料的来源

1、本篇资料中城市居民家庭相关资料来源于城市住户调查年报，由国家统计局青岛调查队城镇住户调查处整理提供。

2、本篇资料中农村居民家庭相关资料来源于农村住户调查年报，由市统计局农村统计处整理提供。

3、人民生活基本情况由市统计局国民经济综合统计处加工整理。

Brief Introduction

I. Main Content

Data in this chapter show the basic conditions of the people's livelihood of the whole city, including income and expenditure of the households, employment, housing condition, consumption and possession of the major consumer goods, etc.

II. Source of Data

(1)Data on conditions of urban households are based on the annual report of sample survey on urban households and compiled by the Division of Urban Household Survey of Survey Office of the National Bureau of Statistics in Qingdao.

(2)Data on conditions of rural households are based on the annual report of sample survey on rural households and compiled by the Division of Countryside Statistics of Qingdao Municipal Bureau of Statistics.

(3)Data on basic statistics on people's living conditions are compiled by the Division of Comprehensive Statistics of Qingdao Municipal Bureau of Statistics.

9-1 人民生活基本情况(1990-2012年)
BASIC STATISTICS ON PEOPLE'S LIVING CONDITIONS(1990-2012)

		单位	Unit	2000	2005	2006	2007	2008
一、城乡居民收入	**Income of Urban and Rural Households**							
城市居民年人均可支配收入	Annual Per Capita Disposable Income of Urban Households	元	yuan	8 016	12 920	15 328	17 856	20 464
农民年人均纯收入	Annual Per Capita Net Income of Rural Households	元	yuan	3 637	5 806	6 546	7 477	8 509
二、城乡居民消费	**Expenditure of Urban and Rural Households**							
城市居民人均消费支出	Per Capita Consumption Expenditure of Urban Households	元	yuan	6 677	9 883	11 945	13 376	14 999
农村居民人均生活消费支出	Per Capita Consumption Expenditure of Rural Households	元	yuan	2 380	3 737	4 203	4 736	5 303
三、城市居民人均现住房建筑面积	**Per Capita Building Space in Urban Areas**	**平方米**	**sq. m**	**20.76**	**22.96**	**23.73**	**23.72**	**26.83**
农村居民人均居住面积	Per Capita Living Space in Rural Areas	平方米	sq. m	25.88	29.54	30.82	30.95	30.73
四、城乡居民人民币储蓄余额	**Savings Deposit of Urban and Rural Households at Year-end(RMB)**	**亿元**	**100 million yuan**	**535.32**	**1 343.10**	**1 567.62**	**1 702.04**	**2 123.36**
人均人民币储蓄余额	Per Capita Savings Deposit at Year-end (RMB)	元	yuan	7 575	18 248	21 038	22 455	27 882
五、学龄儿童入学率	**Attendance Rate of School Age Children**	**%**	**%**	**99.99**	**99.99**	**99.99**	**99.99**	**99.99**
每万人口中大学在校学生	Students Enrollment of University Per 10000 Population	人	person	65	324	347	349	354
六、城市每百户拥有彩色电视机	**Color TV Per 100 Urban Households**	**台**	**set**	**120.00**	**118.25**	**124.5**	**121.84**	**116.00**
城市每百户拥有电冰箱	Refrigerators Per 100 Urban Households	台	set	94.30	94.50	98.5	106.70	102.75
七、每万人口拥有医疗床位	**Hospital Beds Per 10 000 Population**	**张**	**bed**	**34.5**	**41.3**	**38.3**	**39.7**	**42.5**
每万人口拥有医生	Doctors Per 10000 Population	人	person	21.0	20.3	20.6	19.8	21.4
八、城市每一就业者负担人数(包括本人)	**Number of Dependents Per Employee of Urban Household(including the employee himself or herself)**	**人**	**person**	**1.82**	**1.97**	**1.79**	**1.79**	**1.77**
农村每一就业者负担人数(包括本人)	Number of Dependents Per Employee of Rural Household (including the employee himself or herself)	人	person	1.33	1.33	1.34	1.33	1.33
九、农民与城市居民人均年收入对比	**Contrast of Rural and Urban Residents in Annual Per Capita Income**			**1:2.2**	**1:2.2**	**1:2.34**	**1:2.39**	**1:2.41**
农民与城市居民人均年生活费支出对比	Contrast of Rural and Urban Residents in Annual Per Capita Living Expenditure			1:2.8	1:2.6	1:2.84	1:2.82	1:2.83

注：1. 自2002年起城市居民年人均可支配收入为新口径。农民与城市居民人均年收入对比,农民以纯收入,城市居民以可支配收入计算。

2. 城乡居民住房面积分别根据城乡住户抽样调查取得。

Note: 1. Since 2002, new calibre has been adopted in per capita annual disposable income of urban households. The calculation of contrast of rural and urban residents in per capita annual income is using net income of rural residents and disposable income of urban residents.

2. Figures relating to floor space among urban and rural dwellers were based on a survey.

9-1 续表
continued

		单位	Unit	2009	2010	2011	2012
一、城乡居民收入	**Income of Urban and Rural Households**						
城市居民年人均可支配收入	Annual Per Capita Disposable Income of Urban Households	元	yuan	22 368	24 998	28 567	32 145
农民年人均纯收入	Annual Per Capita Net Income of Rural Households	元	yuan	9 249	10 550	12 370	13 990
二、城乡居民消费	**Expenditure of Urban and Rural Households**						
城市居民人均消费支出	Per Capita Consumption Expenditure of Urban Households	元	yuan	16 080	17 531	19 297	20 391
农村居民人均生活消费支出	Per Capita Consumption Expenditure of Rural Households	元	yuan	5 832	6 662	7 661	8 653
三、城市居民人均现住房建筑面积	**Per Capita Building Space in Urban Areas**	**平方米**	**sq. m**	**26.71**	**27.42**	**27.67**	**27.86**
农村居民人均居住面积	Per Capita Living Space in Rural Areas	平方米	sq. m	31.39	30.97	31.73	32.32
四、城乡居民人民币储蓄余额	**Savings Deposit of Urban and Rural Households at Year-end (RMB)**	**亿元**	**100 million yuan**	**2 527.87**	**2 912.33**	**3 198.51**	**3 757.60**
人均人民币储蓄余额	Per Capita Savings Deposit at Year-end (RMB)	元	yuan	33 134	38 137	41 736	48 828
五、学龄儿童入学率	**Attendance Rate of School Age Children**	**%**	**%**	**99.99**	**99.99**	**99.99**	**99.99**
每万人口中大学在校学生	Students Enrollment of University Per 10000 Population	人	person	361	373	380	386
六、城市每百户拥有彩色电视机	**Color TV Per 100 Urban Households**	**台**	**set**	**117.50**	**118.5**	**117.25**	**115.00**
城市每百户拥有电冰箱	Refrigerators Per 100 Urban Households	台	set	105.00	106.75	108.25	108.00
七、每万人口拥有医疗床位	**Hospital Beds Per 10 000 Population**	**张**	**bed**	**43.0**	**47.2**	**52.2**	**61.4**
每万人口拥有医生	Doctors Per 10000 Population	人	person	21.9	23.2	23.9	28.1
八、城市每一就业者负担人数(包括本人)	**Number of Dependents Per Employee of Urban Household (including the employee himself or herself)**	**人**	**person**	**1.73**	**1.75**	**1.71**	**1.69**
农村每一就业者负担人数(包括本人)	Number of Dependents Per Employee of Rural Household (including the employee himself or herself)	人	person	1.34	1.33	1.48	1.46
九、农民、城市居民人均年收入对比	**Contrast of Rural and Urban Residents in Annual Per Capita Income**			**1:2.42**	**1:2.37**	**1:2.31**	**1:2.30**
农民、城市居民人均年生活费支出对比	Contrast of Rural and Urban Residents in Annual Per Capita Living Expenditure			1:2.76	1:2.63	1:2.52	1:2.36

9-2 城市居民家庭收支情况（2012年）

BASIC CONDITIONS ON INCOME AND EXPENDITURE OF URBAN HOUSEHOLDS(2012)

单位：元(yuan)

指标名称	Name	2012	2011	2012年比2011年增长(±%) 2012/2011(±%)
人均家庭总收入	**Per Capita Total Income of Household**	**35 146**	**31 492**	**11.6**
其中 人均可支配收入	of which: Per Capita Disposable Income	32 145	28 567	12.5
（一）工资性收入	Income from Wages and Salaries	22 811	20 100	13.5
（二）经营性净收入	Net Income from Household Operations	2 980	2 710	10.0
（三）财产性收入	Income from Properties	1 141	1 055	8.1
（四）转移性收入	Income from Transfers	8 214	7 627	7.7
人均消费性支出	**Per Capita Consumption Expenditure**	**20 391**	**19 297**	**5.7**
（一）食品	Food	7 450	7 241	2.9
（二）衣着	Clothing	2 851	2 593	10.0
（三）居住	Residence	1 971	1 783	10.5
（四）家庭设备用品及服务	Household Facilities, Articles and Services	1 272	1 139	11.7
（五）医疗保健	Health Care and Medical Services	1 149	1 085	6.0
（六）交通和通讯	Transportation and Communication	2 664	2 901	-8.2
（七）教育文化娱乐服务	Education, Cultural and Recreation Services	2 067	1 930	7.1
（八）其他商品和服务	Other Goods and Services	966	626	54.4

9-3 城市居民家庭基本情况（2012 年）
BASIC CONDITIONS OF URBAN HOUSEHOLDS(2012)

项　目	Item	单位	Unit
调查户数	Number of Households Surveyed	户	household
平均每户人口数	Average Household Size	人	person
户均有收入者人数	Average Number of Persons Having Income Per Household	人	person
户均就业人口数	Average Number of Employed Persons Per Household	人	person
#国有经济单位职工人数	Working in State-owned Units	人	person
集体经济单位职工人数	Working in Collective-owned Units	人	person
聘留离退休人员数	Number of Retired Persons Employed Again	人	person
户均离退休人数	Average Number of Retired Persons Per Household	人	person
户均其他有收入者人数	Average Number of Other Persons Having Income Per Household	人	person
户均无收入者人数	Average Number of Persons Having No Income Per Household	人	person
平均每人期初手存现金	Per Capita Cash on Hand Term-beginning	元	yuan
平均每人每年家庭总收入	Per Capita Annual Income	元	yuan
#平均每人每年可支配收入	Per Capita Annual Disposable Income	元	yuan
平均每人每年出售财物收入	Per Capita Annual Income of Selling Properties	元	yuan
平均每人每年借贷收入	Per Capita Annual Savings and Lending Income	元	yuan
平均每人每年家庭总支出	Per Capita Annual Expenditure	元	yuan
#平均每人每年消费支出	Per Capita Annual Consumption Expenditure	元	yuan
平均每人每年储蓄借贷支出	Per Capita Annual Savings and Lending Expenditure	元	yuan
平均每人期末手存现金	Per Capita Cash on Hand Term-end	元	yuan
平均每一就业者负担人口(包括本人)	Number of Dependents Per Employee(including the employee himself or herself)	人	person

全[illegible]平均 A[illegible]erage	最低收入户 Lowest Income Households	低收入户 Low Income Households	较低收入户 Lower Middle Income Households
400	40	40	80
2.82	2.98	3.08	2.82
2.29	2.05	2.39	2.32
1.67	1.87	1.7	1.64
0.72	0.56	0.65	0.67
0.14	0.24	0.05	0.1
0.29		0.03	0.02
0.6	0.17	0.67	0.64
0.02		0.03	0.04
0.53	0.92	0.69	0.50
1 [illegible]87.50	1 119.83	879.31	1 751.35
[illegible]5 145.94	15 190.44	21 300.40	25 505.05
[illegible]2 144.73	12 709.63	18 771.13	22 558.36
[illegible]62.89		1.42	0.12
[illegible]2 [illegible]28.72	9 499.91	11 952.37	12 177.32
25 [illegible]83.12	14 306.56	18 512.66	20 260.64
20 391.08	11 024.24	14 811.73	16 021.24
20 523.65	10 467.62	14 124.24	16 812.27
3 196.11	602.49	2 087.14	2 984.06
1.69	1.59	1.81	1.72

9-3 续表
continued

项　目	Item	单位	Unit
调查户数	Number of Households Surveyed	户	household
平均每户人口数	Average Household Size	人	person
户均有收入者人数	Average Number of Persons Having Income Per Household	人	person
户均就业人口数	Average Number of Employed Persons Per Household	人	person
#国有经济单位职工人数	Working in State-owned Units	人	person
集体经济单位职工人数	Working in Collective-owned Units	人	person
聘留离退休人员数	Number of Retired Persons Employed Again	人	person
户均离退休人数	Average Number of Retired Persons Per Household	人	person
户均其他有收入者人数	Average Number of Other Persons Having Income Per Household	人	person
户均无收入者人数	Average Number of Persons Having No Income Per Household	人	person
平均每人期初手存现金	Per Capita Cash on Hand Term-beginning	元	yuan
平均每人每年家庭总收入	Per Capita Annual Income	元	yuan
#平均每人每年可支配收入	Per Capita Annual Disposable Income	元	yuan
平均每人每年出售财物收入	Per Capita Annual Income of Selling Properties	元	yuan
平均每人每年借贷收入	Per Capita Annual Savings and Lending Income	元	yuan
平均每人每年家庭总支出	Per Capita Annual Expenditure	元	yuan
#平均每人每年消费支出	Per Capita Annual Consumption Expenditure	元	yuan
平均每人每年储蓄借贷支出	Per Capita Annual Savings and Lending Expenditure	元	yuan
平均每人期末手存现金	Per Capita Cash on Hand Term-end	元	yuan
平均每一就业者负担人口(包括本人)	Number of Dependents Per Employee(including the employee himself or herself)	人	person

中间收入户 Middle Income Households	较高收入户 Upper Middle Income Households	高收入户 High Income Households	最高收入户 Highest Income Households
80	80	40	40
[illegible].78	2.8	2.61	2.72
[illegible].33	2.29	2.29	2.3
[illegible].71	1.62	1.61	1.56
[illegible].61	0.76	0.7	1.18
[illegible].24	0.14	0.11	0.03
[illegible].05	0.02	0.01	0.03
[illegible].62	0.64	0.65	0.74
	0.03	0.03	
[illegible].45	0.51	0.32	0.42
1 36[illegible].02	1 919.36	2 745.41	2 208.81
32 22[illegible].07	38 218.92	49 528.41	81 240.87
28 97[illegible].02	35 489.90	46 000.27	77 399.62
[illegible].49	0.10		674.72
10 78[illegible].24	10 509.17	12 750.90	22 157.40
23 32[illegible].83	26 694.31	36 482.15	48 235.28
18 29[illegible].72	22 475.68	30 469.33	37 449.21
18 13[illegible].61	19 832.18	23 748.37	51 351.40
2 93[illegible].04	4 347.46	3 209.22	5 950.73
1.63	1.73	1.62	1.74

9－4 农村居民家庭基本情况(1990－2012 年)
BASIC CONDITIONS OF RURAL HOUSEHOLDS(1990－2012)

项　目	Item
调查户数(户)	**Number of Households Surveyed(household)**
常住人口(人)	Number of Permanent Residents(person)
平均每户常住人口(人)	Average Number of Permanent Residents Per Household(person)
平均每户整半劳力(人)	Average Number of Full/Semi Labour Force Per Household(person)
平均每个劳动力负担人口(含本人)(人)	Average Number of Dependents Per Labour Force(including the labour force himself or herself)(person)
总收入(元)	**Total Income(yuan)**
工资性收入	Income from Wages and Salaries
家庭经营收入	Income from Household Operations
财产性收入	Income from Properties
转移性收入	Income from Transfers
现金收入(元)	**Cash Income(yuan)**
工资性收入	Income from Wages and Salaries
家庭经营收入	Income from Household Operations
财产性收入	Income from Properties
转移性收入	Income from Transfers
总支出(元)	**Total Expenditure(yuan)**
家庭经营费用支出	Expenditure for Household Operations
购置生产性固定资产	Purchase of Productive Fixed Assets
税费支出	Taxes and Fees
生活消费支出	Expenditure on Household Consumption
转移性和财产性支出	Expenditure on Properties and Transfers
现金支出(元)	**Cash Expenditure(yuan)**
家庭经营费用支出	Expenditure for Household Operations
购买生产性固定资产	Purchase of Productive Fixed Assets
税费支出	Taxes and Fees
生活消费支出	Expenditure on Household Consumption
转移性和财产性支出	Expenditure on Properties and Transfers
平均每人年纯收入(元)	**Per Capita Annual Net Income(yuan)**
工资性收入	Income from Wages and Salaries
家庭经营纯收入	Income from Household Operations
财产性收入	Income from Properties
转移性收入	Income from Transfers

1990	1995	2000	2005	2006	2007	2008	2009	2010	2011	2012
2 300	**770**	**820**	**860**	**900**	**900**	**900**	**900**	**900**	**680**	**680**
9 598	2 919	2 856	2 964	3 073	3 066	3 077	3 069	3 061	2 263	2 222
4.17	3.79	3.48	3.45	3.41	3.41	3.42	3.41	3.40	3.33	3.27
2.6	2.69	2.61	2.59	2.58	2.58	2.59	2.56	2.58	2.37	2.38
1.6	1.41	1.33	1.33	1.32	1.32	1.32	1.33	1.32	1.40	1.38
1 398	**3 516**	**5 394**	**8 370**	**9 464**	**10 881**	**12 381**	**13 299**	**14 993**	**17 156**	**19 567**
267	816	1 481	2 402	2 783	3 178	3 518	3 820	4 361	5 418	6 308
1 095	2 600	3 802	5 565	6 297	7 230	8 257	8 778	9 840	10 840	12 216
36	42	32	236	192	226	293	334	364	281	309
	58	79	167	192	247	314	367	427	617	734
1 087	**2 126**	**4 554**	**7 403**	**8 633**	**10 188**	**11 487**	**12 668**	**14 090**	**15 589**	**18 112**
267	816	1 479	2 400	2 775	3 177	3 512	3 819	4 361	5 367	6 282
784	1 207	2 428	4 603	5 460	6 544	7 395	8 203	8 882	9 420	10 857
	31	24	233	212	226	270	288	425	222	284
36	72	135	167	186	241	309	358	422	580	689
1 104	**3 093**	**4 223**	**6 363**	**7 198**	**8 144**	**9 144**	**9 871**	**11 031**	**13 192**	**14 832**
349	1 127	1 536	2 244	2 560	2 937	3 401	3 570	3 931	4 222	4 919
21	59	144	192	148	121	98	108	104	280	310
74	98	103	27	14	12	9	9	7	8	8
633	1 723	2 380	3 737	4 203	4 736	5 303	5 832	6 662	7 661	8 653
27	86	60	162	271	333	329	351	327	1 019	936
1 004	**2 377**	**3 883**	**5 700**	**6 737**	**7 851**	**8 771**	**9 474**	**10 655**	**12 779**	**14 462**
224	539	941	1 833	2 279	2 809	3 245	3 482	3 812	4 095	4 797
20	59	144	192	148	121	98	108	104	280	310
66	98	96	27	13	9	9	8	6	8	8
494	1 295	2 080	3 486	4 026	4 575	5 088	5 524	6 406	7 389	8 420
34	78	117	162	269	332	329	351	327	1 006	922
952	**2 225**	**3 637**	**5 806**	**6 546**	**7 477**	**8 509**	**9 249**	**10 550**	**12 370**	**13 990**
267	816	1 481	2 402	2 783	3 178	3 518	3 820	4 361	5 418	6 308
65[illegible]	1 320	2 059	3 026	3 406	3 859	4 419	4 775	5 453	6 122	6 718
	42	32	236	192	226	293	334	364	281	309
30	47	65	142	165	214	280	319	372	549	656

9-5 城市住户每百户家庭主要耐用品拥有量（1980-2012年）
OWNERSHIP OF MAJOR DURABLE CONSUMER GOODS PER 100 URBAN HOUSEHOLDS(1980-2012)

年份 Year	家用电脑（台）Computer (set)	钢琴（架）Piano (set)	空调器（台）Air Conditioner (set)	淋浴热水器（台）Water Heater (set)	洗衣机（台）Washing Machine (set)	电冰箱（台）Refrigerator (set)	家用汽车（辆）Automobile (unit)	彩色电视机（台）Color TV (set)	移动电话（部）Cell Phone (unit)	照相机（架）Camera (set)
1980										2.0
1981					12.0			1.0		2.0
1982					22.0			2.0		4.0
1983					27.0	1.0		6.0		6.0
1984					30.0	2.0		8.0		8.0
1985					35.5	3.5		17.5		13.5
1986					40.0	4.5		24.5		15.0
1987					51.5	18.0		33.5		17.5
1988					60.5	33.0		47.0		20.5
1989					67.0	50.0		59.0		22.0
1990					66.0	62.0		68.0		26.0
1991					70.0	76.0		82.0		33.0
1992		1.0		12.5	72.5	83.0		81.0		38.5
1993		2.0	0.5	18.0	82.5	85.5		87.5		49.5
1994		4.0	1.0	17.0	81.0	88.5		92.0		51.0
1995		4.0	3.0	33.5	81.5	89.0		100.0		60.5
1996		4.5	6.5	39.5	83.0	91.5		105.0		63.0
1997	1.0	4.5	9.0	46.5	83.0	93.0		110.5	2.5	63.0
1998	8.3	5.3	16.5	53.0	83.0	91.8		110.8	6.8	69.4
1999	10.5	3.8	21.8	61.3	83.0	93.5		117.3	15.0	68.5
2000	19.3	2.0	24.5	65.8	83.3	94.3		120.0	30.3	69.5
2001	20.0	2.3	24.3	65.8	84.0	92.8		127.5	36.0	68.5
2002	31.5	2.3	38.3	75.3	89.3	93.0	0.5	123.3	80.0	72.8
2003	40.8	3.3	47.5	76.3	90.5	92.8	0.3	124.8	105.5	70.0
2004	46.0	3.0	55.0	79.0	92.5	92.5	2.0	123.5	128.0	68.3
2005	55.0	4.3	69.3	83.8	91.8	94.8	3.8	118.3	152.8	72.3
2006	71.3	7.8	89.3	88.0	97.3	98.5	6.3	124.5	187.0	81.8
2007	75.4	7.4	98.3	93.3	99.8	106.7	7.9	121.8	193.8	82.9
2008	75.0	5.0	93.8	90.3	94.5	102.8	12.8	116.0	190.8	67.0
2009	81.8	6.5	98.3	90.5	96.3	105.0	18.0	117.5	199.0	70.8
2010	86.0	7.5	99.3	90.8	97.3	106.8	20.3	118.5	207.5	71.0
2011	95.0	8.0	103.0	91.5	98.0	108.3	22.0	117.3	218.8	76.5
2012	100.8	9.0	103.5	92.8	97.5	108.0	28.5	115.0	230.5	78.8

9-6 城市居民家庭居住情况
HOUSING CONDITIONS OF URBAN HOUSEHOLDS

类别	Category	2005	2006	2007	2008	2009	2010	2011	2012
现住房总建筑面积（平方米/人）	**Floor Space of Houses (sq. m/person)**	**22.96**	**23.73**	**23.71**	**26.83**	**26.71**	**27.42**	**27.67**	**27.86**
房屋产权（合计）	**Housing Property**	**100.00**	**100.00**	**100.00**	**100.00**	**100.00**	**100.00**	**100.00**	**100.00**
租赁公房（%）	Leasehold of Public Housing(%)	11.00	11.00	7.50	2.25	1.75	2.00	5.25	5.25
租赁私房（%）	Leasehold of Private Housing(%)	1.75	2.00	2.25	3.75	3.25	3.00	2.25	2.50
原有私房（%）	Original Private Housing(%)	17.50	14.00	3.75	12.00	14.25	14.00	9.50	6.75
房改私房（%）	Private Housing After Housing Reform(%)	59.25	52.25	53.75	53.25	51.00	52.25	49.50	46.25
商品房（%）	Condominium(%)	10.00	20.00	32.00	27.75	29.00	27.75	32.00	37.00
借用房									2.00
其它（%）	Others(%)	0.50	0.75	0.75	1.00	0.75	1.00	1.50	0.25
住宅建筑式样（合计）	**Style of Residential Building**	**100.00**	**100.00**	**100.00**	**100.00**	**100.00**	**100.00**	**100.00**	**100.00**
单栋住宅（%）	Monomer House(%)	1.75	1.75	0.25	2.50	3.00	2.75	0.75	0.25
四居室（%）	Four Bedrooms Department(%)	1.50	2.00	3.50	1.00	1.75	2.75	3.75	2.75
三居室（%）	Three Bedrooms Department(%)	16.75	19.75	20.00	26.00	25.75	26.50	29.00	27.50
二居室（%）	Two Bedrooms Department(%)	64.75	63.25	60.50	55.75	55.25	53.75	51.75	56.00
一居室（%）	One Bedroom Department(%)	5.75	5.75	3.25	2.25	2.25	2.25	3.00	3.50
普通楼房（%）	Ordinary Building(%)	5.75	5.25	9.50	10.00	8.00	8.00	9.75	7.75

9－6 续表
continued

类　别	Category	2005	2006	2007	2008	2009	2010	2011	2012
平房及其它(%)	Bungalow and Others(%)	3.75	2.25	3.00	2.50	4.00	4.00	2.00	2.25
卫生设备(合计)	**Sanitary Equipment**	**100.00**	**100.00**	**100.00**	**100.00**	**100.00**	**100.00**	**100.00**	**100.00**
无卫生设备(%)	No Sanitary Equipment(%)			0.25	0.25				
有厕所浴室(%)	Having Toilet and Bathroom(%)	89.00	92.75	92.50	89.00	89.75	89.75	90.75	91.5
有厕所无浴室(%)	Having Toilet but No Bathroom (%)	6.50	3.25	3.25	8.75	8.25	8.00	5.75	4.75
公用(%)	Public Sanitary Equipment(%)	4.50	4.00	4.00	2.00	2.00	2.25	3.50	3.75
取暖设备(合计)	**Heating Equipment**	**100.00**	**100.00**	**100.00**	**100.00**	**100.00**	**100.00**	**100.00**	**100.00**
无取暖设备(%)	No Heating Equipment(%)	2.75	2.50	3.25	6.00	2.75	2.75	2.75	1.75
空调设备(%)	Having Air Conditioner(%)	41.75	43.25	35.25	24.00	25.50	25.50	22.00	14.75
暖气(%)	Having Heater(%)	36.00	43.50	46.25	57.50	60.75	62.00	68.00	77.5
其它(%)	Others(%)	19.50	10.75	15.25	12.50	11.00	9.75	7.25	6.00
炊用燃料使用情况(合计)	**Conditions of Cooking Fuel**	**100.00**	**100.00**	**100.00**	**100.00**	**100.00**	**100.00**	**100.00**	**100.00**
管道煤气(%)	Tap Gas(%)	55.00	61.00	61.25	58.50	61.50	61.75	67.50	76.96
液化石油气(%)	Liquid Natural Gas(%)	42.75	36.50	37.25	36.75	35.50	36.25	31.00	22.3
煤(%)	Coal(%)	2.25	2.00	0.75	4.50	2.75	1.75	1.25	0.74
其他(%)	Others(%)		0.50	0.75	0.25	0.25	0.25	0.25	

9-7 城市居民家庭消费构成
COMPOSITION OF URBAN HOUSEHOLDS CONSUMPTION

项目	Item	2012		2011	
		年人均支出金额(元) Per Capita Annual Expenditure(yuan)	占消费支出的比重(%) Percentage to Consumption Expenditure(%)	年人均支出金额(元) Per Capita Annual Expenditure(yuan)	占消费支出的比重(%) Percentage to Consumption Expenditure(%)
消费支出	**Consumption Expenditure**	**20 391.08**	**100.0**	**19 296.56**	**100.0**
一、食品	**Food**	**7 449.95**	**36.5**	**7 240.95**	**37.5**
#1.粮食	Grain	394.07	1.9	415.84	2.2
2.油脂	Oil or Fat	171.62	0.8	165.97	0.9
3.肉禽及其制品	Meat,Poultry and Processed Products	1 185.10	5.8	1 231.74	6.4
4.蛋类	Eggs	183.41	0.9	197.28	1.0
5.水产品	Aquatic Products	1 000.20	4.9	926.96	4.8
6.菜类	Vegetables	654.72	3.2	637.65	3.3
7.烟草	Tobacco	248.36	1.2	248.59	1.3
8.酒和饮料	Liquor and Beverages	662.85	3.3	647.31	3.4
9.干鲜果品	Dried and Fresh Melons and Fruits	819.97	4.0	758.03	3.9
10.奶及奶制品	Milk and Its Products	340.54	1.7	342.03	1.8
二、衣着	**Clothing**	**2 851.41**	**14.0**	**2 592.52**	**13.4**
#1.服装	Garments	2 109.18	10.3	1 830.37	9.5
2.衣着材料	Clothing Materials	18.11	0.1	14.90	0.1
三、家庭设备用品及服务	**Household Facilities, Articles and Services**	**1 272.15**	**6.2**	**1 138.59**	**5.9**
#日用耐用消费品	Daily Use Durable Consumer Goods	538.86	2.6	399.11	2.1
四、医疗保健	**Health Care and Medical Sevices**	**1 149.45**	**5.6**	**1 084.56**	**5.6**
五、交通与通讯	**Transportation and Communication**	**2 664.32**	**13.1**	**2 901.06**	**15.0**
六、娱乐教育文化服务	**Education, Cultural and Recreation Services**	**2 066.97**	**10.1**	**1 930.02**	**10.0**
1.文化娱乐用品	Cultural and Recreational Articles	635.43	3.1	587.33	3.0
2.文化娱乐服务	Cultural and Recreational Services	730.48	3.6	551.00	2.9
3.教育	Education	701.06	3.4	791.69	4.1
七、居住	**Residence**	**1 971.14**	**9.7**	**1 783.37**	**9.2**
八、杂项商品与服务	**Miscellaneous Goods and Services**	**965.70**	**4.7**	**625.50**	**3.2**

9－8 城市居民家庭年人均消费支出（2012年）
PER CAPITA ANNUAL CONSUMPTION EXPENDITURE OF URBAN HOUSEHOLDS (2012)

项　目	Item	全市平均 Average	最低收入户 Lowest Income Households	低收入户 Low Income Households
一、食品	**Food**	**7 449.95**	**5 283.38**	**6 098.11**
（一）粮油类	Grain and Oil	675.49	678.30	645.38
1. 粮食	Grain	394.07	371.64	364.43
2. 淀粉及薯类	Starches and Tubers	55.73	61.15	57.05
3. 干豆类及豆制品	Beans and Bean Products	54.07	49.39	58.30
4. 油脂类	Oil or Fat	171.62	196.11	165.60
（二）肉禽蛋水产品类	Meat, Poultry, Eggs and Aquatic Products	2 368.71	1 783.53	1 982.63
1. 肉类	Meat	983.69	751.65	917.99
2. 禽类	Poultry	201.41	163.40	182.04
3. 蛋类	Eggs	183.41	154.46	168.89
4. 水产品类	Aquatic Products	1 000.20	714.03	713.71
（三）蔬菜类	Vegetables	654.72	523.08	599.54
1. 鲜菜	Fresh Vegetables	605.88	486.61	547.82
2. 干菜	Dried Vegetables	34.86	28.01	43.81
3. 菜制品	Vegetable Products	13.97	8.47	7.91
（四）调味品	Flavoring	87.78	28.01	43.81
（五）糖烟酒饮料类	Carbohydrate, Tobacco, Liquor and Beverages	972.87	8.47	7.91
1. 糖类	Carbohydrate	61.66	47.13	49.88
2. 烟草类	Tobacco	248.36	178.84	201.29
3. 酒类	Liquor	386.86	226.18	259.15
4. 饮料	Beverages	275.99	218.53	200.33
（六）干鲜瓜果类	Dried and Fresh Melons and Fruits	819.97	561.57	647.82
1. 鲜果	Fresh Fruits	531.09	346.80	4[illegible]1.22
2. 鲜瓜	Fresh Melons	48.42	35.61	40.49
（七）糕点、奶及奶制品	Cake, Milk and Its Products	498.86	407.01	386.22
1. 糕点	Cake	158.31	132.69	131.08
2. 奶及奶制品	Milk and Its Products	340.54	274.31	255.14
（八）其他食品	Other Foods	130.89	62.25	6[illegible].48
（九）饮食服务	Catering Services	1 240.65	533.04	967.07
1. 食品加工服务费	Manufacturing Services	1.60	2.21	[illegible].27
2. 在外饮食	Outward Dinner	1 239.05	530.83	966.80
非食品类	**Non-food**	**4 992.04**	**3 282.32**	**3 700.93**
二、衣着	**Clothing**	**2 851.41**	**1 339.70**	**1 504.69**
（一）服装	Garments	2 109.18	1 013.33	1 068.59

单位:元(yuan)

较低收入户 Lower Middle Income Households	中间收入户 Middle Income Households	较高收入户 Upper Middle Income Households	高收入户 High Income Households	最高收入户 Highest Income Households
7 [illegible]0[illegible].63	**7 586.27**	**8 267.37**	**8 803.71**	**8 941.37**
[illegible]1[illegible].41	673.22	680.99	623.73	660.02
[illegible]2[illegible].10	400.82	402.78	336.56	417.47
5[illegible].71	50.73	53.10	55.20	55.94
5[illegible].94	55.83	51.65	54.82	49.18
17[illegible].65	165.84	173.46	177.15	137.43
2 40[illegible].02	2 566.20	2 396.48	2 482.97	2 845.74
1 02[illegible].48	1 015.85	1 005.85	1 048.80	1 066.13
2[illegible]4.09	242.28	194.74	206.41	186.39
1[illegible]1.05	184.53	188.51	190.16	197.67
9[illegible]4.40	1 123.55	1 007.39	1 037.60	1 395.55
6[illegible]5.73	681.25	697.77	682.80	626.60
6[illegible]6.09	629.21	643.73	633.13	567.81
[illegible]0.10	37.94	38.08	32.51	31.48
[illegible]0.54	14.10	15.96	17.17	27.31
[illegible]0.10	37.94	38.08	32.51	31.48
[illegible]0.54	14.10	15.96	17.17	27.31
63.73	62.27	69.46	55.56	75.73
[illegible]51.34	219.40	274.01	419.38	216.07
[illegible]14.55	448.81	467.72	444.63	507.66
[illegible]54.59	232.63	298.38	457.70	343.56
[illegible]02.46	826.77	896.87	841.13	943.08
[illegible]67.98	538.80	578.59	562.53	645.44
58.21	54.26	52.97	44.03	33.46
[illegible]25.82	502.45	598.19	571.58	602.76
[illegible]36.84	159.12	171.38	159.09	236.34
[illegible]88.98	343.33	426.81	412.48	366.43
117.82	105.77	159.06	261.48	184.97
[illegible]90.55	1 175.63	1 621.78	1 868.17	1 844.61
4.23	1.01	0.18	1.26	1.39
886.32	1 174.62	1 621.60	1 866.92	1 843.21
4 239.40	**5 022.11**	**4 128.63**	**6 012.82**	**10 786.07**
[illegible] 573.30	**2 669.05**	**3 156.99**	**4 055.89**	**5 354.41**
1 853.89	1 911.22	2 315.24	3 014.64	4 257.60

9-8 续表1
continued

项　　目	Item	全市平均 Average	最低收入户 Lowest Income Households	低收入户 Low Income Households
（二）衣着材料	Clothing Materials	18.11	24.25	18.68
（三）鞋类	Shoes	614.65	257.33	369.08
（四）其他衣着用品	Other Clothing Articles	99.27	41.71	41.98
（五）衣着加工服务费	Clothing Manufacturing Services	10.21	3.08	6.37
三、家庭设备用品及服务	**Household Facilities, Articles and Services**	**1 272.15**	**468.42**	**950.27**
（一）耐用消费品	Durable Consumer Goods	538.86	158.75	409.92
1. 家具	Furniture	131.40	0.98	173.48
2. 家庭设备	Household Facilities	407.45	157.77	236.44
（1）洗衣机	Washing Machine	62.89	26.23	24.15
（2）电冰箱	Household Refrigerator	69.24	8.61	32.76
（3）微波炉	Microwave Oven	14.91	11.48	49.63
（4）空调器	Air Conditioner	54.03	49.19	
（5）淋浴热水器	Water Heater	36.31		49.27
（6）消毒碗柜	Sterilized Cabinet	0.89		8.13
（7）洗碗机	Dishwasher			
（8）其他	Others	169.18	62.27	72.50
（二）室内装饰品	Interior Decorations	39.94	0.71	20.86
（三）床上用品	Bed Articles	114.56	21.32	86.05
（四）家庭日用杂品	Daily Use Household Articles	520.87	278.02	360.18
（五）家具材料	Furniture Materias	31.48		13.27
（六）家庭服务	Household Services	26.45	9.61	59.99
1. 家政服务	Household Management Services	5.71		1.63
2. 加工维修服务费	Maintenance and Renovation Services	20.74	9.61	58.37
四、医疗保健	**Health Care and Medical Sevices**	**1 149.45**	**484.82**	**867.49**
（一）医疗器具	Medical Articles	6.87		29.11
（二）保健器具	Health Protection Articles	27.44	5.89	38.72
（三）药品费	Medicines	381.63	111.81	347.08
（四）滋补保健品	Health Protection Products	359.60	207.48	125.31
（五）医疗费	Medical Services	355.98	154.76	316.09
（六）其他	Others	17.93	4.89	11.17
五、交通和通讯	**Transportation and Communication**	**2 664.32**	**1 174.75**	**1 577.21**
（一）交通	Transportation	1 632.58	463.45	608.55
1. 家庭交通工具	Traffic Instruments	367.96	10.03	0.17

单位：元（yuan）

较低收入户 Lower Middle Income Households	中间收入户 Middle Income Households	较高收入户 Upper Middle Income Households	高收入户 High Income Households	最高收入户 Highest Income Households
1[illegible].88	19.76	15.82	23.94	15.21
505.03	624.97	673.99	892.08	920.44
8[illegible].13	104.18	142.49	106.14	144.88
1[illegible].36	8.91	9.44	19.09	16.27
1 025.96	**1 176.15**	**1 493.99**	**1 743.16**	**2 379.85**
450.78	497.12	611.46	712.28	1 087.79
85.40	21.45	157.53	268.68	375.07
365.38	475.67	453.94	443.60	712.72
[illegible]5.42	85.70	72.31	48.89	112.94
39.40	39.83	126.04	94.84	161.34
12.31	7.72	11.84	13.59	6.72
56.90	52.22	60.16	84.86	121.02
32.85	52.20	34.19	29.33	49.07
188.49	238.01	149.38	172.09	261.63
29.21	47.96	19.32	110.62	90.49
94.32	75.50	160.31	248.48	152.60
416.49	492.08	640.42	666.06	879.86
26.29	48.41	34.39	0.49	89.48
11.88	15.07	28.09	5.23	79.62
1.37	1.34	1.19		51.44
10.51	13.73	26.90	5.23	28.18
521.59	**1 038.42**	**1 528.05**	**2 150.44**	**2 054.55**
	1.46	3.48	0.06	29.21
26.87	32.27	37.49	11.49	24.11
232.18	401.99	473.46	453.05	750.68
136.42	295.40	513.29	702.12	764.68
120.69	297.97	485.19	939.37	419.16
5.42	9.32	15.15	44.35	66.71
1 480.86	**1 786.50**	**3 189.15**	**4 969.32**	**6 717.46**
562.09	802.84	2 076.32	3 715.71	5 283.03
14.44	32.30	500.34	1 621.12	1 181.37

9 -8 续表 2
continued

项　　目	Item	全市平均 Average	最低收入户 Lowest Income Households	低收入户 Low Income Households
(1)摩托车	Motor	16.70		
(3)助力车	Motorbike	6.02		
(4)家用汽车	Automobile	338.24		
(5)其他交通工具	Other Traffic Instruments	7.00	10.03	0.17
2.车辆用燃料及零配件	Fuels and Automobile Spare Parts	697.60	180.60	293.37
(1)燃料	Fuels	676.82	180.60	273.05
(2)零配件	Automobile Spare Parts	5.01		
(3)其他	Others	15.78		20.33
3.交通工具服务支出	Expenditure on Traffic Instrument Services	274.79	39.26	35.20
(1)维修费	Mending Cost	57.64	27.79	16.24
(2)车辆使用税费	Vehicle Usage Tax	158.97	11.07	16.80
(3)其它车辆使用费用	Other Cost of Vehicle Usage	58.18	0.41	2.15
4.交通费	Traffic Expenses	292.23	233.56	273.81
(1)飞机	Air Plane	53.18	20.90	20.98
(2)火车	Train	42.02	64.79	38.81
(3)长途汽车	Long-distance Bus	20.67	12.81	17.50
(4)市内公共交通	Bus	118.72	98.41	145.39
(5)出租汽车费	Taxi	48.30	35.03	49.57
(6)其他交通费	Other Traffic Expenses	9.34	1.62	1.56
(二)通信	Communication	1 031.74	711.30	968.66
1.通信工具	Communication Instruments	236.70	109.17	164.30
(1)电话机	Telephone	15.71	32.38	7.86
(2)移动电话	Cell Phone	213.18	73.43	154.61
(3)其他通信工具	Other Communication Instruments	7.80	3.36	1.83
2.通信服务	Communication Services	795.03	602.13	804.36
(1)电信费	Telecommunications	776.58	597.75	774.26
(2)邮费	Postage	2.32		2.80
(3)其他	Others	16.14	4.38	27.30
六、教育文化娱乐服务	**Education, Cultural and Recreation Services**	**2 066.97**	**945.75**	**1 567.62**
(一)文化娱乐用品	Cultural and Recreational Articles	635.43	132.80	323.95
1.彩色电视机	Color TV Set	181.61	0.15	81.13
2.家用电脑	Computer	135.32	1.62	64.46
(1)整机电脑	Entire Computer	116.96		43.89

单位：元（yuan）

较低收入户 Lower Middle Income Households	中间收入户 Middle Income Households	较高收入户 Upper Middle Income Households	高收入户 High Income Households	最高收入户 Highest Income Households
7.93	27.29	35.16	29.33	
		7.82		48.02
		439.51	1 591.79	1 133.34
[illegible].51	5.00	17.84		
26[illegible].54	485.05	1 088.12	1 308.13	1 713.02
24[illegible].82	474.43	1 080.33	1 237.58	1 655.33
1[illegible].88	1.42	4.89	16.33	0.66
[illegible].84	9.20	2.90	54.23	57.03
[illegible]5.33	68.24	215.39	468.74	1 730.38
7.30	52.76	70.18	120.51	172.50
[illegible]1.91	7.92	86.92	225.37	1 232.16
6.12	7.56	58.29	122.86	325.72
2[illegible]6.80	217.24	272.47	317.72	658.26
12.77	13.97	46.72	75.48	292.15
51.41	26.37	24.60	30.30	81.23
18.57	11.03	34.61	36.28	12.80
[illegible]25.73	118.23	103.36	104.39	144.42
33.63	29.24	50.92	66.01	111.52
4.69	18.42	12.26	5.26	16.12
[illegible]18.77	983.66	1 112.84	1 253.61	1 434.43
223.30	229.43	224.56	340.98	440.35
2.69	2.39	9.71	14.90	75.92
203.06	226.13	209.25	311.32	353.05
17.55	0.91	5.59	14.76	11.38
695.47	754.23	888.28	912.63	994.08
685.53	735.10	861.88	905.77	961.68
0.17	1.86	1.02	1.69	13.58
9.77	17.27	25.38	5.17	18.82
[illegible]195.08	**1 664.36**	**2 159.55**	**2 590.65**	**6 005.64**
431.79	555.80	735.55	872.88	1 752.55
170.18	168.37	192.44	253.68	471.35
59.63	118.85	166.40	181.53	462.22
50.25	107.35	142.70	134.93	432.21

9-8 续表3
continued

项　目	Item	全市平均 Average	最低收入户 Lowest Income Households	低收入户 Low Income Households
(2)计算机外部设备	External Equipment	8.96		5.53
(3)各种零配件及耗材	Various Spare Parts	9.39	1.62	15.03
5.组合音响	Hi-Fi Stereo Component System	0.74		
7.摄像机	Pick-up Camera	11.21		13.01
8.照相机	Camera	44.18		5.68
9.钢琴	Piano	4.24		
10.其他中高档乐器	Other Medium and Top Grade Music Instruments	11.03		
11.健身器材	Body Building Equipment	9.63	13.26	
12.电子辞典	Electronic Dictionary	2.60		3.97
13.音像制品及软件	Audio-visual Products and Software	5.45	0.80	11.59
14.体育用品	Sports Articles	6.80	2.10	0.97
15.书报杂志	Books, Newspapers and Magazines	58.92	29.36	51.37
16.纸张文具	Paper and Stationery Goods	21.10	13.77	14.79
17.其他文娱用品	Other Recreation and Culture Articles	142.59	71.74	77.98
(二)文化娱乐服务	Recreation and Culture Services	730.48	188.89	363.65
1.参观游览	Sightseeing	120.84	18.73	35.59
2.健身活动	Body Building Activities	41.98	3.20	16.46
3.团体旅游	Team Tour	441.30	101.46	243.45
4.其它文娱活动	Other Recreation and Culture Activities	120.93	61.16	68.14
5.文娱用品修理服务费	Service Charges for Recreation and Culture Articles Mending	5.42	4.34	
(三)教育	Education	701.06	624.05	880.02
1.教材	Teaching Material	26.26	22.62	18.12
(1)课本及参考书	Text Books and Reference Books	21.61	21.56	11.60
(2)教育软件	Teaching Software	0.60		0.24
(3)其它教材	Other Teaching Material	4.06	1.07	6.27
2.教育费用	Education Cost	674.80	601.43	861.90
(1)非义务教育学杂费	Tuition Fee for Non-compulsory Education	118.97	20.49	208.31
(2)义务教育学杂费	Tuition Fee for Compulsory Education	31.99	109.83	29.75
(3)托幼费	Child-care Fee	139.45	198.92	281.92
(4)成人教育费	Adult Education Expenses	49.44	42.38	4.59
(5)家教费	Family Education Expenses	38.42	7.70	49.53
(6)培训班	Training Fee	241.61	125.82	266.15

单位:元(yuan)

较低收入户 Lower Middle Income Households	中间收入户 Middle Income Households	较高收入户 Upper Middle Income Households	高收入户 High Income Households	最高收入户 Highest Income Households
[illegible].29	4.30	17.05	34.40	8.54
[illegible].59	7.20	6.65	12.19	21.47
2.[illegible]2	1.20	0.09		
	35.94	10.11	8.06	
3.[illegible]3	12.19	38.83	56.91	286.99
	0.32	20.66		
5.[illegible]7	13.19	29.01	7.43	7.68
1.[illegible]2	4.12	5.54		63.64
	4.95		5.46	7.66
5.01	0.35	2.09	15.70	12.68
8.72	7.82	8.28	4.99	11.44
[illegible]6.71	61.42	48.36	77.34	108.20
13.38	27.61	23.56	29.60	25.39
[illegible]9.32	99.46	190.20	232.20	295.30
304.93	560.40	790.39	1 241.25	2 453.02
21.74	85.99	174.14	356.30	283.19
4.62	2.27	49.41	40.48	268.07
[illegible]65.52	355.66	449.12	659.12	1 624.57
[illegible]11.38	108.91	114.84	170.06	264.62
1.67	7.58	2.87	15.29	12.57
[illegible]5[illegible].36	548.15	633.61	476.51	1 800.06
[illegible].16	23.94	39.09	11.53	68.76
[illegible].11	18.99	29.99	9.43	66.45
[illegible].73	0.45	1.66		
[illegible].32	4.50	7.45	2.10	2.31
44[illegible].20	524.21	594.52	464.98	1 731.30
8[illegible].75	112.72	14.42	11.05	546.73
	15.71	38.59	51.89	13.64
9[illegible].64	82.90	131.21	76.59	196.14
[illegible]48.40	25.29	26.26	1.17	262.02
[illegible]6.69	63.97	28.93	28.26	107.15
1[illegible]3.98	136.75	328.55	258.62	466.89

9-8 续表4
continued

项　目	Item	全市平均 Average	最低收入户 Lowest Income Households	低收入户 Low Income Households
(7)学校住宿费	Accommodation Expenses at School	4.18	15.57	2.44
(8)其他	Others	50.74	80.71	19.14
七、居住	**Residence**	**1 971.14**	**976.09**	**1 846.30**
(一)住房	Housing	447.19	19.98	502.75
1.租赁房房租	House Rental	27.08	3.16	11.14
2.住房装潢支出	Decoration Expenses	332.91		190.99
3.维修用建筑材料	Construction Material for Mending	44.04	2.62	121.51
4.其他	Others	43.16	14.20	179.11
(二)水电燃料及其他	Water, Electricity, Fuel and Others	1 357.09	905.30	1 262.57
1.水	Water	74.96	60.08	67.23
2.电	Electricity	378.38	302.37	374.13
3.燃料	Fuels	174.57	147.93	172.52
(1)煤炭	Coal	19.63	22.34	26.29
(2)液化石油气	Liquefied Petroleum Gas	26.77	35.78	19.11
(3)管道煤气	Pipeline Gas	127.55	89.81	126.30
(4)柴油	Diesel Oil	0.07		0.61
(5)其他燃料	Other Fuels	0.56		0.20
4.取暖费	Heating Fees	487.65	245.23	434.19
5.其他	Others	241.53	149.69	214.49
(三)居住服务费	Residence Service Charges	166.86	50.80	80.98
1.物业管理费	Property Management Fee	99.83	36.85	38.52
2.维修服务费	Mending Serivce Charges	10.17	2.91	30.78
3.其它	Others	56.86	11.04	11.68
八、杂项商品和服务	**Miscellaneous Goods and Services**	**965.70**	**351.34**	**400.05**
(一)杂项商品	Miscellaneous Goods	806.97	212.03	258.64
1.金银珠宝饰品	Gold, Silver and Jewellery	471.68	80.93	129.01
2.手表	Watch	34.24	3.27	2.69
3.理发美容用具	Haircut and Cosmetology Articles	6.78	4.50	5.33
4.化妆品	Cosmetics	213.32	111.27	73.23
5.其他杂品	Other Miscellaneous Goods	80.95	12.06	48.39
(二)服务	Services	158.73	139.31	141.41
1.旅馆住宿费	Accommodation Expenses at Inn	24.86	11.15	61.06
2.理发洗澡费	Washing and Haircut Service Charges	59.24	43.96	43.00
3.美容费	Cosmetology Service Charges	43.58	83.39	22.57
4.其他服务	Others	31.05	0.80	14.78

单位:元(yuan)

较低收入户 Lower Middle Income Households	中间收入户 Middle Income Households	较高收入户 Upper Middle Income Households	高收入户 High Income Households	最高收入户 Highest Income Households
	4.09	2.24		10.57
17.73	82.77	24.32	37.41	128.18
1 571.62	**1 590.64**	**1 863.08**	**4 365.41**	**2 843.54**
13[illegible].05	123.59	297.33	2 220.52	831.73
75.44	1.82		109.51	
42.08	38.81	246.18	1 989.93	707.78
9.18	24.35	40.54	47.68	122.75
3.35	58.62	10.61	73.41	1.20
1 3[illegible]9.91	1 359.32	1 453.18	1 486.25	1 628.56
72.51	73.14	75.82	85.93	98.04
374.92	371.26	353.14	475.94	454.36
1[illegible]1.57	162.50	188.01	134.84	228.07
22.21	13.46	11.59		52.83
32.75	15.23	37.58	23.64	16.02
126.60	133.83	138.84	111.20	153.41
				5.81
46.25	493.55	512.24	628.40	720.69
394.67	258.86	323.97	161.14	127.40
66.66	107.73	112.57	658.64	383.24
50.51	85.21	90.25	205.53	301.59
3.03	1.73	9.30	4.38	35.34
13.13	20.79	13.02	448.73	46.30
548.19	**788.32**	**817.48**	**1 790.75**	**3 152.39**
457.66	626.60	650.95	1 592.26	2 864.15
154.08	266.51	224.43	1 081.42	2 401.58
16.88	70.07	58.77	30.95	19.65
4.46	8.53	11.02	8.52	1.54
195.14	204.49	245.57	373.51	328.88
87.09	77.00	111.16	97.86	112.50
90.53	161.73	166.53	198.49	288.24
19.31	6.41	40.44	20.63	19.39
37.50	59.37	68.63	87.78	94.87
24.04	45.34	44.83	33.81	67.50
9.69	50.61	12.63	56.27	106.48

9－9 城市居民家庭年人均购买主要商品(2012 年)

PER CAPITA ANNUAL PURCHASES OF MAJOR COMMODITIES OF URBAN HOUSEHOLDS (2012)

项　目	Item	单位	Unit	全市平均 Average	最低收入户 Lowest Income Households	低收入户 Low Income Households
大米	Rice	千克	kg	17.44	16.26	19.61
面粉	Flour	千克	kg	14.18	13.00	18.21
食用植物油	Edible Vegetable Oil	千克	kg	7.32	8.19	7.3
猪肉	Pork	千克	kg	19.78	15.18	20.06
牛肉	Beef	千克	kg	2.12	1.92	1.75
羊肉	Mutton	千克	kg	1.29	1.04	0.74
鸡	Chicken	千克	kg	5.08	4.49	4.69
鲜蛋	Fresh Eggs	千克	kg	18.85	16.31	17.85
鱼	Fish	千克	kg	12.27	9.98	10.61
虾	Shrimp	千克	kg	4.17	3.17	3.42
白酒	Liquor	千克	kg	2.00	1.56	1.28
果酒	Fruit Wine	千克	kg	0.53	0.37	0.7
啤酒	Beer	千克	kg	15.24	18.98	14.11
碳酸饮料	Carbonated Beverage	千克	kg	1.73	0.91	1.32
瓶装饮用水	Bottled Drinking Water	千克	kg	8.78	4.61	9.4
茶叶	Tea	千克	kg	0.86	1.09	0.76
鲜果	Fresh Fruits	千克	kg	62.35	44.83	53.42
鲜瓜	Fresh Melons	千克	kg	12.16	9.78	9.39
糕点	Cake	千克	kg	7.47	7.14	6.43
鲜乳品	Fresh Milk Products	千克	kg	20.14	13.86	17.48
奶粉	Milk Power	千克	kg	0.67	0.91	0.3
酸奶	Yoghurt	千克	kg	5.88	3.72	3.31
服装	Garments	件	piece	9.62	7.41	6.27
鞋类	Shoes	双	pair	3.17	1.88	2.33
水	Water	吨	ton	29.75	24.85	26.52
电	Electricity	度	watt-hour	688.06	544.00	682.04
煤炭	Coal	千克	kg	21.22	29.59	23.78
液化石油气	Liquefied Petroleum Gas	千克	kg	3.93	4.89	2.28
管道燃气	Pipeline Gas	立方米	cu. m	51.28	38.60	53.88

较低收入户 Lower Middle Income Households	中间收入户 Middle Income Households	较高收入户 Upper Middle Income Households	高收入户 High Income Households	最高收入户 Highest Income Households
1[illegible].[illegible]	16.89	15.13	17.45	18.78
1[illegible].[illegible]2	13.88	13.10	12.81	12.42
[illegible].[illegible]7	7.12	7.50	7.15	5.60
2[illegible].[illegible]3	20.78	19.25	20.74	19.79
2.[illegible]5	1.88	2.21	2.39	3.00
1.[illegible]3	1.35	1.26	0.75	2.65
4.[illegible]3	6.76	4.96	4.36	4.22
[illegible]9.[illegible]5	18.91	18.81	20.55	19.18
12.[illegible]9	13.39	13.40	11.66	11.81
4.38	4.27	4.16	5.52	4.26
1.89	2.17	3.13	1.26	1.52
0.41	0.67	0.64	0.24	0.56
12.66	16.53	16.59	12.52	14.83
1.04	2.50	2.33	2.02	1.45
10.24	4.01	9.28	12.52	15.00
[illegible].98	0.64	0.83	1.07	0.80
6[illegible].76	63.06	66.83	63.21	71.70
1[illegible].65	12.91	13.50	11.29	9.10
[illegible].74	7.36	8.19	7.03	9.74
[illegible].71	22.93	21.29	23.15	24.64
[illegible].36	0.40	0.93	0.77	1.39
5.63	7.00	6.02	7.03	8.19
9.04	8.81	10.72	12.49	13.88
3.14	3.37	3.47	3.67	4.21
[illegible]9.24	28.60	29.76	35.47	37.18
[illegible]4.16	671.11	644.66	878.50	837.91
[illegible]5.13	17.29	12.53		48.02
4.82	2.74	5.46	3.39	2.53
55.35	53.98	53.78	40.66	53.45

9-10 每百户城市居民家庭年末耐用品拥有量

OWNERSHIP OF MAJOR DURABLE CONSUMER GOODS PER 100 URBAN HOUSEHOLDS AT YEAR-END

项　目	Item	单位	Unit	全市平均 Average	最低收入户 Lowest Income Households	低收入户 Low Income Households
摩托车	Motor	辆	unit	7.5	5.0	10.0
助力车	Motorbike	辆	unit	6.3		12.5
家用汽车	Automobile	辆	unit	28.5	20.0	20.0
洗衣机	Washing Machine	台	set	97.5	92.5	100.0
电冰箱	Household Refrigerator	台	set	108.0	97.5	112.5
彩色电视机	Color TV Set	台	set	115.0	105.0	132.5
家用电脑	Computer	台	set	100.8	85.0	92.5
组合音响	Hi-Fi Stereo Component System	套	set	29.0	27.5	32.5
摄像机	Pickup Camera	架	set	23.8	10.0	22.5
照相机	Camera	架	set	78.8	80.0	77.5
钢琴	Piano	架	set	9.0		7.5
其他中高档乐器	Other Medium and Top Grade Music Instruments	件	unit	11.5	7.5	15.0
微波炉	Microwave Oven	台	set	82.0	72.5	72.5
空调器	Air Conditioner	台	set	103.5	85.0	112.5
淋浴热水器	Water Heater	台	set	92.8	85.0	92.5
消毒碗柜	Sterilized Cabinet	台	set	10.8		7.5
洗碗机	Dishwasher	台	set	3.0		
健身器材	Body Building Equipment	套	set	11.0	10.0	12.5
普通电话	Telephone	部	set	62.8	45.0	65.0
移动电话	Cell Phone	部	set	230.5	235.0	225.0

较低收入户 Lower Middle Income Households	中间收入户 Middle Income Households	较高收入户 Upper Middle Income Households	高收入户 High Income Households	最高收入户 Highest Income Households
8.8	5.0	8.8	10.0	5.0
1.3	6.3	12.5	2.5	7.5
20.0	32.5	27.5	37.5	47.5
9[illegible].3	95.0	97.5	100.0	105.0
10[illegible].5	108.8	107.5	112.5	110.0
11[illegible].3	108.8	110.0	117.5	125.0
10[illegible].3	103.8	95.0	100.0	120.0
[illegible]0.0	31.3	33.8	20.0	40.0
[illegible]7.5	26.3	25.0	22.5	45.0
[illegible]8.8	83.8	71.3	82.5	100.0
3.8	10.0	16.3	5.0	17.5
11.3	7.5	15.0	10.0	15.0
80.0	83.8	83.8	90.0	90.0
100.0	101.3	98.8	110.0	127.5
88.8	98.8	88.8	97.5	100.0
5.0	10.0	10.0	17.5	32.5
3.8	1.3	3.8	2.5	10.0
6.3	3.8	11.3	12.5	32.5
53.8	62.5	71.3	60.0	82.5
255.0	231.3	217.5	212.5	225.0

9－11 分市、区农村住户基本情况(2012 年)
BASIC CONDITIONS OF RURAL HOUSEHOLDS BY REGION(2012)

指 标	Indicators	青岛市 Qingdao	#崂山区 Laoshan District
调查户数(户)	Number of Households Surveyed(household)	680	50
平均每户常住人口(人)	Average Number of Permanent Residents Per Household (person)	3.27	3.37
平均每户整半劳动力(人)	Average Number of Full/Semi Labour Force Per Household(person)	2.38	2.38
全年纯收入	Per Capita Annual Net Income	13 990	15 800
生活消费支出	Expenses on Household Consumption	8 653	11 071
1. 食品消费支出	Food	3 130	4 310
2. 衣着消费支出	Clothing	798	1 329
3. 居住消费支出	Residence	1 486	1 494
4. 家庭设备、用品消费支出	Household Facilities and Articles	549	598
5. 交通和通讯消费支出	Transportation and Communication	1 345	1 352
6. 文化教育、娱乐消费支出	Culture, Education and R ecreation	678	1 143
7. 医疗保健消费支出	Health Care and Medical Services	487	517
8. 其他商品和服务消费支出	Other Goods and Services	181	327
平均每户年内新建(购)房屋面积(平方米)	Floor Space Newly Built(Bought) Per Household in the Year(sq. m)	0.62	
平均每户期末拥有住房面积(平方米)	Living Space Per Household at Year-end(sq. m)	108.50	100.38

单位:元(yuan)

原黄岛区 Original Huangdao District	城阳区 Chengyang District	即墨市 Jimo	胶州市 Jiaozhou	原胶南市 Original Jiaonan	平度市 Pingdu	莱西市 Laixi
50	80	100	100	100	100	100
3.06	3.04	3.19	3.20	3.10	3.63	3.46
2.1[illegible]	2.25	2.21	2.39	2.30	2.42	2.66
15 93[illegible]	14 702	13 939	13 923	13 593	13 879	13 623
11 424	10 280	9 883	8 595	7 581	8 404	7 505
[illegible] 6[illegible]	3 813	2 932	3 255	2 739	3 082	2 815
3[illegible]1	1 020	635	949	486	857	837
[illegible]97	1 988	1 926	1 503	1 450	1 359	1 034
[illegible]45	608	564	638	523	465	491
1 [illegible]92	1 137	2 203	1 187	1 180	1 267	1 154
[illegible]64	1 086	663	541	533	762	658
[illegible]17	471	788	322	512	439	340
227	157	173	198	159	174	175
		2.90		0.90		
1[illegible].55	132.25	120.74	104.00	87.24	89.19	134.07

9－12 农村住户基本情况(1990－2012 年)
BASIC CONDITIONS OF RURAL HOUSEHOLDS(1990－2012)

项目	Item	单位	Unit
调查户数	**Number of Households Surveyed**	户	**household**
常住人口	**Number of Permanent Residents**	人	**person**
一、平均每户常住人口	**Average Number of Permanent Residents Per Household**	人	**person**
1.年龄结构	Age Distribution	人	person
(1)6 岁及以下	6 Year-old and Under	人	person
(2)7－15 岁	Between 7 and 15 Year-old	人	person
(3)16－60 岁	Between 16 and 60 Year-old	人	person
(4)61 岁及以上	61 Year-old and Above	人	person
2.在校学生人数	Students Enrollment	人	person
其中:7－15 岁在校学生人数	of which:Between 7 and 15 Year-old	人	person
3.平均每户整半劳动力	Average Number of Full/Semi Labour Force Per Household	人	person
(1)整劳动力	Full Labour Force	人	person
(2)半劳动力	Semi Labour Force	人	person
整半劳动力占常住人口的比重	Percentage of Full/Semi Labour Force to Permanent Residents	%	%
平均每个劳动力负担人口	Average Number of Dependents Per Labour Force	人	person
二、平均每百个劳动力中	**Among Per 100 Labour Force**		
文盲半文盲人数	Illiterate and Semiliterate	人	person
小学程度人数	Primary School	人	person
初中程度人数	Junior High School	人	person
高中程度人数	Senior High School	人	person
中专程度人数	Secondary School	人	person
大专程度人数	Junior College	人	person
三、经营耕地面积(人均)	**Area of Cultivated Land under Management(per capita)**	亩	**mu**
#承包耕地面积	Area of Cultivated Land Contracted	亩	mu
占经营耕地面积的比重	Percentage to Area of Cultivated Land under Management	%	%
四、平均每户年末生产性固定资产原值	**Productive Original Value of Fixed Assets Per Household(year-end)**	元	**yuan**
1.役畜、产品畜	Draught Animal and Commodity Animal	元	yuan
2.大中型铁木农具	Large and Medium Iron and Wooden Farm Tools	元	yuan
3.农林牧渔业机械	Agricultural Machinery	元	yuan
4.工业机械	Industrial Machinery	元	yuan
5.运输机械	Transport Machinery	元	yuan
6.生产用房	Buildings for Production	元	yuan
7.其他	Others	元	yuan
五、平均每户年末拥有汽车	**Ownership of Automobiles Per Household(year-end)**	辆	**set**
大中型拖拉机	Large and Medium Tractors	台	set
小型和手扶拖拉机	Small and Walking Tractors	台	set

注:平均每百个劳动力中文化程度人数,2010 年及以前为整半劳动力文化程度,2011 年为就业劳动力文化程度。

Note:In the education attainment statistics among per 100 labour force,the labour force refers to full/semi labour force before 2010,and refers to employed labour force since 2011.

2005	2006	2007	2008	2009	2010	2011	2012
860	**900**	**900**	**900**	**900**	**900**	**680**	**680**
2 964	**3 073**	**3 066**	**3 077**	**3 069**	**3 061**	**2 263**	**2 222**
3.45	**3.41**	**3.41**	**3.42**	**3.41**	**3.40**	**3.33**	**3.27**
0.15	0.15	0.14	0.12	0.12	0.11	0.15	0.17
0.33	0.35	0.35	0.35	0.35	0.31	0.36	0.36
2.74	2.73	2.69	2.71	2.69	2.70	2.50	2.44
0.23	0.19	0.23	0.24	0.25	0.28	0.30	0.30
0.60	0.60	0.59	0.60	0.60	0.58	0.56	0.51
0.33	0.35	0.35	0.35	0.34	0.30	0.36	0.37
2.59	2.58	2.58	2.59	2.56	2.58	2.37	2.38
1.73	1.76	1.72	1.66	1.57	1.51	1.52	1.54
0.86	0.82	0.86	0.93	0.99	1.06	0.85	0.84
75.1	75.6	75.67	75.63	75.20	75.76	71.24	72.70
1.33	1.32	1.32	1.32	1.33	1.30	1.40	1.38
2.07	1.46	1.64	1.68	1.60	1.38	1.65	1.62
15.72	12.78	12.24	12.46	12.52	9.36	13.45	13.46
54.04	54.43	53.10	53.89	56.63	58.52	60.59	59.06
21.6	24.01	24.48	23.12	19.89	20.53	16.53	17.39
4.27	4.69	5.30	5.20	5.24	5.56	2.70	3.20
2.29	2.62	3.23	3.65	4.12	4.66	5.07	5.27
1.40	**1.31**	**1.26**	**1.27**	**1.30**	**1.47**	**1.38**	**1.60**
1.40	1.31	1.26	1.27	1.30	1.30	1.30	1.52
100.00	100.00	100.00	100.00	100.00	88.44	94.20	95.00
13 845	**16 191**	**21 568**	**21 993**	**21 626**	**22 950**	**24 349**	**27 949**
1 103	871	1 264	1 320	1 358	1 333	1 037	1 527
217	275	435	299	265	293	140	143
3 204	2 912	4 261	4 658	4 062	4 118	4 153	5 167
1 247	1 759	1 899	1 710	1 718	2 008	2 899	3 452
1 623	1 169	1 768	1 110	1 138	1 234	2 421	3 434
3 746	4 479	7 247	7 079	6 372	7 238	8 042	9 548
315	482	739	774	858	819	1 112	1 339
0.04	**0.05**	**0.07**	**0.06**	**0.07**	**0.08**	**0.09**	**0.08**
0.05	0.03	0.03	0.04	0.05	0.05	0.05	0.06
0.31	0.34	0.29	0.30	0.30	0.30	0.22	0.23

9－13 农村住户居住情况(2005－2012 年)
HOUSING CONDITIONS OF RURAL HOUSEHOLDS(2005－2012)

类　别	Category	单位	Unit
一、期末住房情况	**Housing Conditions at Term-end**		
(一)住房面积	Floor Space of Houses	平方米/人	sq. m/person
(二)住房价值	Value of Houses	元/平方米	yuan/sq. m
(三)住房类型	Type of Houses		
1. 楼房面积	Floor Space of Apartment	平方米/人	sq. m/person
2. 砖瓦平房面积	Floor Space of Brick Bungalow	平方米/人	sq. m/person
3. 其他	Others	平方米/人	sq. m/person
(四)住房结构	Structure of Houses		
1. 钢筋混泥土结构面积	Reinforced Concrete Structure	平方米/人	sq. m/person
2. 砖木结构面积	Brick and Wood Structure	平方米/人	sq. m/person
3. 其他	Others	平方米/人	sq. m/person
二、期内新建(购)住房情况	**Conditions of Houses Newly Built (Bought) This Term**		
(一)新建(购)住房面积	Floor Space of Houses Newly Built (Bought)	平方米/人	sq. m/person
(二)新建(购)住房价值	Value of Houses Newly Built (Bought)	元/平方米	yuan/sq. m
(三)新建(购)住房类型	Type of Houses Newly Built (Bought)		
1. 楼房面积	Floor Space of Apartment	平方米/人	sq. m/person
2. 砖瓦平房面积	Floor Space of Brick Bungalow	平方米/人	sq. m/person
3. 其他	Others	平方米/人	sq. m/person
(四)新建(购)住房结构	Structure of Newly Building Housing		
1. 钢筋混泥土结构面积	Reinforced Concrete Structure	平方米/人	sq. m/person
2. 砖木结构面积	Brick and Wood Structure	平方米/人	sq. m/person
3. 其他	Residental Buildings	平方米/人	sq. m/person

2005	2006	2007	2008	2009	2010	2011	2012
29.5[illegible]	30.82	30.95	30.73	31.39	32.06	31.73	32.32
39[illegible]	537	676	732	750	880	1 345	1 369
3.[illegible]2	7.04	6.08	5.96	6.34	6.33	4.15	4.13
25.[illegible]5	23.48	24.52	24.54	24.81	24.58	27.57	28.18
0.[illegible]6	0.30	0.35	0.23	0.24	0.47		
6.53	7.94	5.37	6.05	6.71	6.57	5.26	4.80
23.0[illegible]	22.77	25.47	24.58	24.56	24.71	26.47	27.52
	0.11	0.11	0.11	0.12	0.10		
[illegible].9[illegible]	0.72	0.23	0.30	0.43	0.16	0.55	0.19
52[illegible]	549	545	708	930	1 221	1 199	1 927
[illegible].[illegible]9	0.38		0.07	0.11	0.08	0.16	0.05
0.[illegible]0	0.34	0.23	0.23	0.32	0.08	0.39	0.14
0[illegible]67	0.42	0.08	0.11	0.18	0.08	0.20	0.13
[illegible]31	0.30	0.15	0.19	0.25	0.08	0.35	0.06

9－13 续表
continued

类 别	Category	单位	Unit
三、居住条件	**Living Condition**		
（一）住房卫生设备使用情况	Condition of Health Equipment		
1. 使用水冲式厕所的户数	Having Flushing Toilet	户/百户	household/100 households
2. 使用旱厕的户数	Having Old Toilet	户/百户	household/100 households
3. 无厕所的户数	No Toilet	户/百户	household/100 households
（二）取暖设备使用情况	Condition of Heating Equipment		
1. 使用空调的户数	Having Air Conditioner	户/百户	household/100 households
2. 使用暖气的户数	Having Heater	户/百户	household/100 households
3. 使用火炕的户数	Having Kang	户/百户	household/100 households
4. 无取暖设备的户数	No Heating Equipment	户/百户	household/100 households
（三）炊事使用的主要能源	Major Source of Cooking		
1. 使用液化气的户数	Liquid Natural Gas	户/百户	household/100 households
2. 使用煤炭的户数	Coal	户/百户	household/100 households
3. 使用柴草的户数	Fuelwood	户/百户	household/100 households
4. 使用电的户数	Electricity	户/百户	household/100 households
5. 使用其他燃料的户数	Other Fuels	户/百户	household/100 households
（四）饮用水来源情况	Source of Drinking Water		
1. 饮用自来水的户数	Tap Water	户/百户	household/100 households
2. 饮用深井水的户数	Deep Well Water	户/百户	household/100 households
3. 饮用浅井水的户数	Other Water	户/百户	household/100 households
（五）住宅外道路路面状况	Condition of Road Near Residential		
1. 水泥或柏油路面的户数	Cement or Asphalt	户/百户	household/100 households
2. 沙石或石板等硬质路面的户数	Stone, Sand and Gravel or Other Hard Materials	户/百户	household/100 households
3. 其他路面的户数	Others	户/百户	household/100 households

2005	2006	2007	2008	2009	2010	2011	2012
40	42	45	46	46	46	51	50
60	58	55	54	54	54	49	51
7	8	6	7	6	6	9	9
23	18	21	22	22	22	19	20
70	73	71	69	69	69	60	61
						11	11
50	62	82	82	83	83	66	65
	1						
40	37	16	16	16	16	35	29
	1	1	1	1	1	1	7
77	85	92	95	95	95	94	97
2[illegible]	15	7	5	5	5	5	2
						2	2
[illegible]4	40	54	62	71	75	81	84
[illegible]2	53	42	34	25	22	13	12
[illegible]3	7	5	4	3	3	6	5

9－14 农村住户人均总收入和纯收入(2012 年)

PER CAPITA TOTAL INCOME AND NET INCOME OF RURAL HOUSEHOLDS (2012)

单位:元(yuan)

项　目	Item	金额 Sum
一、总收入	**Total Income**	**19 567**
(一)工资收入	Income from Wages and Salaries	6 308
1. 在非企业组织中劳动得到收入	Gained from Non-enterprise Organization	582
2. 在本乡地域内劳动得到收入	Gained in Local Area	4 000
(1)在企业中劳动得到收入	Gained From Enterprises	3 472
(2)在国家投资基建项目得到收入	Gained From Capital Construction Programs Invested by State	6
(3)提供其他劳务收入	Other Labour Services	521
3. 外出从业得到收入	Gained from Out-city Enterprise by Permanent Person	1 726
(1)在乡外县内从业得到收入	Out of Countryside and in County	1 326
(2)在县外省内从业得到收入	Out of County and in Province	325
(3)在省外国内从业得到收入	Out of Province and in County	20
(4)在国外从业得到收入	From Abroad	56
(二)家庭经营收入	Income from Household Operations	12 216
1. 第一产业收入	Primary Industry	8 015
(1)农业收入	Farming	4 965
(2)林业收入	Forestry	73
(3)牧业收入	Animal Husbandry	2 665
(4)渔业收入	Fishery	311
2. 第二产业收入	Secondary Industry	2 005
(1)工业收入	Industry	1 706
(2)建筑业收入	Construction	300

9－14 续表
continued

单位：元（yuan）

项　目	Item	金额 Sum
3. 第三产业收入	Tertiary Industry	2 196
（1）其他产品收入	Other Products	3
（2）第三产业服务性收入	Services of Tertiary Industry	2 193
①交通、运输和邮电业收入	Transport and Postal Services	579
②批发零售贸易、餐饮业收入	Wholesale, Retail Trade and Catering	1 097
③社会服务业收入	Social Services	308
④文教卫生业收入	Culture, Education and Health Care	82
⑤其他行业收入	Other Household Business	127
（三）财产性收入	Income from Properties	309
1. 利息	Interest	16
2. 租金（包括农业机械）	Rental	113
3. 土地征用补偿收入	Compensation for Land Requisition	
4. 转让承包土地经营权收入	Making over Business Power of Land	39
5. 其他投资收益	Others	89
（四）转移性收入	Income from Transfers	734
其中：1. 家庭住户成员寄回和带回		2
2. 城市亲友赠送收入	Presentation from relatives and Friends	20
3. 农村亲友赠送收入	From Outside The Country	79
4. 退耕还林还草补贴收入	Subsidy For Giving back Cultivation to Forest or Grass	2
二、全年人均纯收入	**Per Capita Annual Net Income**	**13 990**

9－15 农村住户人均总支出(2012 年)
PER CAPITA TOTAL EXPENDITURE OF RURAL HOUSEHOLDS (2012)

单位:元(yuan)

项 目	Item	金额 Sum
总支出	**Total Expenditure**	**14 832**
(一)家庭经营费用支出	Expenditure for Household Operations	4 919
1. 第一产业生产费用支出	Primary Industry	3 408
(1)农业生产费用支出	Farming	1 607
(2)林业生产费用支出	Forestry	44
(3)牧业生产费用支出	Animal Husbandry	1 660
(4)渔业生产费用支出	Fishery	96
2. 第二产业生产费用支出	Secondary Industry	772
(1)工业生产费用支出	Industry	680
(2)建筑业生产费用支出	Construction	92
3. 第三产业生产费用支出	Tertiary Industry	739
(1)交通、运输和邮电业生产费用支出	Transport, Postal and Telecommunication Services	201
(2)批发贸易餐饮业生产费用支出	Wholesale, Retail Trade and Catering	457
(3)社会服务业生产费用支出	Social Services	53
(4)文教卫生业生产费用支出	Culture, Education and Health Care	2
(5)其他行业生产费用支出	Other	26
(二)购置生产用固定资产支出	Purchase of Productive Fixed Assets	310
(三)建造生产性固定资产雇工支出	Employee for Building Productive Fixed Assets	5
(四)税费支出	Taxes and Fees	8
1. 第一产业税	Primary Industry	
2. 第二产业税	Secondary Industry	2
3. 第三产业生产税	Tertiary Industry	1
4. 其他各种收费	Other Various Payment	6

9－15 续表
continued

单位：元(yuan)

项　目	Item	金额 Sum
(五)生活消费支出	Expenditure on Household Consumption	8 653
1. 食品消费支出	Food	3 130
2. 衣着消费支出	Clothing	798
3. 居住消费支出	Residence	1 486
4. 家庭设备、用品消费支出	Household Facilities, Articles and Services	549
5. 交通通讯消费支出	Transportation and Communication	1 345
6. 文化教育、娱乐消费支出	Cultural, Education and Recreation	678
7. 医疗保健消费支出	Medicines and Medical Services	487
8. 其他商品和服务消费支出	Other Goods and Services	181
(六)财产性支出	Expenditure on Properties	11
1. 宅基地有偿使用费	Unfree Use of Land for Building House	10
2. 承包其他农户转让费	Expenditure for Making Over	
3. 其他	Others	1
(七)转移性支出	Expenditure on Transfers	925
1. 寄给带给家庭非常住人口	Expenditure to Outside City	
2. 赠送农村亲友	Presentation to Relatives and Friends in Rural Area	222
3. 赠送城市亲友	Presentation to Relatives and Friends in Urban Area	31

9-16 农村住户人均生活消费支出(2012年)

PER CAPITA EXPENDITURE ON HOUSEHOLD CONSUMPUTION OF RURAL HOUSEHOLDS (2012)

单位:元(yuan)

项　目	Item	金额 Sum
生活消费支出	**Expenditure on Household Consumption**	**8 653**
(一)食品	Food	3 130
购买食品支出	Buying Food	2 824
食品消费服务性支出	Services of Food Consumption	306
(二)衣着	Clothing	798
购买衣着支出	Buying Clothing	796
衣着消费服务性支出	Services ofClothing Consumption	1
(三)居住	Residence	1 486
1. 购买居住消费品支出	Buying Residential Consumption	1 166
2. 居住消费服务性支出	Services for Residential Consumption	321
(四)家庭设备、用品及服务	Household Facilities, Articles and Services	549
1. 购买家庭设备、用品支出	Buying Household Facilities and Articles	538
2. 家庭设备服务消费支出	Services for Household Facilities	11
(五)交通和通讯	Transportation and Communication	345
1. 购买交通和通讯用品支出	Buying Traffic and Communications Articles	1 007
2. 交通和通讯服务消费支出	Services for Traffic and Communications	338
(六)文化教育、娱乐用品及服务	Culture, Education and Recreation Articles and Services	678
1. 购买文化教育、娱乐用品	Culture, Education and Recreation Articles	272
2. 教育服务消费	Services for Education	258
3. 文化体育、娱乐服务消费	Services for Culture, Sports and Recreation	148
(七)医疗保健	Health Care and Medical Services	487
1. 购买医疗保健用品	Buying Articles of Medicines and Medical Services	131
2. 医疗保健服务消费支出	Services for Health care	3[illegible]6
(八)其他商品和服务	Other Goods and Services	181
1. 购买其他商品支出	Goods	116
2. 其他消费服务支出	Services	65

9-17 农村住户人均年购买消费品情况
PEF CAPITA ANNUAL PURCHASES OF MAJOR COMMODITIES OF RURAL HOUSEHOLDS

商品名称	Name	计量单位	Unit	数量 Amount
蔬菜	Vegetables	千克	kg	48.78
豆制品	Bean Products	千克	kg	6.38
猪肉	Pork	千克	kg	13.47
牛羊肉	Beef and Mutton	千克	kg	0.87
食糖	Carbohydrate	千克	kg	0.74
糕点	Cake	千克	kg	4.49
糖果	Sweet	千克	kg	1.03
卷烟	Cigarette	盒	case	26.60
酒	Liquor	千克	kg	18.38
#啤酒	Beer	千克	kg	11.75
茶叶	Tea	千克	kg	0.59
水果	Fruits	千克	kg	28.24
服装	Garments	件	piece	5.71
购买洗衣机	Washing Machine	台	unit	0.01
购买电风扇	Electric Fan	台	unit	0.02
购买电冰箱	Refrigerator	台	unit	0.02
购买手机	Cell Phone	部	unit	0.10
购买彩色电视机	Color TV Set	台	unit	0.02
购买照相机	Camera	只	unit	0.003
购买家用计算机(电脑)	Computer	台	unit	0.02

注:抽样调查资料。
Note The data is from sampling.

9-18 农村住户每百户家庭主要耐用品拥有量(1985-2012 年)
OWNERSHIP OF MAJOR DURABLE CONSUMER GOODS PER 100 RURAL HOUSEHOLDS(1985-2012)

年份 Year	家用电脑(台) Computer (unit)	空调器(台) Air Conditioner (unit)	热水器(台) Water Heater (unit)	自行车(辆) Bicycle (unit)	洗衣机(台) Washing Machine (unit)	电冰箱(台) Household Refrigerator (unit)	彩色电视机(台) Color TV Set (unit)	移动电话(部) Cell Phone (unit)	照相机(架) Camera (unit)	家用汽车(辆) Automobile (unit)
1985				147	0.3		3		1	
1986				165	1.1	0.3	4.5		1	
1987				148	2.4	0.5	7		2	
1988				154	2.4	1	9		2	
1989				170	3	1	12		2	
1990				164	4	2	13		2	
1991				173	5	4	16		2	
1992				178	5	7	20		2	
1993				203	7	14	26		2	
1994				204	9	21	35		7	
1995				203	16	28	43		6	
1996				198	13	33	46		8	
1997				191	15	36	56		13	
1998				184	17	39	63		15	
1999				185	20	42	74		10	
2000				165	28	47	86		13	
2001				153	28	53	92		13	
2002				152	36	58	98		16	
2003	6	5	33	137	39	60	100	45	16	2
2004	8	8	39	142	48	68	105	68	21	2
2005	14	14	53	138	57	77	109	91	21	5
2006	17	15	54	116	63	87	112	114	14	7
2007	19	19	63	118	70	94	113	132	17	8
2008	25	23	68	124	76	97	114	148	19	9
2009	28	25	71	127	79	99	115	160	21	11
2010	34	30	75	128	82	102	117	170	21	12
2011	44	32	76	114	85	100	112	202	18	15
2012	55	37	85	119	91	102	114	216	21	16

9-19 农村住户平均每百户购买生产资料和建筑材料(2012年)

PURCHASES OF PRODUCTION MEANS AND CONSTRUCTION MATERIALPERS PER 100 RURAL HOUSEHOLDS(2012)

商品名称	Name	计量单位	Unit	数量 Amount	金额(元) Sum(yuan)
化肥	Chemical Fertilizer	千克	kg	81 501.02	255 486.85
饼肥	Cake Fertilizer	千克	kg	186.28	620.92
农药	Farm Pesticides	千克	kg	1 887.84	14 159.78
农用薄膜	Plastic Fim	千克	kg	1 290.87	15 882.55
生产用燃料(生产用柴油、汽油及用煤合并)	Fuels for Production	千克	kg	12 418.46	90 226.62
汽车	Automobile	辆	set	0.59	51 659.41
大中型拖拉机	Large and Medium Tractors	台			
小型和手扶拖拉机	Small and Walking Tractors	台	set	0.59	3 014.71
机动脱粒机	Motorized Thresher	台	set	1.18	641.18
胶轮大车	Cart with Rubber Tires	辆	set		
胶轮手推车	Trolley with Rubber Tires	辆	set		
抽水机	Water Pump	台	set		
水泵	Pump	台	set	2.35	1 061.76
役畜	Draught Animal	头	head		
产品畜	Commodity Animal	头	head		
水泥	Cement	千克	kg	4 130.77	2 062.12
木材	Wood	立方米	cu. m	0.34	176.47
维修房屋用木材	Wood for House Mending	立方米	cu. m		
钢材	Rolled Steel	千克	kg	359.48	1 202.63
玻璃	Glass	平方米	sq. m	0.59	8.82
维修房屋用玻璃	Glass for Housing Mending	平方米	sq. m		
砖瓦	Brick and Tile	块	piece	5 545.82	2 604.61

注:抽样调查资料。

Note: The data is from sampling.

9－20 农村住户人均主要食品消费量(1990－2012 年)

PER CAPITA CONSUMPTIONS OF MAJOR COMMODITIES OF RURAL HOUSEHOLDS(1990－2012)

项目	Item	单位	Unit	1990	1995	2000	2005
1. 粮食	Grain	千克	kg	248.33	185.01	216.45	155.79
2. 蔬菜	Vegetables	千克	kg	135.38	129.66	103.98	69.51
3. 食用油	Edible Oil	千克	kg	6.56	7.54	9.03	6.01
(1)植物油	Vegetable Oil	千克	kg	5.75	7.36	8.93	5.95
(2)动物油	Animal Fats	千克	kg	0.81	0.18	0.07	0.06
4. 肉类	Meat	千克	kg	9.22	9.62	12.36	23.53
(1)猪肉	Pork	千克	kg	8.55	9.08	11.85	12.82
(2)牛羊肉	Beef and Mutton	千克	kg	0.67	0.54	0.51	0.76
5. 牛羊奶	Milk	千克	kg	0.09	0.62	1.79	3.29
6. 家禽	Poultry	千克	kg	0.91	1.31	2.55	3.81
7. 蛋类	Eggs	千克	kg	4.79	9.29	14.41	11.52
8. 水产品	Aquatic Products	千克	kg	4.44	10.77	12.70	14.28
9. 食糖	Carbohydrate	千克	kg	0.76	0.83	0.86	0.52
10. 卷烟	Cigarette	盒	case	23.21	22.43	23.18	24.36
11. 酒	Liquor	千克	kg	8.97	14.07	22.81	20.13
12. 茶叶	Tea	千克	kg	0.43	0.61	0.06	0.51
13. 糖果	Sweet	千克	kg	0.60	0.58	0.52	0.41
14. 糕点	Cake	千克	kg	2.91	3.65	4.51	3.10
15. 水果及水果制品	Fruits and Fruit Products	千克	kg	7.75	28.11	39.73	20.11

注：抽样调查资料。

Note: The data is from sampling.

9-20 续表
continued

2006	2007	2008	2009	2010	2011	2012
144.[illegible]6	116.52	133.16	141.91	127.63	133.03	124.04
68.[illegible]1	56.79	59.21	58.78	55.51	71.00	66.16
6.[illegible]5	5.36	6.03	6.58	6.31	7.56	7.67
6.04	5.33	6.01	6.55	6.29	7.55	7.65
0.01	0.04	0.02	0.03	0.03	0.01	0.02
25.32	26.05	23.93	25.86	26.33	23.97	26.58
13.86	12.87	11.92	12.73	12.04	12.45	13.47
1.00	1.13	0.92	1.04	1.00	0.83	0.87
14.87	14.40	12.12	10.51	11.80	10.26	11.18
2.08	2.75	2.70	2.48	2.19	2.52	2.75
12.75	11.03	12.25	12.78	11.26	10.10	11.34
18.2	17.89	20.46	22.06	23.72	17.88	17.17
0.63	0.74	0.75	0.61	0.79	0.63	0.74
26.94	26.63	25.61	26.78	26.96	25.67	26.60
21.86	20.56	19.41	20.21	19.47	17.92	18.60
0.60	0.65	0.76	0.64	0.88	0.83	0.59
0.50	0.53	0.17	0.76	0.78	1.25	1.03
3.63	3.89	0.81	3.88	2.13	3.83	4.49
24.25	22.5	22.16	21.88	21.16	24.31	29.30

主要统计指标解释

城市家庭人口 指居住在一起,经济上合在一起共同生活的家庭成员。凡计算为家庭人口的成员其全部收支都包括在本家庭中。

城市就业者负担人数 指家庭人口与就业人口之比。

城市居民家庭总收入、可支配收入 城市居民家庭总收入指生活在一起的所有家庭成员得到的工资性收入、经营净收入、财产性收入、转移性收入之和,不包括出售财务收入和借贷收入。城市居民家庭可支配收入 指家庭成员得到可用于最终消费支出和其他非义务性支出以及储蓄的总和,即居民家庭可以用来自由支配的收入。它是家庭总收入扣除交纳的个人所得税、个人交纳的社会保障费以及记账补贴后的收入。计算公式为:

可支配收入 = 家庭总收入 - 交纳个人所得税 - 个人交纳的社会保障支出 - 记账补贴

城市居民消费性支出 指被调查的城市居民家庭用于日常生活的全部支出,包括购买商品支出和文化生活、服务等支出。包括用于赠送的商品或服务。不包括罚没、丢失款和缴纳的各种税款(如个人所得税、牌照税、房产税等),也不包括个体劳动者生产经营过程中发生的各项费用。

农村居民家庭整、半劳动力整劳动力 指男子18周岁到50周岁,女子18周岁到45周岁;半劳动力指男子16周岁到17周岁,51周岁到60周岁;女子16周岁到17周岁,46周岁到55周岁,同时具有劳动能力的人。虽然在劳动年龄之内,但已丧失劳动能力的人,不应算为劳动力;超过劳动年龄,但能经常参加劳动,计入半劳动力数内。常住人口中的职工,若这些职工为劳动力,就包括在本户的整半劳动力中。

农村居民家庭总收入、纯收入农村居民家庭总收入 指调查期内农村住户和住户成员从各种来源渠道得到的收入总和。按收入的性质划分为工资性收入、家庭经营收入、财产性收入和转移性收入。农民人均纯收入指按人口平均的纯收入水平,反映的是一个地区或一个农户农村居民的平均收入水平。纯收入指农村住户当年从各个来源得到的总收入相应地扣除所发生的费用后的收入总和。纯收入主要用于再生产投入和当年生活消费支出,也可用于储蓄和各种非义务性支出。计算方法:

纯收入 = 总收入 - 家庭经营费用支出 - 税费支出 - 生产性固定资产折旧 - 赠送农村外部亲友支出

农村居民家庭生活消费支出 指农村常住居民家庭用于日常生活的全部开支,是反映和研究农民家庭实际生活消费水平高低的重要指标。

Explanatory Notes on Main Statistical Indicators

Population of Urban Households refer to members of the household living and sharing economically together. All income and expenditure of the population of the household are included in the income and expenditure of the household.

Number of Dependents per Urban Employee refers to the ratio between number of persons in urban households and the number of dependents.

Total Income and Disposable Income of Urban Households Total Income of Urban Households refers to the sum of wage income, net business income, income from properties, and income from transfers of members of the households, excluding income from selling of properties and income from borrowings. Disposable Income of Urban Households refers to the actual income at the disposal of members of the households which can be used for final consumption, other non-compulsory expenditure and savings. This equals to total income minus income tax, personal contribution to social security and sample household subsidy for keeping dairies. Following formula is used:

Disposable income = total income - income tax - personal contribution to social security - sample household subsidy for keeping dairies.

Consumption Expenditure of Urban Households refers to total expenditure of the sample households for consumption in daily life, including expenditure for various commodities and expenses for non-commodity items such as culture and service, including commodities and service give the other person as a present, but excluding fines and confiscation, loss, tax payments (such as income tax, real estates tax, etc,) and various expenses by individual laborers for business purposes.

Rural Full/Semi Labour Force Full labour force refers to persons capable of work, aged 18-50 for males and 18-45 for females. Semi labour force refers to persons capable of work, aged 16-17 and 51-60 for males and 16-17 and 46-55 for females. Persons at their working ages but not capable of work are not to be included as labour force. Persons not at working ages but participating regularly in work are included in semi labour force. For staff and workers as resident population of the household, they are included as full or semi labour force of the household if they are in the labour force.

Total Income and Net Income of Rural Households Total Income of Rural Households refers to the sum of income earned from various sources by the rural households and their members during the reference period, and is classified as income from wages and salaries, income from from household operations, income from properties and income from transfers.

Net Income of Rural Households refers to the total income of rural households from all sources minus all corresponding expenses. the formula for calculation is an follows:

Net income = total income household operation expenses taxes and fees depreciation of fixed assets for production subsidy for participating in household survey gifts to non rural relatives.

Consumption Expenditure of Rural Households refers to total expenses of rural households on daily life. This indicator is used to show the actual consumption level of peasants.

10 城市建设、环境保护
CITY CONSTRUCTION AND ENVIRONMENT PROTECTION

简要说明

一、本篇资料的主要内容

本篇资料主要反映了全市城市基础设施基本情况，包括市政设施、供水、供电、公共交通、园林绿化、燃气供热、城市环卫、环境保护及工业“三废”排放情况等方面的资料。

二、本篇资料的来源

1、本篇资料中市政设施、供水、公共交通、园林绿化、燃气供热、城市环卫相关资料来源于市建设委员会的城市建设统计年报，由市统计局固定资产投资统计处整理提供。

2、本篇资料中供电资料来源于青岛供电公司，由市统计局能源统计处整理提供。

3、本篇资料中环境保护、环境质量及工业“三废”排放情况来源于市环境保护局，由市统计局能源统计处整理提供。

Brief Introduction

I. Main Content

Data in this chapter show the basic conditions of public facilities of the whole city, including urban construction and infrastructure, water supply, electricity supply, public communications, urban greenery, gas and heating, urban sanitation, environmental protection and discharge conditions of industrial waste water, waste gas and solid waste, etc.

II. Source of Data

(1)Data on conditions of urban construction and infrastructure, water supply, public communications, urban greenery, gas and heating, urban sanitation are based on the annual report of city construction provided by Qingdao Municipal Construction Commission, and compiled by the Division of Investment and Construction Statistics of Qingdao Municipal Bureau of Statistics.

(2)Data on electricity supply are provided by Qingdao Power Corporation, and compiled by the Division of Energy Statistics of Qingdao Municipal Bureau of Statistics.

(3)Data on environmental protection, environmental conditions and discharge conditions of industrial waste water, waste gas and solid waste are provided by Qingdao Municipal Bureau of Environmental Protection ,and compiled by the Division of Energy Statistics of Qingdao Municipal Bureau of Statistics.

10－1 主要年份城市建设和公用事业

MAJOR YEAR'S CITY CONSTRUCTION AND PUBLIC UTILITIES

年份 Year	建成区面积 (平方公里) Developed Areas(sq. km)	年末道路长度 (公里) Length of Roads at Year-end(km)	年末道路面积 (万平方米) Area of Roads at Year-end (10000 sq. m)	公共汽车、电车线路网长度(公里) Network Length of Bus and Trolley Bus(km)
1949	27	243	206	26.4
1952	29	245	213	124.4
1957	36	248	217	232.3
1962	55	266	235	252.8
1965	57	266	235	308.1
1970	59	374	346	358.5
1975	63	392	355	389.3
1978	66	408	368	422.1
1980	72	408	377	474.1
1985	79	462	464	611.3
1987	81	578	575	581
1989	92.5	541	583	661
1990	94.3	667	786	777
1991	94.7	673	826	922
1992	95.4	683	840	988
1993	99.9	764	944	1 094
1994	103.9	811	985	1 372
1995	106	936	1 177	1 101
1996	110	991	1 339	1 211
1997	112	1 047	1 436	1 492
1998	114	1 106	1 436	1 859
1999	116	1 171	1 698	2 339
2000	119.1	1 192	1 789	2 711
2001	123	1 248	2 169	2 521
2002	133	1 426	2 594	896
2003	145.9	1 595	2 816	973
2004	154.8	1 755	3 254	1 185
2005	178.8	1 862	3 547	1 159
2006	227.5	3 160	5 218	1 362
2007	250.7	3 288	5 411	1 480
2008	267.1	3 318	5 596	1 470
2009	272.9	3 402	5 763	1 216
2010	282.3	3 409	5 893	1 383
2011	291.5	3 705	6 605	1 719
2012	374.6	4 281	7 528	1 978

注：1. 自2002年起人均公共绿地面积按辖区内全部人口计算。

2. 2005年以前所用园林绿地面积；公共绿地面积；人均公共绿地面积；公园、动物园个数；公园、动物园面积指标分别改为现在的绿地面积；公园绿地面积；人均公园绿地面积；公园个数；公园面积。

3. 2012年城市建设数据由建委提供，包括范围：市南区、市北区、李沧区、崂山区、黄岛区、城阳区。黄岛区包含开发区、保税区和原胶南划入的6个街道办事处的数据。与以前年度范围不同，数据不可比。

Note：1. Per capita public green areas is calculated at total population in the area under jurisdiction since 2002.

2. Before 2005, the corresponding indicators of greenbelt area, park greenbelt area, per capita park greenbelt area, coverage rate of greenbelt, number of parks and area of parks were greenland area , public greenbelt area , per capita public greenbelt area, coverage rate of green, number of parks and zoos, area of parks and zoos.

3. In 2012, the data on city construction are provided by Qingdao Urban and Rural Construction Commision, include: Shinan, Shibei, Licang, Laoshan, Huangdao, Chengyang. The statistics of Huangdao include Development Zone. Free Trade Zone and 6 sub-districts to be under the jurisdiction of original Jiaonan. The figures are not comparable with those over the years.

10－1 续表1
continued

年　份 Year	自来水供水管道长度（公里）Length of Tap Water Pipelines（km）	全年供水总量（万立方米）Annual Volume of Tap Water Supply（10000 cu. m）	#全年售水量（万立方米）Annual Volume of Tap Water Sale（10000 cu. m）	#居民家庭用水 of which: Consumption for Residential Use	用水普及率（%）Coverage Rate of Population with Access to Tap Water（%）	排水管道长度（公里）Length of Sewage Pipes（km）	全年用电量（亿千瓦时）Annual Volume of Electricity Supply（100 million kW·h）	#居民生活用电 of which: Consumption for Residential Use
1949	308	721	456	331	89.0	200	0.88	0.14
1952	341	778	612	310	90.0	227	1.85	0.14
1957	412	1 392	1 296	606	93.0	273	2.61	0.26
1962	483	2 700	2 512	937	98.0	290	3.77	0.57
1965	500	3 220	2 979	929	98.0	295	5.92	0.68
1970	521	4 503	4 106	1 085	99.0	350	9.83	1.02
1975	564	6 726	6 302	1 950	99.0	361	12.41	1.43
1978	572	5 334	4 975	1 314	99.0	382	16.34	1.62
1980	588	8 224	7 874	2 577	99.0	394	21.48	2.78
1985	685	7 557	7 038	2 628	99.9	505	26.39	2.87
1987	749	10 716	9 155	3 691	99.9	569	34.15	4.01
1989	853	10 349	8 606	3 666	97.0	620	38.36	3.38
1990	873	11 896	10 211	4 270	96.9	645	41.08	4.32
1991	908	13 865	11 760	4 990	96.6	649	44.51	5.34
1992	1 035	16 385	13 070	5 931	96.5	672	51.78	6.84
1993	1 123	16 137	14 027	6 124	99.1	734	55.02	7.66
1994	1 124	17 367	14 716	6 405	100	811	60.74	8.78
1995	1 046	22 513	15 810	7 050	100	990	67.23	10.16
1996	1 182	23 277	16 566	7 731	100	1 051	72.87	12.23
1997	1 266	24 130	17 215	8 787	100	1 167	77.82	13.73
1998	1 390	23 845	17 271	9 115	100	1 210	79.65	14.28
1999	1 471	23 849	18 558	10 032	100	1 301	88.12	15.31
2000	1 524	25 414	20 642	11 405	100	1 460	106.80	16.00
2001	1 665	22 225	18 556	10 555	100	1 539	116.10	17.52
2002	1 781	27 662	21 684	10 129	100	1 641	131.44	18.31
2003	2 060	27 594	21 483	10 142	100	1 884	147.68	19.88
2004	2 566	30 877	23 864	11 695	100	2 002	167.95	23.63
2005	2 876	33 265	25 874	12 536	100	2 309	193.81	33.76
2006	3 984	30 524	25 572	10 682	100	3 994	215.35	34.87
2007	4 187	31 533	26 454	11 408	100	4 079	236.42	37.42
2008	4 642	32 675	27 396	11 301	100	4 229	250.07	40.31
2009	4 767	33 490	28 274	12 250	100	4 555	259.42	43.29
2010	4 926	34 909	29 617	12 524	100	4 708	292.97	49.50
2011	5 121	34 109	28 837	10 049	100	5 187	313.44	50.13
2012	5 243	38 945	33 039	12 121	100	6 814	318.36	51.64

10－1 续表2
continued

年 份 Year	公共汽车、电车营运车辆(辆) Number of Bus and Trolley Bus under Operation(unit)	全年客运量(万人次) Annual Passenger Traffic(10000 person-times)	出租汽车(辆) Number of Taxi(unit)	使用液化气、煤气、天然气人数(万人) Population with Access to Gas (10000 persons)	液化气 Liquefied Petroleum	煤 气 Coal Gas	天然气 Natural Gas	液化气供气量(吨) Volume of Liquefied Petroleum Supply(ton)
1949	32	298						
1952	76	932						
1957	112	4 110						
1962	127	4 747						
1965	173	6 092						
1970	224	13 002						
1975	324	14 426		2	2			184.9
1978	409	27 351		17	17			3 246
1980	485	38 981	48	24	24			4 345
1985	621	48 852	219	42.1	42.1			10 619
1987	679	56 102	652	56.4	45.4	11.0		12 947
1989	751	63 212	782	62.5	47.5	15.0		14 503
1990	801	63 495	832	75.0	57.4	17.6		17 512
1991	1 372	67 552	1 070	76.2	57.4	18.8		17 963
1992	1 470	73 529	1828	82.8	62.0	20.8		19 565
1993	1 875	72 427	4 874	88.4	64.6	23.8		22 224
1994	1 850	78 231	5 806	103.6	77.4	26.2		24 684
1995	1 891	71 867	5 887	116.2	82.9	33.3		32 443
1996	2 012	49 077	6 660	126.0	88.0	38.0		40 651
1997	2 148	55 642	6 861	133.6	92.9	40.7		38 717
1998	2 184	51 042	7 469	146.8	97.8	49.0		45 381
1999	2 470	55 414	7 839	154.9	98.3	56.6		40 537
2000	3 141	59 879	7 933	164.1	93.3	70.8		46 951
2001	3 453	60 167	8 110	168.8	87.5	81.3		45 295
2002	3 681	61 713	8 376	224.2	133.8	90.4		60 123
2003	3 648	58 792	8 109	246.7	138.3	93.1	15.3	67 803
2004	3 848	66 463	8 144	258.4	140.6	78.8	39.0	58 548
2005	4 039	68 776	8 121	265.0	132.6	45.7	86.7	78 000
2006	4 167	73 726	8 146	271.0	112.5	49.5	109.0	97 343
2007	4 524	78 702	8 221	275.6	104.1	12.1	159.4	79 715
2008	4 701	82 460	9 241	276.3	91.9	10.5	173.9	81 987
2009	4 288	81 768	9 316	276.1	59.8	12.3	204.0	96 721
2010	4 664	85 251	9 539	276.3	36.7	12.6	227.0	80 073
2011	5 419	89 614	9 683	277.1	25.8	12.6	238.7	79 812
2012	5 640	97 922	9 693	313.7	36.7	13.1	263.9	54 341

注：1990 年以前公共营运车辆不包括系统外及个体。

Note: Vehicles not belonging to system and individual vehicles are not contained in public operating vehicles before 1990.

10－1 续表3
continued

年　份 Year	煤气供气量（万立方米） Volume of Coal Gas Supply (10000 cu. m)	天然气供气量（万立方米） Volume of Natural Gas Supply (10000 cu. m)	燃气普及率（%） Coverage Rate of Population with Access to Gas(%)	绿地面积（公顷） Area of Green Areas (hectare)	公园绿地面积（公顷） Park Green Areas (hectare)	人均公园绿地面积(平方米) Per Capita Park Green Areas(sq. m)	建成区绿化覆盖率(%) Green Coverage Rate of Developed Areas(%)	公园（个） Number of Parks and Zoos(unit)	公园面积（公顷） Area of Parks and Zoos (hectare)
1949				133	42	0.7	4.9	3	43
1952				134	43	0.7	4.4	4	45
1957				245	132	1.7	6.9	10	122
1962				771	184	2.2	14.0	12	174
1965				777	184	2.1	13.7	12	174
1970				772	184	2.1	13.0	6	117
1975			2.3	465	162	1.8	7.6	5	134
1978			18.6	469	162	1.7	7.6	6	165
1980			24.5	625	206	2.1	10.4	6	152
1985			36.3	1 072	255	2.3	17.3	7	153
1987	491		47.0	1 790	427	3.6	21.8	20	372
1989	2 585		47.3	1 941	459	3.5	21.7	22	381
1990	3 073		56.2	2 120	492	3.7	22.8	26	404
1991	3 439		56.5	2 318	500	3.7	24.4	28	443
1992	3 824		60.0	2 471	515	3.7	25.9	28	417
1993	4 215		63.1	2 488	543	3.9	26.5	31	453
1994	4 116		63.1	2 866	572	4.0	27.9	31	463
1995	4 734		79.2	4 547	771	5.3	30.1	33	675
1996	5 447		83.9	4 679	836	5.6	30.4	33	675
1997	5 920		87.3	4 717	924	6.0	31.3	34	730
1998	5 959		92.5	6 812	1 047	6.6	35.0	35	775
1999	7 319		96.0	7 007	1 186	7.4	35.9	36	791
2000	9 567		98.0	7 439	1 423	8.5	37.0	37	790
2001	11 814		99.0	7 688	1 588	9.3	37.5	39	832
2002	13 500		99.5	7 967	1 791	8.1	36.4	43	926
2003	14 826	1 181	100	8 829	2 305	9.3	37.5	45	1 034
2004	15 503	2 710	100	10 047	2 842	11	38.0	48	1 421
2005	16 573	7 456	100	11 137	3 132	11.8	38.8	47	1 110
2006	9 821	13 876	100	11 756	3 198	11.8	39.2	47	1 188
2007	9 516	18 103	100	15 369	3 661	13.3	37.8	73	1 258
2008	8 691	21 780	100	15 630	4 014	14.5	41.5	77	1 815
2009	7 523	26 948	100	16 003	4 003	14.5	43.4	71	1 897
2010	9 153	35 681	100	16 619	4 027	14.6	43.38	72	1 9[illegible]7
2011	9 137	46 147	100	18 013	4 041	14.6	44.69	74	1 951
2012	8 148	68 397	100	21 471	4 573	14.6	44.7	78	2 112

注：1. 自2002年起人均公共绿地面积按辖区内全部人口计算。

2. 2005年以前所用园林绿地面积；公共绿地面积；人均公共绿地面积；公园、动物园个数；公园、动物园面积指标分别改为现在的绿地面积；公共绿地面积；人均公园绿地面积；公园个数；公园面积。

Note: 1. Per capita public green areas is calculated at total population in the area under jurisdiction since 2002.

2. Before 2005, the corresponding indicators of greenbelt area, park greenbelt area, per capita park greenbelt area, coverage rate of greenbelt, number of parks and area of parks were greenland area, public greenbelt area, per capita public greenbelt area, coverage rate of green, number of parks and zoos, area of parks and zoos.

10－2 全年供电(2012 年)
ANNUAL ELECTRICITY SUPPLY(2012)

全年供电 项　目	Item	单位	Unit	2012
发电设备总容量	Total Capacity of Generation Equipment	万千瓦	10000 kW	411.26
#青岛电厂	Qingdao Power Plant	万千瓦	10000 kW	120
黄岛电厂	Huangdao Power Plant	万千瓦	10000 kW	177
全年发电量	Annual Electricity Generation	亿千瓦时	100 million kW · h	189.43
#青岛电厂	Qingdao Power Plant	亿千瓦时	100 million kW · h	62.5
黄岛电厂	Huangdao Power Plant	亿千瓦时	100 million kW · h	97.43
全年实际用电量	Annual Electricity Consumption	亿千瓦时	100 million kW · h	318.36
#工业	Industrial Consumption	亿千瓦时	100 million kW · h	199.99
农业	Agricultural Consumption	亿千瓦时	100 million kW · h	1.4
生活	Residential Consumption	亿千瓦时	100 million kW · h	51.64
平均每日用电量	Average Daily Consumption	万千瓦时	10000 kW · h	8 722.1

10－3 分行业用电(2012 年)
ELECTRICITY CONSUMPTION BY SECTOR(2012)

单位:万千瓦时(10 000 kW · h)

行业	Sector	2012	2012 年比 2011 年增长(%) Growth Rate in 2012 over 2011(%)
全社会用电总计	**Total Electricity Consumption**	**3 183 560**	**1.57**
一、农、林、牧、渔业	Farming, Forestry, Animal Husbandryand Fishery	43 348	-16.95
二、工业	Industry	1 999 928	2.02
三、建筑业	Construction	46 902	-1.62
四、交通运输、仓储和邮政业	Transport, Storage and Post	84 625	-4.98
五、信息传输、计算机服务和软件业	Information Transmission, Computer Services and Software	26 784	9.64
六、商业、住宿和餐饮业	Trade, Hotels and Catering Services	151 033	4.23
七、金融、房地产、商务及居民服务业	Financial Intermediation, Real Estate and Business Services	163 778	3.24
八、公共事业及管理组织	Public Management and Social Organization	150 732	5.05
九、城乡居民生活用电	Household Consumption	516 430	3.02
城镇居民	Urban Area	289 234	-5.30
乡村居民	Rural Area	227 196	15.99

10－4 城市供水(2012 年)
URBAN WATER SUPPLY(2012)

项　目	Item	单位	Unit	2012
自来水供水管道长度	Length of Tap Water Pipelines	公里	km	5 643
综合生产能力	Synthesis Production Capacity	万立方米/日	10000 cu. m/day	141
全年供水总量	Annual Volume of Tap Water Supply	万立方米	10000 cu. m	38 945
#售水量	of which: Volume of Tap Water Sale	万立方米	10000 cu. m	33 039
#生产运营用水	of which: Consumption for Production Use	万立方米	10000 cu. m	13 635
公共服务用水	Consumption for Public Services Use	万立方米	10000 cu. m	6 962
居民家庭用水	Consumption for Residential Use	万立方米	10000 cu. m	12 121
其他用水	Consumption for Other Uses	万立方米	10000 cu. m	320
平均每日供水量	Daily Volume of Tap Water Supply	万立方米	10000 cu. m	106.7
#生产用	of which: Consumption for Production Use	万立方米	10000 cu. m	37.36
生活用	Consumption for Residential Use	万立方米	10000 cu. m	33.21
用水户数	Households with Access to Water	户	household	1 123 385
用水人口	Population with Access to water	万人	10000 persons	300.38
工业用水量重复利用率	Recycle Rate of Water for Industrial Use	%	%	87.53

10－5 城市公共交通(2012 年)
URBAN PUBLIC TRAFFIC(2012)

项　目	Item	单位	Unit	2012
公共汽车、电车线路网长度	Network Length of Bus and Trolley Bus	公里	km	1 978
公共汽车、电车营运车辆	Number of Bus and Trolley Bus under Operation	辆	unit	5 640
#汽车	Bus	辆	unit	5 485
电车	Trolley Bus	辆	unit	155
公共汽车、电车全年客运量	Annual Passenger Traffic of Bus and Trolley Bus	万人次	10000 person-times	97 922
公共汽车、电车平均每日客运量	Daily Passenger Traffic of Bus and Trolley Bus	万人	10000 persons	268.3
出租汽车数	Number of Taxi	辆	unit	9 693
轮渡运营船数	Number of Ferry Boat under Operation	艘	ship	38
轮渡客运总量	Passenger Traffic of Ferry Boat	万人次	10000 person-times	220.5
轮渡平均每日客运量	Daily Passenger Traffic of Ferry Boat	万人	10000 persons	0.6

10－6 城市供气(2012 年)
URBAN GAS SUPPLY(2012)

项 目	Item	单位	Unit	2012
煤气供应总量	Volume of Coal Gas Supply	万立方米	10000 cu. m	8 148
#家庭用量	Household Consumption	万立方米	10000 cu. m	1 255
煤气用气户数	Households with Access to Coal Gas	户	household	47 207
#家庭用户	Household Users	户	household	47 111
液化石油气供应总量	Volume of Liquefied Petroleum Supply	吨	ton	54 341
#家庭用量	Household Consumption	吨	ton	22 335
液化石油气用气户数	Households with Access to Liquefied Petroleum	户	household	200 863
#家庭用户	Household Users	户	household	199 081
天然气供应总量	Volume of Natural Gas Supply	万立方米	10000 cu. m	68 397
#家庭用量	Household Consumption	万立方米	10000 cu. m	15 808
天然气用气户数	Households with Access to Natural Gas	户	household	1 054 644
#家庭用户	Household Users	户	household	1 050 632
燃气普及率	Coverage Rate of Population with Access to Gas	%	%	100

10－7 城市环境卫生(2012 年)
URBAN ENVIRONMENTAL SANITATION(2012)

项 目	Item	单位	Unit	2012
市容环卫专用车辆总数	Number of Special Vehicles for Environmental Sanitation	辆	unit	1 262
生活垃圾清运量	Volume of Garbage Disposal	万吨	10000 tons	147
生活垃圾无害化处理厂(场)数	Number of Bio-safety Disposal Plant of Garbage	座	unit	4
生活垃圾无害化处理能力	Bio-safety Disposal Capacity of Garbage	吨/日	ton/day	4 936
生活垃圾无害化处理量	Bio-safety Disposal Volume of Garbage	万吨	10000 tons	147
道路清扫保洁面积	Area under Cleaning Program	万平方米	10000 sq. m	5 127
#机械化	of which: Mechanization	万平方米	10000 sq. m	2 646
粪便清运量	Volume of Excrement and Urine Disposal	万吨	10000 tons	9.93
粪便无害化处理量	Bio-safety Disposal Volume of Excrement and Urine	万吨	10000 tons	9.93
公共厕所	Public Toilets	个	unit	553

10－8 城市道路、下水道及绿化(2012 年)
URBAN ROAD,SEWAGE AND GREEN(2012)

项　目	Item	单位	Unit	2012
道路	**Road**			
年末道路长度	Length of Roads at Year-end	公里	km	4 281
年末道路面积	Area of Roads at Year-end	万平方米	10000 sq. m	7 528
#人行道面积	of which:Area of Pavements	万平方米	10000 sq. m	1 585.27
排水管道长度	Length of Sewage Pipes	公里	km	6 813.72
园林绿化	**Greening**			
绿化覆盖面积	Area of Green Coverage Areas	公顷	hectare	23 720
绿地面积	Area of Green Areas	公顷	hectare	21 471
公园绿地面积	Area of Park Green Areas	公顷	hectare	4 573
公园数	Number of Parks and Zoos	个	unit	78
公园面积	Area of Parks and Zoos	公顷	hectare	2 112
游人量	Number of Tourists	万人次	10000 person-times	1 269.3
城市每人平均公园绿地面积	Per Capita Park Green Area	平方米	sq. m	14.58
建成区绿化覆盖率	Green Coverage Rate of Developed Areas	%	%	44.7

10 -9 环境保护基本情况(2012 年)
BASIC CONDITIONS OF ENVIRONMENTAL PROTECTION(2012)

项目	Item	单位	Unit	2012	2011	2012 年比 2011 年增(+)减(-)% 2012 Compared to 2011(+/-)
二氧化硫排放总量	Sulphur Dioxide Emission	吨	ton	99 623	102 837.75	-3.13
氮氧化物排放总量	Discharge Amount of Nitrogenoxides	吨	ton	119353.19	130 845.62	-8.78
烟尘排放总量	Soot Emission	吨	ton	40753.56	42 390.32	-3.86
工业粉尘排放总量	Industrial Dust Emission	吨	ton	40753.56	42 390.32	-3.86
工业固体废物排放总量	Industrial Solid Wastes Discharged	吨	ton			
化学需氧量排放总量	Discharge Amount of Chemical Oxygen Demand	吨	ton	149429.67	158 338.73	-5.63
氨氮排放总量	Discharge Amount of Ammonia and Nitrogen	吨	ton	12573.29	13 231.17	-4.97
废水排放总量	Waste Water Discharged	万吨	10 000 tons	42796.99	41 157.04	3.98

10 -10 环境质量状况(2012 年)
ENVIRONMENT CONDITION(2012)

项目	Item	单位	Unit	2012	2011	2012 年比 2011 年增(+)减(-)% 2012 Compared to 2011(+/-)
市区空气质量优良率	The Percentages of Excellent Or Good Air Quality of Urban Area	%	%	92.9	91.5	1.53
空气质量功能区达标率	The Reaching Rate of Air Quality For Corresponding Functional Regions	%	%	100	100	0.00
近岸海域功能区达标率	The Reaching Rate of The Offshore Sea Water for Corresponding Functional Regions	%	%	81.3	84.4	-3.67
市区区域环境噪声平均等效声级	The Average Equivalent Sound Level of the Urban Regional Environmental Noise	分贝(A)	db(A)	53.7	53.7	0.00
市区道路交通噪声平均等效声级	The Average Equivalent Sound Level of the Urban Road Traffic Noise	分贝(A)	db(A)	68.4	68.1	0.44

10－11 工业“三废”排放情况(2012 年)

DISCHARGE CONDITIONS OF INDUSTRIAL WASTE WATER,WASTE GAS AND SOLID WASTE(2012)

项　目	Item	单位	Unit	2012	2011	2012年比2011年增(+)减(-)% 2012 Compared to 2011(+/-)
工业废水排放总量	Industrial Waste Water Discharged	万吨	10000 tons	11 145.44	11 229.75	-0.75
废水治理设施数	Number of Facilities for Treatment of Waste Water	套	set	476	486	-2.06
废水治理设施处理能力	Capacity of Facilities for Treatment of Waste Water	万吨/日	10000 tons/day	172.1	112	53.66
进入城市污水处理厂量	Volume Handled by Sewage Treatment Plant	万吨	10000 tons	8 099.65	8 138.74	-0.48
工业废水排放达标量	Industrial Waste Water Meeting Discharge Standards	万吨	10000 tons			
化学需氧量排放量	Discharge Amount of Chemical Oxygen Demand	吨	ton	8 280.95	7 621.28	8.66
氨氮排放量	Discharge Amount of Ammonia and Nitrogen	吨	ton	749.57	755.67	-0.81
工业废气排放总量	Industrial Waste Air Discharged	万标立方米	10000 cu. m	24 297 552	24 383 323	-0.35
废气治理设施数	Number of Facilities for Treatment of Waste Air	套	set	1 175	1 197	-1.84
其中:脱硫设施数	of which:Desulphurization Facilities	套	set	280	298	-6.04
废气治理设施处理能力	Capacity of Facilities for Treatment of Waste Air	万标立方米/时	10000 cu. m/hr	8 335.78	8 562.45	-2.65
其中:脱硫能力	of which:Desulphurization Capacity	万立方米/时	ton/hr	2 385	2 792.39	
二氧化硫去除量	Sulphur Dioxide Removed	吨	ton	190 869.29	173 459.02	10.04
二氧化硫排放量	Sulphur Dioxide Emission	吨	ton	72 562.62	75 777.43	-4.24
其中:达标排放量	of which:Amount Meeting Discharge Standards	吨	ton			
烟尘排放量	Soot Emission	吨	ton	26 308.03	26 845.17	-2.00
其中:达标排放量	of which:Amount Meeting Discharge Standards	吨	ton			
工业粉尘排放量	Industrial Dust Emission	吨	ton			
其中:达标排放量	of which:Amount Meeting Discharge Standards	吨	ton			
工业固体废物产生量	Industrial Solid Wastes Producted	万吨	10000 tons	888.45	891.38	-0.33
其中:危险废物	of which:Hazardous Wastes	吨	ton	35 521	35 996	-1.32
工业固体废物综合利用量	Industrial Solid Wastes Comprehensive Utilized	万吨	10000 tons	876.02	883.55	-0.85
工业固体废物排放量	Industrial Solid Wastes Discharged	万吨	10000 tons			
其中:危险废物	of which:Hazardous Wastes	吨	ton			
污染治理项目完成投资	Investment in Treatment Projects of Pollution	万元	10000 yuan	13 301	10 219	30.16
污染治理项目数	Number of Treatment Projects of Pollution	个	item	25	25	
当年竣工治理项目数	Number of Completed Treatment Projects in the Year	个	item	24	19	26.32

主要统计指标解释

供水综合生产能力　指按供水设施取水、净化、送水、出厂输水干管等环节设计能力计算的综合生产能力。

年末供水管道长度　指从送水泵至用户水表之间所有管道的长度。不包括新安装尚未使用的管道。

用水普及率　指城市用水人口数与城市人口总数的比率。计算公式：

$$用水普及率=\frac{城市用水人口数}{城市人口总数}\times100\%$$

全年供水总量　指报告期供水企业(单位)供出的全部水量。包括有效供水量和漏损水量。

全年供气总量　指全年燃气企业(单位)向用户供应的燃气数量。包括销售量和损失量。

用气普及率　指报告期末使用燃气的城市人口数与城市人口总数的比率。计算公式为：

$$用气普及率=\frac{城市用气人口数}{城市人口总数}\times100\%$$

年末道路长度　指年末道路长度和与道路相通的广场、桥梁、隧道的长度，按车行道中心线计算。在统计时只统计路面宽度在3.5米(含3.5米)以上的各种铺装道路，包括开放型工业区和住宅区道路在内。

工业废气排放量　指报告期内企业厂区内燃料燃烧和生产工艺过程中产生的各种排入大气的含有污染物的气体的总量，以标准状态(273K，101325Pa)计算。

工业废水排放量　指经过企业厂区所有排放口排到企业外部的工业废水量。包括生产废水、外排的直接冷却水、超标排放的矿井地下水和与工业废水混排的厂区生活污水，不包括外排的间接冷却水(清污不分流的间接冷却水应计算在内)。

工业废水排放达标量　指各项指标都达到国家或地方排放标准的外排工业废水量，包括未经处理外排达标的和经过处理后外排达标的和两部分。国家排放标准见GB8978—88。

工业固体废物产生量　指企业在生产过程中产生的固体状、半固体状和高浓度液体状废弃物的总量，包括危险废物、冶炼废渣、粉煤灰、炉渣、煤矸渣、尾矿、放射性废物和其他废物等；不包括矿山开采的剥离废石和掘进废石(煤矸石和呈酸性或碱性的废石除外)酸性或碱性废石是指采掘的废石其流经水、雨淋水的pH值小于4或pH值大于10.5者。

工业粉尘排放量　指企业在生产工艺过程中排放的能在空气中悬浮一定时间的固体颗粒物排放量。如钢铁企业的耐火材料粉尘、焦化企业的筛焦系统粉尘、烧结机的粉尘、石灰窑的粉尘、建材企业的水泥粉尘等。不包括电厂排入大气的烟尘。

化学需氧量(COD)　测量有机和无机物质化学分解所消耗氧的质量浓度的水污染指数。

Explanatory Notes on Main Statistical Indicators

Production Capacity of Water Supply　refers to the designed comprehensive production capacity of water facilities, covering the 4 links of water collection, purification, conveyance, and outflow through trunk pipelines.

Length of Water Supply Pipelines at the Year-end　refers to the total length of all the pipelines between the water pumps and the user water meters, excluding pipelines newly installed but not used yet.

Coverage Rate of Urban Population with Access to Tap Water　refers to the ratio of the urban population with access to tap water to the total urban population. The formula is:

Coverage rate of urban population with access to tap water = (Urban population with access to tap water)/(Urban population) × 100%

Annual Volume of Water Supply refers to the total volume of water supplied by water-works(units) during the reference period, including both the effective water supply and loss during the water supply.

Annual Volume of Gas Supply refers to the total volume of gas provided to users by gas-producing enterprises(units) in a year, including the volume sold and the volume lost.

Coverage Rate of Urban Population with Access to Gas refers to the ratio of the urban population with access to gas to the total urban population at the end of the reference period. The formula is:

Coverage rate of urban population with access to gas = (Urban population with access to gas/Urban population) × 100%

Length of Paved Roads at the Year-end refers to the length of roads with paved surface including squares bridges and tunnels connected with roads by the end of the year. Length of the roads is measured by the central lines for vehicles for paved roads with a width of 3.5 meters and over, including roads in open-ended factory compounds and residential quarters.

Industrial Waste Air Emission refers to discharge into atmosphere of waste air containing pollutants generated from fuel burning and production process in enterprises within a given period of time. It is calculated at standard status(273K, 101325Pa).

Waste Water Discharged by Industry refers to the volume of waste water discharged by industrial enterprises through all their outlets, including waste water from production process, directly cooled water, groundwater from mining wells which does not meet discharge standards and sewage from households mixed with waste water produced by industrial activities, but excluding indirectly cooled water discharged(It should be included if the discharge is not separated with waste water).

Industrial Waste Water Meeting Discharge Standards refers to volume of industrial waste water discharge which, with or without treatment, reaches national or local standards with regard to all pollutants. National Discharge standards see GB8978—88.

Industrial Solid Wastes Produced refers to total volume of solid, semi-solid and high concentration liquid residues produced by industrial enterprises from production process in a given period of time, including hazardous wastes, slag, coal ash, gangue, tailings, radioactive residues and other wastes, but excluding stones stripped or dug out in mining(gangue and acid or alkaline stones not included). A stone is acid or alkaline depending on the pH value of the water below 4 or above 10.5 when the stone is in, or soaked by, the water.

Industrial Dust Emission refers to volume of dust emitted by production process of enterprises and suspended in the air for a given period of time, including dust from refractory material of iron and steel works, dust from coke-screening systems and sintering machines of coke plants, dust from lime kilns and dust from cement production in building material enterprises, but excluding soot and dust emitted from power plants.

Chemical Oxygen Demand(COD) refers to index of water pollution measuring the mass concentration of oxygen consumed by the chemical breakdown of organic and inorganic matter.

11 农　业
AGRICULTURE

简要说明

一、本篇资料的主要内容

本篇资料主要反映了全市农业生产和农村经济的基本情况，主要包括农林牧渔业总产值、中间消耗、增加值、农村劳动力、耕地、主要农产品产量、农业机械年末拥有量、农业机械化和电气化以及农田水利建设等方面的资料。

二、本篇资料的来源

1、本篇资料中耕地面积资料来源于市国土资源房屋管理局。

2、水产品产量等相关资料来源于市海洋与渔业局。

3、农业机械化等相关资料来源于市农机局。

4、农田水利灌溉等相关资料来源于市水利局。

5、植树造林等相关资料来源于市林业局。

本篇资料由市统计局农村统计处、国家统计局青岛调查队农村调查处整理提供。

Brief Introduction

I. Main Content

Data in this chapter show the basic conditions of agricultural production and rural economy, mainly including agricultural output, intermediate consumption, value added, rural labor force, cultivated land, output of main agricultural produces, agricultural machinery and electrification in rural areas and basic construction on irrigation and drainage.

II. Source of Data

(1)Data on area of cultivated land are provided by Qingdao Municipal Bureau of Land Resources and Housing Management.

(2)Data on output of aquatic products are provided by Qingdao Municipal Bureau of Ocean and Fishery.

(3)Data on Agricultural machinery are provided by Qingdao Municipal Bureau of Agricultural Machinery.

(4)Data on farmland water conservancy are provided by Qingdao Municipal Bureau of Water Conservancy.

(5)Data on forest planting are provided by Qingdao Municipal Forestry Bureau.

Data in this chapter are compiled by the Division of Countryside Statistics of Qingdao Municipal Bureau of Statistics and Division of Rural Household Survey of Survey Office of the National Bureau of Statistics in Qingdao.

11-1 农村基本情况(1980-2012年)

BASIC STATISTICS ON RURAL AREA (1980-2012)

项目	Item	单位	Unit	1980	1990	1995	2000	2005	2006
一、乡村户数、人口、劳动力	**Rural Households, Population and Labor Force**								
乡村户数	Rural Households	万户	10000 households	110.56	133.73	145.71	148.20	151.06	151.1
乡村人口	Rural Population	万人	10000 persons	477.53	495.45	496.93	483.39	478.78	478.32
乡村劳动力	Rural Labor Force	万人	10000 persons	194.10	247.29	258.66	254.62	257.87	264.7
男劳动力	Male	万人	10000 persons	113.67	137.28	139.62	137.09	137.66	141.27
女劳动力	Female	万人	10000 persons	80.43	110.01	119.04	117.53	120.21	123.43
二、年末实有耕地面积	**Year-end Area of Cultivated Land**	**万公顷**	**10000 hectares**					**50.90**	**51.19**
三、农用机械总动力	**Total Agricultural Machinery Power**	**万千瓦**	**10000 kW**	**110.44**	**253.52**	**289.23**	**459.21**	**619.69**	**650.65**
拖拉机	Tractors	台	unit	24 278	55 363	56 391	126 981	163 032	171 155
农用汽车	Agricultural Automobiles	辆	unit	728	3 880	6 314	9 613	11 552	11 098
四、农村用电量	**Electricity Consumed in Rural Areas**	**万千瓦时**	**10000 kW·h**	**20 492**	**67 616**	**134 284**	**189 651**	**372 645**	**413 762**
五、农用化肥施用量(折纯)	**Consumption of Chemical Fertilizer (convert to pure amount)**	**万吨**	**10000 tons**	**12.06**	**20.47**	**31.45**	**32.53**	**33.01**	**32.64**
六、有效灌溉面积	**Irrigated Area**	**万公顷**	**10000 hectares**	**29.66**	**27.47**	**28.70**	**29.52**	**29.65**	**30.31**

11-1 续表
continued

项目	Item	单位	Unit	2007	2008	2009	2010	2011	2012
一、乡村户数、人口、劳动力	**Rural Households, Population and Labor Force**								
乡村户数	Rural Households	万户	10000 households	151.19	151.75	152.37	154.92	154.91	155.66
乡村人口	Rural Population	万人	10000 persons	478.06	480.22	484.81	487.04	488.57	491.10
乡村劳动力	Rural Labor Force	万人	10000 persons	268.31	270.71	274.74	276.03	277.24	276.97
男劳动力	Male	万人	10000 persons	144.04	144.36	146.20	147.09	146.67	146.48
女劳动力	Female	万人	10000 persons	124.27	126.35	128.54	128.94	130.57	130.49
二、年末实有耕地面积	**Year-end Area of Cultivated Land**	**万公顷**	**10000 hectares**	**51.25**	**51.31**	**53.50**			
三、农用机械总动力	**Total Agricultural Machinery Power**	**万千瓦**	**10000 kW**	**680.16**	**697.38**	**719.33**	**763.61**	**784.06**	**797.71**
拖拉机	Tractors	台	unit	173 326	176 156	180 171	200 208	202 022	206 290
农用汽车	Agricultural Automobiles	辆	unit	11 408	11 408	11 408			
四、农村用电量	**Electricity Consumed in Rural Areas**	**万千瓦时**	**10000 kW·h**	**425 715**	**424 292**	**426 306**	**426 819**	**431 646**	**426 815**
五、农用化肥施用量（折纯）	**Consumption of Chemical Fertilizer (convert to pure amount)**	**万吨**	**10000 tons**	**33.89**	**31.05**	**30.17**	**29.89**	**29.37**	**29.09**
六、有效灌溉面积	**Irrigated Area**	**万公顷**	**10000 hectares**	**30.58**	**31.39**	**32.27**	**32.90**	**33.17**	**33.39**

11 -2 农村劳动力(1985 -2012 年)

RURAL LABOR FORCE(1985 -2012)

单位:万人(10 000 persons)

年 份 Year	合 计 Total	农林牧渔业 Farming, Forestry, Animal Husbandry and Fishery	工 业 Industry	建 筑 业 Construction
1985	225.09	147.89	32.92	15.62
1988	238.93	146.00	44.46	17.51
1989	242.70	151.16	44.65	16.46
1990	247.29	155.20	44.48	16.17
1991	253.01	160.31	45.49	15.87
1992	258.23	160.04	47.00	17.25
1993	259.18	159.22	44.04	20.20
1994	258.34	155.74	43.70	21.52
1995	258.66	154.08	44.06	22.33
1996	256.34	151.10	43.08	21.80
1997	258.60	153.07	41.66	22.02
1998	258.50	152.79	40.79	21.68
1999	256.82	149.11	42.18	22.32
2000	254.62	143.59	42.76	22.99
2001	253.98	132.46	47.76	24.66
2002	254.08	119.98	53.66	26.52
2003	257.67	118.27	55.65	26.65
2004	258.91	112.05	60.32	28.36
2005	257.87	103.03	65.59	29.03
2006	264.70	102.28	71.46	28.16
2007	268.31	100.63	74.70	30.97
2008	270.71	100.90	74.82	30.87
2009	274.74	102.64	75.42	31.23
2010	276.04	102.45	76.32	32.10
2011	277.24	102.73	76.87	32.57
2012	276.97	102.24	76.82	32.36

11－2 续表
continued

单位：万人(10 000 persons)

年份 Year	交通运输仓储和邮电业 Transport, Postal and Telecommunication Services	批发零售贸易、餐饮业 Wholesale and Retail Trades and Catering Services	金融保险业 Finance and Insurance	其他劳动力 Other Labor Force
1985	5.23	0.06	19.76	3.61
1988	5.89	0.09	20.40	4.58
1989	6.00	0.12	19.95	4.36
1990	6.11	0.12	20.71	4.50
1991	6.09	0.13	20.52	4.60
1992	7.02	0.16	21.74	5.02
1993	8.93	0.16	20.65	5.58
1994	6.48	10.10		20.80
1995	7.11	10.71		20.37
1996	7.33	11.78		21.25
1997	7.62	12.40		21.83
1998	8.02	13.32		21.90
1999	8.19	14.03		20.99
2000	8.39	16.10		20.79
2001	9.02	17.80		22.28
2002	10.00	20.07		23.85
2003	9.96	20.60		26.54
2004	10.20	24.08		22.95
2005	10.70	25.88		22.34
2006	11.66	25.31		24.37
2007	11.61	27.61		21.16
2008	11.06	28.76		22.09
2009	11.40	29.03		22.75
2010	11.78	28.85		22.01
2011	11.89	29.34		21.02
2012	11.96	29.56		21.11

11－3 分市、区乡村户数、人口、劳动力(2012 年)
RURAL HOUSEHOLDS, POPULATION AND LABOR FORCE BY REGION(2012)

市、区名称	Region	乡村户数（万户）Rural Households (10000 households)	乡村人口（万人）Rural Population (10000 persons)	乡村劳动力(万人) Labor Force of Village (10000 persons)	男劳动力 Male Laborer	女劳动力 Female Laborer	农林牧渔业 Farming, Forestry, Animal Husbandry and Fishery	#林牧渔业 Forestry, Animal Husbandry and Fishery
总　计	**Total**	**155.66**	**491.10**	**276.97**	**146.48**	**130.49**	**102.24**	**19.58**
市　区	Urban Area	25.87	73.66	40.10	21.12	18.98	6.09	2.87
#崂山区	Laoshan District	5.56	16.05	9.09	4.88	4.21	1.87	0.62
原黄岛区	Original Huangdao District	5.06	16.72	9.42	4.99	4.44	1.06	0.69
城阳区	Chengyang District	15.24	40.89	21.59	11.25	10.34	3.15	1.56
即墨市	Jimo	29.71	97.58	55.86	29.42	26.44	16.86	2.96
胶州市	Jiaozhou	19.60	63.01	36.11	18.72	17.39	9.91	0.83
原胶南市	Original Jiaonan	22.12	70.41	36.70	19.69	17.01	13.64	2.75
平度市	Pingdu	37.54	122.80	71.41	37.65	33.76	37.56	8.77
莱西市	Laixi	20.83	63.63	36.79	19.88	16.91	18.19	1.41

11－3 续表
continued

市、区名称	Region	工　业 Industry	建筑业 Construction	交通运输仓储和邮电业 Transportation, Storage, Postal and Telecommunications	批发零售贸易、餐饮业 Wholesale, Retail and Catering Business	其他劳动力 Other Labor Force
总　计	**Total**	**76.82**	**32.36**	**11.96**	**29.56**	**21.11**
市　区	Urban Area	15.54	5.22	2.56	5.60	4.29
#崂山区	Laoshan District	2.75	1.37	0.60	1.10	1.24
原黄岛区	Original Huangdao District	3.26	1.91	0.67	1.26	0.98
城阳区	Chengyang District	9.53	1.94	1.30	3.24	2.07
即墨市	Jimo	20.68	6.05	2.13	5.75	3.99
胶州市	Jiaozhou	11.60	4.68	1.56	4.63	3.47
原胶南市	Original Jiaonan	9.77	5.39	1.22	3.00	3.24
平度市	Pingdu	12.93	7.22	2.93	7.20	2.96
莱西市	Laixi	6.30	3.81	1.56	3.37	3.16

11 -4 主要年份农、林、牧、渔业总产值(按现价计算)
MAJOR YEAR'S GROSS OUTPUT VALUE OF FARMING, FORESTRY, ANIMAL HUSBANDRY AND FISHERY (CURRENT PRICE)

单位:万元(10 000 yuan)

年份 Year	农、林、牧、渔业总产值 Gross Output Value of Farming, Forestry, Animal Husbandry and Fishery	农业产值 Farming	林业产值 Forestry	牧业产值 Animal Husbandry	渔业产值 Fishery
1949	16 511	14 755	325	1 200	231
1952	24 428	21 353	479	1 888	708
1957	26 189	22 717	644	2 218	610
1962	15 356	13 257	230	1 243	626
1965	25 123	21 488	854	2 110	671
1970	44 078	36 889	1 851	3 817	1 521
1975	93 213	79 208	2 144	7 923	3 938
1978	121 497	94 397	3 112	17 293	6 695
1980	149 436	117 547	2 953	22 215	6 721
1985	299 139	215 729	8 986	53 894	20 530
1987	378 981	263 066	5 949	73 271	36 695
1989	463 952	303 679	19 134	91 885	49 254
1990	579 877	381 287	13 801	119 208	65 581
1991	664 779	417 111	12 875	144 909	89 884
1992	703 433	400 471	15 252	150 942	136 763
1993	989 763	509 601	20 845	232 143	227 174
1994	1 424 074	763 366	23 101	356 734	280 873
1995	1 923 771	1 021 413	26 765	503 999	371 594
1996	2 317 434	1 145 399	29 100	692 362	450 573
1997	2 047 712	939 922	24 052	578 443	505 295
1998	2 386 303	1 198 043	16 760	633 735	537 765
1999	2 382 320	1 169 596	17 122	618 020	577 582
2000	2 483 256	1 116 397	19 102	692 782	654 975
2001	2 615 228	1 135 816	20 433	758 313	700 666
2002	2 688 532	1 110 671	23 157	796 007	758 697
2003	2 759 692	1 062 576	36 183	859 915	801 018
2004	2 967 389	1 181 009	32 831	937 494	816 055
2005	3 205 057	1 265 695	25 246	1 070 831	843 285
2006	3 396 096	1 360 755	23 546	1 076 254	855 131
2007	3 429 877	1 483 733	20 842	975 032	830 479
2008	4 008 540	1 778 404	24 452	1 214 648	856 227
2009	4 086 146	1 856 753	22 264	1 160 558	898 608
2010	4 831 806	2 339 238	19 241	1 264 028	1 051 452
2011	5 359 343	2 365 300	19 237	1 560 108	1 232 720
2012	5 665 217	2 492 493	20 461	1 582 549	1 370 622

11－5 分市、区农、林、牧、渔业总产值(2012 年,现价)

GROSS OUTPUT VALUE OF FARMING, FORESTRY, ANIMAL HUSBANDRY AND FISHERY BY REGION(2012, CURRENT PRICE)

单位:万元(10 000 yuan)

市、区名称	Region	农、林、牧、渔业总产值 Gross Output Value of Farming, Forestry, Animal Husbandry and Fishery	农业 Farming	林业 Forestry	牧业 Animal Husbandry	渔业 Fishery
总计	**Total**	**5 665 217**	**2 492 493**	**20 461**	**1 582 549**	**1 370 622**
市区	Urban Area	462 752	46 207	1 304	45 024	352 996
#崂山区	Laoshan District	97 665	8 532	186	5 170	74 747
原黄岛区	Original Huangdao District	77 319	14 317	343	10 707	45 952
城阳区	Chengyang District	287 768	23 358	775	29 147	232 297
即墨市	Jimo	955 756	354 316	4 271	207 643	342 094
胶州市	Jiaozhou	789 141	320 541	3 800	205 463	227 049
原胶南市	Original Jiaonan	910 699	263 248	2 792	192 516	419 258
平度市	Pingdu	1 586 284	1 043 045	4 652	484 118	15 240
莱西市	Laixi	960 585	465 136	3 642	447 785	13 985

注 本表按当年价格计算。

Note: Data in this form are calculated at current price.

11－6 农、林、牧、渔业总产值、增加值(2012 年)
VALUE-ADDED OF FARMING, FORESTRY, ANIMAL HUSBANDRY AND FISHERY(2012)

单位:万元(10 000 yuan)

		总计 Total	农业 Farming	#种植业 Planting	林业 Forestry	牧业 Animal Husbandry	渔业 Fishery
总产值	**Gross Output Value**	**5 665 217**	**2 492 493**	**2 492 493**	**20 461**	**1 582 549**	**1 370 622**
中间消耗	**Intermediate Expenditure**	**2 421 106**	**879 602**	**879 602**	**9 555**	**900 885**	**538 580**
中间物质消耗	Intermediate Expenditure of Matter	1 808 697	669 875	669 875	6 904	677 617	395 165
对非农生产部门的劳动支出	Expenditure of Labor Services to Nonagricultural Production Development	612 409	209 727	209 727	2 651	223 268	143 415
增加值	**Added Value**	**3 244 111**	**1 612 891**	**1 612 891**	**10 906**	**681 664**	**832 042**

11－7 分市、区农、林、牧、渔业增加值(2012 年)
VALUE-ADDED OF FARMING, FORESTRY, ANIMAL HUSBANDRY FISHERY BY REGION(2012)

单位:万元(10 000 yuan)

市、区名称	Region	增加值 Added Value	农业 Farming	林业 Forestry	牧业 Animal Husbandry	渔业 Fishery
总　计	**Total**	**3 244 111**	**1 612 891**	**10 906**	**681 664**	**832 042**
市　区	Urban Area	260 697	28 926	764	19 064	202 362
#崂山区	Laoshan District	54 150	5 420	102	2 702	41 101
原黄岛区	Original Huangdao District	45 635	9 524	121	4 734	27 534
城阳区	Chengyang District	160 912	13 982	541	11 628	133 677
即墨市	Jimo	568 004	239 234	2 336	101 122	199 509
胶州市	Jiaozhou	476 822	213 193	2 100	87 076	156 881
原胶南市	Original Jiaonan	523 126	164 430	970	85 676	255 090
平度市	Pingdu	890 462	680 173	3 015	177 806	9 284
莱西市	Laixi	525 000	286 935	1 721	210 920	8 916

11－8 主要年份耕地面积与播种面积
MAJOR YEAR'S CULTIVATED AND SOWN AREA

单位:万公顷(10 000 hectares)

年份 Year	年末实有耕地面积 Year-end Area of Cultivated Land	农作物播种面积 Sown Area of Farm Crops	#粮食作物 Grain Crops	经济作物 Economic Crops
1949		93.47	84.00	7.20
1952		97.53	85.07	10.80
1957		97.87	87.07	10.53
1962		81.47	72.53	5.80
1965		82.80	71.80	8.33
1970		80.73	68.27	10.07
1975		79.82	65.84	11.01
1978		77.60	63.60	10.40
1980		75.87	60.33	12.00
1985		78.27	57.33	15.73
1987		76.67	55.87	15.93
1989		74.78	54.28	16.06
1990		76.85	56.99	15.53
1991		76.98	56.89	15.69
1992		76.96	56.37	15.64
1993	56.90	77.75	56.22	15.71
1994		76.61	54.08	16.20
1995		76.54	53.71	15.65
1996	55.01	77.26	54.81	14.90
1997		75.04	52.32	14.40
1998		77.18	53.05	14.54
1999		77.56	50.61	13.24
2000		76.47	45.07	13.98
2001		73.69	41.91	14.54
2002		72.32	40.83	13.95
2003	53.20	67.82	36.05	14.50
2004	52.23	71.33	41.40	14.11
2005	50.90	75.02	49.93	11.89
2006	51.19	74.86	49.79	11.75
2007	51.25	72.79	47.56	12.11
2008	51.31	74.09	51.06	11.29
2009	53.50	75.00	52.92	11.34
2010		75.39	53.56	11.00
2011		75.70	54.56	10.69
2012		74.96	54.08	10.69

注:年末实有耕地面积由市国土资源和房屋管理局提供。由于第二次国土资源普查未结束,2012年无数据。

Note: The data on year-end area of cultivated land are provided by Qingdao Municipal Bureau of Land Resources and Housing Management. There is no data in 2012, because the Second National Land Survey has not been finished.

11－9 分市、区耕地面积(2012 年)
AREA OF CULTIVATED LAND BY REGION(2012)

单位:公顷(hectare)

市、区名称	Region	年末耕地面积 Year-end Area of Cultivated Land	#旱田 Dry Farmland	当年增加的耕地 Area of Cultivated Land Increased in the Year	#新开荒地 Wasteland Newly Opened up
总计	**Total**				
市区	Urban Area				
#崂山区	Laoshan District				
原黄岛区	Original Huangdao District				
城阳区	Chengyang District				
即墨市	Jimo				
胶州市	Jiaozhou				
原胶南市	Original Jiaonan				
平度市	Pingdu				
莱西市	Laixi				

11－9 续表
continued

单位:公顷(hectare)

市、区名称	Region	当年减少的耕地 Area of Cultivated Land Decreased in the Year	国家基建占地 Government Capital Construction	乡镇集体基建占地 Rural Capital Construction	农民个人建房占地 Private Building
总计	**Total**				
市区	Urban Area				
#崂山区	Laoshan District				
原黄岛区	Original Huangdao District				
城阳区	Chengyang District				
即墨市	Jimo				
胶州市	Jiaozhou				
原胶南市	Original Jiaonan				
平度市	Pingdu				
莱西市	Laixi				

注:由于第二次国土资源普查未结束,分市、区耕地面积(2012 年)无数据。

Note:There is no data on area of cultivated land by region in 2012,because the Second National Land Survey has not been finished.

11－10 分市、区农作物播种面积(2012 年)
SOWN AREA OF FARM CROPS BY REGION(2012)

单位:公顷(hectare)

市、区名称	Region	总播种面积 Total Sown Area	粮食 Grain	#棉花 Cotton	花生 Peanut	烟叶 Tobacco	蔬菜 Vegetable
总计	**Total**	**749 564**	**540 787**	**2 741**	**95 297**	**579**	**101 136**
市区	Urban Area	11 090	7 273		1 095		2 457
#崂山区	Laoshan District	711	227		220		256
原黄岛区	Original Huangdao District	2 612	1 333		826		269
城阳区	Chengyang District	7 767	5 713		49		1 932
即墨市	Jimo	115 886	86 733		18 215		10 187
胶州市	Jiaozhou	105 480	74 680		8 243		21 913
原胶南市	Original Jiaonan	88 463	58 567		20 172	490	8 747
平度市	Pingdu	293 531	216 667	2 741	28 570	89	40 985
莱西市	Laixi	135 114	96 867		19 002		16 846

11－11 分市、区部分农作物产量(2012 年)
OUTPUT OF FARM CROPS BY REGION(2012)

单位:吨(ton)

市、区名称	Region	粮食 Grain	棉花 Cotton	花生 Peanut	烟叶 Tobacco	蔬菜 Vegetable
总计	**Total**	**3 699 600**	**4 301**	**459 464**	**1 615**	**5 697 564**
市区	Urban Area	40 900		4 231		99 687
#崂山区	Laoshan District	1 600		648		8 128
原黄岛区	Original Huangdao District	8 700		3 431		11 201
城阳区	Chengyang District	30 600		152		80 358
即墨市	Jimo	547 100		81 148		625 262
胶州市	Jiaozhou	477 400		40 310		1 196 468
原胶南市	Original Jiaonan	321 700		96 220	1 306	404 111
平度市	Pingdu	1 631 500	4 301	144 634	309	2 339 287
莱西市	Laixi	681 000		92 921		1 032 748

11－12 分市、区部分农作物播公顷单产量(2012 年)

OUTPUT OF FARM CROPS PER HECTARE BY REGION(2012)

单位:千克(kg)

市、区名称	Region	棉　花 Cotton	花　生 Peanut	烟　叶 Tobacco	蔬　菜 Vegetable
总　　计	**Total**	**1 569**	**4 821**	**2 789**	**56 336**
市　　区	Urban Area		3 864		40 566
#崂山区	Laoshan District		2 952		31 782
原黄岛区	Original Huangdao District		4 155		41 566
城阳区	Chengyang District		3 065		41 589
即墨市	Jimo		4 455		61 380
胶州市	Jiaozhou		4 890		54 600
原胶南市	Original Jiaonan		4 770	2 667	46 200
平度市	Pingdu	1 569	5 063	3 458	57 076
莱西市	Laixi		4 890		61 305

11-13 主要年份农作物总产量
MAJOR YEAR'S OUTPUT OF FARM CROPS

单位：吨(ton)

年份 Year	粮食 Grain	#小麦 Wheat	玉米 Corn	棉花 Cotton	花生 Peanut	水果 Fruit	蔬菜 Vegetable
1949	723 190	158 815	25 810	1 280	71 080	9 955	356 015
1952	967 640	200 380	58 130	6 025	115 585	13 468	284 050
1957	921 920	210 690	141 540	3 520	90 445	18 869	625 220
1962	628 930	104 340	53 010	1 280	35 470	8 366	524 455
1965	917 635	180 610	135 595	6 090	88 390	16 034	465 850
1970	1 175 985	243 945	244 530	16 490	96 280	33 907	541 145
1975	1 899 540	430 135	420 095	15 390	98 495	59 206	693 970
1978	1 900 850	514 570	510 635	8 720	114 370	82 819	921 140
1980	2 164 415	520 045	819 930	19 630	160 670	80 840	996 565
1985	2 331 060	961 055	739 455	19 335	475 270	200 515	1 253 075
1987	2 626 029	996 165	1 030 926	13 819	394 296	249 655	1 489 250
1989	2 654 334	993 406	1 084 441	14 638	391 782	288 757	1 664 238
1990	2 998 246	1 265 157	1 210 687	17 490	413 636	292 366	1 786 041
1991	3 180 893	1 421 143	1 285 043	25 965	446 880	294 349	1 837 265
1992	2 675 641	1 235 755	981 490	8 160	321 145	341 415	2 030 327
1993	3 164 812	1 463 759	1 248 780	15 344	419 109	383 368	2 705 349
1994	3 106 562	1 392 977	1 252 952	8 326	494 827	423 024	3 002 318
1995	3 291 587	1 480 385	1 365 167	8 177	510 662	478 685	3 221 507
1996	3 390 033	1 513 479	1 466 668	4 001	486 574	505 711	3 405 056
1997	2 523 064	1 584 478	743 199	2 000	308 233	438 398	3 333 181
1998	3 469 821	1 627 261	1 484 182	4 159	546 786	529 592	4 036 992
1999	3 331 124	1 501 182	1 499 775	3 668	572 941	606 800	5 459 140
2000	2 780 481	1 353 445	1 169 649	2 077	534 174	651 591	6 649 322
2001	2 539 257	1 143 679	1 178 851	3 409	579 441	675 244	6 250 361
2002	2 383 802	1 085 936	1 094 731	3 755	557 714	579 703	6 847 570
2003	2 221 697	931 787	1 117 704	5 324	568 798	677 361	7 305 618
2004	2 650 952	1 301 791	1 202 063	7 216	580 290	748 516	6 720 886
2005	3 150 203	1 535 471	1 478 616	4 042	503 941	737 300	5 792 110
2006	3 039 266	1 548 928	1 372 166	3 954	471 853	827 755	6 051 239
2007	3 007 443	1 395 643	1 497 343	4 330	495 972	793 859	6 157 471
2008	3 336 643	1 620 734	1 620 910	4 173	471 447	806 815	6 118 876
2009	3 539 075	1 727 966	1 723 279	4 529	468 022	820 887	5 679 434
2010	3 514 081	1 646 745	1 795 187	3 952	441 443	803 092	5 807 761
2011	3 630 046	1 653 376	1 906 374	3 917	443 713	805 192	5 838 183
2012	3 699 600			4 301	459 464	798 685	5 697 564

11－14 分市、区大牲畜头数(2012 年)
NUMBER OF LARGE LIVESTOCK BY REGION(2012)

单位:万头(10 000 head)

市、区名称	Region	年末大牲畜头数 Number of Large Livestock (year-end)	牛 Cattle and Buffaloes	#奶　牛 Cows	马 Horses	驴 Donkeys	骡 Mules
总　计	**Total**	**26.18**	**26.13**	**11.99**	**0.02**	**0.02**	
市　区	Urban Area	0.59	0.59	0.59			
#崂山区	Laoshan District	0.02	0.02	0.02			
原黄岛区	Original Huangdao District	0.01	0.01	0.01			
城阳区	Chengyang District	0.55	0.55	0.55			
即墨市	Jimo	2.69	2.69	1.55			
胶州市	Jiaozhou	3.15	3.14	0.59			
原胶南市	Original Jiaonan	2.02	2.01	0.09		0.02	
平度市	Pingdu	6.81	6.81	0.67			
莱西市	Laixi	10.92	10.91	8.50	0.02		

11－15 分市、区猪、羊及家禽存养量(2012 年)
HOGS, SHEEP, GOATS AND POULTRY IN STOCK BY REGION(2012)

单位:万只(10 000 head)

市、区名称	Region	年末生猪存养量 Hogs in Stock (year-end)	年末羊存养量 Sheep and Goats in Stock (year-end)	#山　羊 Goats	绵　羊 Sheep	家　禽 Poultry
总　计	**Total**	**224.40**	**19.09**	**14.49**	**4.61**	**5 975.61**
市　区	Urban Area	6.42	0.28	0.28		229.32
#崂山区	Laoshan District	0.84	0.04	0.04		50.67
原黄岛区	Original Huangdao District	1.06	0.09	0.09		8.08
城阳区	Chengyang District	4.52	0.14	0.14		170.57
即墨市	Jimo	27.48	1.18	0.90	0.28	955.09
胶州市	Jiaozhou	36.08	3.62	3.21	0.41	430.98
原胶南市	Original Jiaonan	41.33	5.21	4.68	0.52	450.23
平度市	Pingdu	68.87	5.85	2.80	3.04	1 843.60
莱西市	Laixi	44.22	2.96	2.61	0.35	2 066.39

11－16 分市、区肉、蛋、奶、蜂蜜产量(2012 年)
OUTPUT OF MEAT,EGGS AND MILK BY REGION(2012)

单位:万吨(10000 tons)

市、区名称	Region	肉类产量 Output of Meat	#猪肉 Pork	牛肉 Beef	羊肉 Mutton	禽肉 Poultry Meat	禽蛋 Poultry Eggs	牛羊奶 Milk
总　计	**Total**	**61.37**	**27.12**	**0.89**	**0.20**	**32.91**	**19.12**	**37.64**
市　区	Urban Area	1.38	0.79			0.58	1.73	1.72
#崂山区	Laoshan District	0.25	0.10			0.15	0.35	0.07
原黄岛区	Original Huangdao District	0.14	0.13			0.02	0.07	0.06
城阳区	Chengyang District	0.99	0.56			0.42	1.31	1.59
即墨市	Jimo	7.41	3.32	0.09	0.02	3.98	4.69	4.60
胶州市	Jiaozhou	5.73	4.36	0.12	0.04	1.20	3.10	2.56
原胶南市	Original Jiaonan	7.13	4.96	0.11	0.06	1.80	2.30	1.56
平度市	Pingdu	19.80	8.26	0.28	0.05	11.19	3.92	2.66
莱西市	Laixi	19.92	5.44	0.28	0.03	14.16	3.38	24.53

11－17 分市、区渔业养殖面积
AQUACULTURE AREA BY REGION

单位:公顷(hectare)

市、区名称	Region	2012			2011		
		养殖面积 Aquaculture Area	海水 Seawater	淡水 Fresh Water	养殖面积 Aquaculture Area	海水 Seawater	淡水 Fresh Water
总　计	**Total**	**52 279**	**35 947**	**16 332**	**54 857**	**38 743**	**16 114**
市　区	Urban Area	15 060	13 086	1 974	16 896	15 053	1 843
#崂山区	Laoshan District	1 600	1 600		1 568	1 568	
原黄岛区	Original Huangdao District	3 741	3 528	213	3 482	3 400	82
城阳区	Chengyang District	9 719	7 958	1 761	11 846	10 085	1 761
即墨市	Jimo	13 253	12 079	1 174	13 253	12 079	1 174
胶州市	Jiaozhou	4 708	2 308	2 400	5 439	3 137	2 302
原胶南市	Original Jiaonan	10 754	8 474	2 280	10 741	8 474	2 267
平度市	Pingdu	3 800		3 800	3 800		3 800
莱西市	Laixi	4 704		4 704	4 728		4 728

11－18 分市、区水产品总产量(2012 年)
OUTPUT OF AQUATIC PRODUCTS BY REGION(2012)

单位:吨(ton)

市、区名称	Region	水产品总产量 Output of Aquatic Products	#养殖产量 Aquaculture Outpu	鱼　类 Fish	甲壳类 Crust	贝　类 Shellfish	藻　类 Algae
总　计	**Total**	**1 124 409**	**852 318**	**229 730**	**75 703**	**735 476**	**12 010**
市　区	Urban Area	365 702	255 869	56 218	20 531	237 971	9 210
#崂山区	Laoshan District	71 437	19 377	19 926	11 588	19 036	1 760
原黄岛区	Original Huangdao District	34 346	25 271	7 254	426	23 513	200
城阳区	Chengyang District	259 919	211 221	29 038	8 517	195 422	7 250
即墨市	Jimo	297 894	232 846	26 305	30 605	231 063	
胶州市	Jiaozhou	128 014	96 462	39 101	5 976	81 483	
原胶南市	Original Jiaonan	310 620	244 962	85 986	18 552	184 959	2 800
平度市	Pingdu	11 005	11 005	10 973	28		
莱西市	Laixi	11 174	11 174	11 147	11		

11－19 分市、区植树及造林面积(2012 年)
AREA OF FORESTATION AND AFFORESTATION BY REGION(2012)

市、区名称	Region	当年造林面积(公顷) Area of Afforestation in the Year(hectare)	本年新增育苗面积(公顷) Nursery Garden Area(hectare)	未成林抚育作业面积(公顷) Laid out Area of Young Trees(hectare)	成林抚育面积(公顷) Laid out Area of Grown-up Trees (hectare)	零星(四旁)植树(万株) Surrounding Tree Planting(10 000 trees)
总　计	**Total**	**9 173**	**4 167**	**18 107**	**25 466**	**531**
市　区	Urban Area	464	196		3 504	55
#崂山区	Laoshan District	147			1 333	2
原黄岛区	Original Huangdao District	160	63		1 838	30
城阳区	Chengyang District	157	133		333	23
即墨市	Jimo	1 263	333		1 334	80
胶州市	Jiaozhou	1 533	133		467	10
原胶南市	Original Jiaonan	1 625	133		3 333	100
平度市	Pingdu	2 388	362	11 769	6 986	126
莱西市	Laixi	1 900	3 010	6 338	9 842	160

11－20 分市、区果园面积、水果总产量(2012 年)
AREA OF ORCHARDS AND OUTPUT OF FRUITS BY REGION(2012)

单位:吨(ton)

市、区名称	Region	果园总面积(公顷) Area of Orchards (hectare)	水果总产量(吨) Output of Fruits(ton)	#苹果 Apple	梨 Pear	桃 Peach	葡萄 Grape	杏 Apricot	山楂 Hawthorn
总　计	**Total**	**26 901**	**798 685**	**528 124**	**69 199**	**75 340**	**84 493**	**5 758**	**5 407**
市　区	Urban Area	2 098	24 493	2 595	379	11 210	3 006	2 826	76
#崂山区	Laoshan District	579	7 497	1 119	265	3 467	20	1 593	13
原黄岛区	Original Huangdao District	280	3 032	649	16	1 720	12	112	23
城阳区	Chengyang District	1 238	13 964	828	98	6 023	2 974	1 121	40
即墨市	Jimo	902	23 182	7 631	1 893	4 765	853	83	146
胶州市	Jiaozhou	1 725	57 809	22 850	6 176	19 960	5 365	1 955	90
原胶南市	Original Jiaonan	4 670	113 213	92 169	8 036	9 375	443	215	346
平度市	Pingdu	9 611	355 544	246 642	11 930	23 458	58 701	646	2 044
莱西市	Laixi	7 894	224 444	156 237	40 786	6 572	16 125	33	2 706

11－21 分市、区茶园、桑园面积和茶叶、蚕茧产量(2012 年)
AREA OF TEA AND MULBERRY PLANTATIONS AND OUTPUT OF TEA AND SILKWORM COCOONS BY REGION(2012)

市、区名称	Region	茶园面积(公顷) Area of Tea Plantations(hectare)	茶叶产量(吨) Output of Tea(ton)	桑园面积(公顷) Area of Mulberry Plantations(hectare)	蚕茧产量(吨) Output of Silkworm Cocoons(ton)
总　计	**Total**	**4 235**	**2 103**		**807**
市　区	Urban Area	1 390	1 105		
崂山区	Laoshan District	1 230	1 072		
原黄岛区	Original Huangdao District	49	15		
城阳区	Chengyang District	111	18		
即墨市	Jimo	302	547		2
胶州市	Jiaozhou				
原胶南市	Original Jiaonan	2 530	451		321
平度市	Pingdu	13			445
莱西市	Laixi				39

11－22 主要年份主要农业机械拥有量
MAJOR YEAR'S OWNERSHIP OF AGRICULTURAL MACHINERY

年份 Year	农业机械总动力(万千瓦) Total Agricultural Machinery Power (10 000 kW)	农用拖拉机 Agricultural Tractors		大、中型机引农具(万台) Large and Medium Towing Farm Machinery (10 000 sets)	农用汽车(辆) Agricultural Automobiles (vehicle)	排灌机械 Drainage and Irrigation Machinery	
		混合台 set	千瓦 kW			台 set	万千瓦 10 000 kW
1949							
1952					1		
1957	0.22	59	2.2	0.01	2		
1962	2.47	254	11.47	0.06	13		
1965	3.49	296	13.2	0.08	15		
1970	10.40	602	7 963	0.07	12		
1975	43.94	6 447	103 476	0.48	90		
1978	75.45	15 576	309 287	1.02	261		
1980	110.44	24 278	502 731	1.72	728		
1985	174.76	33 097	506 217	1.71	2 645	67 794	54.92
1987	228.00	50 904	649 340	1.91	3 961	86 314	62.90
1989	241.00	53 556	661 400	1.96	3 982	93 437	70.46
1990	253.52	55 363	680 903	2.03	3 880	105 574	74.63
1991	250.58	57 404	691 332	2.20	3 706	134 900	73.77
1992	253.94	57 182	684 182	2.28	3 948	124 800	82.68
1993	261.24	56 335	678 161	2.34	4 378	144 460	78.96
1994	278.41	58 698	688 886	2.39	5 474	147 259	80.81
1995	289.23	56 391	657 025	2.28	6 314	138 625	73.58
1996	303.57	59 698	680 447	2.32	7 263	148 313	81.53
1997	326.72	66 841	744 424	2.42	8 085	155 629	88.09
1998	364.21	87 226	894 985	2.48	8 409	156 565	86.68
1999	411.44	105 743	1 075 907	3.06	9 363	170 875	96.20
2000	459.21	126 981	1 253 210	3.30	9 613	182 646	108.26
2001	496.27	141 409	1 394 114	4.33	10 212	178 437	104.18
2002	534.92	152 920	1 537 544	4.79	10 411	182 799	107.35
2003	560.94	160 676	1 666 185	5.07	11 201	192 930	109.44
2004	598.87	168 061	1 818 276	5.31	11 085	192 144	110.38
2005	619.69	163 032	1 757 177	5.66	11 552	188 689	112.16
2006	650.65	171 155	1 890 402	6.20	11 098	192 010	116.08
2007	680.16	173 326	1 958 047	6.57	11 408	195 050	118.22
2008	697.38	176 156	2 034 453	7.98	11 408	208 711	134.10
2009	719.33	180 171	2 266 697	8.60	11 408	207 648	133.99
2010	763.61	200 208	2 331 867	9.80		190 770	123.33
2011	784.06	202 022	2 649 283	9.77		189 834	127.16
2012	797.71	206 290	2 759 004	9.91		190 134	127.34

11－23 主要年份农业机械化、用电量、化肥施用量
MAJOR YEAR'S MECHANIZATION, ELECTRICITY AND CHEMICAL FERTILIZER CONSUMPTION

年　份 Year	有效灌溉面积(公顷) Irrigated Area (hectare)	配套机电井(眼) Number of Electromechanical Well (well)	机耕面积(公顷) Area of Motorized Cultivation (hectare)	机播面积(公顷) Area of Motorized Planting (hectare)	机收面积(公顷) Area of Motorized Harvesting (hectare)	农村用电量(万千瓦时) Electricity Consumption in Rural Area (10 000 kW·h)	化肥施用量(折纯万吨) Chemical Fertilizer Consumption (convert to 10 000 tons)
1949	8 340						
1952	14 980						
1957	59 353		12 800	13			0.19
1962	55 213	191	65 680	927	927	55	0.10
1965	80 000	125	11 433	573	247	128	0.55
1970	147 613	3 947	143 700	2 527	133	1 208	1.76
1975	233 980	12 820	248 867	54 507	953	2 522	2.77
1978	276 660	21 017	329 213	178 533	15 060	13 975	3.64
1980	296 606	22 472	444 800	187 980	55 333	20 492	12.06
1985	302 647	42 925	366 786	148 433	56 447	41 524	11.66
1987	260 800	48 497	410 820	187 680	104 240	58 280	13.87
1989	267 440	61 570	540 413	208 527	107 320	62 859	17.91
1990	274 680	56 821	426 680	220 593	143 133	67 616	20.47
1991	281 500	58 987	431 293	254 266	192 946	81 200	22.53
1992	281 610	62 100	438 533	270 453	207 780	88 024	22.60
1993	284 080	63 954	439 300	260 287	225 807	102 501	28.04
1994	286 750	64 877	436 820	262 846	238 693	121 307	28.73
1995	287 020	64 651	435 213	271 707	250 267	134 284	31.45
1996	289 320	65 237	438 947	280 480	235 933	143 740	31.36
1997	292 130	66 783	442 213	308 267	266 147	150 971	28.99
1998	294 120	64 109	442 920	359 447	285 513	153 113	31.95
1999	294 790	64 734	440 967	396 180	286 367	169 337	32.58
2000	295 190	65 179	439 980	346 480	292 787	189 651	32.53
2001	296 980	65 547	436 576	382 870	265 730	228 069	31.73
2002	294 310	65 588	433 660	364 680	267 690	256 453	31.07
2003	292 410	65 406	415 790	404 980	256 600	299 425	31.89
2004	292 520	65 501	415 220	454 800	314 680	330 609	32.45
2005	296 450	65 303	409 610	493 240	367 740	372 644	33.01
2006	303 070	65 981	403 980	493 750	398 700	413 762	32.64
2007	305 760	66 400	400 480	499 590	429 630	425 715	33.89
2008	313 920	66 828	404 080	517 540	455 120	424 292	31.05
2009	322 710	67 027	404 080	538 220	481 176	426 306	30.17
2010	328 960	67 242		558 611	499 248	426 819	29.89
2011	331 690	62 104		567 947	547 108	431 646	29.37
2012	333 850	62 112	410 440	627 701	566 653	426 815	29.09

11－24 分市、区农业机械化和电气化(2012 年)

MECHANIZATION AND ELECTRIFICATION IN AGRICULTURE BY REGION(2012)

市、区名称	Region	机耕作业面积 Area of Motorized Cultivation		机播地面积 Area of Motorized Planting	
		面积(公顷) Area(hectare)	占播种面积比重(%) Percentage to Area of Cultivated Land(%)	面积(公顷) Area(hectare)	占播种面积比重(%) Percentage to Sown Area(%)
总　计	**Total**	**410 440**	**54.8**	**627 701**	**83.7**
市　区	Urban Area	6 051	54.6	6 860	61.9
#崂山区	Laoshan District				
原黄岛区	Original Huangdao District	1 412	54.1		
城阳区	Chengyang District	4 639	59.7	6 860	88.3
即墨市	Jimo	75 757	65.4	112 161	96.8
胶州市	Jiaozhou	55 268	52.4	91 000	86.3
原胶南市	Original Jiaonan	49 772	56.3	57 300	64.8
平度市	Pingdu	164 333	56.0	243 724	83.0
莱西市	Laixi	59 259	43.9	116 656	86.3

11－24 续表

continued

市、区名称	Region	机收面积 Area of Motorized Harvesting		农村用电量(万千瓦小时) Electricity Consumed in Rural Areas(10 000 kW·h)
		面积(公顷) Area(hectare)	占播种面积比重(%) Percentage to Sown Area(%)	
总　计	**Total**	**566 653**	**75.6**	**426 815**
市　区	Urban Area	5 276	47.6	80 827
#崂山区	Laoshan District			16 414
原黄岛区	Original Huangdao District	610	23.4	12 536
城阳区	Chengyang District	4 666	60.1	51 877
即墨市	Jimo	102 216	88.2	76 049
胶州市	Jiaozhou	85 600	81.2	86 000
原胶南市	Original Jiaonan	47 500	53.7	42 300
平度市	Pingdu	224 148	76.4	106 981
莱西市	Laixi	101 913	75.4	34 659

11－25 分市、区农用化肥施用量(2012 年)
CONSUMPTION OF CHEMICAL FERTILIZERS BY REGION(2012)

单位:折纯吨(ton converted to pure amount)

市、区名称	Region	农用化肥施用量 Consumption of Chemical Fertilizers	氮 肥 Nitrogenous Fertilizer	磷 肥 Phosphate Fertilizer	钾 肥 Potash Fertilizer	复合肥 Compound Fertilizer	附:平均每公顷耕地施用化肥量(＊) Annotation:Consumption of Chemical Fertilizer Per Hectare
总 计	**Total**	**290 899**	**57 382**	**14 011**	**20 077**	**199 428**	
市 区	Urban Area	3 403	915	196	241	2 050	
#崂山区	Laoshan District	838	214	68	60	496	
原黄岛区	Original Huangdao District	730	146	7	64	512	
城阳区	Chengyang District	1 835	555	121	117	1 041	
即墨市	Jimo	38 964	16 509	2 843	1 206	18 406	
胶州市	Jiaozhou	36 996	7 240	936	5 300	23 520	
原胶南市	Original Jiaonan	36 266	10 445	3 398	5 142	17 281	
平度市	Pingdu	119 999	10 670	2 663	7 903	98 763	
莱西市	Laixi	55 272	11 603	3 975	285	39 409	

注:(＊)单位为[折纯千克] Note:The(＊)mark refers to kilogram converted to pure amount.

11－26 分市、区农田水利(2012 年)
FARMLAND WATER CONSERVANCY BY REGION(2012)

市、区名称	Region	有效灌溉面积(公顷) Irrigated Area (hectare)	#机、电排灌面积 of which:Area with Motorized Irrigation Facilities	有效灌溉面积占耕地面积比重(%) Percentage of Irrigated Area to Area of Cultivated Land(%)	农业排灌机械拥有量(万台/万千瓦) Ownership of Drainage and Irrigation Machinery (10 000 sets/10 000 kW)	农用水泵(万台) Agricultural Pump (10 000 sets)	喷灌机械(套) Spraying Irrigation Machinery (set)	机电井数(眼) Number of Electromechanical Well (well)
总 计	**Total**	**333 850**	**306 510**		**19.01/127.34**	**14.20**	**88 374**	**70 706**
市 区	Urban Area	6 460	4 270		0.81/6.40	0.42	2 746	2 174
#崂山区	Laoshan District	520	910					319
原黄岛区	Original Huangdao District	1 200	900		0.17/1.92	0.01	74	233
城阳区	Chengyang District	2 780	2 460		0.64/4.47	0.42	2 672	1 424
李沧区	Licang District	220						198
即墨市	Jimo	56 930	52 300		2.11/14.91	2.13	18 521	5 541
胶州市	Jiaozhou	40 930	35 550		1.33/10.32	0.81	13 650	5 547
原胶南市	Original Jiaonan	44 650	30 850		0.58/4.72	1.20	9 000	6 269
平度市	Pingdu	128 290	128 570		12.45/80.50	7.36	18 077	37 456
莱西市	Laixi	58 330	54 970		1.74/10.50	2.28	26 380	13 719

11－27 分市、区主要农业机械拥有量(2012 年)

OWNERSHIP OF MAJOR AGRICULTURAL MACHINERY BY REGION(2012)

市、区名称	Region	农业机械总动力(万千瓦) Agricultural Machinery Power (10 000 kW)	平均每公顷耕地拥有量(千瓦) Power Per Hectare of Cultivated Land(kW)	大中型拖拉机 Large and Medium Tractors		小型拖拉机 Small Tractors	
				台 set	千瓦 kW	台 set	千瓦 kW
总　计	**Total**	**797.71**		**38 588**	**1 469 904**	**167 702**	**1 289 100**
市　区	Urban Area	47.27		590	18 012	1 990	12 148
#崂山区	Laoshan District						
原黄岛区	Original Huangdao District	12.98		156	3 723	452	1 563
城阳区	Chengyang District	34.29		434	14 289	1 538	10 585
即墨市	Jimo	123.93		6 755	199 887	32 862	271 275
胶州市	Jiaozhou	112.01		4 649	258 045	19 008	147 901
原胶南市	Original Jiaonan	73.89		3 460	96 950	44 200	309 400
平度市	Pingdu	312.80		18 176	730 865	34 482	310 338
莱西市	Laixi	127.81		4 958	166 145	35 160	238 038

11－27 续表 1
continued

市、区名称	Region	大、中、小播种机(部) Large, Medium and Small Seeders(set)	机引犁(部) Towing Ploughs(unit)	机引耙(部) Towing Rakes(unit)	脱粒机(部) Threshers (unit)
总　计	**Total**	**57 190**	**129 885**	**28 705**	**34 457**
市　区	Urban Area	772	1 205	207	
#崂山区	Laoshan District				
原黄岛区	Original Huangdao District		5		
城阳区	Chengyang District	772	1 200	207	
即墨市	Jimo	11 749	19 952	1 680	6 574
胶州市	Jiaozhou	8 720	14 355	5 000	3 568
原胶南市	Original Jiaonan	1 340	38 600	1 200	7 300
平度市	Pingdu	26 480	21 845	16 543	12 016
莱西市	Laixi	8 129	33 928	4 075	4 999

11－27 续表 2
continued

市、区名称	Region	粮食加工机械(台) Grain Processing Machinery(unit)	棉花加工机械(部) Cotton Processing Machinery(unit)	油料加工机械(部) Oil Processing Machinery(unit)	饲料粉碎机(部) Pulverizers (unit)
总　计	**Total**	**25 551**	**125**	**9 141**	**22 964**
市　区	Urban Area	1 617	17	690	341
#崂山区	Laoshan District				
原黄岛区	Original Huangdao District	12		170	4
城阳区	Chengyang District	1 605	17	520	337
即墨市	Jimo	3 259		1 472	1 449
胶州市	Jiaozhou	2 950		2 025	3 620
原胶南市	Original Jiaonan	1 100		243	3 540
平度市	Pingdu	4 365	6	1 411	7 504
莱西市	Laixi	12 260	102	3 300	6 510

主要统计指标解释

农林牧渔业总产值　农林牧渔业总产值是以货币表现的农林牧渔业的全部产品总量和对农林牧渔业生产活动进行的各种支持性服务活动的价值。它反映一定时期内农林牧渔业生产总规模和总成果。

农林牧渔业总产值的统计范围是辖区内各种经济组织类型、各个系统的全部农林牧渔业生产单位和非农行业单位附属的农林牧渔业生产活动单位。

粮食产量　指稻谷、小麦、玉米、高粱等谷物及薯类、豆类和杂粮的全社会产量。其产量计算方法,豆类按去豆荚后的干豆计算;薯类(包括甘薯和马铃薯,不包括芋头和木薯)按5公斤鲜薯折1公斤粮食计算。城市郊区作为蔬菜的薯类(如马铃薯等)按鲜品计算,并且不作粮食统计。其他粮食一律按脱粒后的原粮计算。

水产品产量　指人工养殖的水产品和天然生长的水产品的捕捞量.包括海水的鱼类、虾蟹类、贝类和藻类以及内陆水域的鱼类、虾蟹类和贝类,不包括淡水生植物。

猪、牛、羊肉产量　指当年出栏并已屠宰、除去头蹄下水后带骨头肉(即胴体重)的重量。其统计范围为全社会。

农用化肥施用量　指本年内实际用于农业生产的化肥数量,包括氮肥、磷肥、钾肥和复合肥。化肥施用量要求按折纯量计算数量。折纯量是指把氮肥、磷肥、钾肥分别按含氮、含五氧化二磷、含氧化钾的百分之百成分进行折算后的数量。复合肥按其所含主要成分折算。

公式:折纯量 = 实物量 × 某种化肥有效成分含量的百分比

农业机械总动力　指用于农、林、牧、渔业生产的各种动力机械的动力总和。动力机械包括耕作、排灌、种植、植物保护、收获、农产品加工、运输、畜牧、渔业、农田水利等各种机械。不包括专门用于乡办工业、基本建设、非农业运输、科学试验和教学等非农业生产方面用的动力机械与作业机械的数量。

Explanatory Notes on Main Statistical Indicators

Gross Output Value of Agriculture, Forest, Animal Husbandry and Fishery　refers to the total value of products of agriculture, forestry, animal husbandry and fishery, and total value of services in support of agriculture, forest, animal husbandry and fishery activities . It reflects the total scale and results of agriculture, production during a given period.

Statistics on agriculture, forest, animal husbandry and fishery cover rural economic units of various types, all production units of agriculture and activity units of agriculture attached to non-agricultural production units. within the jurisdiction.

Grain Output　refers to the total output of rice, wheat, corn, sorghum, millet, beans and other miscellaneous grains. Output of beans refers to dry beans without pods, the output of tubers (sweet potatoes and potatoes, excluding taros and cassava) was converted into that of grain at the ratio 5∶1, i. e. 5 kilograms of fresh tubers was equivalent to 1 kilogram of grain, tubers supplies as vegetable (such as potatoes) in cities and suburbs are calculated as fresh vegetables and their output is not included in the output of grain output of all other grains refers to husked grain.

Output of Aquatic Products　refers to catches of both artificially cultured and naturally grown aquatic products, including fish, shrimps, crabs and shellfish in sea and inland water as well as seaweed. Freshwater plants are not included.

Output of Pork, Beef, and Mutton　refers to the meat of slaughtered hogs, cattle, sheep and goats with head, feet, and offal taken away. Data refers to the production of the whole country.

Consumption of Chemical Fertilizers in Agriculture　refers to the quantity of chemical fertilizers applied in agriculture in the year, including nitrogenous fertilizer, phosphate fertilizer, potash fertilizer, and compound fertilizer. The consumption of chemical fertilizers is required in calculation to convert the gross weight into weight containing 100% effective component (e. g. 100% nitrogen content in nitrogenous fertilizer, 100% phosphorous pent oxide contents in phosphate fertilizer, 100% potassium oxide contents in potash fertilizer). Compound fertilizer is converted with its major component. The formula is:

Volume of effective component = physical quantity x effective component of certain chemical fertilizer (%)

Total Power of Agriculture Machinery Refers to the total mechanical power of machinery used in farming forestry animal husbandry and fishery, including machines used for ploughing, irrigation and drainage, crop growing, plant protection, harvesting, farm product processing, transport, stock breeding, fishery and water conservancy, Machinery employed for non agricultural purposes such as township industry capital construction, non-agricultural transport, scientific experiments and for teaching is excluded.

12 工　业
INDUSTRY

简 要 说 明

一、本篇资料的主要内容

本篇资料主要反映了全市工业生产和基本效益情况，主要包括工业企业单位数、历年工业总产值、规模以上工业、国有控股工业、国有工业、集体工业、外商投资和港澳台投资工业、大中型工业企业的主要经济指标、相关的财务分析指标和主要工业产品产量等方面的内容。

二、本篇资料的来源

1、本篇中规模以上工业资料来源于工业统计年报，由市统计局工业统计处整理提供。

2、规模以下工业资料产值与单位数均来源于抽样调查推算，工业单位数除普查年度外无分市（区）数据，由国家统计局青岛调查队工业与投资建筑业调查处整理提供。

Brief Introduction

I. Main Content

Data in this chapter show the basic condition of industrial production and benefit in Qingdao, mainly including the number of industrial enterprises, gross industrial output value and indices, the output of major industrial products and major economic and relevant financial indicators of industrial enterprises. Industrial enterprises include enterprises above designated size, state share-holding enterprises, state owned enterprises, collective owned enterprises, foreign funded enterprises, enterprises with funds from Hong Kong, Macao and Taiwan, large and medium sized enterprises.

II. Source of Data

(1)Data on industry above designated size are based on the annual report of industrial statistics, and prepared by the Division of Industry Statistics of Qingdao Municipal Bureau of Statistics.

(2)Data on output value and unit number of industry below designated size are based on the sample survey, and there is no data on number of enterprises by region except census year. The Data are complied by the Division of Industry, Investment and Construction Survey of Survey Office of the National Bureau of Statistics in Qingdao.

12－1 规模以上工业企业单位数
NUMBER OF INDUSTRIAL ENTERPRISES ABOVE DESIGNATEO SIZE

单位:个(unit)

项　目	Item	1985	1990	1995	2000	2005	2006
总　计	**Total**	**2 411**	**2 997**	**4 987**	**1 504**	**3 697**	**4 567**
一、按隶属关系分	**Grouped by Subordination**						
中央工业	Central Industry	24	16	102	18	26	17
省属工业	Provincial Industry	26	22	64	7	37	33
地方工业	Local Industry	2 361	2 959	4 821	1 479	3 634	4 517
二、按经济类型分	Grouped by Economic Types						
国有企业	State-owned	502	568	1 084	179	76	74
集体企业	Collective-owned	1 907	2 386	2 731	226	87	72
其他经济类型企业	Other Economic Types	2	43	1 172	1 099	3 534	4 421
#外商及港澳台商投资企业	Foreign Funded Enterprises and Enterprises with Funds from Hong Kong,Macao and Taiwan		35	1 027	593	1 658	1 952
三、按轻重工业分	Grouped by Light and Heavy Industries						
轻工业	Light Industry	1 398	1 730	2 858	891	1 942	2 313
重工业	Heavy Industry	1 013	1 267	2 129	613	1 755	2 254
四、按企业规模分	Grouped by Size of Enterprises						
大型企业	Large	26	42	89	202	51	51
中型企业	Medium	80	168	216	229	441	469
小型企业	Small	2 305	2 787	4 480	1 073	3 205	4 047
五、按行业分	Grouped by Sectors						
黑色金属矿采选业	Mining of Ferrous Metal Ores		4	6	1	2	5
有色金属矿采选业	Mining of Non-ferrous Metal Ores	2	7	9	7	5	5
非金属矿采选业	Mining and Processing of Nonmetal Ores	43	70	87	29	34	31
食品制造业	Manufacture of Foods	244	324	437	170	121	137
#粮食及饲料加工	Processing of Grain and Feed	62	57	60	27		
饮料制造业	Manufacture of Beverage	31	44	74	23	29	28
#饮料酒	Beverage Liquor	20	28	27	19	20	25

注:1. 规模以上工业企业为年主营业务收入2000万元及以上的工业法人企业。
2. 2010年以前为国有及年主营业务收入500万元以上的非国有工业企业。
3. 本表1998年以前为乡及乡以上工业企业单位数 。
4. 2012年行业分类按2011年发布的《国民经济行业分类》(GB/T4754－2011)重新划分。

Note:1. Industrial enterprises above designated size refers to industrial enterprises with revenue from principal business over 20 million yuan.
2. Before 2010, industrial enterprises above designated size refered to all the state-owned enterprises and non-state enterprises with revenue from principal business over 5 million yuan.
3. Before 1998, the number of industial enterprises refer to those at and above county level.
4. The sectors are grouped by "Classification and Code of the Sectors of the National Economy" (GB/T4754－2011) in 2012.

12－1 续表 1

项　目	Item	2007	2008	2009	2010	2011
总　计	**Total**	**5 032**	**5 628**	**5 895**	**5 674**	**4 727**
一、按隶属关系分	**Grouped by Subordination**					
中央工业	Central Industry	9	40	44	31	31
省属工业	Provincial Industry	34	28	25	25	17
地方工业	Local Industry	4 989	5 560	5 826	5 618	4 679
二、按经济类型分	Grouped by Economic Types					
国有企业	State-owned	63	65	163	61	147
集体企业	Collective-owned	72	61	59	53	31
其他经济类型企业	Other Economic Types	4 897	5 502	5 673	5 560	4 549
#外商及港澳台商投资企业	Foreign Funded Enterprises and Enterprises with Funds from Hong Kong, Macao and Taiwan	2 091	2 217	2 244	2 037	1 618
三、按轻重工业分	Grouped by Light and Heavy Industries					
轻工业	Light Industry	2 489	2 704	2 805	2 635	2 131
重工业	Heavy Industry	2 543	2 924	3 090	3 039	2 596
四、按企业规模分	Grouped by Size of Enterprises					
大型企业	Large	53	48	50	52	50
中型企业	Medium	489	519	502	525	516
小型企业	Small	4 490	5 061	5 343	5 097	4 161
五、按行业分	Grouped by Sectors					
黑色金属矿采选业	Mining of Ferrous Metal Ores	7	23	22	12	12
有色金属矿采选业	Mining of Non-ferrous Metal Ores	5	6	6	4	
非金属矿采选业	Mining and Processing of Nonmetal Ores	33	30	26	26	23
食品制造业	Manufacture of Foods	156	158	174	167	127
#粮食及饲料加工	Processing of Grain and Feed					
饮料制造业	Manufacture of Beverage	33	40	42	42	36
#饮料酒	Beverage Liquor					

12-1 续表2
continued

单位：个(unit)

项 目	Item	1985	1990	1995	2000	2005	2006
烟草制品业	Manufacture of Tobacco	2	2	5	3	2	2
纺织业	Manufacture of Textile	169	225	330	132	300	327
纺织服装、鞋、帽制造业	Manufacture of Textile Wearing Apparel, Footware and Caps	171	194	322	95	272	339
皮革、毛皮、羽毛(绒)及其制品业	Manufacture of Leather, Fur, Feather and Related Products	56	64	161	64	167	194
木材加工制品业	Processing of Wood and Wood Products	71	89	116	19	40	53
家具制造业	Manufacture of Furniture	61	72	88	10	72	103
造纸及纸制品业	Manufacture of Paper and Paper Products	66	74	110	56	102	128
印刷业和记录媒介的复制	Printing, Reproduction of Recording Media	61	81	215	23	44	59
文教体育用品制造业	Manufacture of Articles For Culture, Education and Sport Activities	31	27	93	48	89	91
石油加工、炼焦及核燃料加工业	Processing of Petroleum, Coking, Processing of Nuclear Fuel	2	3	13	5	10	6
化学原料及制品	Manufacture of Raw Chemical Materials and Chemical Products	106	156	278	81	178	233
医药制造业	Manufacture of Medicines	16	14	39	20	30	46
化学纤维制造业	Manufacture of Chemical Fibers	2	4	26	15	14	13
橡胶制品业	Manufacture of Rubber	53	57	143	48	116	170
塑料制品业	Manufacture of Plastics	103	131	237	64	153	179
非金属矿物制品业	Manufacture of Non-metallic Mineral Products	230	245	275	62	161	218
黑色金属压延加工业	Smelting and Pressing of Ferrous Metals	11	13	31	15	41	45
有色金属压延加工业	Smelting and Pressing of Non-ferrous Metals	6	8	19	9	28	40
金属制品业	Manufacture of Metal Products	161	186	372	88	186	250
通用设备制造业	Manufacture of General Purpose Machinery	320	398	320	94	299	397
交通运输制造业	Manufacture of Transport Equipment	104	114	358	52	151	194
电气机械及器材制造业	Manufacture of Electrical Machinery and Equipment	86	96	211	79	214	249
通信设备、计算机及其他电子设备制造业	Manufacture of Communication Equipment, Computers and Other Electronic Equipment	32	31	79	34	123	140
仪器仪表及文化、办公用机械制造业	Manufacture of Measuring Instruments and Machinery for Cultural Activity and Office Work	28	33	70	20	40	44
水的生产和供应业	Production and Supply of Water	8	12	12	8	10	10
电力、热力的生产和供应业	Production and Supply of Electric Power and Heat Power	10	16	20	17	27	32
燃气生产和供应业	Production and Supply of Gas	1	4	3	2	5	6
其他工业	Other Industrial Sectors	46	48	209	63	166	534

12－1 续表3

continued

单位：个（unit）

项　目	Item	2007	2008	2009	2010	2011
烟草制品业	Manufacture of Tobacco	2	2	2	1	1
纺织业	Manufacture of Textile	340	330	322	287	229
纺织服装、鞋、帽制造业	Manufacture of Textile Wearing Apparel, Footware and Caps	362	418	434	392	295
皮革、毛皮、羽毛（绒）及其制品业	Manufacture of Leather, Fur, Feather and Related Products	197	209	210	211	160
木材加工制品业	Processing of Wood and Wood Products	64	66	68	68	49
家具制造业	Manufacture of Furniture	119	130	133	117	97
造纸及纸制品业	Manufacture of Paper and Paper Products	126	133	133	138	101
印刷业和记录媒介的复制	Printing, Reproduction of Recording Media	63	74	79	92	58
文教体育用品制造业	Manufacture of Articles For Culture, Education and Sport Activities	97	96	99	90	75
石油加工、炼焦及核燃料加工业	Processing of Petroleum, Coking, Processing of Nuclear Fuel	7	7	9	8	7
化学原料及制品	Manufacture of Raw Chemical Materials and Chemical Products	261	276	275	262	231
医药制造业	Manufacture of Medicines	48	49	56	52	44
化学纤维制造业	Manufacture of Chemical Fibers	12	13	14	12	10
橡胶制品业	Manufacture of Rubber	183	211	214	196	187
塑料制品业	Manufacture of Plastics	199	227	234	233	169
非金属矿物制品业	Manufacture of Non-metallic Mineral Products	259	311	320	327	303
黑色金属压延加工业	Smelting and Pressing of Ferrous Metals	39	24	27	31	29
有色金属压延加工业	Smelting and Pressing of Non-ferrous Metals	40	41	40	35	34
金属制品业	Manufacture of Metal Products	271	347	376	361	294
通用设备制造业	Manufacture of General Purpose Machinery	473	535	592	597	521
交通运输制造业	Manufacture of Transport Equipment	217	264	290	296	253
电气机械及器材制造业	Manufacture of Electrical Machinery and Equipment	274	303	300	281	230
通信设备、计算机及其他电子设备制造业	Manufacture of Communication Equipment, Computers and Other Electronic Equipment	152	163	168	167	124
仪器仪表及文化、办公用机械制造业	Manufacture of Measuring Instruments and Machinery for Cultural Activity and Office Work	47	47	55	54	39
水的生产和供应业	Production and Supply of Water	10	13	14	14	11
电力、热力的生产和供应业	Production and Supply of Electric Power and Heat Power	34	36	39	38	36
燃气生产和供应业	Production and Supply of Gas	7	13	13	14	11
其他工业	Other Industrial Sectors	895	1 033	1 109	1 049	921

12－1 续表4
continued

单位：个(unit)

项　目	Item	2012年
总　计	**Total**	**4 817**
一、按隶属关系分	**Grouped by Subordination Relation**	
中央工业	Central Industry	15
省属工业	Provincial Industry	18
地方工业	Local Industry	4 784
二、按经济类型分	**Grouped by Economic Types**	
国有企业	State-owned	144
集体企业	Collective-owned	28
其他经济类型企业	Other Economic Types	4 645
#外商及港澳台商投资企业	Foreign Funded Enterprises and Enterprises with Funds from Hong Kong, Macao and Taiwan	1 599
三、按轻重工业分	**Grouped by Light and Heavy Industries**	
轻工业	Light Industry	2 153
重工业	Heavy Industry	2 664
四、按企业规模分	**Grouped by Size of Enterprises**	
大型企业	Large	98
中型企业	Medium	596
小型企业	Small	4 123
五、按行业分	**Grouped by Sectors**	
黑色金属矿采选业	Mining of Ferrous Metal Ores	10
非金属矿采选业	Mining and Processing of Nonmetal Ores	14
农副食品加工业	Processing of Food from Agricultural Products	454
食品制造业	Manufacture of Foods	129
酒、饮料和精制茶制造业	Manufacture of Liquor, Beverage and Refind Tea	34
烟草制品业	Manufacture of Tobacco	1
纺织业	Manufacture of Textile	181
纺织服装、服饰业	Manufacture of Textile Wearing Apparel	312
皮革、毛皮、羽毛及其制品和制鞋业	Manufacture of Leather, Fur, Feather & Its Products Footwear	177

12－1 续表 5
continued

单位：个（unit）

项　　目	Item	2012 年
木材加工和木、竹、藤、棕、草制品业	Processing of Timbers, Manufacture of Wood, Bamboo, Rattan, Palm and Straw Products	34
家具制造业	Manufacture of Furniture	103
造纸和纸制品业	Manufacture of Paper and Paper Products	100
印刷和记录媒介复制业	Printing, Reproduction of Recording Media	80
文教、工美、体育和娱乐用品制造业	Manufacture of Articles for Culture, Arts & Crafts, Sports and Entertainment	253
石油加工、炼焦和核燃料加工业	Processing of Petroleum, Coking, Processing of Nucleus Fuel	8
化学原料和化学制品制造业	Manufacture of Chemical Raw Material and Chemical Products	224
医药制造业	Manufacture of Medicines	45
化学纤维制造业	Manufacture of Chemical Fiber	9
橡胶和塑料制品业	Manufacture of Rubber and Plastic	352
非金属矿物制品业	Manufacture of Non-metallic Mineral Products	325
黑色金属冶炼和压延加工业	Smelting and Pressing of Ferrous Metals	105
有色金属冶炼和压延加工业	Smelting and Pressing of Non-ferrous Metals	37
金属制品业	Manufacture of Metal Products	399
通用设备制造业	Manufacture of General Purpose Machinery	362
专用设备制造业	Manufacture of Special Purpose Machinery	312
汽车制造业	Manufacture of Vehicle	136
铁路、船舶、航空航天和其他运输设备制造业	Manufacture of Transport Equipment for Railway, Shipping, Aerospace and other uses	145
电气机械和器材制造业	Manufacture of Electrical Machinery & Equipment	202
计算机、通信和其他电子设备制造业	Manufacture of Computer, Communication Equipment and Other Electronic Equipment	137
仪器仪表制造业	Manufacture of Measuring Instrument	41
其他制造业	Manufacture of Other Products	18
废弃资源综合利用业	Recycling and Disposal of Waste Resources	4
金属制品、机械和设备修理业	Maintenance of Metal Products, Machinery and Equipment	7
电力、热力的生产和供应业	Production and Supply of Electric Power and Heat Power	36
燃气生产和供应业	Production and Supply of Gas	12
水的生产和供应业	Production and Supply of Water	11

12－2 分市、区全部工业企业单位数(2012 年)
NUMBER OF ALL INDUSTRIAL ENTERPRISES BY REGION(2012)

单位:个(unit)

市、区名称	Region	合计 Total	规模以上 Above Designated Size	按轻重工业分 Grouped by Light and Heavy Industries		按企业规模分 Grouped by Size of Enterprises		
				轻工业 Light Industry	重工业 Heavy Industry	大型企业 Large	中型企业 Medium	小型企业 Small
总　计	**Total**	**73 160**	**4 817**	**2 153**	**2 664**	**98**	**596**	**4 123**
市　区	Urban Area		1 020	389	631	54	220	746
#崂山区	Laoshan District		104	44	60	4	22	78
原黄岛区	Original Huangdao District		271	60	211	16	62	193
城阳区	Chengyang District		446	215	231	16	93	337
即墨市	Jimo		759	418	341	12	107	640
胶州市	Jiaozhou		858	396	462	10	113	735
原胶南市	Original Jiaonan		732	241	491	9	44	679
平度市	Pingdu		677	289	388	6	45	626
莱西市	Laixi		698	394	304	6	49	643
高新区	High-tech Zone		73	26	47	1	18	54

12－2 续表
continued

单位:个(unit)

市、区名称	Region	按经济类型分 Grouped by Economic Types				规模以下 Below Designated Size	#个体 Individual
		国有企业 State-owned	集体企业 Collective-owned	其他经济 Others	#外资及港澳台商企业 Foreign Funded Enterprises and Enterprises with Funds from Hong Kong, Macao and Taiwan		
总　计	**Total**	**144**	**28**	**4 645**	**1 599**	**68 343**	**46 224**
市　区	Urban Area	93	8	919	528		
#崂山区	Laoshan District	9	1	94	39		
原黄岛区	Original Huangdao District	28	2	241	151		
城阳区	Chengyang District	11	1	434	269		
即墨市	Jimo	10	3	746	253		
胶州市	Jiaozhou	9	1	848	234		
原胶南市	Original Jiaonan	8	1	723	151		
平度市	Pingdu	13	6	658	197		
莱西市	Laixi	7	9	682	199		
高新区	High-tech Zone	4	0	69	37		

注:规模以下工业资料产值与单位数均来源于抽样调查推算,工业单位数除普查年度外无分市(区)数据。

Note: The data of output and number of industrial enterprises below designated size are caculated according to the sampling survey. There are no data of the number of industrial enterprises by region except in the census year.

12 -3 历年全部工业总产值
GROSS INDUSTRIAL OUTPUT VALUE OVER THE YEARS

单位:万元（10 000 yuan）

年 份 Year	工业总产值 Gross Industrial Output Value	轻工业产值 Light Industry	重工业产值 Heavy Industry
1949	21 605	18 494	3 111
1950	34 010	28 720	5 290
1951	53 538	44 600	8 938
1952	84 295	69 258	15037
1953	115 222	74 716	40 506
1954	126 064	80 604	45 460
1955	118 935	86 956	31 979
1956	144 833	93 809	51 024
1957	142 920	101 202	41 718
1958	217 648	92 407	125 241
1959	282 610	84 376	198 234
1960	291 451	77 043	214 408
1962	120 738	64 233	56 505
1963	139 542	83 630	55 912
1964	177 273	108 884	68 389
1965	215 536	141 765	73 771
1966	252 896	152 304	100 592
1967	287 739	163 627	124 112
1968	299 814	175 791	123 489
1969	296 814	188 860	107 954
1970	345 212	202 903	142 309

注:本表按当年价格计算,1995 年开始工业总产值按新规定计算。

Note: The data in this form are calculated at current price. Since 1995, new regulations have been adopted in calculating gross industrial output value.

12－3 续表1
continued

单位:万元(10 000 yuan)

年　份 Year	工业总产值 Gross Industrial Output Value	轻工业产值 Light Industry	重工业产值 Heavy Industry
1971	365 770	216 172	149 598
1972	378 266	230 309	147 957
1973	377 943	245 371	132 572
1974	237 219	154 054	83 165
1975	402 541	261 418	141 123
1976	439 793	278 514	161 279
1977	490 669	296 728	193 941
1978	565 503	336 817	228 686
1979	625 227	379 276	245 951
1980	677 690	442 078	235 612
1981	707 434	479 954	227 480
1982	732 705	474 767	257 938
1983	816 793	513 759	303 034
1984	918 364	569 080	349 284
1985	1 113 891	699 524	414 367
1986	1 316 230	833 864	482 366
1987	1 703 830	1 065 873	637 957
1988	2 481 594	1 451 215	1 030 379
1989	3 191 643	1 857 019	1 334 624
1990	3 571 845	2 057 968	1 513 878

12-3 续表 2
continued

单位：万元（10 000 yuan）

年　份	Year	工业总产值 Gross Industrial Output Value	轻工业产值 Light Industry	重工业产值 Heavy Industry
1991	1991	3 986 427	2 318 257	1 668 170
1992	1992	4 826 834	2 835 728	1 991 106
1993	1993	5 929 236	3 422 107	2 507 129
1994	1994	8 456 974	4 931 262	3 525 712
1995	1995	9 412 635	5 579 637	3 832 998
1996	1996	11 173 672	6 793 007	4 380 665
1997	1997	13 704 735	8 620 710	5 084 025
1998	1998	15 794 106	10 153 634	5 640 472
1999	1999	16 822 436	10 918 827	5 903 609
2000	2000	19 408 338	12 433 214	6 975 124
2001	2001	22 398 464	14 368 582	8 029 882
2002	2002	25 794 324	14 811 106	10 983 218
2003	2003	31 195 595	17 306 539	13 889 056
2004	2004	39 590 783	21 473 202	18 117 581
2005	2005	50 017 829	24 697 792	25 320 037
2006	2006	59 188 120	28 686 826	30 501 294
2007	2007	74 306 364	33 463 071	40 843 293
2008	2008	89 467 300	37 871 227	51 596 073
2009	2009	102 556 155	42 715 781	59 840 374
2010	2010	116 148 345	44 954 630	71 193 715
2011	2011	132 779 629	50 854 938	81 924 691
2012	2012	153 102 565	60 521 444	92 581 121
“一五”时期合计	“First Five-Year Plan” Period	647 974	437 287	210 687
“二五”时期合计	“Second Five-Year Plan” Period	1 077 075	388 406	688 669
1963-1965 年合计	1963-1965	532 351	334 279	198 072
“三五”时期合计	“Third Five-Year Plan” Period	1 481 941	883 485	598 456
“四五”时期合计	“Fourth Five-Year Plan” Period	1 761 739	1 107 324	654 415
“五五”时期合计	“Fifth Five-Year Plan” Period	2 798 882	1 733 413	1 065 469
“六五”时期合计	“Sixth Five-Year Plan” Period	4 289 187	2 737 084	1 552 103
“七五”时期合计	“Seventh Five-Year Plan” Period	12 265 142	7 265 939	4 999 204
“八五”时期合计	“Eighth Five-Year Plan” Period	32 612 106	19 087 323	13 524 783
“九五”时期合计	“Ninth Five-Year Plan” Period	76 903 287	48 919 392	27 983 895
“十五”时期合计	“Tenth Five-Year Plan” Period	168 996 995	92 657 221	76 339 774
“十一五”时期合计	“Eleventh Five-Year Plan” Period	175 336 465	73 641 456	101 695 009

12－4 分市、区全部工业总产值(2012 年)
GROSS INDUSTRIAL OUTPUT VALUE BY REGION(2012)

单位:万元(10 000 yuan)

市、区名称	Region	工业总产值 Gross Industrial Output Value	规模以上 Above Designated Size	#外商及港澳台商投资企业 Foreign Funded Enterprises and Enterprises with Funds from Hong Kong, Macao and Taiwan	规模以下 Below Designated Size
总　计	**Total**	**153 102 565**	**140 533 565**	**39 213 844**	**12 569 000**
市　区	Urban Area	68 186 900	64 274 200	18 093 517	3 912 700
#崂山区	Laoshan District	4 603 885	4 107 285	776 880	496 600
原黄岛区	Original Huangdao District	29 904 733	29 202 633	9 049 069	702 100
城阳区	Chengyang District	17 586 737	15 555 537	6 212 034	2 031 200
即墨市	Jimo	21 744 223	19 538 023	7 099 818	2 206 200
胶州市	Jiaozhou	18 729 694	17 008 194	3 854 900	1 721 500
原胶南市	Original Jiaonan	17 490 806	15 864 506	2 883 091	1 626 300
平度市	Pingdu	14 716 391	13 027 191	3 750 396	1 689 200
莱西市	Laixi	10 633 537	9 220 437	2 653 515	1 413 100
高新区	High-tech Zone	1 601 015	1 601 015	878 607	

注:高新区为北部园区口径.
Note: In this from, high-tech zone reffers to the northern park.

12－5 分市、区规模以上工业总产值(2012 年)
GROSS INDUSTRIAL OUTPUT VALUE ABOVE DESIGNATED SIZE BY REGION(2012)

指　标	Indicator	总计 Total	市内四区 Four Districts in Urban Area	崂山区 Laoshan District	原黄岛区 Original Huangdao District	城阳区 Chengyang District
总　计	**Total**	**140 533 565**	**15 408 744**	**4 107 285**	**29 202 633**	**15 555 537**
按隶属关系分	**Grouped by Subordination**					
中央	Centrality	14 943 997	3 431 653	238 383	7 931 566	2 910 782
省(自治区、直辖市)	Province(Autonomous Region,Municipality)	2 392 040	240 298	1 099 844	10 618	515 524
市(地级)	Municipality(local level)	18 120 357	9 412 999	1 046 873	5 379 785	819 075
县级市(区)	Municipality at County Level(District)	4 396 962	227 504	238 937	77 264	1 155 245
镇、街道	Town and Subdistrict Office	7 480 475	26 926	51 110	10 811	1 871 656
乡	Country	75 265				
其它	Others	93 124 469	2 069 364	1 432 138	15 792 590	8 283 256
按登记注册类型分	**Grouped by Status of Registration**					
国有经济	State-owned	30 558 320	8 267 240	1 293 826	15 306 193	3 134 059
集体经济	Collective-owned	7 757 526	4 227 493	831 067	1 635 164	475 483
其他经济	Others	102 217 719	2 914 011	1 982 392	12 261 276	11 395 995
#外资与港澳台企业	Foreign Funded Enterprises and Enterprises with Funds from Hong Kong,Macao and Taiwan	39 213 844	2 055 534	776 880	9 049 069	6 212 034
按轻重工业分	**Grouped by Light and Heavy Industries**					
轻工业	Light Industry	55 546 558	6 846 781	2 569 098	6 971 538	4 908 925
重工业	Heavy Industry	84 987 007	8 561 963	1 538 187	22 231 096	10 646 512
按企业规模分	**Grouped by Size of Enterprises**					
大型企业	Large	41 503 654	11 987 195	1 562 436	12 476 053	6 833 059
中型企业	Medium	33 791 022	2 027 595	864 133	12 556 999	3 742 507
小型企业	Small	65 238 890	1 393 954	1 680 717	4 169 582	4 979 970

单位:万元(10 000 yuan)

即墨市 Jimo	胶州市 Jiaozhou	原胶南市 Original Jiaonan	平度市 Pingdu	莱西市 Laixi	高新区 High-tech Zone
19 53[illegible] 023	**17 008 194**	**15 864 506**	**13 027 191**	**9 220 437**	**1 601 015**
4 343	181 757	21 045	167 891	9 909	46 669
137 315		133 520	69 038		135 883
[illegible]74 324	171 800	759 366	108 506	94 371	53 260
1 [illegible]13 008	199 275	812 069	361 017	212 643	
440 933	2 991 175	1 512 072	487 738	56 818	31 237
	4 518			70 747	
1[illegible] 518 099	13 459 669	12 626 436	11 833 002	8 775 949	1 333 966
383 835	353 624	916 107	414 149	177 801	261 486
127 656	61 358	44 798	243 262	111 245	
[illegible]9 026 532	16 593 212	14 903 602	12 369 780	8 931 390	1 339 529
7 099 818	3 854 900	2 883 091	3 750 396	2 653 515	878 607
11 226 594	7 019 352	4 908 310	5 048 007	5 597 536	450 417
8 311 429	9 988 842	10 956 196	7 979 185	3 622 901	1 150 597
2 839 486	1 137 718	2 316 950	417 431	1 840 353	92 974
5 175 528	3 706 985	1 644 478	1 911 151	1 232 219	929 427
11 523 009	12 163 491	11 903 078	10 698 610	6 147 865	578 615

12－5 续表
continued

指　　标	Indicator	总计 Total	市内四区 Four Districts in Urban Area	崂山区 Laoshan District
按行业分	**Grouped by Industrial Sector**	**140 533 565**	**15 408 744**	**4 107 285**
煤炭开采和洗选业	Mining and Washing of Coal			
石油和天然气开采业	Extraction of Petroleum and Natural Gas			
黑色金属矿采选业	Mining of Ferrous Metal Ores	166 759		
有色金属矿采选业	Mining of Non-ferrous Metal Ores			
非金属矿采选业	Mining and Processing of Nonmetal Ores	291 339		
开采辅助活动	Auxiliary Activities of Mining			
其他采矿业	Mining of Other Ores			
农副食品加工业	Processing of Food from Agricultural Products	12 145 813	354 317	32 949
食品制造业	Manufacture of Foods	2 496 281	59 717	114 073
酒、饮料和精制茶制造业	Manufacture of Liquor, Beverage and Refind Tea	1 634 341	833 163	205 585
烟草制品业	Manufacture of Tobacco	1 096 785		1 096 785
纺织业	Manufacture of Textile	3 698 517	185 416	3 806
纺织服装、服饰业	Manufacture of Textile Wearing Apparel	6 322 897	71 974	17 756
皮革、毛皮、羽毛及其制品和制鞋业	Manufacture of Leather, Fur, Feather & Its Products Footwear	3 400 301	19 748	7 842
木材加工和木、竹、藤、棕、草制品业	Processing of Timbers, Manufacture of Wood, Bamboo, Rattan, Palm, and Straw Products	563 824		
家具制造业	Manufacture of Furniture	1 592 589	20 120	
造纸和纸制品业	Manufacture of Paper and Paper Products	1 750 814	6 311	34 856
印刷和记录媒介复制业	Printing, Reproduction of Recording Media	1 191 527	139 974	
文教、工美、体育和娱乐用品制造业	Manufacture of Articles for Culture, Arts & Crafts, Sports and Entertainment	3 283 799	87 776	13 341
石油加工、炼焦和核燃料加工业	Processing of Petroleum, Coking, Processing of Nucleus Fuel	8 953 155	1 757 511	55 456
化学原料和化学制品制造业	Manufacture of Chemical Raw Material and Chemical Products	6 579 213	1 288 717	27 144
医药制造业	Manufacture of Medicines	965 373	41 475	137 861
化学纤维制造业	Manufacture of Chemical Fiber	148 782	24 055	
橡胶和塑料制品业	Manufacture of Rubber and Plastic	8 284 769	296 162	74 105
非金属矿物制品业	Manufacture of Non-metallic Mineral Products	5 285 649	145 639	95 128
黑色金属冶炼和压延加工业	Smelting and Pressing of Ferrous Metals	4 823 183	1 953 050	5 193
有色金属冶炼和压延加工业	Smelting and Pressing of Non-ferrous Metals	1 266 929		2 637
金属制品业	Manufacture of Metal Products	9 991 428	25 454	7 328
通用设备制造业	Manufacture of General Purpose Machinery	8 321 651	463 099	30 176
专用设备制造业	Manufacture of Special Purpose Machinery	6 617 090	63 621	106 697
汽车制造业	Manufacture of Vehicle	5 757 479	1 198 461	8 349
铁路、船舶、航空航天和其他运输设备制造业	Manufacture of Transport Equipment for Railway, Shipping, Aerospace and other uses	7 669 238	398 135	120 339
电气机械和器材制造业	Manufacture of Electrical Machinery & Equipment	14 088 716	4 402 851	1 474 328
计算机、通信和其他电子设备制造业	Manufacture of Computer, Communication Equipment and Other Electronic Equipment	7 920 896	690 233	185 273
仪器仪表制造业	Manufacture of Measuring Instrument	779 709	20 286	212 368
其他制造业	Manufacture of Other Products	184 868	9 555	12 539
废弃资源综合利用业	Recycling and Disposal of Waste Resources	47 616		
金属制品、机械和设备修理业	Maintenance of Metal Products, Machinery and Equipment	108 951		
电力、热力生产和供应业	Production and Supply of Electric Power and Heat Power	2 536 784	630 861	21 321
燃气生产和供应业	Production and Supply of Gas	450 366	164 316	
水的生产和供应业	Production and Supply of Water	116 138	56 747	

单位:万元(10 000 yuan)

原黄岛区 Original Huangdao District	城阳区 Chengyang District	即墨市 Jimo	胶州市 Jiaozhou	原胶南市 Original Jiaonan	平度市 Pingdu	莱西市 Laixi	高新区 High-tech Zone
29 202 [illegible]33	**15 555 537**	**19 538 023**	**17 008 194**	**15 864 506**	**13 027 191**	**9 220 437**	**1 601 015**
					98 412	68 347	
		2 980			156 400	131 959	
825 947	1 648 734	1 180 169	1 576 404	880 555	2 214 347	3 164 921	266 471
115 185	215 623	75 162	430 379	810 498	309 118	366 527	
	4 962	164 833	164 833	218 551	140 334	45 358	
16 888	887 958	893 830	627 378	253 745	450 859	378 637	
120 023	683 446	3 569 533	725 149	542 929	246 300	300 103	45 686
53 064	175 975	1 234 265	1 061 912	301 341	51 297	484 859	
48 223		35 700	35 700	88 458	35 606	128 258	
	330 094	35 363	35 363	174 990	179 824	79 972	11 684
54 846	87 853	509 993	233 130	520 465	180 235	123 125	
	206 186	528 629	21 761	282 329	6 123		6 525
63 391	278 892	611 510	647 880	505 261	761 080	308 533	6 134
6 433 257	683 995	3 030	6 665		13 241		
[illegible] 881 928	318 603	620 972	739 307	695 761	482 182	439 892	84 708
90 068	112 324	149 004	179 902	106 826	25 099	63 549	59 266
49 195		11 450	49 000	15 082			
2 019 828	290 097	804 002	810 032	2 243 757	1 087 147	572 699	86 940
551 844	500 627	131 806	744 478	561 615	1 467 866	1 079 865	6 781
927 517	509 879	145 409	176 822	254 855	830 476	16 982	
129 435	15 606	127 506	280 005	0	534 407	9 426	167 907
1 213 567	692 208	4 210 813	2 246 060	821 789	437 889	237 292	99 029
1 134 800	497 735	516 340	2 373 564	1 398 505	1 390 633	280 251	236 548
960 949	614 545	486 490	943 999	2 746 802	430 246	242 727	21 014
2 880 122	564 866	116 160	287 472	244 180	254 070	67 416	135 883
1 993 813	3 142 967	220 213	249 970	1 150 543	157 417	122 298	113 043
3 167 947	839 071	2 162 802	1 175 560	519 495	138 091	180 105	28 466
3 920 233	1 587 151	521 465	71 208	131 581	513 429	109 323	191 001
4 291	114 133	44 773	52 553	116 516	168 872	20 963	24 955
	27 732	34 448	22 376	14 563	42 012	12 619	8 975
				14 614		33 002	
12 146		64 610		32 195			
449 545	478 538	222 818	196 049	194 886	218 645	124 120	
53 573	42 289	89 747	65 941	16 663	35	17 801	
20 009	3 450	12 200	3 564	5 158	5 502	9 509	

12－6 规模以上工业企业主要指标(2012 年)

MAIN INDICATORS OF INDUSTRIAL ENTERPRISES ABOVE DESIGNATED SIZE(2012)

项　　目	Indicator	企业单位数(个) Number of Enterprises (unit)
总　计	**Total**	**4 817**
按注册登记类型分	**Grouped by Status of Registration**	
国有及国有控股企业	State-owned and State-holding Enterprises	144
集体企业	Collective-owned Enterprises	28
股份有限公司	Share-holding Corporations Ltd	112
外商投资企业	Foreign Funded Enterprises	1 321
港澳台商投资企业	Invested by HongKong, Macao and Taiwan	278
按轻重工业分	**Grouped by Light and Heavy Industries**	
轻工业	Light Industry	2 153
重工业	Heavy Industry	2 664
按企业规模分	**Grouped by Size of Enterprises**	
大型企业	Large	98
中型企业	Medium	596
小型企业	Small	4 123
按所在地分	**Grouped by Location**	
市　区	Urban Area	1 020
#崂山区	Laoshan District	104
原黄岛区	Original Huangdao District	271
城阳区	Chengyang District	445
即墨市	Jimo	759
胶州市	Jiaozhou	858
原胶南市	Original Jiaonan	732
平度市	Pingdu	677
莱西市	Laixi	698
高新区	High-tech Zone	73
按行业分	**Grouped by Sector**	
煤炭开采和洗选业	Mining and Washing of Coal	
石油和天然气开采业	Extraction of Petroleum and Natural Gas	
黑色金属矿采选业	Mining of Ferrous Metal Ores	10
有色金属矿采选业	Mining of Non-ferrous Metal Ores	
非金属矿采选业	Mining and Processing of Nonmetal Ores	14
开采辅助活动	Auxiliary Activities of Mining	
其他采矿业	Mining of Other Ores	

单位:万元(10 000 yuan)

工业总产值 Gross Industrial Output Value	资产合计 Total Assets	流动资产合计 Total Current Assets	固定资产净值 Net Value of Fixed Assets
140 533 565	**78 284 627**	**45 780 867**	**20 571 189**
30 558 320	24 920 733	13 871 936	6 945 526
7 757 526	7 256 242	5 981 669	666 818
10 512 309	8 224 283	5 307 709	1 436 142
32 388 096	20 422 959	12 130 972	5 194 426
6 825 748	3 746 656	2 386 593	985 070
55 546 558	29 666 229	18 468 440	6 564 934
84 987 007	48 618 397	27 312 427	14 006 254
41 503 654	35 197 051	23 464 097	6 721 710
33 791 022	20 177 859	10 447 146	6 471 710
65 238 890	22 909 717	11 869 623	7 377 769
64 274 200	49 832 563	31 480 515	10 767 725
4 107 285	3 468 193	2 464 159	506 106
29 202 633	18 942 887	11 472 660	5 296 631
15 555 537	11 580 652	7 585 502	1 902 999
19 538 023	5 775 693	2 841 243	1 732 188
17 008 194	7 409 091	4 244 128	2 318 518
15 864 506	5 775 411	2 620 529	2 112 357
13 027 191	4 336 376	2 132 966	1 647 269
9 220 437	3 365 316	1 567 387	1 398 236
1 601 015	1 790 177	894 098	594 896
166 759	22 708	7 054	11 529
291 339	55 806	25 686	24 460

12－6 续表 1
continued

项　　目	Indicator	主营业务收入 Revenue from Principal Business
总　计	**Total**	**138 296 575**
按注册登记类型分	**Grouped by Status of Registration**	
国有及国有控股企业	State-owned and State-holding Enterprises	32 332 132
集体企业	Collective-owned Enterprises	9 211 645
股份有限公司	Share-holding Corporations Ltd	9 868 100
外商投资企业	Foreign Funded Enterprises	30 832 386
港澳台商投资企业	Invested by HongKong Macao and Taiwan	6 698 999
按轻重工业分	**Grouped by Light and Heavy Industries**	
轻工业	Light Industry	56 261 167
重工业	Heavy Industry	82 035 407
按企业规模分	**Grouped by size of Enterprises**	
大型企业	Large	45 120 015
中型企业	Medium	32 127 347
小型企业	Small	61 049 213
按所在地分	**Grouped by Location**	
市　区	Urban Area	63 730 668
#崂山区	Laoshan District	3 401 095
原黄岛区	Original Huangdao District	29 825 414
城阳区	Chengyang District	12 217 994
即墨市	Jimo	19 107 682
胶州市	Jiaozhou	16 467 209
原胶南市	Original Jiaonan	15 581 888
平度市	Pingdu	12 862 991
莱西市	Laixi	8 909 998
高新区	High-tech Zone	1 636 140
按行业分	**Grouped by Sector**	
煤炭开采和洗选业	Mining and Washing of Coal	
石油和天然气开采业	Extraction of Petroleum and Natural Gas	
黑色金属矿采选业	Mining of Ferrous Metal Ores	163 541
有色金属矿采选业	Mining of Non-ferrous Metal Ores	
非金属矿采选业	Mining and Processing of Nonmetal Ores	283 499
开采辅助活动	Auxiliary Activities of Mining	
其他采矿业	Mining of Other Ores	

单位:万元(10 000 yuan)

主营业务成本 Cost of Principal Business	主营业务税金及附加 Taxes and Extra Charges on Principal Business	利润总额 Total Profits	本年应交增值税 Value-added Tax Payable	全部从业人员年平均人数(人) Annual Average Employed Persons(person)
116 454 061	**2 311 939**	**7 435 774**	**4 418 223**	**1 103 554**
27 458 706	1 279 847	934 510	1 164 995	136 796
7 078 093	63 992	546 343	204 056	28 843
8 534 051	45 379	463 112	235 583	78 299
26 014 641	389 420	1 765 688	915 114	371 177
5 796 654	56 219	352 584	169 765	61 371
46 633 273	532 935	3 422 750	1 706 039	561 204
69 820 788	1 779 004	4 013 024	2 712 184	542 350
37 858 966	570 910	2 054 794	1 069 913	304 633
27 577 051	1 026 526	1 185 606	1 209 001	326 333
51 018 044	714 503	4 195 375	2 139 309	472 588
53 866 326	1 451 403	2 300 044	1 926 567	396 954
2 646 479	22 780	251 779	109 280	34 213
25 017 533	1 006 167	1 055 936	1 317 392	122 961
10 597 382	46 409	529 336	174 072	139 248
16 347 696	338 606	1 112 256	580 340	180 853
13 466 532	205 569	1 247 176	664 942	180 729
12 652 257	226 000	1 185 801	604 045	106 174
10 958 078	62 490	929 993	454 928	95 249
7 747 195	24 185	561 524	154 962	123 055
1 415 976	3 686	98 980	32 439	20 540
135 163	1 965	15 753	4 274	1 176
208 576	2 149	17 952	8 897	2 169

12－6 续表2
continued

项 目	Indicator	企业单位数(个) Number of Enterprises (unit)
农副食品加工业	Processing of Food from Agricultural Products	454
食品制造业	Manufacture of Foods	129
酒、饮料和精制茶制造业	Manufacture of Liquor, Beverage and Refind Tea	34
烟草制品业	Manufacture of Tobacco	1
纺织业	Manufacture of Textile	[illegible]
纺织服装、服饰业	Manufacture of Textile Wearing Apparel	[illegible]
皮革、毛皮、羽毛及其制品和制鞋业	Manufacture of Leather, Fur, Feather & Its Products Footwear	177
木材加工和木、竹、藤、棕、草制品业	Processing of Timbers, Manufacture of Wood, Bamboo, Rattan, Palm, and Straw Products	34
家具制造业	Manufacture of Furniture	103
造纸和纸制品业	Manufacture of Paper and Paper Products	100
印刷和记录媒介复制业	Printing, Reproduction of Recording Media	80
文教、工美、体育和娱乐用品制造业	Manufacture of Articles for Culture, Arts & Crafts, Sports and Entertainment	263
石油加工、炼焦和核燃料加工业	Processing of Petroleum, Coking, Processing of Nucleus Fuel	8
化学原料和化学制品制造业	Manufacture of Chemical Raw Material and Chemical Products	224
医药制造业	Manufacture of Medicines	45
化学纤维制造业	Manufacture of Chemical Fiber	9
橡胶和塑料制品业	Manufacture of Rubber and Plastic	350
非金属矿物制品业	Manufacture of Non-metallic Mineral Products	325
黑色金属冶炼和压延加工业	Smelting and Pressing of Ferrous Metals	105
有色金属冶炼和压延加工业	Smelting and Pressing of Non-ferrous Metals	37
金属制品业	Manufacture of Metal Products	399
通用设备制造业	Manufacture of General Purpose Machinery	362
专用设备制造业	Manufacture of Special Purpose Machinery	312
汽车制造业	Manufacture of Vehicle	136
铁路、船舶、航空航天和其他运输设备制造业	Manufacture of Transport Equipment for Railway, Shipping, Aerospace and other uses	145
电气机械和器材制造业	Manufacture of Electrical Machinery & Equipment	202
计算机、通信和其他电子设备制造业	Manufacture of Computer, Communication Equipment and Other Electronic Equipment	137
仪器仪表制造业	Manufacture of Measuring Instrument	41
其他制造业	Manufacture of Other Products	18
废弃资源综合利用业	Recycling and Disposal of Waste Resources	4
金属制品、机械和设备修理业	Maintenance of Metal Products, Machinery and Equipment	7
电力、热力生产和供应业	Production and Supply of Electric Power and Heat Power	36
燃气生产和供应业	Production and Supply of Gas	12
水的生产和供应业	Production and Supply of Water	11

单位:万元(10 000 yuan)

工业总产值 Gross Industrial Output Value	资产合计 Total Assets	流动资产合计 Total Current Assets	固定资产净值 Net Value of Fixed Assets
22 145 813	4 418 675	2 556 087	1 293 562
2 496 281	1 512 064	942 259	330 266
1 634 341	1 863 009	629 166	301 259
1 096 785			
3 698 517	1 378 329	713 298	415 473
6 322 897	2 676 751	1 385 359	796 086
3 400 301	979 160	562 972	306 695
563 824	144 377	64 767	54 382
1 592 589	567 620	311 187	188 088
1 750 814	699 106	337 730	260 691
1 191 527	477 075	212 812	135 455
3 283 799	1 098 353	590 028	397 836
8 953 155	2 842 729	1 046 537	1 389 329
6 579 213	3 828 920	1 952 801	1 250 676
965 373	831 595	392 144	229 021
148 782	114 327	70 161	29 804
8 284 769	3 871 927	2 154 211	1 244 687
5 285 649	2 617 651	1 423 453	925 723
4 823 183	2 608 901	1 454 638	636 189
1 266 929	514 468	216 034	221 628
9 991 428	3 719 466	2 052 363	1 146 543
8 321 651	4 277 924	2 357 724	1 140 950
6 617 090	3 584 600	2 172 425	767 556
5 757 479	5 469 014	4 041 778	823 180
7 669 238	8 383 878	5 400 765	1 978 440
14 088 716	10 519 466	8 066 813	1 194 550
7 920 896	4 564 309	3 152 272	760 480
779 709	501 930	349 696	115 894
184 868	127 998	53 252	22 808
47 616	13 759	5 708	7 935
108 951	42 197	23 525	8 780
2 536 784	2 676 320	729 338	1 509 299
450 366	741 857	182 014	332 472
116 138	538 358	144 813	319 464

12 -6 续表3
continued

项　目	Indicator	主营业务收入 Revenue from Principal Business
农副食品加工业	Processing of Food from Agricultural Products	11 575 548
食品制造业	Manufacture of Foods	2 446 859
酒、饮料和精制茶制造业	Manufacture of Liquor, Beverage and Refind Tea	2 103 805
烟草制品业	Manufacture of Tobacco	
纺织业	Manufacture of Textile	3 600 885
纺织服装、服饰业	Manufacture of Textile Wearing Apparel	5 993 879
皮革、毛皮、羽毛及其制品和制鞋业	Manufacture of Leather, Fur, Feather & Its Products Footwear	3 247 315
木材加工和木、竹、藤、棕、草制品业	Processing of Timbers, Manufacture of Wood, Bamboo, Rattan, Palm, and Straw Products	537 313
家具制造业	Manufacture of Furniture	1 493 508
造纸和纸制品业	Manufacture of Paper and Paper Products	1 655 052
印刷和记录媒介复制业	Printing, Reproduction of Recording Media	1 100 818
文教、工美、体育和娱乐用品制造业	Manufacture of Articles for Culture, Arts & Crafts, Sports and Entertainment	3 196 546
石油加工、炼焦和核燃料加工业	Processing of Petroleum, Coking, Processing of Nucleus Fuel	8 754 348
化学原料和化学制品制造业	Manufacture of Chemical Raw Material and Chemical Products	6 104 465
医药制造业	Manufacture of Medicines	873 346
化学纤维制造业	Manufacture of Chemical Fiber	148 247
橡胶和塑料制品业	Manufacture of Rubber and Plastic	8 347 336
非金属矿物制品业	Manufacture of Non-metallic Mineral Products	4 908 097
黑色金属冶炼和压延加工业	Smelting and Pressing of Ferrous Metals	5 350 128
有色金属冶炼和压延加工业	Smelting and Pressing of Non-ferrous Metals	1 240 135
金属制品业	Manufacture of Metal Products	9 599 788
通用设备制造业	Manufacture of General Purpose Machinery	8 105 922
专用设备制造业	Manufacture of Special Purpose Machinery	6 129 506
汽车制造业	Manufacture of Vehicle	5 733 575
铁路、船舶、航空航天和其他运输设备制造业	Manufacture of Transport Equipment for Railway, Shipping, Aerospace and other uses	7 714 063
电气机械和器材制造业	Manufacture of Electrical Machinery & Equipment	15 319 998
计算机、通信和其他电子设备制造业	Manufacture of Computer, Communication Equipment and Other Electronic Equipment	8 638 211
仪器仪表制造业	Manufacture of Measuring Instrument	737 405
其他制造业	Manufacture of Other Products	198 338
废弃资源综合利用业	Recycling and Disposal of Waste Resources	47 636
金属制品、机械和设备修理业	Maintenance of Metal Products, Machinery and Equipment	110 282
电力、热力生产和供应业	Production and Supply of Electric Power and Heat Power	2 323 257
燃气生产和供应业	Production and Supply of Gas	402 028
水的生产和供应业	Production and Supply of Water	111 485

单位:万元(10 000 yuan)

主营业务成本 Cost of Principal Business	主营业务税金及附加 Taxes and Extra Charges on Principal Business	利润总额 Total Profits	本年应交增值税 Value-added Tax Payable	全部从业人员年平均人数(人) Annual Average Employed Persons(person)
1[illegible] 111 606	69 554	580 682	276 053	107 990
[illegible] 817 659	21 859	174 247	82 299	21 517
[illegible] 557 348	60 001	174 095	96 995	15 362
				1 484
3 102 312	37 947	178 151	95 833	35 867
5 130 745	66 863	374 765	178 890	112 602
2 744 617	32 012	233 272	114 781	71 137
450 269	7 522	42 848	21 871	4 753
1 243 841	16 528	99 970	62 343	19 611
1 402 128	24 465	121 456	64 691	13 606
897 734	15 871	74 972	36 334	9 558
2 646 294	35 175	217 517	104 862	45 714
7 595 255	1 107 129	-155 612	541 046	3 475
5 279 134	70 283	248 413	203 798	38 755
587 345	6 030	117 877	44 709	10 357
131 466	1 263	2 824	3 981	1 517
7 269 478	86 309	380 104	308 389	62 593
4 113 458	42 352	343 865	163 854	40 126
4 940 256	12 728	108 270	82 813	22 210
1 103 983	9 982	71 999	26 177	5 883
8 198 646	141 757	568 323	289 025	71 974
6 697 749	74 714	567 106	264 574	67 117
5 023 495	61 230	542 693	240 944	47 621
4 928 697	78 343	357 937	162 131	44 629
5 826 126	42 833	564 129	185 150	53 474
12 272 380	116 510	834 785	373 761	77 831
7 513 336	50 062	372 055	275 985	59 398
536 368	5 216	98 752	28 867	8 366
164 318	2 356	14 741	5 311	3 799
38 686	235	4 260	158	477
94 745	1 068	7 736	3 528	553
2 216 912	6 970	41 830	50 159	14 835
345 053	1 764	43 672	9 378	3 015
128 885	895	-5 663	6 364	3 003

12-7 按行业分国有及国有控股工业企业主要指标（2012 年）
MAIN INDICATORS OF STATE-OWNED AND STATE-HOLDING INDUSTRIAL ENTERPRISES BY INDUSTRIAL SECTOR(2012)

项　目	Indicator	企业单位数(个) Number of Enterprises(unit)
总　计	**Total**	**144**
煤炭开采和洗选业	Mining and Washing of Coal	
石油和天然气开采业	Extraction of Petroleum and Natural Gas	
黑色金属矿采选业	Mining of Ferrous Metal Ores	
有色金属矿采选业	Mining of Non-ferrous Metal Ores	
非金属矿采选业	Mining and Processing of Nonmetal Ores	1
开采辅助活动	Auxiliary Activities of Mining	
其他采矿业	Mining of Other Ores	
农副食品加工业	Processing of Food from Agricultural Products	2
食品制造业	Manufacture of Foods	1
酒、饮料和精制茶制造业	Manufacture of Liquor, Beverage and Refind Tea	6
烟草制品业	Manufacture of Tobacco	1
纺织业	Manufacture of Textile	
纺织服装、服饰业	Manufacture of Textile Wearing Apparel	4
皮革、毛皮、羽毛及其制品和制鞋业	Manufacture of Leather, Fur, Feather & Its Products Footwear	1
木材加工和木、竹、藤、棕、草制品业	Processing of Timbers, Manufacture of Wood, Bamboo, Rattan, Palm, and Straw Products	
家具制造业	Manufacture of Furniture	
造纸和纸制品业	Manufacture of Paper and Paper Products	1
印刷和记录媒介复制业	Printing, Reproduction of Recording Media	1
文教、工美、体育和娱乐用品制造业	Manufacture of Articles for Culture, Arts & Crafts, Sports and Entertainment	
石油加工、炼焦和核燃料加工业	Processing of Petroleum, Coking, Processing of Nucleus Fuel	4
化学原料和化学制品制造业	Manufacture of Chemical Raw Material and Chemical Products	15
医药制造业	Manufacture of Medicines	5
化学纤维制造业	Manufacture of Chemical Fiber	
橡胶和塑料制品业	Manufacture of Rubber and Plastic	6
非金属矿物制品业	Manufacture of Non-metallic Mineral Products	9
黑色金属冶炼和压延加工业	Smelting and Pressing of Ferrous Metals	3
有色金属冶炼和压延加工业	Smelting and Pressing of Non-ferrous Metals	3
金属制品业	Manufacture of Metal Products	3
通用设备制造业	Manufacture of General Purpose Machinery	8
专用设备制造业	Manufacture of Special Purpose Machinery	4
汽车制造业	Manufacture of Vehicle	7
铁路、船舶、航空航天和其他运输设备制造业	Manufacture of Transport Equipment for Railway, Shipping, Aerospace and other uses	16
电气机械和器材制造业	Manufacture of Electrical Machinery & Equipment	3
计算机、通信和其他电子设备制造业	Manufacture of Computer, Communication Equipment and Other Electronic Equipment	2
仪器仪表制造业	Manufacture of Measuring Instrument	2
其他制造业	Manufacture of Other Products	1
废弃资源综合利用业	Recycling and Disposal of Waste Resources	
金属制品、机械和设备修理业	Maintenance of Metal Products, Machinery and Equipment	
电力、热力生产和供应业	Production and Supply of Electric Power and Heat Power	27
燃气生产和供应业	Production and Supply of Gas	1
水的生产和供应业	Production and Supply of Water	7

单位:万元(10 000 yuan)

工业总产值 Gross Industrial Output Value	资产合计 Total Assets	流动资产合计 Total Current Assets	固定资产净值 Net Value of Fixed Assets
30 558 320	**24 920 733**	**13 871 936**	**6 945 526**
5 664	9 458	5 423	1 888
86 736	22 870	6 824	11 333
5 340	5 531	3 847	1 412
1 125 853	1 625 528	516 873	209 257
1 096 785			
57 173	56 172	42 519	11 060
17 084	11 331	7 545	1 997
149 812	80 700	37 392	25 742
3 374	12 567	5 564	943
8 874 763	2 799 066	1 026 868	1 374 725
689 006	927 188	370 667	221 497
184 753	292 640	127 916	62 707
703 352	1 033 084	708 927	223 481
129 868	191 554	124 819	38 659
2 252 521	1 741 061	1 102 359	384 318
69 038	81 887	13 817	55 524
225 661	83 623	50 535	28 939
170 372	358 477	208 274	96 776
501 925	316 699	256 797	49 749
3 331 586	3 396 786	2 890 133	267 220
4 796 317	5 332 064	3 035 846	1 626 689
592 096	501 413	323 445	54 623
3 286 940	2 528 760	2 101 298	252 481
10 657	6 191	5 231	611
9 555	16 231	13 189	1 286
1 972 538	2 551 703	682 261	1 459 380
115 671	439 594	79 211	179 335
93 881	498 557	124 358	303 895

12 -7 续表
continued

项　目	Indicator	主营业务收入 Revenue from Principal Business
总　计	**Total**	**32 [illegible]32 132**
煤炭开采和洗选业	Mining and Washing of Coal	
石油和天然气开采业	Extraction of Petroleum and Natural Gas	
黑色金属矿采选业	Mining of Ferrous Metal Ores	
有色金属矿采选业	Mining of Non-ferrous Metal Ores	
非金属矿采选业	Mining and Processing of Nonmetal Ores	7 697
开采辅助活动	Auxiliary Activities of Mining	
其他采矿业	Mining of Other Ores	
农副食品加工业	Processing of Food from Agricultural Products	83 796
食品制造业	Manufacture of Foods	5 340
酒、饮料和精制茶制造业	Manufacture of Liquor, Beverage and Refind Tea	1 562 147
烟草制品业	Manufacture of Tobacco	
纺织业	Manufacture of Textile	
纺织服装、服饰业	Manufacture of Textile Wearing Apparel	59 [illegible]86
皮革、毛皮、羽毛及其制品和制鞋业	Manufacture of Leather, Fur, Feather & Its Products Footwear	13 [illegible]96
木材加工和木、竹、藤、棕、草制品业	Processing of Timbers, Manufacture of Wood, Bamboo, Rattan, Palm, and Straw Products	
家具制造业	Manufacture of Furniture	
造纸和纸制品业	Manufacture of Paper and Paper Products	126 2[illegible]1
印刷和记录媒介复制业	Printing, Reproduction of Recording Media	3 922
文教、工美、体育和娱乐用品制造业	Manufacture of Articles for Culture, Arts & Crafts, Sports and Entertainment	
石油加工、炼焦和核燃料加工业	Processing of Petroleum, Coking, Processing of Nucleus Fuel	8 677 025
化学原料和化学制品制造业	Manufacture of Chemical Raw Material and Chemical Products	737 05[illegible]
医药制造业	Manufacture of Medicines	159 430
化学纤维制造业	Manufacture of Chemical Fiber	
橡胶和塑料制品业	Manufacture of Rubber and Plastic	933 205
非金属矿物制品业	Manufacture of Non-metallic Mineral Products	126 105
黑色金属冶炼和压延加工业	Smelting and Pressing of Ferrous Metals	3 187 023
有色金属冶炼和压延加工业	Smelting and Pressing of Non-ferrous Metals	69 087
金属制品业	Manufacture of Metal Products	231 128
通用设备制造业	Manufacture of General Purpose Machinery	188 506
专用设备制造业	Manufacture of Special Purpose Machinery	421 371
汽车制造业	Manufacture of Vehicle	3 344 340
铁路、船舶、航空航天和其他运输设备制造业	Manufacture of Transport Equipment for Railway, Shipping, Aerospace and other uses	4 838 626
电气机械和器材制造业	Manufacture of Electrical Machinery & Equipment	849 601
计算机、通信和其他电子设备制造业	Manufacture of Computer, Communication Equipment and Other Electronic E-quipment	4 619 541
仪器仪表制造业	Manufacture of Measuring Instrument	9 071
其他制造业	Manufacture of Other Products	12 072
废弃资源综合利用业	Recycling and Disposal of Waste Resources	
金属制品、机械和设备修理业	Maintenance of Metal Products, Machinery and Equipment	
电力、热力生产和供应业	Production and Supply of Electric Power and Heat Power	1 910 199
燃气生产和供应业	Production and Supply of Gas	65 482
水的生产和供应业	Production and Supply of Water	90 848

单位:万元(10 000 yuan)

主营业务成本 Cost of Principal Business	主营业务 税金及附加 Taxes and Extra Charges on Principal Business	利润总额 Total Profits	本年应 交增值税 Value-added Tax Payable	全部从业人员 年平均人数(人) Annual Average Employed Persons(person)
27 453 706	**1 279 847**	**934 510**	**1 164 995**	**136 796**
5 448	352	200	503	248
37 036	363	2 515	513	400
3 309	113	726	447	344
1 119 819	53 848	139 419	74 583	11 181
				1 484
56 710	245	163	1 202	2 365
10 981	47	804	392	230
120 376	208	1 052	1 800	1 416
2 244	40	297	332	149
7 535 462	1 106 526	-163 682	538 966	2 996
654 495	2 235	-6 977	13 713	8 388
84 566	1 365	21 545	10 620	2 242
870 163	3 365	7 859	11 624	8 825
104 504	483	7 006	3 811	1 912
3 059 982	1 545	7 301	17 537	10 054
50 318	88	9 838	672	857
216 620	1 261	4 310	1 910	1 451
153 483	1 003	546	3 859	4 437
339 193	205	1 815	25 183	2 454
2 905 228	58 079	242 936	106 181	10 767
3 414 883	16 300	306 181	91 721	24 630
770 418	1 869	18 165	16 724	6 618
3 908 141	23 152	296 245	187 535	15 033
5 740	122	343	599	217
10 365	139	161	324	128
1 845 076	6 140	34 125	48 447	13 864
60 052		10 816	501	1 363
114 096	754.7	-9 202	5 296	2 743

12－8 按行业分规模以上外商投资和港澳台商投资工业企业主要指标（2012 年）

MAIN INDICATORS OF FOREIGN FUNDED ENTERPRISES AND ENTERPRISES WITH FUNDS FROM HONG KONG, MACAO AND TAIWAN ABOVE DESIGNATED SIZE BY INDUSTRIAL SECTOR(2012)

项　目	Indicator	企业单位数(个) Number of Enterprises(unit)
总　计	**Total**	**1 599**
煤炭开采和洗选业	Mining and Washing of Coal	
石油和天然气开采业	Extraction of Petroleum and Natural Gas	
黑色金属矿采选业	Mining of Ferrous Metal Ores	1
有色金属矿采选业	Mining of Non-ferrous Metal Ores	
非金属矿采选业	Mining and Processing of Nonmetal Ores	1
开采辅助活动	Auxiliary Activities of Mining	
其他采矿业	Mining of Other Ores	
农副食品加工业	Processing of Food from Agricultural Products	162
食品制造业	Manufacture of Foods	63
酒、饮料和精制茶制造业	Manufacture of Liquor, Beverage and Refind Tea	9
烟草制品业	Manufacture of Tobacco	
纺织业	Manufacture of Textile	72
纺织服装、服饰业	Manufacture of Textile Wearing Apparel	161
皮革、毛皮、羽毛及其制品和制鞋业	Manufacture of Leather, Fur, Feather & Its Products Footwear	101
木材加工和木、竹、藤、棕、草制品业	Processing of Timbers, Manufacture of Wood, Bamboo, Rattan, Palm, and Straw Products	6
家具制造业	Manufacture of Furniture	31
造纸和纸制品业	Manufacture of Paper and Paper Products	29
印刷和记录媒介复制业	Printing, Reproduction of Recording Media	16
文教、工美、体育和娱乐用品制造业	Manufacture of Articles for Culture, Arts & Crafts, Sports and Entertainment	139
石油加工、炼焦和核燃料加工业	Processing of Petroleum, Coking, Processing of Nucleus Fuel	1
化学原料和化学制品制造业	Manufacture of Chemical Raw Material and Chemical Products	73
医药制造业	Manufacture of Medicines	11
化学纤维制造业	Manufacture of Chemical Fiber	5
橡胶和塑料制品业	Manufacture of Rubber and Plastic	101
非金属矿物制品业	Manufacture of Non-metallic Mineral Products	58
黑色金属冶炼和压延加工业	Smelting and Pressing of Ferrous Metals	20
有色金属冶炼和压延加工业	Smelting and Pressing of Non-ferrous Metals	5
金属制品业	Manufacture of Metal Products	110
通用设备制造业	Manufacture of General Purpose Machinery	78
专用设备制造业	Manufacture of Special Purpose Machinery	61
汽车制造业	Manufacture of Vehicle	59
铁路、船舶、航空航天和其他运输设备制造业	Manufacture of Transport Equipment for Railway, Shipping, Aerospace and other uses	36
电气机械和器材制造业	Manufacture of Electrical Machinery & Equipment	63
计算机、通信和其他电子设备制造业	Manufacture of Transport Equipment for Railway, Shipping, Aerospace and other uses	91
仪器仪表制造业	Manufacture of Measuring Instrument	14
其他制造业	Manufacture of Other Products	9
废弃资源综合利用业	Recycling and Disposal of Waste Resources	1
金属制品、机械和设备修理业	Maintenance of Metal Products, Machinery and Equipment	3
电力、热力生产和供应业	Production and Supply of Electric Power and Heat Power	1
燃气生产和供应业	Production and Supply of Gas	7
水的生产和供应业	Production and Supply of Water	1

单位：万元(10 000 yuan)

工业总产值 Gross Industrial Output Value	资产合计 Total Assets	流动资产合计 Total Current Assets	固定资产净值 Net Value of Fixed Assets
[illegible] 213 844	**24 169 615**	**14 517 565**	**6 179 496**
62 289	7 142	625	3 686
37 914	9 513	5 314	4 199
3 915 927	1 920 095	1 285 497	489 004
1 533 783	1 150 545	765 694	209 039
1 112 208	1 695 395	548 208	236 730
1 283 844	574 929	262 329	222 432
2 473 429	961 206	457 398	292 298
1 722 491	520 216	302 472	179 632
99 118	33 279	11 619	17 664
330 073	131 720	79 370	41 436
520 858	272 782	176 545	73 148
430 103	251 639	126 361	49 940
1 509 496	620 712	392 722	170 419
55 456	35 075	14 518	11 167
2 826 913	1 728 112	948 553	673 577
297 361	93 249	48 529	31 355
82 407	93 235	56 226	23 802
1 718 188	1 226 313	590 612	509 546
942 345	649 009	321 866	270 060
1 230 846	521 615	202 144	86 814
118 773	116 742	54 505	51 021
3 915 497	1 479 451	852 453	459 945
2 033 953	1 300 188	805 785	399 283
938 980	786 483	514 401	160 752
2 910 337	3 076 910	2 444 746	526 128
1 136 474	2 181 205	1 801 501	275 640
1 338 383	593 731	372 430	145 294
3 891 328	1 678 223	819 970	445 688
312 241	173 238	134 118	34 796
104 173	85 834	25 419	13 103
12 453	7 262	3 552	3 710
26 943	15 886	12 360	2 361
20 299	1 621	192	678
266 035	172 218	75 805	64 123
2 926	4 846	3 728	1 028

12 -8 续表
continued

项 目	Indicator	主营业务收入 Revenue from Principal Business
总 计	**Total**	**37 531 385**
煤炭开采和洗选业	Mining and Washing of Coal	
石油和天然气开采业	Extraction of Petroleum and Natural Gas	
黑色金属矿采选业	Mining of Ferrous Metal Ores	62 289
有色金属矿采选业	Mining of Non-ferrous Metal Ores	
非金属矿采选业	Mining and Processing of Nonmetal Ores	37 189
开采辅助活动	Auxiliary Activities of Mining	
其他采矿业	Mining of Other Ores	
农副食品加工业	Processing of Food from Agricultural Products	4 046 320
食品制造业	Manufacture of Foods	1 567 393
酒、饮料和精制茶制造业	Manufacture of Liquor, Beverage and Refind Tea	1 536 559
烟草制品业	Manufacture of Tobacco	
纺织业	Manufacture of Textile	1 247 051
纺织服装、服饰业	Manufacture of Textile Wearing Apparel	2 259 503
皮革、毛皮、羽毛及其制品和制鞋业	Manufacture of Leather, Fur, Feather & Its Products Footwear	1 615 098
木材加工和木、竹、藤、棕、草制品业	Processing of Timbers, Manufacture of Wood, Bamboo, Rattan, Palm, and Straw Products	93 994
家具制造业	Manufacture of Furniture	327 275
造纸和纸制品业	Manufacture of Paper and Paper Products	507 358
印刷和记录媒介复制业	Printing, Reproduction of Recording Media	347 161
文教、工美、体育和娱乐用品制造业	]Manufacture of Articles for Culture, Arts & Crafts, Sports and Entertainment	1 490 804
石油加工、炼焦和核燃料加工业	Processing of Petroleum, Coking, Processing of Nucleus Fuel	55 631
化学原料和化学制品制造业	Manufacture of Chemical Raw Material and Chemical Products	2 220 893
医药制造业	Manufacture of Medicines	237 634
化学纤维制造业	Manufacture of Chemical Fiber	84 379
橡胶和塑料制品业	Manufacture of Rubber and Plastic	1 659 267
非金属矿物制品业	Manufacture of Non-metallic Mineral Products	916 287
黑色金属冶炼和压延加工业	Smelting and Pressing of Ferrous Metals	857 620
有色金属冶炼和压延加工业	Smelting and Pressing of Non-ferrous Metals	117 683
金属制品业	Manufacture of Metal Products	3 834 584
通用设备制造业	Manufacture of General Purpose Machinery	1 947 995
专用设备制造业	Manufacture of Special Purpose Machinery	796 988
汽车制造业	Manufacture of Vehicle	2 858 633
铁路、船舶、航空航天和其他运输设备制造业	Manufacture of Transport Equipment for Railway, Shipping, Aerospace and other uses	1 098 741
电气机械和器材制造业	Manufacture of Electrical Machinery & Equipment	1 242 906
计算机、通信和其他电子设备制造业	Manufacture of Computer, Communication Equipment and Other Electronic E-quipment	3 321 656
仪器仪表制造业	Manufacture of Measuring Instrument	310 534
其他制造业	Manufacture of Other Products	112 374
废弃资源综合利用业	Recycling and Disposal of Waste Resources	13 559
金属制品、机械和设备修理业	Maintenance of Metal Products, Machinery and Equipment	25 463
电力、热力生产和供应业	Production and Supply of Electric Power and Heat Power	18 898
燃气生产和供应业	Production and Supply of Gas	268 743
水的生产和供应业	Production and Supply of Water	2 926

单位:万元(10 000 yuan)

主营业务成本 Cost of Principal Business	主营业务税金及附加 Taxes and Extra Charges on Principal Business	利润总额 Total Profits	本年应交增值税 Value-added Tax Payable	全部从业人员年平均人数(人) Annual Average Employed Persons(person)
31 8[illegible]1 295	**445 639**	**2 118 272**	**1 084 878**	**432 548**
[illegible]2 204	856	5 914	1 345	289
[illegible]5 727	55	2 065	1 061	284
3 568 734	17 569	185 421	106 736	38 682
1 105 801	13 071	116 073	54 688	11 630
1 [illegible]75 440	52 409	149 897	80 038	10 296
1 [illegible]94 010	21 728	55 262	31 693	15 398
1 [illegible]50 052	27 161	114 261	52 553	56 061
1 583 147	20 832	78 467	43 843	50 617
82 760	849	6 525	3 052	516
[illegible]79 800	2 656	19 684	11 168	5 311
[illegible]37 177	5 336	30 326	19 456	4 412
295 812	2 764	19 249	8 017	3 699
1 252 060	13 136	74 597	38 265	31 682
40 903	561	6 017	1 781	383
2 181 853	41 252	103 705	117 317	11 756
202 729	954	16 065	5 777	2 009
74 356	540	-1 319	598	1 074
1 422 789	11 876	75 881	37 933	21 388
786 584	4 450	49 018	27 979	7 739
804 342	1 353	5 759	23 376	2 755
114 270	313	1 573	32	659
[illegible] 389 183	71 761	172 682	98 459	28 462
648 064	11 378	149 876	31 316	19 731
646 156	5 953	55 632	22 484	8 698
2 327 694	60 466	305 004	119 470	22 497
873 755	10 655	151 296	28 438	11 969
983 473	20 111	50 800	23 440	18 372
3 027 045	21 887	40 136	68 214	37 806
224 032	733	42 571	15 396	4 026
87 065	1 150	5 437	1 816	2 851
10 452		1 743	5	233
20 864	284	1 773	469	226
13 229	87	1 543	964	78
227 398	1 432	24 997	7 527	942
2 336	21	347	176	17

12 -9 按行业分大中型工业企业主要指标 (2012 年)

MAIN INDICATORS OF LARGE AND MEDIUM-SIZED INDUSTRIAL ENTERPRISES BY INDUSTRIAL SECTOR(2012)

项　目	Indicator	企业单位数(个) Number of Enterprises(unit)
总　计	**Total**	**694**
煤炭开采和洗选业	Mining and Washing of Coal	
石油和天然气开采业	Extraction of Petroleum and Natural Gas	
黑色金属矿采选业	Mining of Ferrous Metal Ores	
有色金属矿采选业	Mining of Non-ferrous Metal Ores	
非金属矿采选业	Mining and Processing of Nonmetal Ores	1
开采辅助活动	Auxiliary Activities of Mining	
其他采矿业	Mining of Other Ores	
农副食品加工业	Processing of Food from Agricultural Products	52
食品制造业	Manufacture of Foods	19
酒、饮料和精制茶制造业	Manufacture of Liquor, Beverage and Refind Tea	7
烟草制品业	Manufacture of Tobacco	
纺织业	Manufacture of Textile	22
纺织服装、服饰业	Manufacture of Textile Wearing Apparel	78
皮革、毛皮、羽毛及其制品和制鞋业	Manufacture of Leather, Fur, Feather & Its Products Footwear	50
木材加工和木、竹、藤、棕、草制品业	Processing of Timbers, Manufacture of Wood, Bamboo, Rattan, Palm, and Straw Products	3
家具制造业	Manufacture of Furniture	8
造纸和纸制品业	Manufacture of Paper and Paper Products	5
印刷和记录媒介复制业	Printing, Reproduction of Recording Media	6
文教、工美、体育和娱乐用品制造业	Manufacture of Articles for Culture, Arts & Crafts, Sports and Entertainment	35
石油加工、炼焦和核燃料加工业	Processing of Petroleum, Coking, Processing of Nucleus Fuel	4
化学原料和化学制品制造业	Manufacture of Chemical Raw Material and Chemical Products	27
医药制造业	Manufacture of Medicines	8
化学纤维制造业	Manufacture of Chemical Fiber	2
橡胶和塑料制品业	Manufacture of Rubber and Plastic	40
非金属矿物制品业	Manufacture of Non-metallic Mineral Products	20
黑色金属冶炼和压延加工业	Smelting and Pressing of Ferrous Metals	5
有色金属冶炼和压延加工业	Smelting and Pressing of Non-ferrous Metals	5
金属制品业	Manufacture of Metal Products	56
通用设备制造业	Manufacture of General Purpose Machinery	50
专用设备制造业	Manufacture of Special Purpose Machinery	25
汽车制造业	Manufacture of Vehicle	28
铁路、船舶、航空航天和其他运输设备制造业	Manufacture of Transport Equipment for Railway, Shipping, Aerospace and other uses	29
电气机械和器材制造业	Manufacture of Electrical Machinery & Equipment	43
计算机、通信和其他电子设备制造业	Manufacture of Computer, Communication Equipment and Other Electronic Equipment	38
仪器仪表制造业	Manufacture of Measuring Instrument	7
其他制造业	Manufacture of Other Products	2
废弃资源综合利用业	Recycling and Disposal of Waste Resources	
金属制品、机械和设备修理业	Maintenance of Metal Products, Machinery and Equipment	
电力、热力生产和供应业	Production and Supply of Electric Power and Heat Power	15
燃气生产和供应业	Production and Supply of Gas	2
水的生产和供应业	Production and Supply of Water	2

单位:万元(10 000 yuan)

工业总产值 Gross Industrial Output Value	资产合计 Total Assets	流动资产合计 Total Current Assets	固定资产净值 Net Value of Fixed Assets
75 294 676	**55 374 910**	**33 911 243**	**13 193 419**
51 761	5 451	1 862	3 589
5 956 002	2 405 459	1 401 843	729 375
825 495	777 107	482 000	127 040
1 282 100	1 702 115	541 510	253 527
1 322 316	713 021	421 492	186 352
3 137 132	1 850 874	1 020 378	490 664
1 574 706	519 658	304 137	158 206
93 152	21 260	14 279	6 981
390 552	156 936	100 555	30 407
248 552	148 516	81 895	43 576
204 663	137 194	82 951	41 528
612 046	344 197	209 558	107 667
8 727 731	2 712 692	980 563	1 342 914
3 618 132	2 323 531	1 102 870	739 452
366 432	614 882	297 754	134 362
53 389	57 285	32 412	17 411
3 747 908	2 536 281	1 445 378	867 963
885 281	1 049 411	565 666	354 189
2 491 847	1 808 564	1 132 742	419 499
337 759	231 159	82 370	119 956
3 751 966	1 986 021	1 228 326	491 261
3 477 062	2 504 357	1 460 975	513 785
1 681 703	1 806 937	1 252 012	263 976
4 605 817	4 719 774	3 602 055	617 914
6 190 390	7 535 377	4 917 935	1 745 246
10 896 769	9 420 985	7 449 699	947 501
6 514 716	3 908 625	2 762 777	622 841
315 804	276 585	200 335	55 163
55 654	35 789	5 621	10 490
1 646 561	2 152 606	567 179	1 244 955
164 316	556 299	98 844	262 888
66 960	355 964	63 271	242 744

12 -9 续表
continued

项 目	Indicator	主营业务收入 Revenue from Principal Business
总 计	**Total**	**77 247 362**
煤炭开采和洗选业	Mining and Washing of Coal	
石油和天然气开采业	Extraction of Petroleum and Natural Gas	
黑色金属矿采选业	Mining of Ferrous Metal Ores	
有色金属矿采选业	Mining of Non-ferrous Metal Ores	
非金属矿采选业	Mining and Processing of Nonmetal Ores	49 792
开采辅助活动	Auxiliary Activities of Mining	
其他采矿业	Mining of Other Ores	
农副食品加工业	Processing of Food from Agricultural Products	5 381 802
食品制造业	Manufacture of Foods	896 310
酒、饮料和精制茶制造业	Manufacture of Liquor, Beverage and Refind Tea	1 755 489
烟草制品业	Manufacture of Tobacco	
纺织业	Manufacture of Textile	1 326 538
纺织服装、服饰业	Manufacture of Textile Wearing Apparel	2 935 599
皮革、毛皮、羽毛及其制品和制鞋业	Manufacture of Leather, Fur, Feather & Its Products Footwear	1 517 001
木材加工和木、竹、藤、棕、草制品业	Processing of Timbers, Manufacture of Wood, Bamboo, Rattan, Palm, and Straw Products	90 530
家具制造业	Manufacture of Furniture	324 490
造纸和纸制品业	Manufacture of Paper and Paper Products	224 397
印刷和记录媒介复制业	Printing, Reproduction of Recording Media	204 595
文教、工美、体育和娱乐用品制造业	Manufacture of Articles for Culture, Arts & Crafts, Sports and Entertainment	595 893
石油加工、炼焦和核燃料加工业	Processing of Petroleum, Coking, Processing of Nucleus Fuel	8 536 183
化学原料和化学制品制造业	Manufacture of Chemical Raw Material and Chemical Products	3 224 968
医药制造业	Manufacture of Medicines	353 800
化学纤维制造业	Manufacture of Chemical Fiber	53 716
橡胶和塑料制品业	Manufacture of Rubber and Plastic	3 962 100
非金属矿物制品业	Manufacture of Non-metallic Mineral Products	697 780
黑色金属冶炼和压延加工业	Smelting and Pressing of Ferrous Metals	3 294 789
有色金属冶炼和压延加工业	Smelting and Pressing of Non-ferrous Metals	355 307
金属制品业	Manufacture of Metal Products	3 641 698
通用设备制造业	Manufacture of General Purpose Machinery	3 420 231
专用设备制造业	Manufacture of Special Purpose Machinery	1 516 666
汽车制造业	Manufacture of Vehicle	4 593 129
铁路、船舶、航空航天和其他运输设备制造业	Manufacture of Transport Equipment for Railway, Shipping, Aerospace and other uses	6 242 749
电气机械和器材制造业	Manufacture of Electrical Machinery & Equipment	12 364 475
计算机、通信和其他电子设备制造业	Manufacture of Computer, Communication Equipment and Other Electronic Equipment	7 406 072
仪器仪表制造业	Manufacture of Measuring Instrument	288 940
其他制造业	Manufacture of Other Products	55 254
废弃资源综合利用业	Recycling and Disposal of Waste Resources	
金属制品、机械和设备修理业	Maintenance of Metal Products, Machinery and Equipment	
电力、热力生产和供应业	Production and Supply of Electric Power and Heat Power	1 756 029
燃气生产和供应业	Production and Supply of Gas	114 127
水的生产和供应业	Production and Supply of Water	66 917

单位：万元（10 000 yuan）

主营业务成本 Cost of Principal Business	主营业务 税金及附加 Taxes and Extra Charges on Principal Business	利润总额 Total Profits	本年应交 增值税 Value-added Tax Payable	全部从业人员 年平均人数（人） Annual Average Employed Persons （person）
65 435 017	**1 597 436**	**7 126 348**	**2 278 914**	**630 966**
58 619	498	5 906	653	434
4 884 427	29 115	259 380	70 970	62 525
623 145	4 531	85 571	28 929	8 864
1 283 115	54 452	279 103	82 860	12 452
1 [illegible]39 868	3 838	70 409	23 683	16 382
2 617 331	20 566	256 122	74 462	80 075
1 395 510	9 172	155 050	40 977	51 171
30 174	612	12 900	3 177	1 205
282 044	1 515	14 677	3 780	6 901
209 287	359	8 192	4 155	2 851
167 716	1 323	21 773	5 798	2 374
499 966	4 065	43 775	12 385	18 773
7 598 268	1 086 672	1 450 834	519 441	3 220
2 916 756	37 512	202 819	104 539	18 682
167 081	3 140	108 850	27 364	5 679
49 424	123	−982	310	841
3 572 723	24 983	319 120	164 105	29 677
602 280	4 831	51 438	20 051	12 251
3 150 835	1 804	36 926	33 342	11 207
312 820	707	25 976	5 965	2 402
5 171 295	49 757	323 112	87 248	34 364
2 917 116	24 117	318 245	77 386	31 706
1 211 059	5 670	169 885	56 181	16 935
3 949 431	68 061	493 364	124 472	31 024
4 624 134	23 166	599 488	121 672	41 347
9 832 352	88 192	1 034 014	282 866	59 910
5 426 071	41 534	612 038	240 864	46 330
200 629	602	53 380	8 555	4 277
52 953	136	3 990	621	1 903
1 680 752	5 833	89 228	46 969	11 469
103 344	61	19 935	967	1 886
85 495	491	1 831	4 170	1 849

12－10 按行业分规模以上工业企业主要经济效益指标（2012 年）

MAIN INDICATORS ON ECONOMIC BENEFIT OF INDUSTRIAL ENTERPRISES ABOVE DESIGNATED SIZE BY INDUSTRIAL SECTOR(2012)

行　业	Sector	总资产贡献率(%) Ratio of Total Assets to Industrial Output Value(%)
总　计	**Total**	**19.03**
按轻重工业分	**Grouped by Light and Heavy Industries**	
轻工业	Light Industry	19.76
重工业	Heavy Industry	18.59
按行业分	**Grouped by Sector**	
煤炭开采和洗选业	Mining and Washing of Coal	
石油和天然气开采业	Extraction of Petroleum and Natural Gas	
黑色金属矿采选业	Mining of Ferrous Metal Ores	97.5
有色金属矿采选业	Mining of Non-ferrous Metal Ores	
非金属矿采选业	Mining and Processing of Nonmetal Ores	54.7
开采辅助活动	Auxiliary Activities of Mining	
其他采矿业	Mining of Other Ores	
农副食品加工业	Processing of Food from Agricultural Products	22.37
食品制造业	Manufacture of Foods	19.6
酒、饮料和精制茶制造业	Manufacture of Liquor, Beverage and Refind Tea	18.83
烟草制品业	Manufacture of Tobacco	
纺织业	Manufacture of Textile	23.76
纺织服装、服饰业	Manufacture of Textile Wearing Apparel	24.43
皮革、毛皮、羽毛及其制品和制鞋业	Manufacture of Leather, Fur, Feather & Its Products Footwear	39.73
木材加工和木、竹、藤、棕、草制品业	Processing of Timbers, Manufacture of Wood, Bamboo, Rattan, Palm, and Straw Products	50.67
家具制造业	Manufacture of Furniture	32.84
造纸和纸制品业	Manufacture of Paper and Paper Products	31.21
印刷和记录媒介复制业	Printing, Reproduction of Recording Media	27.12
文教、工美、体育和娱乐用品制造业	Manufacture of Articles for Culture, Arts & Crafts, Sports and Entertainment	33.33
石油加工、炼焦和核燃料加工业	Processing of Petroleum, Coking, Processing of Nucleus Fuel	55.01
化学原料和化学制品制造业	Manufacture of Chemical Raw Material and Chemical Products	15.39
医药制造业	Manufacture of Medicines	21.12
化学纤维制造业	Manufacture of Chemical Fiber	9.68
橡胶和塑料制品业	Manufacture of Rubber and Plastic	21.65
非金属矿物制品业	Manufacture of Non-metallic Mineral Products	21.91
黑色金属冶炼和压延加工业	Smelting and Pressing of Ferrous Metals	9.38
有色金属冶炼和压延加工业	Smelting and Pressing of Non-ferrous Metals	23.02
金属制品业	Manufacture of Metal Products	27.70
通用设备制造业	Manufacture of General Purpose Machinery	22.27
专用设备制造业	Manufacture of Special Purpose Machinery	24.57
汽车制造业	Manufacture of Vehicle	11.34
铁路、船舶、航空航天和其他运输设备制造业	Manufacture of Transport Equipment for Railway, Shipping, Aerospace and other uses	9.70
电气机械和器材制造业	Manufacture of Electrical Machinery & Equipment	12.79
计算机、通信和其他电子设备制造业	Manufacture of Computer, Communication Equipment and Other Electronic Equipment	15.15
仪器仪表制造业	Manufacture of Measuring Instrument	26.71
其他制造业	Manufacture of Other Products	18.08
废弃资源综合利用业	Recycling and Disposal of Waste Resources	33.82
金属制品、机械和设备修理业	Maintenance of Metal Products, Machinery and Equipment	32.92
电力、热力生产和供应业	Production and Supply of Electric Power and Heat Power	5.99
燃气生产和供应业	Production and Supply of Gas	8.94
水的生产和供应业	Production and Supply of Water	0.83

资产负债率（%）Assets-Liability Ratio(%)	流动资产周转次数(次/年) Number of Times of Annualof Turnover Current Assets(time/year)	工业成本费用利润率(%) Ratio of Profits to Industrial Costs(%)	产品销售率(%) Ratio of Sales to Output(%)
58.69	**3.08**	**5.67**	**98.01**
55.41	3.11	6.37	99.56
60.69	3.06	5.19	96.99
21.77	23.18	10.58	98.07
32.95	11.04	7.12	97.06
52.81	4.55	5.29	97.64
49.82	2.66	7.82	99.28
38.87	3.53	8.37	140.18
0.00	0.00	0.00	100.04
55.32	5.06	5.19	98.57
47.10	4.35	6.54	97.99
52.84	5.79	7.65	97.21
48.61	8.30	9.00	97.84
56.32	4.80	7.33	97.56
42.58	4.95	7.95	98.06
48.56	5.21	7.23	98.46
40.82	5.43	7.50	98.34
79.45	8.70	-1.91	96.66
58.35	3.27	4.19	92.99
30.06	2.25	15.53	98.46
49.52	2.15	1.87	96.91
66.92	3.90	4.82	98.96
61.04	3.45	7.55	96.99
68.95	3.70	2.01	99.28
59.40	5.75	6.15	98.31
52.52	4.72	6.39	93.91
52.67	3.47	7.46	97.76
54.47	2.84	9.64	96.06
61.55	1.49	6.45	101.08
66.93	1.45	8.53	98.64
63.54	1.93	5.73	98.27
50.99	2.94	4.15	99.59
36.06	2.12	16.09	95.64
57.10	3.74	8.30	97.51
40.21	8.35	10.48	98.17
68.67	4.76	7.32	94.54
74.65	3.21	1.64	92.69
50.5	2.54	10.53	95.27
55.89	0.84	-3.61	99.35

12－11 按行业分国有控股工业企业主要经济效益指标(2012 年)

MAIN INDICATORS ON ECONOMIC BENEFIT OF STATE-OWNED AND STATE-HOLDING INDUSTRIAL ENTERPRISES BY INDUSTRIAL SECTOR(2012)

行 业	Sector	总资产贡献率(%) Ratio of Total Assets to Industrial Output Value(%)
总 计	**Total**	**14.58**
煤炭开采和洗选业	Mining and Washing of Coal	
石油和天然气开采业	Extraction of Petroleum and Natural Gas	
黑色金属矿采选业	Mining of Ferrous Metal Ores	
有色金属矿采选业	Mining of Non-ferrous Metal Ores	
非金属矿采选业	Mining and Processing of Nonmetal Ores	11.15
开采辅助活动	Auxiliary Activities of Mining	
其他采矿业	Mining of Other Ores	
农副食品加工业	Processing of Food from Agricultural Products	16.82
食品制造业	Manufacture of Foods	23.05
酒、饮料和精制茶制造业	Manufacture of Liquor, Beverage and Refind Tea	17.57
烟草制品业	Manufacture of Tobacco	
纺织业	Manufacture of Textile	
纺织服装、服饰业	Manufacture of Textile Wearing Apparel	4.37
皮革、毛皮、羽毛及其制品和制鞋业	Manufacture of Leather, Fur, Feather & Its Products Footwear	12.58
木材加工和木、竹、藤、棕、草制品业	Processing of Timbers, Manufacture of Wood, Bamboo, Rattan, Palm, and Straw Products	
家具制造业	Manufacture of Furniture	
造纸和纸制品业	Manufacture of Paper and Paper Products	6.22
印刷和记录媒介复制业	Printing, Reproduction of Recording Media	5.37
文教、工美、体育和娱乐用品制造业	Manufacture of Articles for Culture, Arts & Crafts, Sports and Entertainment	
石油加工、炼焦和核燃料加工业	Processing of Petroleum, Coking, Processing of Nucleus Fuel	55.45
化学原料和化学制品制造业	Manufacture of Chemical Raw Material and Chemical Products	2.29
医药制造业	Manufacture of Medicines	12.27
化学纤维制造业	Manufacture of Chemical Fiber	
橡胶和塑料制品业	Manufacture of Rubber and Plastic	3.70
非金属矿物制品业	Manufacture of Non-metallic Mineral Products	7.29
黑色金属冶炼和压延加工业	Smelting and Pressing of Ferrous Metals	4.41
有色金属冶炼和压延加工业	Smelting and Pressing of Non-ferrous Metals	13.75
金属制品业	Manufacture of Metal Products	11.30
通用设备制造业	Manufacture of General Purpose Machinery	1.85
专用设备制造业	Manufacture of Special Purpose Machinery	8.82
汽车制造业	Manufacture of Vehicle	11.88
铁路、船舶、航空航天和其他运输设备制造业	Manufacture of Transport Equipment for Railway, Shipping, Aerospace and other uses	8.13
电气机械和器材制造业	Manufacture of Electrical Machinery & Equipment	7.73
计算机、通信和其他电子设备制造业	Manufacture of Computer, Communication Equipment and Other Electronic Equipment	19.59
仪器仪表制造业	Manufacture of Measuring Instrument	17.19
其他制造业	Manufacture of Other Products	4.55
废弃资源综合利用业	Recycling and Disposal of Waste Resources	
金属制品、机械和设备修理业	Maintenance of Metal Products, Machinery and Equipment	
电力、热力生产和供应业	Production and Supply of Electric Power and Heat Power	5.83
燃气生产和供应业	Production and Supply of Gas	4.30
水的生产和供应业	Production and Supply of Water	-0.27

资产负债率(%) Assets-Liability Ratio(%)	流动资产周转次数(次/年) Number of Times of Annual of Turnover Current Assets(time/year)	工业成本费用利润率(%) Ratio of Profits to Industrial Costs(%)	产品销售率(%) Ratio of Sales to Output(%)
55.73	**2.44**	**2.97**	**100.30**
78.48	1.42	2.93	92.88
25.42	12.28	6.21	96.61
19.34	2.17	9.68	100.00
37.04	3.24	8.89	158.78
			100.04
97.84	1.72	0.22	99.27
56.71	1.83	6.11	104.82
62.71	3.39	0.84	96.00
46.98	0.70	8.23	116.13
79.97	8.79	-2.02	96.63
61.39	2.11	-0.89	100.00
35.59	1.27	15.15	98.67
76.74	1.34	0.80	102.38
71.44	1.02	5.66	100.24
81.92	2.91	0.23	100.64
54.26	5.03	16.52	100.00
87.45	4.58	1.90	97.17
60.55	0.92	0.28	97.56
87.44	1.65	0.43	87.80
62.04	1.24	7.38	101.64
65.84	1.62	7.62	98.46
75.75	2.63	2.16	101.27
54.64	2.48	6.02	99.79
43.03	1.74	3.95	89.11
60.08	0.92	1.37	100.00
74.13	2.82	1.65	90.86
45.58	1.19	12.74	81.77
56.74	0.81	-6.58	100.00

12－12 按行业分规模以上外商及港澳台商投资工业企业主要经济效益指标(2012年)

MAIN INDICATORS ON ECONOMIC BENEFIT OF FOREIGN FUNDED ENTERPRISES AND ENTERPRISES WITH FUNDS FROM HONG KONG, MACAO AND TAIWAN ABOVE DESIGNATED SIZE BY INDUSTRIAL SECTOR(2012)

行　业	Sector	总资产贡献率(%) Ratio of Total Assets to Industrial Output Value(%)
总　计	**Total**	**15.87**
煤炭开采和洗选业	Mining and Washing of Coal	
石油和天然气开采业	Extraction of Petroleum and Natural Gas	
黑色金属矿采选业	Mining of Ferrous Metal Ores	114.33
有色金属矿采选业	Mining of Non-ferrous Metal Ores	
非金属矿采选业	Mining and Processing of Nonmetal Ores	33.91
开采辅助活动	Auxiliary Activities of Mining	
其他采矿业	Mining of Other Ores	
农副食品加工业	Processing of Food from Agricultural Products	17.74
食品制造业	Manufacture of Foods	17.06
酒、饮料和精制茶制造业	Manufacture of Liquor, Beverage and Refind Tea	17.65
烟草制品业	Manufacture of Tobacco	
纺织业	Manufacture of Textile	19.28
纺织服装、服饰业	Manufacture of Textile Wearing Apparel	21.11
皮革、毛皮、羽毛及其制品和制鞋业	Manufacture of Leather, Fur, Feather & Its Products Footwear	28.44
木材加工和木、竹、藤、棕、草制品业	Processing of Timbers, Manufacture of Wood, Bamboo, Rattan, Palm, and Straw Products	32.01
家具制造业	Manufacture of Furniture	27.21
造纸和纸制品业	Manufacture of Paper and Paper Products	21.09
印刷和记录媒介复制业	Printing, Reproduction of Recording Media	12.15
文教、工美、体育和娱乐用品制造业	Manufacture of Articles for Culture, Arts & Crafts, Sports and Entertainment	21.11
石油加工、炼焦和核燃料加工业	Processing of Petroleum, Coking, Processing of Nucleus Fuel	26.55
化学原料和化学制品制造业	Manufacture of Chemical Raw Material and Chemical Products	17.31
医药制造业	Manufacture of Medicines	25.88
化学纤维制造业	Manufacture of Chemical Fiber	2.55
橡胶和塑料制品业	Manufacture of Rubber and Plastic	11.66
非金属矿物制品业	Manufacture of Non-metallic Mineral Products	13.60
黑色金属冶炼和压延加工业	Smelting and Pressing of Ferrous Metals	5.95
有色金属冶炼和压延加工业	Smelting and Pressing of Non-ferrous Metals	2.71
金属制品业	Manufacture of Metal Products	24.09
通用设备制造业	Manufacture of General Purpose Machinery	15.02
专用设备制造业	Manufacture of Special Purpose Machinery	11.23
汽车制造业	Manufacture of Vehicle	16.02
铁路、船舶、航空航天和其他运输设备制造业	Manufacture of Transport Equipment for Railway, Shipping, Aerospace and other uses	8.58
电气机械和器材制造业	Manufacture of Electrical Machinery & Equipment	16.50
计算机、通信和其他电子设备制造业	Manufacture of Computer, Communication Equipment and Other Electronic E-quipment	7.82
仪器仪表制造业	Manufacture of Measuring Instrument	34.10
其他制造业	Manufacture of Other Products	10.47
废弃资源综合利用业	Recycling and Disposal of Waste Resources	24.06
金属制品、机械和设备修理业	Maintenance of Metal Products, Machinery and Equipment	23.93
电力、热力生产和供应业	Production and Supply of Electric Power and Heat Power	160.68
燃气生产和供应业	Production and Supply of Gas	20.15
水的生产和供应业	Production and Supply of Water	12.13

资产负债率 (%) Assets-Liability Ratio(%)	流动资产周转次数(次/年) Number of Times of Annual of Turnover Current Assets(time/year)	工业成本费用利润率(%) Ratio of Profits to Industrial Costs(%)	产品销售率(%) Ratio of Sales to Output(%)
51.86	**2.62**	**5.90**	**98.59**
8.48	99.60	9.98	100.00
16.36	7.00	5.89	98.09
56.71	3.17	4.82	98.38
49.03	2.13	8.08	98.45
36.18	3.20	9.13	160.40
51.62	4.76	4.53	99.06
38.35	4.95	5.19	98.98
54.87	5.35	5.13	96.84
28.37	8.09	7.36	96.91
60.15	4.13	6.42	93.72
38.04	2.91	6.44	97.71
48.65	2.75	5.39	99.01
40.29	3.80	5.37	98.92
41.04	3.83	12.23	100.32
58.68	2.72	4.26	91.10
27.31	5.00	7.00	95.00
52.94	1.55	-1.51	95.01
54.83	2.85	4.71	97.89
43.79	2.85	5.67	96.65
45.44	4.32	0.59	98.48
50.82	2.17	1.26	98.81
55.85	4.55	4.66	88.31
45.72	2.44	8.03	98.11
51.28	1.60	7.44	92.56
56.86	1.19	12.00	101.05
72.50	0.63	15.66	98.58
49.59	3.34	4.76	95.26
42.64	4.09	1.18	99.76
38.42	2.33	16.71	99.39
63.10	4.05	5.77	95.97
36.98	3.82	16.23	104.55
78.00	2.06	7.57	93.41
6.31	100.28	8.51	100.00
54.20	3.55	10.27	99.94
14.21	0.78	13.52	100.00

12－13 按行业分大中型工业企业主要经济效益指标（2012 年）

MAIN INDICATORS ON ECONOMIC BENEFIT OF LARGE AND MEDIUM-SIZED INDUSTRIAL ENTERPRISES BY INDUSTRIAL SECTOR(2012)

行 业	Sector	总资产贡献率(%) Ratio of Total Assets to Industrial Output Value(%)
总 计	**Total**	**13.79**
煤炭开采和洗选业	Mining and Washing of Coal	
石油和天然气开采业	Extraction of Petroleum and Natural Gas	
黑色金属矿采选业	Mining of Ferrous Metal Ores	
有色金属矿采选业	Mining of Non-ferrous Metal Ores	
非金属矿采选业	Mining and Processing of Nonmetal Ores	108.34
开采辅助活动	Auxiliary Activities of Mining	
其他采矿业	Mining of Other Ores	
农副食品加工业	Processing of Food from Agricultural Products	12.72
食品制造业	Manufacture of Foods	12.17
酒、饮料和精制茶制造业	Manufacture of Liquor, Beverage and Refind Tea	17.43
烟草制品业	Manufacture of Tobacco	
纺织业	Manufacture of Textile	11.40
纺织服装、服饰业	Manufacture of Textile Wearing Apparel	15.24
皮革、毛皮、羽毛及其制品和制鞋业	Manufacture of Leather, Fur, Feather & Its Products Footwear	30.89
木材加工和木、竹、藤、棕、草制品业	Processing of Timbers, Manufacture of Wood, Bamboo, Rattan, Palm, and Straw Products	61.02
家具制造业	Manufacture of Furniture	11.31
造纸和纸制品业	Manufacture of Paper and Paper Products	7.80
印刷和记录媒介复制业	Printing, Reproduction of Recording Media	15.81
文教、工美、体育和娱乐用品制造业	Manufacture of Articles for Culture, Arts & Crafts, Sports and Entertainment	13.38
石油加工、炼焦和核燃料加工业	Processing of Petroleum, Coking, Processing of Nucleus Fuel	56.09
化学原料和化学制品制造业	Manufacture of Chemical Raw Material and Chemical Products	10.88
医药制造业	Manufacture of Medicines	18.38
化学纤维制造业	Manufacture of Chemical Fiber	1.68
橡胶和塑料制品业	Manufacture of Rubber and Plastic	14.20
非金属矿物制品业	Manufacture of Non-metallic Mineral Products	5.50
黑色金属冶炼和压延加工业	Smelting and Pressing of Ferrous Metals	4.76
有色金属冶炼和压延加工业	Smelting and Pressing of Non-ferrous Metals	13.72
金属制品业	Manufacture of Metal Products	17.25
通用设备制造业	Manufacture of General Purpose Machinery	13.73
专用设备制造业	Manufacture of Special Purpose Machinery	10.33
汽车制造业	Manufacture of Vehicle	10.73
铁路、船舶、航空航天和其他运输设备制造业	Manufacture of Transport Equipment for Railway, Shipping, Aerospace and other uses	8.13
电气机械和器材制造业	Manufacture of Electrical Machinery & Equipment	11.12
计算机、通信和其他电子设备制造业	Manufacture of Computer, Communication Equipment and Other Electronic Equipment	15.33
仪器仪表制造业	Manufacture of Measuring Instrument	19.11
其他制造业	Manufacture of Other Products	12.55
废弃资源综合利用业	Recycling and Disposal of Waste Resources	
金属制品、机械和设备修理业	Maintenance of Metal Products, Machinery and Equipment	
电力、热力生产和供应业	Production and Supply of Electric Power and Heat Power	6.75
燃气生产和供应业	Production and Supply of Gas	5.16
水的生产和供应业	Production and Supply of Water	0.95

资产负债率(%) Assets-Liability Ratio(%)	流动资产周转次数(次/年) Number of Times of Annual of Turnover Current Assets(time/year)	工业成本费用利润率(%) Ratio of Profits to Industrial Costs(%)	产品销售率(%) Ratio of Sales to Output(%)
62.44	**2.34**	**4.30**	**98.26**
5.50	26.74	11.51	96.20
53.69	3.87	2.95	96.74
59.99	1.96	5.97	98.80
37.71	3.46	8.03	151.56
57.40	3.16	3.28	98.00
48.93	2.90	5.63	98.64
52.54	5.01	7.24	95.87
64.49	6.34	11.13	99.22
64.00	3.23	2.85	93.96
58.35	2.82	1.59	96.87
46.19	2.47	7.32	97.43
45.46	2.86	4.77	98.56
81.36	9.06	-1.95	96.64
65.03	3.03	1.85	90.24
26.54	1.20	27.54	101.79
39.49	1.66	-2.74	93.81
73.59	2.76	3.32	99.77
75.16	1.24	3.68	93.89
79.16	2.94	0.05	100.29
69.55	4.32	5.59	98.74
53.34	3.01	5.34	87.26
59.10	2.39	6.33	97.58
62.56	1.22	7.40	94.26
61.53	1.34	6.74	101.96
69.32	1.29	8.52	98.64
64.78	1.69	5.54	98.57
50.66	2.90	4.20	99.84
32.32	1.45	18.37	92.26
87.30	9.91	5.73	94.34
72.34	3.11	1.90	98.90
48.95	1.75	10.91	87.17
52.82	1.15	-2.74	100.00

12－14 主要年份主要工业产品产量

MAJOR YEAR'S PRODUCTS OUTPUT OF INDUSTRY ABOVE DESIGNATED SIZE

年份 Year	原盐（万吨）Salt (10000 tons)	发电量（亿千瓦小时）Electricity (100 million kW·h)	饮料酒（万吨）Beverage Liquor (10000 tons)	#啤酒 Beer	卷烟（万箱）Cigarettes (10000 cases)	罐头（吨）Canned Food (ton)	化学纤维（吨）Chemical Fiber (ton)	纱（吨）Yarn (ton)
1949	15.16	1.21	0.18	0.12	2.36			27 447
1952	35.08	2.11	0.37	0.18	12.27			59 674
1957	44.34	2.92	0.96	0.58	23.41			50 699
1962	38.60	3.86	1.58	0.79	16.59		28	17 939
1965	41.34	6.80	2.04	1.34	31.34		205	68 082
1970	29.96	10.57	3.39	2.55	42.16		621	85 591
1975	34.52	10.98	5.30	2.98	36.00		357	79 516
1978	60.68	13.63	6.25	3.75	44.00	4 743	1 413	85 233
1980	41.19	12.50	8.49	4.84	48.79	3 521	2 116	83 389
1985	47.34	26.97	13.76	10.05	51.81	6 400	1 747	91 839
1987	50.64	28.97	23.40	13.85	55.84	16 000	3 442	108 003
1988	53.28	29.35	26.61	15.58	57.01	27 200	3 393	107 720
1989	55.37	29.87	24.57	15.40	58.64	13 200	3 700	118 379
1990	35.70	40.22	29.18	19.61	61.94		2 900	100 381
1991	31.39	54.60	36.75	27.38	56.19	130 510	5 200	96 271
1992	46.24	58.63	44.59	37.01	59.37	3 200	6 000	99 043
1993	48.88	59.39	54.74	45.92	63.46	1 900	27 100	91 351
1994	53.02	59.62	60.00	50.92	69.20	2 300	21 400	86 744
1995	50.84	64.69	60.85	54.16	70.96	4 609	20 973	79 492
1996	41.39	83.02	61.79	54.40	73.04	1 719	22 945	66 832
1997	34.11	95.12	66.64	56.06	88.32	554	26 300	70 402
1998	19.08	79.65	47.33	42.79	77.10		23 858	66 504
1999	30.30	82.00	126.21	120.10	149.00	379	29 967	56 431
2000	41.83	90.84	211.47	206.50	148.10	225	65 362	69 561
2001	31.40	85.73	279.37	274.28	142.95	99	89 989	72 933
2002	42.50	89.70	323.20	320.60	138.10	11 690	91 394	70 888
2003	36.85	87.69	353.90	351.80	148.00		101 752	65 919
2004	34.36	89.01	393.30	390.60	147.10	10 889	115 187	71 931
2005	10.00	98.63	439.70	435.20	150.70	10 097	95 887	72 140
2006	15.30	124.54	101.60（本地）	95.60（本地）	95.16（本地）	1 668	72 381	56 128
2007	19.23	155.30	118.10（本地）	112.50（本地）	100.08（本地）	1 850	68 746	47 850
2008	15.90	164.58	132.07（本地）	124.75（本地）	100.02（本地）	1 510	51 751	43 102
2009	5.90	172.66	137.21（本地）	127.12（本地）	100.08（本地）	4 706	59 852	38 566
2010	11.25	181.93	144.66（本地）	141.65（本地）	102.55（本地）	1 092	68 654	35 278
2011		173.69	164.04（本地）	156.50（本地）	104.51（本地）	41 204	38 640	18 556
2012		174.72	174.03（本地）	163.95（本地）	106.03（本地）	35 026	32 371	19 404

注：1998 年以前为乡及乡以上工业。

Note: Before 1998, the data refer to those at and above county level.

12 -14 续表 1

continued

年 份 Year	布(万米) Cloth (10000 m)	印染布 (万米) Printed Fabric (10000 m)	机制纸及纸板(万吨) Machine-made Paper and Paperboards (10000 tons)	硫 酸 (万吨) Sulfuric Acid (10000 tons)	烧 碱 (万吨) Caustic Soda (10000 tons)	纯 碱 (万吨) Soda Ash (10000 tons)
1949	10 608	2 947	0.98		0.01	
1952	30 069	13 658	0.44		0.17	
1957	27 806	16 053	1.54		0.74	
1962	7 444	7 375	1.45	0.06	0.89	
1965	29 538	13 670	2.22		1.66	5.32
1970	33 660	21 994	3.14	0.04	2.14	12.01
1975	31 242	22 828	3.10	0.53	2.36	9.15
1978	36 877	25 797	4.55	1.32	3.61	14.04
1980	34 937	22 900	5.25	4.11	4.33	18.18
1985	34 998	17 679	6.20	3.34	5.52	26.03
1987	38 155	21 833	6.52	4.40	6.15	29.53
1988	35 890	21 213	7.42	4.88	6.62	31.12
1989	36 188	19 842	6.20	4.30	6.95	32.25
1990	34 066	21 446	6.02	4.86	6.73	30.48
1991	34 076	19 999	5.99	5.62	5.99	29.50
1992	33 682	21 534	5.95	6.70	5.62	34.60
1993	35 912	16 606	8.84	6.96	6.07	40.43
1994	43 241	16 387	12.36	8.33	6.48	43.36
1995	41 170	17 864	11.06	9.69	7.90	43.20
1996	39 023	16 881	11.31	10.12	7.30	46.91
1997	43 615	15 722	7.78	10.16	8.45	50.55
1998	40 440	9 864	6.91	10.33	9.25	52.80
1999	39 576	4 340	7.77	12.56	8.96	53.70
2000	41 783	3 526	10.96	12.96	10.24	56.20
2001	40 640	3 402	23.05	13.03	11.44	58.47
2002	47 609	5 592	29.92	5.00	13.80	60.70
2003	35 922	10 131	31.76	4.50	13.53	62.50
2004	50 111	7 718	36.38	14.70	14.86	60.80
2005	51 307	16 027	31.95	14.80	16.10	62.50
2006	55 093	20 867	15.50	7.00	15.90	63.95
2007	44 251	18 708	24.04	9.22	14.91	71.02
2008	48 399	58 907	22.41	13.02	12.78	72.03
2009	31 048	27 998	34.59	1.40	12.24	68.21
2010	17 457	29 631	35.43	4.07	13.87	69.35
2011	49 617	28 449	32.28	5.06	13.20	70.07
2012	48 987	32 478	22.27	7.22	13.71	63.35

12－14 续表 2
continued

年 份 Year	合成氨 （万吨） Synthetic Ammonia （10000 tons）	化学肥料 （万吨） Chemical Fertilizer （10000 tons）	化学农药 （吨） Chemical Pesticides （ton）	油 漆 （吨） Paint （ton）	染 料 （吨） Dye （ton）
1949				30	599
1952				480	2 855
1957			1 226	1 247	4 307
1962		0.45	213	910	3 560
1965		1.42	2	4 727	3 667
1970	0.98	5.89	2 313	6 380	9 347
1975	3.46	12.46	4 439	7 016	5 967
1978	7.17	23.66	9 714	8 786	5 877
1980	7.24	7.82	8 333	14 556	2 159
1985	6.31	5.16	2 000	26 055	4 448
1987	8.20	8.32	2 200	28 323	5 316
1988	8.72	9.41	2 400	28 943	5 527
1989	8.47	8.84	2 500	27 713	5 784
1990	7.56	7.55	2 500	29 075	5 119
1991	8.52	8.04	2 800	33 548	5 263
1992	10.45	7.85	3 400	35 058	4 821
1993	10.70	8.02	3 600	33 054	4 550
1994	13.04	12.39	3 600	29 437	5 097
1995	14.98	12.62	4 934	37 772	7 185
1996	18.67	12.62	4 976	26 762	7 658
1997	16.94	12.52	4 600	19 743	11 139
1998	22.36	15.30	6 755	17 594	8 274
1999	26.09	20.19	4 480	3 730	7 866
2000	24.64	20.04	3 758	693	9 316
2001	35.53	28.07	3 915	1 349	9 737
2002	20.30	9.80	4 020	1 701	9 826
2003	21.55	9.70	2 039	2 106	10 734
2004	30.30	19.60	5 061	1 955	3 961
2005	33.80	22.10	6 524	1 687	13 979
2006	33.30	21.30	12 544		26 544
2007	28.22	25.70	16 433	2 957	28 269
2008	17.93	21.51	12 848	12 105	18 263
2009	17.71	21.23	49 684		24 893
2010	16.84	14.10	16 450		41 333
2011	10.78	9.26	23 286		
2012	7.71	6.98	28 801		

12－14 续表3
continued

年 份 Year	化学原料药 （吨） Chemical Medicines(ton)	水 泥 （万吨） Cement (10000 tons)	平板玻璃 （万重量箱） Plate Glass (10000 weight cases)	耐火材料 （万吨） Refractory Material (10000 tons)	钢 （万吨） Crude Steel (10000 tons)	钢 材 （万吨） Rolled-steel (10000 tons)
1949						0.06
1952				0.78	0.36	0.41
1957				3.39	1.77	4.30
1962		2.09		2.41	4.59	2.94
1965		6.59		2.91	11.72	8.43
1970		7.35	16.31	3.23	19.38	14.56
1975	55	20.93	19.44	4.88	21.25	20.01
1978	185	35.40	8.86	5.93	31.06	27.61
1980	123	44.66	70.13	5.38	37.14	32.82
1984	7 228	70.27	91.25	7.98	37.81	32.43
1985	4 222	82.70	77.00	4.35	37.51	32.68
1987	7 457	117.20	87.00	4.90	46.51	38.09
1988	7 655	141.00	108.81	4.56	50.17	38.26
1989	8 348	135.00	96.49	3.68	54.64	39.38
1990	6 913	139.48	83.13	3.91	54.55	38.04
1991	4 754	165.66	96.90	3.71	56.96	39.02
1992	5 743	191.50	120.00	3.86	63.75	50.09
1993	6 566	221.30	148.71	3.55	61.75	44.88
1994	4 238	246.50	145.12	3.06	60.82	46.95
1995	1 993	213.82	426.40	3.88	67.27	49.60
1996	5 505	181.45	423.60	3.54	72.02	50.60
1997	1 693	208.04	570.85	2.45	75.71	51.06
1998	910	131.51	509.38	0.99	84.02	64.93
1999	1 691	149.41	576.50	0.59	108.10	86.58
2000	2 131	137.52	556.58	0.62	101.17	93.35
2001	2 534	148.67	421.51	0.51	124.45	119.77
2002	2 712	140.30	405.40	0.45	145.90	142.20
2003	3 288	154.90	361.40	0.47	204.80	204.30
2004	4 394	181.19	163.30	0.69	225.70	230.97
2005	4 430	210.80	297.50	1.04	309.70	330.30
2006	32 232	232.72	418.74	1.21	325.82	375.52
2007	14 139	425.53	397.79	2.38	327.00	365.55
2008	17 910	363.57	599.87	3.65	300.19	350.14
2009	19 086	397.66	681.02	18.46	307.89	349.63
2010	26 170	442.66	662.04	8.17	300.04	333.46
2011	29 337	588.08	510.05	20.02	318.27	325.89
2012	49 290	556.57	494.54	33.44	252.78	274.67

12－14 续表 4
continued

年 份 Year	金属切削机床 （台） Metal-cutting Machine Tools (unit)	锻压机械 （台） Metal Forming Machinery (unit)	汽　车 （辆） Motor Vehicles (set)	交流电动机 （万千瓦） AC Motors (10000 kW)
1949				0.[illegible]2
1952	105			0.50
1957	76			3.61
1962	167	77		3.85
1965	526	111	13	6.45
1970	2 353	531	120	14.53
1975	3 213	788	490	15.56
1978	2 558	379	22	21.72
1980	595	444	1 644	20.1[illegible]
1985	900	607	4 575	26.08
1987	1 175	887	2 304	27.02
1988	1 336	737	3 722	39.60
1989	1 107	1 010	3 404	38.60
1990	1 049	440	2 317	34.28
1991	869	764	1 514	44.17
1992	1 018	982	3 287	61.08
1993	1 532	919	4 828	64.13
1994	1 505	860	2 793	37.71
1995	972	2 563	5 210	39.18
1996	1 084	584	12 247	22.65
1997	449	416	13 020	20.74
1998	280		15 475	6.43
1999	251		20 038	11.10
2000	384		30 053	38.70
2001	472	2 477	40 658	42.72
2002	588		70 079	68.25
2003	990		65 612	95.63
2004	1 287		62 572	96.13
2005	1 347		31 055	63.50
2006	3 636		50 278	702.02
2007	3 392	1 869	61 016	119.23
2008	8 381	1 230	70 161	96.89
2009	668		458 900	728.03
2010	1 120		566 211	101.10
2011	1 194		488 330	74.08
2012	1 014		574 729	104.48

12－14 续表5
continued

年份 Year	钢芯铝绞线(吨) Steel-cored Aluminum Stranded Wire(ton)	家用电冰箱(万台) Home Refrigerators (10000 sets)	家用洗衣机(万台) Home Washing Machines (10000 sets)	彩色电视机(万部) Color TV Sets (10000 sets)
1949				
1952				
1957				
1962				
1965	250			
1970	34			
1975	188			
1978	684			
1980	1 232			
1985	2 327	1.66	0.48	6.60
1987	2 849	9.08	22.08	14.20
1988	1 571	15.22	42.38	17.00
1989	2 805	21.65	35.02	18.11
1990	1 880	27.41	45.86	18.50
1991	2 463	31.51	45.70	22.27
1992	2 248	54.84	46.31	28.07
1993	1 144	50.48	56.59	36.08
1994	287	62.50	71.34	60.15
1995	1 659	107.91	64.34	60.53
1996	2 265	193.80	100.94	56.68
1997	2 616	257.10	171.95	124.86
1998	1 725.3	219.23	183.67	96.83
1999	2 805.2	259.60	256.30	285.20
2000	4 201.5	311.10	318.50	379.40
2001	4 498	396.30	367.89	455.40
2002	5 825	518.20	408.60	593.20
2003	4 940	598.30	471.50	671.70
2004	6 608	815.03	575.06	957.90
2005	116 592	908.80	614.90	1 324.30
2006	46 974	1 290.00	649.40	1 205.60
2007	22 564	1 421.40	769.40	1 243.10
2008	29 507	723.19	407.54	836.66
2009		827.21	488.72	1 064.70
2010		801.22	580.87	1 111.19
2011		718.54	604.55	1 154.20
2012		575.01	583.60	1 439.98

12－15 规模以上工业主要产品产量
OUTPUT OF MAJOR INDUSTRIAL PRODUCTS OF INDUSTRY ABOVE DESIGNATED SIZE

产品名称	Name	计量单位	Unit	2012	2011	2012年比2011年(±%) 2012/2011(±%)
冶金工业产品	**Products of Metallurgical Industry**					
粗钢	Crude Steel	万吨	10000 tons	252.78	318.27	-20.57
钢材	Rolled-steel	万吨	10000 tons	274.67	325.89	-15.72
耐火材料制品	Refractory Material	万吨	10000 tons	33.44	20.02	67.04
电力工业产品	**Products of Electricity Industry**					
发电量	Electricity	亿千瓦小时	100 million kW·h	174.72	173.69	0.59
化学工业产品	**Products of Chemical Industry**					
原油加工量	Processing Amount of Crude Oil	万吨	10000 tons	1 562.04	1 322.36	18.12
汽油	Petrol	万吨	10000 tons	378.91	313.11	21.01
柴油	Diesel Oil	万吨	10000 tons	517.83	526.82	-1.71
燃料油	Fuel Oil	万吨	10000 tons	15.37	16.62	-7.52
硫酸	Sulfuric Acid	万吨	10000 tons	7.22	5.06	42.55
纯碱	Soda Ash	万吨	10000 tons	63.35	72.07	-12.10
烧碱	Caustic Soda	万吨	10000 tons	13.71	13.20	3.84
农用化肥(100%)	Ag-fertilizer(100%)	万吨	10000 tons	6.98	9.26	-24.59
合成氨	Synthetic Ammonia	万吨	10000 tons	7.71	10.78	-28.43
化学农药	Chemical Pesticides	万吨	10000 tons	2.88	2.33	23.68
塑料制品	Plastic	吨	ton	326 453	371 866	-12.21
化学药品(原料)	Chemical Medicines(Raw Materials)	吨	ton	49 290	29 337	68.01

12－15 续表1
continued

产品名称	Name	计量单位	Unit	2012	2011	2012年比2011年（±%）2012/2011（±%）
橡胶轮胎外胎	Tires	万条	10000 tires	5 646.08	4 442.59	27.09
机械工业产品	**Products of Machinery Industry**					
工业锅炉	Industrial Boiler	蒸发量吨	ton(evaporation amount)	6 561.75	5 364.59	22.32
交流电动机	AC Motors	万千瓦	10000 kW	104.48	74.08	41.05
金属切削机床	Metal-cutting Machine	台	set	1 014	1 194	-15.08
汽车	Motor Vehicles	辆	set	574 729	488 330	17.69
改装汽车	Refitted Motor Vehicles	辆	set	13 111	18 120	-27.64
民用钢质船舶	Civil Steel Ships	载重吨	syn-ton	1 253 897	1 661 016	-24.51
电子产品	**Electronic Products**					
彩电电视机	Color TV Sets	万部	10000 sets	1 439.98	1 154.20	24.76
电子元件	Electronics	万只	10000 units	429 574.57	375 775.25	14.32
集成电路	Semiconductor Integrated Circuits	万块	10000 pieces	7.75	1.88	312.23
建材工业产品	**Products of Construction Industry**					
水泥	Cement	万吨	10000 tons	556.57	588.08	-5.36
平板玻璃	Plate Glass	万重量箱	10000 weight cases	494.54	510.05	-3.04
砖（折标准砖）	Bricks	万块	10000 pieces	51 975.90	44 975.80	15.56

12 -15 续表 2
continued

产品名称	Name	计量单位	Unit	2012	2011	2012 年比 2011 年 (±%) 2012/2011 (±%)
纺织工业产品	**Products of Textile Industry**					
纱	Yarn	吨	ton	19 404	18 556	4.57
布	Cloth	万米	10000 m	48 987.23	49 616.89	-1.27
印染布	Printed Fabric	万米	10000 m	32 477.71	28 449.24	14.16
帘子布	Cord Fabrics	吨	ton	1 753	2 283	-23.22
化学纤维	Chemical Fibers	万吨	10000 tons	3.24	3.86	-15.23
轻工产品	**Products of Light Industry**					
机制纸及纸板	Machine-made Paper and Paperboards	万吨	10000 tons	22.27	32.28	-30.99
家用洗衣机	Home Washing Machines	万台	10000 sets	583.6	604.55	-3.47
糖果	Sugar	万吨	10000 tons	515	502	2.53
卷烟	Cigarette	万箱	10000 cases	106.03	104.51	1.45
食用植物油	Vegetable Oil	万吨	10000 tons	60.65	48.03	25.26
饮料酒	Beverage Liquor	万吨	10000 tons	174.03	164.04	6.09
#白酒	Wine	万吨	10000 tons	1.51	1.25	20.95
#啤酒	Beer	万吨	10000 tons	163.95	156.50	4.76
塑料制品	Plastic Products	吨	ton	326 453	371 866	-12.21
家具	Furniture	万件	10000 units	712.98	669.07	6.56
家用电冰箱	Home Refrigerators	万台	10000 sets	575.01	718.54	-19.98
皮革鞋靴	Leather Shoes	万双	10000 pairs	7 232.20	7 189.63	0.59
服装	Clothing	万件	10000 articles	89 118.69	86 234.05	3.35

12－16 规模以上工业主要产品生产能力

PRODUCTION CAPACITY OF MAJOR PRODUCTS OF INDUSTRY ABOVE DESIGNATED SIZE

产品名称	Name	计算单位	Unit	2012 生产能力 Production Capacity of 2012	2011 生产能力 Production Capacity of 2011
发电设备容量总计/发电量	Total Capacity of Generation Equipment	万千瓦/万千瓦小时	10000 kW/10000 kW·h	351	349
卷烟	Cigarettes	万支	10000 pieces	7 155 000	7 074 000
化学纤维	Chemical Fiber	吨	ton	29 219	60 145
棉纺锭/纺纱量	Knitting Spindle	锭/吨	spindle/ton	154 076	135 632
棉布织机/布	Cotton Cloth Loom	台/万米	set/10000 m	33 607	52 100
焦炭	Coke	吨	ton	1 020 000	1 020 000
农用氮、磷、钾化学肥料总计(折纯)	Chemical Fertilizer	吨	ton	175 520	329 520
水泥	Cement	吨	ton	8 836 440	7 960 000
平板玻璃	Plate Glass	重量箱	weight cases	9 207 712	9 225 000
生铁	Pig Iron	吨	ton	4 000 000	4 000 000
粗钢	Crude Steel	吨	ton	4 000 000	4 000 000
钢材	Rolled-steel	吨	ton	3 990 000	3 945 000
金属切削机床	Metal-cutting Machine	台	set	1 964	1 670
汽车	Motor Vehicles	辆	set		575 000
家用电冰箱	Home Refrigerators	台	set	7 230 000	8 400 000
房间空气调节器	Air Conditioner	台	set	7 600 000	7 000 000
移动通信手持机(手机)	Cell Phone	台	set	32 200 000	41 800 000
彩色电视机	Color TV Sets	台	set	15 180 000	13 600 000

说明:2012 年报汽车生产能力国家统计生产轿车的企业,青岛未涉及。

Note: In 2012, the statistical scope of production capacity of motor vehicles is limited to manufacturing enterprise of car according to the national regulation, and there are no related enterprises in Qingdao.

主要统计指标解释

工业总产值　是以货币表现的工业企业在一定时期内生产的已出售或可供出售工业产品总量，它是反映一定时间内工业生产的总规模和总水平。

工业销售产值　是以货币表现的工业企业在一定时期内销售的本企业生产的工业产品产量。包括已销售的成品、半成品价值，以及对外提供的工业性作业价值和对本单位基本建设部门、生活福利部门等提供的产品和工业性作业及自制设备的价值。

工业增加值　指工业企业在报告期内以货币表现的工业生产活动的最终成果。是企业全部生产活动的总成果扣除了在生产过程中消耗或转移的物质产品和劳务价值后的余额，是企业生产过程中新增加的价值。

资产总计　指企业拥有或控制的能以货币计量的经济资源，包括各种财产、债权和其他权利。资产按其流动性（即资产的变现能力和支付能力）划分为：流动资产、长期投资、固定资产、无形资产、递延资产和其他资产。

负债合计　指企业所承担的能以货币计量，将以资产或劳务偿付的债务，偿还形式包括货币、资产或提供劳务。负债一般按偿还期长短分为流动负债和长期负债。

利润总额　指企业生产经营活动的最终成果，是企业在一定时期内实现的盈亏相抵后的利润总额（亏损以“-”号表示），它等于营业利润加上补贴收入加上投资收益加上营业外净收入再加上以前年度损益调整。

Explanatory Notes on Main Statistical Indicators

Gross Industrial Output Value　is the total volume of final industrial products produced and industrial services provided during a given period. It reflects the total achievements and overall scale of industrial production during a given period.

Sales Output Value of Industry　refers to total sales of products produced by industrial enterprises during a given period, including sales of fished goods, value of semi-products, value of industrial services provided to other units, value of products, industrial services provided for capital construction sector, welfare and self produced equipments within enterprise.

Value-added of Industry　refers to the final results of industrial production of industrial enterprises in money terms during the reference period.

Total Assets　refer to all economic resources, in monetary terms, that is owned or controlled by enterprises, including properties, creditors equity and other economic rights of all forms. Classified by the degree of equitability, total assets include circulating assets, long-term investment, fixed assets, intangible assets and deferred assets, and other assets.

Total Liabilities　refer to payable liabilities of enterprises that have to repay in terms of money, assets or labour services. In terms of payment, it can be divided into liquid liabilities and long-term liabilities.

Total Profits　refer to the final achievements of production and operation of the enterprises, represented by the total profits after deducting losses (loss is expressed by the negative figure). It is the sum of profits from operation, income from subsidies, investment earnings, net income from activities other than operation, and adjustment of profits and losses of previous years.

13 建筑业
CONSTRUCTION

简 要 说 明

一、本篇资料的主要内容

本篇资料主要反映了全市建筑业基本情况，主要包括建筑业总产值、增加值、建筑企业生产指标、财务指标、重点建筑企业名单等方面的内容。

二、本篇资料的来源

本篇资料来源于建筑业统计年报，由市统计局固定资产投资统计处整理提供。

Brief Introduction

I. Main Content

Data in this chapter show the basic conditions of construction of the whole city, mainly including the gross output value of construction, value added, major production and financial indicators and list of key enterprises of construction, etc.

II. Source of Data

Data in this chapter are based on the annual report of construction industry, and complied by the Division of Investment and Construction Statistics of Qingdao Municipal Bureau of Statistics.

13－1 建筑业企业生产情况(2012 年)
PRODUCTION SITUATION OF CONSTRUCTION ENTERPRISES(2012)

项 目	Item	单位	Unit	合计 Total	#中央 of which: Central Enterprises	国有企业 State-owned Enterprises	集体企业 Collective-owned Enterprises	其他所有制企业 Other Ownership Enterprises
施工企业单位数	Number of Construction Enterprises	个	unit	596	8	31	23	542
建筑业总产值	Gross Output Value of Construction	万元	10000 yuan	10 131 056	1 805 472	1 129 412	39 964	8 961 680
#建筑工程	of which: Construction	万元	10000 yuan	9 076 822	1 664 766	949 544	38 254	8 089 024
安装工程	Installation	万元	10000 yuan	824 921	140 706	176 049	1 420	647 452
建筑业增加值	Value Added of Construction	万元	10000 yuan	3 609 200				
全年竣工产值	Output Value of Buildings Completed in the Year	万元	10000 yuan	4 398 924	453 633	551 175	19 696	3 828 053
施工房屋面积	Floor Space of Buildings under Construction	万平方米	10000 sq. m	8 282	664	656	27	7 599
#新开工	of which: Newly Operating	万平方米	10000 sq. m	2 802	137	126	14	2 662
投标承包	Bidding and Contracting	万平方米	10000 sq. m	6 827	664	654	22	6 151
竣工房屋面积	Floor Space of Buildings Completed	万平方米	10000 sq. m	2 027	139	132	17	1 878
#住宅	of which: Residential Buildings	万平方米	10000 sq. m	1 339	84	84	12	1 243
年末自有施工机械设备台数	Number of Machinery and Equipment Owned (year-end)	台	set	46 596	6 738	7 025	929	38 642
年末自有施工机械设备净值	Net Value of Machinery and Equipment Owned (year-end)	万元	10000 yuan	225 721	56 297	45 283	1 191	179 247
年末自有施工机械设备总功率	Total Power of Machinery and Equipment Owned(year-end)	万千瓦	10000 kw	125	37	21	2	102
计算建筑业劳动生产率平均人数	Average Number of Persons for Calculating the Labor Productivity	人	person	297 641	48 316	43 600	1 263	252 778

13 −2 建筑业企业财务状况(2012 年)
FINANCIAL SITUATION OF CONSTRUCTION ENTERPRISES(2012)

项　目	Item	单位	Unit	合计 Total
流动资产	Circulating Funds	万元	10000 yuan	8 834 542
#存货	of which: Inventory	万元	10000 yuan	1 807 573
年末固定资产原价	Original Value of Fixed Assets(year-end)	万元	10000 yuan	1 243 438
本年固定资产折旧	Depreciation of Fixed Assets in the Year	万元	10000 yuan	81 939
年末固定资产净值	Net Value of Fixed Assets(year-end)	万元	10000 yuan	696 307
年末资产合计	Total Assets(year-end)	万元	10000 yuan	10 912 329
年末负债合计	Total Liabilities(year-end)	万元	10000 yuan	8 122 390
所有者权益合计	Total Owners' Equity	万元	10000 yuan	2 789 072
#实收资本	Paid-in Capitals	万元	10000 yuan	2 803 552
主营业务收入	Revenue from Principal Business	万元	10000 yuan	10 921 300
主营业务成本	Cost of Principal Business	万元	10000 yuan	9 872 921
主营业务税金及附加	Taxes and Extra Charges on Principal Business	万元	10000 yuan	282 704
管理费用	Management Expenses	万元	10000 yuan	350 897
利润总额	Total Profits	万元	10000 yuan	361 554
利税总额	Total Pre-tax Profits	万元	10000 yuan	660 002
年末应收工程款	Account Receivable(year-end)	万元	10000 yuan	2 452 377
#其中:竣工工程	of which: Projects Completed	万元	10000 yuan	900 143

#中央 of which: Central Enterprises	国有企业 State-owned Enterprises	集体企业 Collective-owned Enterprises	其他所有制企业 Other Ownership Enterprises
2 291 578	1 803 442	58 051	6 973 049
391 155	300 287	10 591	1 496 695
422 153	309 282	15 870	923 286
39 929	25 757	909	55 273
190 183	166 079	9 588	520 640
2 837 665	2 232 957	75 678	8 603 694
2 494 057	1 949 822	50 092	6 122 476
343 608	283 136	25 586	2 480 350
221 541	170 629	23 989	2 608 934
3 329 795	2 699 158	69 726	8 152 416
3 099 477	2 535 351	61 321	7 276 249
60 128	37 536	2 180	242 988
106 722	80 675	3 654	266 568
97 133	86 423	2 244	272 887
162 859	129 108	4 789	526 105
556 992	332 232	1 5807	2 104 338
107 978	76 056	3 864	820 223

13－3 建筑业企业主要经济效益指标(2012 年)
MAIN INDICATORS ON ECONOMIC BENEFIT OF CONSTRUCTION ENTERPRISES(2012)

项目	Item	单位	Unit	合计 Total	#中央 of which: Central Enterprises	国有企业 State-owned Enterprises	集体企业 Collective-owned Enterprises	其它所有制企业 Other Ownership Enterprises
建筑业劳动生产率	Labor Productivity of Construction							
按总产值计算	In Terms of Gross Output Value	元/人	yuan/person	340 378	373 679	259 039	316 421	354 527
竣工率	Rate of Buildings Completed							
按产值计算	In Terms of Gross Output Value	%	%	45.2	25.1	48.8	49.3	44.8
产值工资率	Ratio of Wages to Gross Output Value	%	%	7.4	9.5	12.4	15.7	6.7
资金利润率	Ratio of Profit to Funds	%	%	3.7	4.3	3.9	3.3	3.6
产值利润率	Ratio of Profit to Gross Output Value	%	%	3.6	7.6	5.4	5.6	3.1
技术装备率	Value of Machines per Laborer	元/人	yuan/person	7 454	11 651	10 385	9 285	10 194
流动比率	Current Ratio	%	%	119.2	93.5	93.3	171.2	128.0
资产负债率	Assets-Liability Ratio	%	%	74.4	87.8	87.3	66.2	71.2

13－4 建筑业增加值(2012 年)
VALUE ADDED OF CONSTRUCTION(2012)

单位:亿元(100 million yuan)

市、区名称	Region	增加值 Value Added
总　计	Total	360.92
市南区	Shinan District	30.59
原市北区	Original Shibei District	24.00
原四方区	Original Sifang District	14.08
李沧区	Licang District	9.81
崂山区	Laoshan District	33.76
原黄岛区	Original Huangdao District	60.09
城阳区	Chengyang District	13.93
即墨市	Jimo	42.01
胶州市	Jiaozhou	41.15
原胶南市	Original Jiaonan	38.10
平度市	Pingdu	26.49
莱西市	Laixi	26.91

13-5 重点建筑企业一览表(2012 年)
LIST OF KEY CONSTRUCTION ENTERPRISES(2012)

序号 Precedence	企业单位名称	Name	所在地区 Location		资质等级 Qualification Criteria
1	青建集团股份公司	Qingjian Group Co. ,Ltd.	原市北区	Original Shibei District	A001
2	中交一航局第二工程有限公司	China Communications 1nd Navigational Bureau 2nd Engineering Co. , Ltd.	市南区	Shinan	A104
3	中铁二十局集团第四工程有限公司	China Railway 20th Bureau Group 4th Engineering Co. ,Ltd.	崂山区	Laoshan	A103
4	青岛海尔家居集成股份有限公司	Qingdao Haier Home Corp.	崂山区	Laoshan	B103
5	中启胶建集团有限公司	Zhongqi Jiaozhou Construction Group Co. ,Ltd.	胶州市	Jiaozhou	A001
6	青岛海川建设集团有限公司	Qingdao Haichuan Construction Group Co. ,Ltd.	原市北区	Original Shibei District	A101
7	青岛博海建设集团有限公司	Qingdao Bohai Construction Group Co. ,Ltd.	市南区	Shinan	A101
8	山东莱钢建设有限公司	Shandong Laigang Gonstruction Co. ,Ltd.	市南区	Shinan	A108
9	青岛一建集团有限公司	Qingdao Yijian Group Co. ,Ltd.	原四方区	Original Sifang District	A101
10	中建八局第四建设有限公司	China Construction 8th Devision Corp. Ltd. (Qingdao Branch)	市南区	Shinan	A101
11	青岛建安建设集团有限公司	Shandong Laigang Gonstruction Co. ,Ltd.	市南区	Shinan	A101
12	青岛东亚建筑装饰有限公司	Qingdao Feiyu Construction and Decoration Co. ,Ltd.	市南区	Shinan	B103
13	中建筑港集团有限公司	China State Construction Port Engineering Group Co. ,Ltd.	原四方区	Original Sifang District	A104
14	青岛温泉建设集团有限公司	Qingdao Hot Spring Construction Group Co. ,Ltd.	即墨市	Jimo	A101
15	山东兴华建设集团有限公司	Shandong Xinghua Construction Co. ,Ltd.	原黄岛区	Original Huangdao District	A101
16	莱西市建筑总公司	Laixi Construction Corp.	莱西市	Laixi	A001
17	青岛福瀛建设集团有限公司	Qingdao Fuying Construction Group Co. ,Ltd.	原黄岛区	Original Huangdao District	A101
18	青岛通力建设集团有限公司	Qingdao Tongli Construction Group Co. ,Ltd.	市南区	Shinan	A101
19	青岛公路建设集团有限公司	Qingdao Highway Construction Group Co. ,Ltd.	原四方区	Original Sifang District	A102
20	青岛新华友建工集团股份有限公司	Qingdao Xinhuayou Construction Engineering Group Co. ,Ltd.	原市北区	Original Shibei District	A101
21	山东电力建设第三工程公司	Shandong Power Construction No. 3 Engineering Co. ,Ltd.	崂山区	Laoshan	A106
22	青岛滨海建设集团有限公司	Qingdao Binhai Construction Group Co. ,Ltd.	原黄岛区	Original Huangdao District	A101
23	青岛土木建工集团有限公司	Qingdao Yinghai Construction Co. ,Ltd.	原黄岛区	Original Huangdao District	A101
24	青岛城建集团有限公司	Qingdao City Construction Co. ,Ltd.	原四方区	Original Sifang District	A110
25	青岛第一市政工程有限公司	Qingdao No. 1 Municipal Construction Engineering Co. ,Ltd.	原四方区	Original Sifang District	A110
26	青岛建工集团有限公司	Qingdao Jiangong Group Co. ,Ltd.	崂山区	Laoshan	A102
27	青岛德才装饰安装工程有限公司	Qingdao Decai Decoration and Installation Engineering Co. ,Ltd.	市南区	Shinan	B103
28	通广建工集团有限公司	Qingdao Tongguang Construction Engineering Co. ,Ltd.	即墨市	Jimo	A001
29	青岛瑞源工程集团有限公司	Qingdao Ruiyuan Engineering Group Co. ,Ltd.	原黄岛区	Original Huangdao District	A105
30	青岛星火建筑工程有限公司	Qingdao Xinghuo Construction Engineering Co. ,Ltd.	原胶南市	Original Jiaonan	A301
31	青岛昶德建设集团有限公司	Qingdao Changde Construction Co. ,Ltd.	胶州市	Jiaozhou	A101
32	青岛安装建设股份有限公司	Qingdao Installation and Construction Co. ,Ltd.	原四方区	Original Sifang District	A112
33	中国石油天然气第七建设公司	China Petroluem 7th Construction Company	崂山区	Laoshan	A109

13－5 续表1
continued

序号 Precedence	企业单位名称	Name	所在地区	Location	资质等级 Qualification Criteria
34	青岛建祥建设集团有限公司	Qingdao Jianxiang Construction Group Co. ,Ltd.	胶州市	Jiaozhou	A201
35	青岛胶城建设集团有限公司	Qingdao Jiaocheng Construction Co. ,Ltd.	胶州市	Jiaozhou	A101
36	青岛亿联集团股份有限公司	Qingdao Yilian Group Co. ,Ltd.	原胶南市	Original Jiaonan	A101
37	青岛高新建筑安装工程有限公司	Qingdao Gaoxin Construction and Installation Co. , Ltd.	崂山区	Laoshan	A101
38	青岛金北洋工程有限公司	Qingdao Jinbeiyang Engineering Co. ,Ltd.	原黄岛区	Original Huangdao District	B113
39	青岛环海工程贸易发展有限公司	Qingdao Huanhai Engineering Trade Development Co. ,Ltd.	原市北区	Original Shibei District	A201
40	青岛恒生源集团建设有限公司	Qingdao Hengshengyuan Construction Engineering Co. ,Ltd.	即墨市	Jimo	A101
41	青岛营上建设集团有限公司	Qingdao Yingshang Construction Co. ,Ltd.	即墨市	Jimo	A101
42	青岛三林建筑工程有限公司	Qingdao Sanlin Construction Engineering Co. ,Ltd.	原胶南市	Original Jiaonan	A201
43	青岛港务局港务工程公司	Qingdao Port Engineering Co. ,Ltd.	原黄岛区	Original Huangdao District	A204
44	青岛平建建筑安装股份有限公司	Qingdao Pingjian Construction and Installation Co. , Ltd.	平度市	Pingdu	A101
45	山东巴龙建设集团有限公司	Shandong Ballon Construction Group Co. ,Ltd.	市南区	Shinan	A201
46	青岛市神州建筑工程有限公司	Qingdao Shenzhou Construction Engineering Co. ,Ltd.	胶州市	Jiaozhou	A201
47	青岛地矿岩土工程有限公司	Qingdao Mine Engineering Co. ,Ltd.	市南区	Shinan	B101
48	青岛青房建安集团有限公司	Qingdao Qingfang Construction and Installation Co. ,Ltd.	市南区	Shinan	A101
49	胶州市铺集建筑公司	Jiaozhou Puji Construction Co. ,Ltd.	胶州市	Jiaozhou	A304
50	青岛九龙建设集团有限公司	Qingdao Jiulong Construction Co. ,Ltd.	胶州市	Jiaozhou	A201
51	青岛胶州南关建安股份有限公司	Qingdao Jiaonan Nanguan Construction and Installation Co. ,Ltd.	胶州市	Jiaozhou	A201
52	青岛德泰建设工程有限公司	Qingdao Detai Construction Engineering Co. ,Ltd.	原黄岛区	Original Huangdao District	A101
53	青岛多元建设集团有限公司	Qingdao Duoyuan Construction Group Co. ,Ltd.	原黄岛区	Original Huangdao District	A210
54	青岛金沙滩建设集团有限公司	Qingdao Jinsha Beach Construction Co. ,Ltd.	原黄岛区	Original Huangdao District	A101
55	青岛海德路桥工程股份有限公司	Qingdao Haide Highway & Bridge Engineering Co. ,Ltd.	市南区	Shinan	A210
56	青岛市热电工程公司	Qingdao Thermal Power Engineering Co. ,Ltd.	原市北区	Original Shibei District	A210
57	青岛营海建设集团有限公司	Qingdao Civil Engineering Group Co. ,Ltd.	胶州市	Jiaozhou	A101
58	青岛新城发展建筑工程有限公司	Qingdao New City Development Construction Engineering Co. ,Ltd.	原市北区	Original Shibei District	A201
59	青岛东捷建设工程有限公司	Qingdao Dongjie Construction Engineering Co. ,Ltd.	原市北区	Original Shibei District	A101
60	青岛市一宅建筑集团股份有限公司	Qingdao Yizhai Construction Co. ,Ltd.	原市北区	Original Shibei District	A101
61	青岛颐金建筑装饰工程有限公司	Qingdao Yijin Construction and Installation Co. , Ltd.	市南区	Shinan	B103
62	青岛恒源送变电工程有限公司	Qingdao Hengyuan Transmission and Distribution Project Co. ,Ltd.	城阳区	Chengyang	A201
63	山东省路通工程集团有限公司	Shandong Lutong Engineering Group Co. ,Ltd.	崂山区	Laoshan	A102
64	平度市南预制件厂	Pingdu Nanding Precast Factory	平度市	Pingdu	B306
65	山东兴华建设集团胶南工程有限公司	Shandong Xinghua Construction Group Jiaonan Enginnering Co. ,Ltd.	原黄岛区	Original Huangdao District	A301
66	山东国建工程集团有限公司	Shandong Guojian Construction Project Co. ,Ltd.	崂山区	Laoshan	B201

13 -5 续表 2
continued

序号 Precedence	企业单位名称	Name	所在地区 Location		资质等级 Qualification Criteria
67	青岛市泽惠建设集团有限公司	Qingdao Huize Construction Co. ,Ltd.	城阳区	Chengyang	A101
68	青岛建国工程集团有限公司	Qingdao Jianguo Engineering Co. ,Ltd.	原黄岛区	Original Huangdao District	A201
69	胶南市建筑工程公司	Jiaonan Construction Engineering Co. ,Ltd.	原胶南市	Original Jiaonan	A101
70	青岛康太源建设集团有限公司	Qingdao Kangtaiyuan Construction Group Co. ,Ltd.	李沧区	Licang	A101
71	青岛市市政工程集团有限公司	Qingdao Municipal Engineering Co. ,Ltd.	市南区	Shinan	A110
72	青岛施运机械施工有限责任公司	Qingdao Shiyun Mechanized Construction Co. ,Ltd.	原四方区	Original Sifang District	B101
73	青岛腾达建筑工程有限公司	Qingdao Tengda Construction Engineering Co. ,Ltd.	即墨市	Jimo	A201
74	山东红建建安集团公司	Shandong Hongjian Construction and Installation Co. ,Ltd.	原黄岛区	Original Huangdao District	A201
75	青岛经济技术开发区建筑安装工程总公司	Qingdao Development Zone Construction and Installation Co. ,Ltd.	原黄岛区	Original Huangdao District	A201
76	青岛新世纪路桥工程有限公司	Qingdao New Century Highway & Bridge Engineering Co. ,Ltd.	即墨市	Jimo	A202
77	青岛四机建筑安装有限公司	Qingdao Siji Construction and Installation Co. ,Ltd.	原四方区	Original Sifang District	B201
78	青岛中奥体育专用地板有限公司	Qingdao Zhongao Sport Wooden Floor Co. ,Ltd.	平度市	Pingdu	B159
79	青岛望城三宝建设有限公司	Qingdao Wangcheng Sanbao Construction Co. ,Ltd.	莱西市	Laixi	A101
80	青岛铁路工程建筑有限公司	Qingdao Railway Engineering Co. ,Ltd.	市南区	Shinan	A203
81	青岛城阳兴源建筑工程有限公司	Qingdao Chengyang Xingyuan Construction Co. ,Ltd.	城阳区	Chengyang	A301
82	青岛隆昌达建筑安装有限公司	Qingdao Longchangda Construction and Installation Co. ,Ltd.	胶州市	Jiaozhou	A101
83	青岛阳光东辉建设集团有限公司	Qingdao Yangguang Donghui Construction Group Co. ,Ltd.	胶州市	Jiaozhou	A201
84	青岛亿佰建筑工程有限公司	Qingdao Yibai Construction Engineering Co. ,Ltd.	原胶南市	Original Jiaonan	A201
85	青岛福海洋建设集团有限公司	Qingdao Fuhaiyuang Construction Co. ,ltd.	胶州市	Jiaozhou	A201
86	青岛宏远建筑工程有限公司	Qingdao Hongyuan Construction Engineering Co. , Ltd.	莱西市	Laixi	A201
87	青岛即建建设集团有限公司	Qingdao Jijian Construction Group Co. ,Ltd.	即墨市	Jimo	A101
88	青岛市黄岛区园林绿化工程有限公司	Qingdao Huangdao Green Enginnering Co. ,Ltd.	原黄岛区	Original Huangdao District	B101
89	青岛市胶州水利工程有限公司	Qingdao Jiaozhou Water Engineering Co. ,Ltd.	胶州市	Jiaozhou	A205
90	青岛建设集团建兴工程有限公司	Qingdao Construction Group Jianxing Engineering Co. ,Ltd.	市南区	Shinan	A201
91	青岛宝利建设有限公司	Qingdao Baoli Construction Co. ,Ltd.	莱西市	Laixi	A201
92	青岛胶南万德建筑工程有限公司	Qingdao Jiaonan Wande Construction Engineering Co. ,Ltd.	原胶南市	Original Jiaonan	A301
93	青岛石化检修安装工程有限责任公司	Qingdao Petrochemical Repair and Installation Co. ,Ltd.	李沧区	Licang	B253
94	青岛建设装饰集团有限公司	Qingdao Construction and Decoration Co. ,Ltd.	市南区	Shinan	B103
95	青岛康大诚鑫建筑安装工程有限公司	Qingdao Kangda Chengxin Construction and Installation Co. ,Ltd.	原胶南市	Original Jiaonan	A301
96	青岛市崂山区古建建筑工程有限公司	Qingdao Laoshan Gujian Construction Engineering Co. ,Ltd.	崂山区	Laoshan	A201
97	青岛洋河建设集团有限公司	Qingdao Yanghe Construction Group Co. ,Ltd.	胶州市	Jiaozhou	A201
98	青岛市李沧区东李建筑工程有限公司	Qingdao Licang Dongli Construction Project Co. , Ltd.	李沧区	Licang	A201
99	青岛市益水工程股份有限公司	Qingdao Yishui Engineering Co. ,Ltd.	市南区	Shinan	A210

13－5 续表3
continued

序号 Precedence	企业单位名称	Name	所在地区 Location		资质等级 Qualification Criteria
100	青岛荣宏建筑安装工程有限公司	Qingdao Ronghong Construction and Installation Co. ,Ltd.	原胶南市	Original Jiaonan	A201
101	青岛新业建筑工程有限公司	Qingdao Xinye Construction Engineering Co. ,Ltd.	李沧区	Licang	A301
102	青岛金星科技工程有限公司	Qingdao Jinxing Science and Technology Enginnering Co. ,Ltd.	市南区	Shinan	B111
103	青岛天一建设集团有限公司	Qingdao Tianyi Construction Group Co. ,Ltd.	原胶南市	Original Jiaonan	A201
104	青岛九鼎峰建设集团有限公司	Qingdao Jiudingfeng Construction Co. ,Ltd.	原黄岛区	Original Huangdao District	A201
105	青岛鑫鸿泰建设工程有限公司	Qingdao Hongxintai Construction Engineering Co. ,Ltd.	胶州市	Jiaozhou	A201
106	青岛金坤建筑有限公司	Qingdao Jinkun Construction Co. ,Ltd.	平度市	Pingdu	A201
107	青岛胶东建设集团有限公司	Qingdao Jiaodong Construction Co. ,Ltd.	胶州市	Jiaozhou	A201
108	青岛金楷装饰工程有限公司	Qingdao Jinkai Decoration Engineering Co. ,Ltd.	原市北区	Original Shibei District	B202
109	青岛田横建筑工程有限公司	Qingdao Tianheng Construction Project Co. ,Ltd.	即墨市	Jimo	A201
110	青岛铁路红宇建设集团有限公司	Qingdao Railway Hongyu Construction Group Co. ,Ltd.	市南区	Shinan	A301
111	青岛华天建设集团有限公司	Qingdao Huatian Construction Group Co. ,Ltd.	胶州市	Jiaozhou	A201
112	青岛润达建设工程有限公司	Qingdao Runda Construction Engineering Co. ,Ltd.	原黄岛区	Original Huangdao District	A210
113	青岛爱华工程有限公司	Qingdao Aihua Engineering Co. ,Ltd.	原市北区	Original Shibei District	A201
114	青岛嘉和建造有限公司	Qingdao Jiahe Construcion Co. ,Ltd.	即墨市	Jimo	A201
115	青岛泰能工程股份有限公司	Qingdao Taineng Engineering Co. ,Ltd.	原四方区	Original Sifang District	A210
116	青岛福盛建设集团有限公司	Qingdao Fusheng Construction Group Co. ,Ltd.	城阳区	Chengyang	A101
117	青岛岳海建设集团有限公司	Qingdao Yuehai Construction Group Co. ,Ltd.	市南区	Shinan	A101
118	青岛莱西九联建筑工程有限公司	Qingdao Laixi Jiulian Construction Project Co. ,Ltd.	莱西市	Laixi	A201
119	青岛金原建筑工程有限公司	Qingdao Jinyuan Construction Co. ,Ltd.	原胶南市	Original Jiaonan	A201
120	青岛高科技工业园市政有限公司	Qingdao High-tech Industrial Park Municipal Co. ,Ltd.	崂山区	Laoshan	A210
121	青岛政益达实业有限公司	Qingdao Zhengyida Industrial Co. ,Ltd.	原市北区	Original Shibei District	A210
122	青岛环城建工集团有限公司	Qingdao Huancheng Construction Engineering Group Co. ,Ltd.	原黄岛区	Original Huangdao District	A201
123	青岛红塔建筑工程有限公司	Qingdao Hongta Construction Engineering Co. ,Ltd.	原胶南市	Original Jiaonan	A201
124	青岛经济技术开发区市政工程总公司	Qingdao Development Zone Municipal Administration Engineering Co. ,Ltd.	原黄岛区	Original Huangdao District	A210
125	青岛新奥燃气设施开发有限公司	Qingdao ENN Gas Facilities Development Co. ,Ltd.	原黄岛区	Original Huangdao District	B225
126	青岛市丰水市政工程有限公司	Qingdao Shunyuan Construction Engineering Co. ,Ltd.	即墨市	Jimo	A210
127	青岛泓鑫源建筑安装工程有限公司	Qingdao Hongxinyuan Construction and Installion Project Co. ,Ltd.	胶州市	Jiaozhou	A201
128	青岛市自来水物资工程公司	Qingdao Tap Water Project Co. ,Ltd.	原四方区	Original Sifang District	A310
129	青岛天晟防水建材有限公司	Qingdao Tiansheng Waterproof Material Co. ,Ltd.	胶州市	Jiaozhou	B312
130	青岛泰华集团有限公司	Qingdao Taihua Group Co. ,Ltd.	原胶南市	Original Jiaonan	A201
131	青岛市沙子口第二建筑工程有限公司	Qingdao Shazikou 2nd Construction Engineering Co. ,Ltd.	崂山区	Laoshan	A301
132	青岛兴水实业有限公司	Qingdao Xingshui Industry Co. ,Ltd.	原市北区	Original Shibei District	A210

13 –5 续表 4
continued

序号 Precedence	企业单位名称	Name	所在地区 Location		资质等级 Qualification Criteria
133	青岛伟信建设工程有限公司	Qingdao Weixin Construction Engineering Co., Ltd.	平度市	Pingdu	A201
134	青岛华商工程有限公司	Qingdao Huashang Engineering Co., Ltd.	莱西市	Laixi	A301
135	青岛光大集团工程有限公司	Qingdao Guangda Group Co., Ltd.	原胶南市	Original Jiaonan	A201
136	青岛吉安工程有限公司	Qingdao Jian Engineering Co., Ltd.	莱西市	Laixi	A205
137	青岛盈鑫建设集团有限公司	Qingdao Yingxin Construction Co., Ltd.	城阳区	Chengyang	A201
138	青岛晶城设计装饰工程有限公司	Qingdao Jingcheng Design and Decoration Enginnering Co., Ltd.	市南区	Shinan	B103
139	青岛琅琊建筑有限公司	Qingdao Langyatai Construction Engineering Co., Ltd.	原胶南市	Original Jiaonan	A201
140	青岛飞宇建设集团有限公司	Qingdao Feiyu Construction Engineering Co., Ltd.	原胶南市	Original Jiaonan	A301
141	山东森泰源建设工程有限公司	Shandong Sentaiyuan Construction Engineering Co., Ltd.	原黄岛区	Original Huangdao District	A210
142	青岛汉河电气工程有限公司	Qingdao Hanhe Electrical Engineering Co., Ltd.	崂山区	Laoshan	B349
143	青岛市房产工程公司	Qingdao Real Estate Enginnering Co., Ltd.	市南区	Shinan	B103
144	青岛东方铁塔安装工程有限公司	Qingdao Orient Iron Tower Project Co., Ltd.	胶州市	Jiaozhou	B108
145	青岛通达公路工程有限公司	Qingdao Tongda Road Engineering Co., Ltd.	莱西市	Laixi	A202
146	青岛天润工程有限公司	Qingdao Tianrun Enginnering Co., Ltd.	莱西市	Laixi	A305
147	青岛啤酒工程有限公司	Qingdao Boer Engineering Co., Ltd.	市南区	Shinan	B318
148	即墨市七级建筑工程有限公司	Jimo 7-class Construction Engineering Co., Ltd.	即墨市	Jimo	A201
149	青岛聚源建设集团有限公司	Qingdao Juyuan Construction Group Co., Ltd.	原胶南市	Original Jiaonan	A201
150	青岛枫和建设工程有限公司	Qingdao Fenghe Construction Engineering Co., Ltd.	即墨市	Jimo	A310
151	青岛鲁赫建筑装饰有限公司	Qingdao Luhe Construction and Decoration Co., Ltd.	市南区	Shinan	B203
152	青岛经济技术开发区五岳建筑工程有限公司	Qingdao Development Zone Wuyue Construction Engineering Co., Ltd.	原黄岛区	Original Huangdao District	A301
153	山东省即墨市第二建筑工程公司	Shandong Jimo 2nd Construction Project Co., Ltd.	即墨市	Jimo	A201
154	青岛华联装饰工程有限公司	Qingdao Huanlian Decoration Engineering Co., Ltd.	原四方区	Original Sifang District	B203
155	青岛东部电气工程有限公司	Qingdao Eastern Electrical Engineering Co., Ltd.	崂山区	Laoshan	B349
156	平度市永盛建筑有限公司	Pingdu Yongsheng Construction Co., Ltd.	平度市	Pingdu	A201
157	青岛江河水利工程有限公司	Qingdao Jianghe Water Project Co., Ltd.	平度市	Pingdu	A205
158	青岛暖万家市政工程有限公司	Qingdao Nuanwanjia Municipal Engineering Co., Ltd.	原黄岛区	Original Huangdao District	A210
159	青岛崂峰市政工程有限公司	Qingdao Laofeng Municipal Engineering Co., Ltd.	崂山区	Laoshan	A210
160	青岛金阳光消防工程有限公司	Qingdao Jinyangguang Fire Engineering Co., Ltd.	市南区	Shinan	B111
161	青岛静力工程有限公司	Qingdao Static Project Co., Ltd.	市南区	Shinan	B301
162	平度市光华建筑工程有限公司	Pingdu guanghua Construction Engineering Co., Ltd.	平度市	Pingdu	A301
163	青岛新凯达市政工程有限公司	Qingdao Xinkaida Municipal Enginnering Co., Ltd.	原市北区	Original Shibei District	A210
164	青岛市城阳区上马建筑工程有限公司	Qingdao Chengyang Shangma Construction Co., Ltd.	城阳区	Chengyang	A201
165	青岛鑫鸿飞装饰工程有限公司	Qingdao Xinhongfei Decoration Engineering Co., Ltd.	市南区	Shinan	B137

13－5 续表 5
continued

序号 Precedence	企业单位名称	Name	所在地区	Location	资质等级 Qualification Criteria
156	青岛恒星实业发展有限公司	Qingdao Hengxing Industry Co. ,Ltd.	市南区	Shinan	B303
157	即墨市水利建筑安装工程公司	Jimo Water Construction and Installation Engineering Corp.	即墨市	Jimo	A205
158	青岛恒瑞工程建设有限公司	Qingdao Hengrui Engineering Construction Co. ,Ltd.	原黄岛区	Original Huangdao District	A210
159	青岛易通建安有限公司	Qingdao Yitong Construction and Installation Co. ,Ltd.	原黄岛区	Original Huangdao District	A201
160	青岛鲁城建设有限公司	Qingdao Lucheng Construction Co. ,Ltd.	市南区	Shinan	A201
161	青岛经典建设工程有限公司	Qingdao Classical Construction Project Co. ,Ltd.	胶州市	Jiaozhou	A201
162	青岛平运路桥工程有限公司	Qingdao Pingyun Road & Bridge Project Co. ,Ltd.	平度市	Pingdu	A202
163	青岛金茂建设工程有限公司	Qingdao Jinmao Construction Engineering Co. , Ltd.	原胶南市	Original Jiaonan	A301
164	青岛凯顺建设集团有限公司	Qingdao Kaishun Construction Group Co. ,Ltd.	胶州市	Jiaozhou	A201
165	青岛市红岛建筑工程有限公司	Qingdao Hongdao Construction Engineering Co. , Ltd.	城阳区	Chengyang	A201
166	青岛岩土基础工程公司	Qingdao Geotechnical Engineering Co. ,Ltd.	市南区	Shinan	B201
167	青岛恒辉建设工程有限公司	Qingdao Henghui Construction Enginnering Co. , Ltd.	原黄岛区	Original Huangdao District	A201
168	青岛德惠建筑工程有限公司	Qingdao Dehui Construction Engineering Co. ,Ltd.	即墨市	Jimo	A201
169	青岛城阳恒升建筑安装工程有限公司	Qingdao Chengyang Hengsheng Construction and Installation Co. , Ltd.	城阳区	Chengyang	A201
180	青岛胜利兄弟建筑有限公司	Qingdao Victory Brothers Construction Co. ,Ltd.	胶州市	Jiaozhou	B114
181	青岛易简电力工程有限公司	Qingdao Yijian Power Enginnering Co. ,Ltd.	莱西市	Laixi	B349
182	青岛阳光电器工程有限公司	Qingdao Sunshine Electro-engineering Co. ,Ltd.	市南区	Shinan	B211
183	青岛城阳城建集团有限公司	Qingdao Chengyang Chengjian Group Co. ,Ltd.	城阳区	Chengyang	A201
184	青岛华山广泰建筑工程有限公司	Qingdao Huanshan Guangtai Construction Engineering Co. ,Ltd.	即墨市	Jimo	A301
185	青岛市宏运公路工程有限责任公司	Qingdao Hongyun Road Project Co. ,Ltd.	平度市	Pingdu	A202
186	青岛宇鑫锋建设工程有限公司	Qingdao Xinyufeng Construction Engineering Co. ,Ltd.	原黄岛区	Original Huangdao District	A210
187	青岛国龙市政建设工程有限公司	Qingdao Guolong Municipal Construction Engineering Co. ,Ltd.	城阳区	Chengyang	A310
188	青岛经济技术开发区天龙建筑安装工程有限公司	Qingdao Development Zone Tianlong Construction and Installion Co. ,Ltd.	原黄岛区	Original Huangdao District	A201
189	青岛市李沧建筑安装工程有限公司	Qingdao Licang Construction and Decoration Engineering Co. ,Ltd.	李沧区	Licang	A201
190	青岛和瑞城市建设集团有限公司	Qingdao Herui City Construction Group Co. ,Ltd.	崂山区	Laoshan	A101
191	青岛润佳建筑工程有限公司	Qingdao Runjia Construction Project Co. ,Ltd.	即墨市	Jimo	A201
192	青岛水集建筑有限公司	Qingdao Shuiji Construction Co. ,Ltd.	莱西市	Laixi	A201
193	青岛圣达建筑工程有限公司	Qingdao Shengda Construction Engineering Co. , Ltd.	平度市	Pingdu	A301
194	青岛安得利建筑工程有限公司	Qingdao Andeli Construction Engineering Co. , Ltd.	胶州市	Jiaozhou	A201
195	青岛永鑫幕墙有限公司	Qingdao Yongxin Curtain Wall Co. ,Ltd.	崂山区	Laoshan	B104
196	青岛水建集团有限公司	Qingdao Shuijian Group Co. ,Ltd.	胶州市	Jiaozhou	A205
197	青岛柳源鑫瑞市政园林建设集团有限公司	Qingdao Liuyuan Xinrui Municipal Green Construction Co. ,Ltd.	原黄岛区	Original Huangdao District	A210
198	青岛方圆达建设集团有限公司	Qingdao Fangyuanda Construction Group Co. ,Ltd.	李沧区	Licang	A201
199	青岛华烨建设工程有限公司	Qingdao Huaye Construction Engineering Co. , Ltd.	原黄岛区	Original Huangdao District	A301
200	平度市东苑建筑工程有限公司	Pingdu Dongyuan Construction Engineering Co. ,Ltd.	平度市	Pingdu	A201

主要统计指标解释

建筑业统计单位 指从事房屋、构筑物建造和设备安装活动的法人企业。建筑业法人企业应具有建筑业资质并能够独立核算,同时其应具备以下条件:①依法成立,有自己的名称、组织机构和场所,能够承担民事责任;②独立拥有和使用资产,承担负债,有权与其他单位签订合同;③独立核算盈亏,能够编制资产负债表。

建筑业总产值 是以货币形式表现的建筑业企业在一定时期内生产的建筑业产品和提供的服务的总和。建筑业总产值包括:

(1)建筑工程产值:指列入建筑工程预算内的各种工程价值。

(2)安装工程产值:指设备安装工程价值,不包括被安装设备本身的价值。

(3)其他产值:建筑业总产值中除建筑工程、安装工程以外的产值。包括房屋构筑物修理产值、非标准设备制造产值、总包企业向分包企业收取的管理费以及不能明确划分的施工活动所完成的产值。

建筑业增加值 指建筑业企业在报告期内以货币形式表现的建筑业生产经营活动的最终成果。建筑业增加值 = 劳动者报酬 + 生产税净额 + 本年折旧 + 营业盈余

Explanatory Notes on Main Statistical Indicators

Statistical Unit in Construction refers to corporate enterprise engaged in the construction of buildings and structures and in the installation of equipment. A corporate construction enterprise should have qualification certificates with independent accounting system, and should meet the following 3 requirements: a) being set up in line with relevant legal basis, having its full name, organization and location, and capable of taking civil liabilities; b) independently possessing and using its assets and assuming its liabilities, and entitled to sign contracts with other institutions; and c) making independent accounts of its profits and losses, and capable of compiling its own balance sheet.

Gross Output Value of Construction refers to total of construction products and services, expressed in money terms, produced or rendered by construction and installation enterprises during a given period of time. It includes:

(1) Output value of construction projects, that is the value of projects covered by the project budgets;

(2) Output value of installation projects, that is the value of the installation of equipment, (excluding the value of the equipment to be installed);

(3) Output value of others, that is the output value of construction industry excluding that of construction projects and installation projects. It includes: output value of repair of buildings and structures; output value of non-standard equipment manufacturing; overhead expenses received by contracted enterprises to the sub-contracted enterprises and the completed output value of construction activities that have no clear definition.

Value-added of Construction refers to the final result of the activities of production and management of construction industry in monetary terms in the reference period.

Value-added of Construction = Compensation of Employees + Net Taxes on Production + Depreciation of Fixed Assets + Operating Surplus.

14 运输、邮电

TRANSPORT, POSTAL AND TELECOMMUNICATION SERVICES

简要说明

一、本篇资料的主要内容

本篇资料主要反映了全市交通运输业和邮电业通讯业发展的基本情况，主要包括客货运输及港口吞吐量、民用汽车拥有量、独立核算运输邮电单位主要财务指标、邮电通讯基本情况等方面的内容。

二、本篇资料的来源

1、本篇资料中交通运输资料来源于全市交通运输业统计年报。

2、邮电通讯业资料来源于邮电通讯基本情况统计年报。

3、民用汽车拥有量资料来源于青岛市公安局交警支队车辆管理所。

本篇资料由市统计局工业统计处整理提供。

Brief Introduction

I. Main Content

Data in this chapter show the basic conditions of the development of transport, post and telecommunications in Shandong Province, mainly including the freight traffic and passenger traffic, cargo handled at port, possession of civil motor vehicles, major financial indices and basic conditions of transport, postal and telecommunication services.

II. Source of Data

(1)Data on transport are based on the annual report of transport.

(2)Data on postal and telecommunication are based on the annual report of postal and telecommunication.

(3)Data on possession of civil motor vehicles are provided by Traffic Police Office of Vehicle Management of Qingdao Municipal Bureau of Public Security.

Data in this chapter are prepared and provide by the Division of Industry Statistics of Qingdao Municipal Bureau of Statistics.

14 -1 主要年份客货运输及港口吞吐量

MAJOR YEAR'S PASSENGER & FREIGHT TRAFFIC AND HANDLING CAPACITY OF THE PORTS

年份 Year	客运量(万人) Passenger Traffic(10000 persons)				货运量(万吨) Freight Traffic(10000 tons)				港口吞吐量(万吨)Cargo Handled at Ports(10000 tons)	集装箱吞吐量(万标箱) Containers(10000 TEU)
	铁路 Railways	公路 Highways	海运 Waterways	航空 Civil Aviation	铁路 Railways	公路 Highways	海运 Waterways	航空 Civil Aviation		
1949	327	14	9		386	162	22		73	
1952	571	49	13		447	399	44		181	
1957	1 054	149	13		747	548	118		269	
1962	3 100	141	39		909	524	97		391	
1965	1 424	230	19		1 257	690	158		524	
1970	1 329	373	20		1 856	736	232		695	
1975	1 803	159	30		2 325	817	282		1 542	
1978	1 986	274	49		2 917	1 561	528		2 081	
1980	1 896	713	73		2 596	1 642	941		1 779	
1985	2 063	1 894	86	1.0	3 009	2 303	919	0.03	2 610	
1987	2 019	2 133	159	7.0	3 288	4 948	1 085	0.04	3 070	
1988	2 083	3 300	234	8.8	3 418	6 486	1 160	0.04	3 153	
1989	1 802	3 441	308	11.3	3 717	8 926	1 450	0.10	3 145	
1990	1 488	3 639	316	14.1	3 741	6 433	1 556	0.20	3 068	
1991	1 453	4 144	366	19.0	3 774	6 896	1 789	0.31	3 194	
1992	1 488	4 965	437	27.0	3 899	6 822	1 981	0.45	3 240	
1993	1 499	6 436	499	35.3	4 044	7 685	1 910	0.64	3 650	
1994	1 564	6 787		47.0	4 112	8 336	1 804		4 331	
1995	1 480	9 785		66.6	4 205	11 788	2 185		5 165	
1996	1 230	10 738		79.9	4 415	10 749	474		6 056	81.1
1997	1 308	11 855			4 466	11 232	544		6 944	103.3
1998	1 549	11 754			4 028	14 311	1 792	1.44	7 044	121.3
1999	1 674	12 103			3 919	14 550	1 926	1.96	7 282	154.3
2000	1 780	12 145		124.1	4 256	17 234	2 998	2.30	8 661	212.0
2001	1 678	13 686		143.0	4 778	20 906	3 432	2.40	10 423	264.0
2002	1 530	14 516	777	163.7	5 079	24 480	2 530	3.00	12 252	341.0
2003	1 366	13 132	786	174.7	4 929	27 241	2 773	3.60	14 135	424.0
2004	1 496	16 420	862	241.9	5 119	29 937	3 503	5.30	16 303	514.0
2005	552	17 212	972	280.9	2 299	31 009	4 471	4.60	18 727	630.7
2006	810	17 752	999	320.2	2 790	32 047	4 768	5.10	22 438	770.0
2007	1 101	18 800	1 080	366.9	2 781	33 336	4 019	5.90	2 6507	946.6
2008	1 278	19 909	1 055	377.9	3 225	34 172	5 080	7.20	30 029	1 037.7
2009	1 425	19 612	1 145	440.9	3 772	16 297	4 332	7.19	31 668	1 027.6
2010	537	20 460	1 302	505.5	5 031	17 525	4 407	8.44	35 012	1 201.0
2011	693	21 560	791	537.4	5 697	19 208	4 220	8.93	37 971	1 302.0
2012	881	22 724	413.68	586.57	6 126.4	21 312	1 790.69	9.06	41 465	1 450.0

14－2 民用车辆拥有量(2012 年底)

POSSESSION OF CIVIL MOTOR VEHICLES(END OF 2012)

单位:辆(unit)

项 目	Item	合计 Total 辆数 Number	#个人 of which: Private Vehicles 辆数 Number
一、汽车	**Automobile**	**1 330 843**	**1 057 672**
1.载客汽车	Passenger Vehicles	1 132 219	958 109
其中:轿车	of which:Sedan	703 920	614 071
2.载货汽车	Trucks	164 931	72 048
3.其他汽车	Other Automobile	33 693	27 515
二、电车	**Tram**	**70**	
三、摩托车	**Motorcycle**	**454 451**	**451 975**
四、农用运输车	**Agricultural Camion**		
五、挂车	**Trailer Trucks**	**16 314**	**657**
六、其他类型车	**Other Vehicles**	**237**	**16**

补充资料:机动车驾驶员(人)Motor drivers(person) 1996420

其中:汽车驾驶员(人)of which:Automobile drivers(person) 1846188

14－3 客货运输及港口吞吐量(2012 年)

PASSENGER & FREIGHT TRAFFIC AND HANDLING CAPACITY OF THE PORTS(2012)

项 目	Item	货运量（万吨） Freight Traffic (10000 tons)	货物周转量（亿吨公里） Freight Ton-kilometers(100 million tons · km)	客运量（万人） Passenger Traffic (10000 persons)	旅客周转量（亿人公里） Passenger-Kilometers(100 million person-km)	旅客吞吐量（万人） Volume of Passenger Handled (10000 persons)	货物吞吐量（万吨） Volume of Freight Handled (10000 tons)	集装箱（万标箱） Containers (10000 TEU)
总 计	**Total**	**29 229.09**	**2 064.88**	**25 018.68**	**197.21**	**1 272.68**	**41 482.01**	**1 450.00**
铁路	Railways	6 126.40	186.24	1 881.00	57.37			
公路	Highways	21 312.00	452.61	22 724.00	139.20			
水运	Waterways	1 790.69	1 426.03	413.68	0.64			
民航	Civil Aviation					1 260.12	17.19	
港口	Ports					12.56	41 464.82	1 450.00

14－4 独立核算运输邮电单位主要财务指标(2012 年)

MAIN FINANCIAL INDICATORS OF INDEPENDENT ACCOUNTING UNITS OF TRANSPORT, POSTAL AND TELECOMMUNICATION SERVICES(2012)

单位：万元(10 000 yuan)

项目	Item	主营业务收入 Revenue from principal Business	主营业务成本 Cost of principal Business	营业利润 Operating Profits	营业税金及附加 Operating Taxes and Extra Charges	利润总额 Total Profits
总 计	**Total**	**4 156 371.8**	**3 133 842.8**	**536 296.4**	**82 323.0**	**559 776.9**
铁路	Railways					
公路	Highways	442 722.3	406 710.9	－6 712.3	6 924.2	9 918.1
水运	Waterways	266 035.6	285 136.7	－44 270.9	1 280.5	－40 731.8
民航	Civil Aviation	76 080.9	48 112.5	10 677.1	3 260.1	10 644.0
港口	Ports	2 368 805.2	1 920 632.2	292 451.5	40 232.4	292 663.4
邮政	Postal Services	75 161.4	65 799.0	2 859.6	838.6	3 642.4
电信	Telecommunication Services	927 566.4	407 451.5	281 291.4	29 787.2	283 640.8

14－5 邮电通讯基本情况(2012 年)

BASIC CONDITIONS OF POSTAL AND TELECOMMUNICATION SERVICES(2012)

市、区名称	Region	邮电局(处) Post Office (unit)	#提供邮政全功能服务的 of which:Providing Omni-directional Services	邮路总长度(公里) Length of Postal Routes(km)	邮运汽车(辆) Vehicles for Postal Services(unit)	信筒、信箱(个) Post Boxes (unit)
总　计	**Total**	**668**	**217**	**7 131**	**297**	**743**
市　区	Urban Area	149	33	4 583	139	274
#崂山区	Huangdao District	35	8	127	21	56
原黄岛区	Orginal Huangdao District	40	9	205	21	29
即墨市	Jimo	85	34	522	24	75
胶州市	Jiaozhou	72	29	295	29	63
原胶南市	Original Jiaonan	86	28	463	13	63
平度市	Pingdu	120	50	636	28	127
莱西市	Laixi	70	26	300	22	56

14－5 续表 1

continued

市、区名称	Region	固定电话市话交换机容量(门) Capacity of Urban Fixed Telephone Exchanges(line)	固定电话市话用户数(户) Urban Fixed Telephone Subscribers (subscriber)	固定电话农村交换机容量(门) Capacity of Rural Fixed Telephone Exchanges(line)	固定电话农村用户数(户) Rural Fixed Telephone Subscribers (subscriber)	移动电话交换机容量(户) Capacity of Mobile Telephone Exchanges (subscriber)	年末移动电话用户(户) Mobile Telephone Subscribersat Year-end (subscriber)
总　计	**Total**	**3 466 080**	**1 636 455**	**1 139 090**	**894 991**	**21 200 000**	**11 739 507**
市　区	Urban Area	2 815 819	1 097 432	332 518	329 439	8 991 529	4 225 315
#崂山区	Huangdao District	82 637	104 780	39 521	27 835	833 349	673 211
原黄岛区	Original Huang-dao District	133 412	99 010	28 181	23 978	1 666 989	574 899
即墨市	Jimo	99 888	87 335	166 858	151 666	2 314 848	1 307 637
胶州市	Jiaozhou	108 062	75 957	91 374	71 038	1 614 923	956 553
原胶南市	Original Jiaonan	91 183	69 626	89 521	83 663	1 450 122	944 526
平度市	Pingdu	69 419	58 986	160 861	151 655	1 732 933	1 160 866
莱西市	Laixi	65 660	43 329	80 256	55 717	944 217	756 499

14－5 续表2
continued

市、区名称	Region	函件（出口）（万件） Number of Letters (10000 pcs)	邮政储蓄期末余额（万元） Balance of Postal Savings at Term-end (10 000 yuan)	特快专递（万件） Express Mail Services (10000 pcs)	邮电业务总量（万元 2010 年价）Business Volume of Postal and Telecommunication Services (10000 yuan at 2010 price)	报纸期发份数（万份） Issue of Newspapers (10000 copies)	杂志期发份数（万份） Issue of Magazines (10000 copies)
总　计	**Total**	**8 497.68**	**2 038 435.99**	**96.64**	**2 086 784.04**	**63.42**	**38.15**
市　区	Urban Area	3 602.17	236 869.18	37.16	885 405.24	22.53	19.81
#崂山区	Huangdao District	505.14	102 196.59	13.05	124 364.05	5.36	3.40
原黄岛区	Original Huangdao District	444.10	81 474.65	10.38	187 878.98	4.09	1.74
即墨市	Jimo	710.91	392 080.94	7.96	210 434.05	6.45	1.79
胶州市	Jiaozhou	1 163.09	336 671.38	8.40	96 490.83	5.71	3.31
原胶南市	Original Jiaonan	749.12	224 768.73	6.46	142 982.29	5.16	1.96
平度市	Pingdu	925.30	477 425.10	8.01	149 661.23	9.93	2.65
莱西市	Laixi	397.85	186 949.42	5.22	90 403.44	4.19	3.49

主要统计指标解释

货(客)运量 指在一定时期内,各运输部门实际运送的货物(旅客)数量。是反映运输业为国民经济和人民生活服务的数量指标,也是制定和检查运输生产计划,研究运输发展规模和速度的重要指标。货运按吨计算,客运按人计算。货物不论运输距离长短,货物类别,均按实际重量统计;旅客不论行程远近或票价多少,均按一人一次作为客运量统计。半价票、小孩票也按一人统计。

货物(旅客)周转量 指在一定时期内,由各种运输工具运送的货物(旅客)数量与其相应运输距离的乘积之总和。是反映运输业生产总成果的重要指标,也是编制和检查运输生产计划,计算运输效益、劳动生产率以及核算运输单位成本的主要基础资料。通常以吨公里和人公里为计算单位。计算货物周转量通常按发出站与到达站之间的最短距离,也就是计费距离计算。

港口货物吞吐量 指经水运进出沿海主要港区范围,并经过装卸的货物数量,包括邮件及办理托运手续的行李、包裹以及补给运输船舶的燃、物料和淡水。货物吞吐量按货物流向分为进口、出口吞吐量,按货物交流性质分为外贸货物吞吐量和国内贸易货物吞吐量。货物吞吐量的货类构成及其流向,是衡量港口生产能力大小的重要指标。

邮电业务总量 指以货币表现的邮电部门用于传递信息和提供其他邮电服务的总数量。它综合反映了一定时期邮电工作的总成果,是研究邮电业务量构成和发展趋势的重要指标。根据邮电管理体制不同,分为中央国营业务总量和地方国营业务总量。它用各种邮电分类业务量,如函件件数、电报份数、长话张数、市内电话和农村电话的年均户数、订销报刊累计份数等,分别乘以相应的平均单位(不变价),加总后再加上出租电路和设备的收入、代用户维护电话交换机和线路等设备的收入、其他业务收入求得。

Explanatory Notes on Main Statistical Indicators

Freight (Passenger) Traffic refers to the volume of freight (passenger) transported with various means. Freight transport is calculated in tons and passenger traffic is calculated in the number of persons. Despite the type of freight and traveling distance, the freight transport is calculated in the actual weight of the goods; and despite the traveling dístance and ticket price, the passenger traffic is calculated by the principle that one person can be counted only once in one travel. The passengers who travel with a half price ticket or a child ticket is also calculated as one person. The freight (passenger) traffic provides a quantitative measure to show how the transport industry serves the national economy and people, and is also an important indicator for planning the transport industry and for studying the development scale and speed of the transport industry.

Freight Ton-kilometers (Passenger-kilometers) refer to the sum of the products of the volume of transported cargo (passengers) multiplying by the transport distance. It is an important indicator to reflect the achievement of transportation industry. Normally, the shortest distance between the departure station and the destination station (i. e., the payable distance) is the basis to calculate the freight ton-kilometers. This is an important indicator to show the total results of the transport industry, to prepare and examine the transport plan and to measure the efficiency, the labour productivity and the unit cost of transport.

Volume of Freight Handled in Ports refers to the volume of cargo passing in and out the harbor area of the major coastal ports and having been loaded and unloaded. The volume includes that of the postal matters, registered luggage and fuels, materials and fresh water as supplies of the ships. The volume of freight handled may be classified by direction of flow as freight for import and freight for export, or by nature of cargo as freight for domestic trade and freight for foreign trade. As an important indicator, the volume of freight handled by type of cargo and by main flow direction reflects the production capacity of ports.

Businesss Volume of Postal and Telecommunication Services refers to the total amount of the information delivered and other post and telecommunication services provided by the post and telecommunication departments for the customers. It is arrived by first multiplying the business volume of different types, such as number of letters, telegrams, long distance calls, city and rural telephone (fixed price) and then adding these products together, plus the income from maintenance of telephone switchboards and lines, and the income from other business operations. The service revenue of posts and telecommunications reflects the total achievements by the post and telecommunication departments during a given period of time in a comprehensive way, and is an important indicator to study the composition and development of the post and telecommunication business.

15 批发和零售业 WHOLESALE AND RETAIL TRADES

简要说明

一、本篇资料的主要内容

本篇资料主要反映了全市批发和零售业经营情况和效益情况，主要包括批发和零售业商品流转及财务情况、批发和零售业网点及从业人员、亿元以上商品交易市场、社会消费品零售总额等内容。

二、本篇资料的来源

本篇资料来源于批发和零售业统计年报和定期报表统计资料；网点资料依据市工商局提供的个体私营经济注册登记资料测算。由市统计局外经贸易统计处整理提供。

Brief Introduction

I. Main Content

Data in this chapter show the development of wholesale and retail trade of the whole city, mainly including the circulation and financial indices of commodities in the wholesale and retail trade, outlets and employment of wholesale and retail trade, commodity exchange markets over 100 million yuan, Total retail sales of consumer goods, etc.

II. Source of Data

Data in this chapter are based on annual report and regular reports of wholesale and retail trade. Data on outlets are based on registration information of individual and private economy provided by Qingdao Municipal Bureau of Industry and Commerce.

Data in this chapter are prepared and compiled by the Division of Trade and External Economic Relations Statistics of Qingdao Municipal Bureau of Statistics.

15－1 社会消费品零售总额(1985－2012年)

TOTAL RETAIL SALES OF CONSUMER GOODS(1985-2012)

单位:万元(10 000 yuan)

年份 Year	消费品零售总额 Total Retail Sales of Consumer Goods	批发零售业 Wholesale and Retail Trades	住宿餐饮业 Hotels and Catering Services	其他行业 Others
1985	307 222	231 477	16 996	18 753
1986	364 091	269 418	21 384	27 118
1987	432 569	310 658	23 319	32 617
1988	590 538	434 572	32 304	45 449
1989	619 941	450 812	34 083	56 303
1990	658 264	484 770	35 568	67 863
1991	760 562	566 767	43 320	56 812
1992	888 411	666 911	53 045	67 392
1993	1 384 533	1 031 794	80 077	96 759
1994	1 880 654	1 352 073	127 313	202 937
1995	2 376 776	1 637 349	186 028	305 947
1996	2 708 527	1 873 008	220 322	321 325
1997	3 008 981	2 105 728	241 928	361 248
1998	3 368 736	2 322 209	277 696	411 210
1999	3 762 754	2 715 635	315 307	391 388
2000	4 282 871	3 116 990	387 944	403 854
2001	4 911 735	3 561 731	507 012	433 851
2002	5 574 364	4 162 676	638 358	402 654
2003	6 455 113	5 283 584	849 032	322 497
2004	7 475 022	6 266 750	1 017 193	191 079
2005	8 701 057	7 304 660	1 176 539	219 858
2006	10 163 457	8 458 226	1 443 120	262 111
2007	12 162 246	9 995 772	1 837 754	328 720
2008	14 922 153	12 995 842	1 554 086	372 225
2009	17 302 231	14 232 954	2 549 203	520 074
2010	19 611 331	17 151 504	2 459 827	
2011	23 023 703	20 153 079	2 870 624	
2012	26 356 180	23 043 005	3 313 175	

注:1. 自2003年开始消费品零售总额不再包括制造业零售额和农民对非农居民的销售额分组。
2. 自2005年起,住宿业从其它行业调整到住宿餐饮业中。
3. 根据第二次经济普查结果,对2005年以来的历史数据进行了调整。

Note:1. Since 2003, retail sales of manufacturing and retail sales of rural residents to urban residents are excluded in total retail sales of consumer goods.
2. Since 2005, hotels is adjusted to hotels and catering services from the others.
3. Historical data since 2005 have been adjusted according to results of the Second China Economic Census.

15 -2 分市、区社会消费品零售总额(2012 年)
TOTAL RETAIL SALES OF CONSUMER GOODS BY REGION(2012)

单位:万元(10 000 yuan)

市、区名称	Region	消费品零售总额 Total Retail Sales of Consumer Goods	按行业分 Grouped By Sector	
			批发零售业 Wholesale and Retail Trades	住宿餐饮业 Hotels and Catering Services
总计	**Total**	**26 356 180**	**23 043 005**	**3 313 175**
市区	Urban Area	14 992 355	12 974 969	2 017 386
市南区	Shinan District	3 761 830	3 084 035	677 795
原市北区	Original Shibei District	3 015 333	2 634 141	381 192
原四方区	Original Sifang District	1 713 651	1 632 600	81 051
李沧区	Licang District	2 314 485	2 074 461	240 024
崂山区	Laoshan District	1 241 536	1 113 095	128 441
原黄岛区	Original Huangdao District	1 445 997	1 170 808	275 189
城阳区	Chengyang District	1 499 523	1 265 829	233 694
即墨市	Jimo	2 716 675	2 481 240	235 435
胶州市	Jiaozhou	2 295 011	1 966 280	328 731
原胶南市	Original Jiaonan	1 986 795	1 767 531	219 264
平度市	Pingdu	2 492 785	2 230 566	262 219
莱西市	Laixi	1 872 559	1 622 419	250 140

15-3 限额以上批发和零售业商品购销存总额(2012年)
TOTAL PURCHASES,SALES AND STOCK OF ENTERPRISES ABOVE DESIGNATED SIZE OF WHOLESALE AND RETAIL TRADES(2012)

单位:万元(10 000 yuan)

项目	Item	商品销售总额 Total Sales Value	批发总额 Wholesale Value	零售总额 Retail Value	库存总额 Stock
总计	**Total**	**46 190 644**	**37 023 105**	**9 167 539**	**2 669 178**
#国有企业	State-owned Enterprises	4 688 702	4 566 423	122 279	227 799
集体企业	Collective-owned Enterprises	1 715 061	1 674 910	40 151	59 877
其它企业	Other Enterprises	39 786 881	30 781 772	9 005 109	2 381 502
#农、林、牧产品批发	Wholesale of Farm Produce and Livestock Products	1 250 050	1 249 991	59	85 219
食品、饮料及烟草制品批发	Wholesale of Food, Beverages and Tobaccos	2 017 239	1 995 801	21 438	172 665
纺织、服装及家庭用品批发	Retail of Textiles, Garments and Daily Consumer Articles	7 618 711	7 401 829	216 881	437 306
文化、体育用品及器材批发	Wholesale of Culture, Sports Appliances and Equipments	210 506	206 571	3 935	26 577
医药及医疗器材批发	Wholesale of Medicines and Medical Appliances	895 636	865 352	30 284	51 409
矿产品、建材及化工产品批发	Wholesale of Mineral Products, Building Materials and Chemical Products	21 621 754	20 354 559	1 267 194	726 851
机械设备、五金产品及电子产品批发	Wholesale of Machinery, Hardware and Electronic Equipment	3 278 960	3 245 332	33 628	126 633
贸易经纪与代理	Trade Broker and Agency	288 157	260 942	27 216	426
其它批发业	Other Wholesale not Classified Elsewhere	633 708	633 708		21 935
#综合零售	Integrated Retail Trade	3 224 828	221 681	3 003 147	356 181
食品、饮料及烟草制品专门零售	Retail of Food, Beverages and Tobaccos	71 844	26 793	45 052	13 835
纺织、服装及日用品专门零售	Retail of Textiles, Garments and Daily Consumer Articles	354 512	69 917	284 595	115 911
文化、体育用品及器材专门零售	Retail of Culture, Sports Appliances and Equipments	120 024	42 529	77 495	26 669
医药及医疗器材专门零售	Retail of Medicines and Medical Appliances	136 644	35 426	101 218	38 930
汽车、摩托车、燃料及零配件专门零售	Retail of Motor Vehicles, Motorcycles, Fuel and Parts	3 769 522	214 416	3 555 106	388 298
家用电器及电子产品专门零售	Retail of Household Electric Appliances and Electronic Products	493 054	102 538	390 516	54 170
五金、家具及室内装饰材料专门零售	Retail of Hardware, Furniture and Decoration Materials	95 040	36 501	58 539	10 043
货摊、无店铺及其他零售业	Non-shop and Other Retails	110 455	59 219	51 236	16 120

15－4 限额以上批发和零售业商品分类销售额(2012 年)

SALES VALUE OF ENTERPRISES ABOVE DESIGNATED SIZE OF WHOLESALE AND RETAIL TRADES BY CATEGORY OF COMMODITIES(2012)

单位:万元(10 000 yuan)

项　　目	Item	销售总额 Total Sales Value	#批发总额 Wholesale Value	零售总额 Retail Value
销售总额	**Total Sales Value**	**46 464 297**	**36 953 420**	**9 510 878**
一、粮油、食品、饮料、烟酒类	Grain & Oil,Food, Beverages, Tobacco and Liquor	3 591 803	2 399 649	1 192 154
#粮油、食品类	Grain & Oil and Food	2 034 927	1 157 925	877 002
粮油类	Grain and Oil	457 116	328 759	128 356
肉禽蛋类	Meat, Poultry and Eggs	307 333	137 829	169 505
水产品类	Aquatic Products	150 792	77 945	72 847
蔬果类	Vegetable and Fruit	51 841	26 242	25 599
干鲜果品类	Dried and Fresh Fruit	80 601	38 907	41 694
饮料类	Beverages	181 738	76 365	105 373
烟酒类	Tobacco and Liquor	1 375 138	1 165 359	209 779
二、服装鞋帽、针、纺织品类	Clothing, Shoes, Hats and Textiles	3 039 979	1 694 272	1 345 707
#服装类	Clothing	1 896 935	966 634	930 301
鞋帽类	Shoes and Hats	465 553	144 266	321 287
针、纺织品类	Knitwear and Textiles	677 491	583 372	94 119
三、化妆品类	Cosmetics	259 391	62 808	196 583
四、金银珠宝类	Gold, Silver and Jewellery	284 617	47 493	237 124
五、日用品类	Articles for Daily Use	511 898	212 960	298 938
#洗涤用品类	Washing Articles	113 525	51 444	62 081
儿童玩具类	Children Toys	18 006	5 568	12 438
六、五金、电料类	Hardware and Electrical Materials	330 410	265 671	64 739
七、体育、娱乐用品类	Sports and Recreation Articles	85 905	27 120	58 785
八、书报杂志类	Newspapers and Magazines	124 451	31 065	93 387
九、电子出版物及音像制品类	E-journals and Video Products	8 347	2 088	6 259
十、家用电器和音像器材类	Household Appliances and Video Appliances	5 401 751	4 643 313	758 438
十一、中西药品类	Traditional Chinese and Western Medicines	851 724	707 995	143 729
#西药	Western Medicines	752 445	629 275	123 170
中草药及中成药	Traditional Chinese Medicines	91 137	74 167	16 970
十二、文化办公用品类	Cultural and Offices Appliances	444 938	236 730	208 208
十三、家具类	Furniture	80 366	18 996	61 370
十四、通讯器材类	Communication Appliances	185 903	42 168	143 735
十五、煤炭及制品类	Coal and Related Products	2 054 925	2 039 757	15 168
十六、木材及制品类	Wood and Wooden Products	285 621	285 621	
十七、石油及制品类	Petroleum and Related Products	4 750 051	3 215 400	1 534 651
十八、化工材料及制品类	Chemical Materials and Related Products	2 495 388	2 495 388	
#化肥类	Fertilizers	190 497	190 497	
十九、金属材料类	Metal Materials	12 956 262	12 956 262	
二十、建筑及装潢材料类	Building and Decoration Materials	367 881	256 858	111 023
二十一、机电产品及设备类	Mechanical and Electrical Products	2 218 714	2 203 529	15 185
#农机类	Agricultural Machineries	39 919	39 919	
二十二、汽车类	Automobiles	3 699 697	758 441	2 941 256
二十三、种子饲料类	Seeds and Feedstuff	674 066	674 066	
二十四、棉麻类	Cotton, Hemp	280 057	280 057	
二十五、其他类	Others	1 480 152	1 395 713	84 439

注:此表为定期报表数据。

Note:The data are from regular reports.

15－5 限额以上批发业财务状况(2012年)

FINANCIAL POSITION OF ENTERPRISES ABOVE DESIGNATED SIZE OF WHOLESALE TRADE(2012)

单位:万元(10 000 yuan)

指标	Indicator	合计 Total	国有经济 State-owned Enterprises	集体经济 Collective-owned Enterprises	外商及港澳台经济 Foreign Funded Enterprises and Enterprises with Funds from Hong Kong,Macao and Taiwan	其它 Other Enterprises
单位数	**Number of Enterprises**	**927**	**33**	**7**	**57**	**830**
年末资产负债	**Year-end Assets-Liability**					
资产合计	Total Assets	17 028 807	2 787 845	883 143	363 577	12 994 242
流动资产小计	Sub-total of Current Assets	14 908 184	2 492 937	811 286	322 456	11 281 506
负债合计	Total Liabilities	14 682 173	2 399 288	858 753	231 138	11 192 994
所有者权益合计	Total Owners' Equities	2 346 635	388 557	24 390	132 439	1 801 249
损益及分配	**Loss,Profits and Distribution**					
主营业务收入	Revenue from Principal Business	34 688 433	4 154 020	1 546 091	1 068 677	27 919 644
主营业务成本	Cost of Principal Business	33 002 418	3 866 072	1 501 775	969 564	26 665 007
主营业务税金及附加	Taxes and Extra Charges on Principal Business	95 972	56 124	1 068	2 397	36 383
主营业务利润	Profits from Principal Business	1 590 042	231 824	43 247	96 717	1 218 254
其他业务利润	Profits from other Business	70 986	10 086	1 078	2 984	56 838
营业费用	Operating Costs	704 533	62 945	12 041	50 274	579 273
管理费用	Management Expenses	370 488	66 296	26 085	22 991	255 116
财务费用	Financial Expenses	152 725	5 765	7 011	1 535	138 415
利润总额	Total Profits	686 449	122 462	1 150	28 047	534 790
经济效益	**Economic Benefit**					
商品经营费用率%	Ratio of Operating Costs to Revenue from Principal Business	2.03	1.52	0.78	4.70	2.07
商品销售利润率%	Ratio of Profit to Sales Revenue	4.58	5.58	2.80	9.05	4.36

15－6 限额以上零售业财务状况(2012 年)

FINANCIAL POSITION OF ENTERPRISES ABOVE DESIGNATED SIZE OF RETAIL TRADE(2012)

单位:万元(10 000 yuan)

指标	Indicator	合计 Total	国有经济 State-owned Enterprises	集体经济 Collective-owned Enterprises	外商及港澳台经济 Foreign Funded Enterprises and Enterprises with Funds from Hong Kong, Macao and Taiwan	其它 Other Enterprises
单位数	**Number of Enterprises**	**573**	**13**	**5**	**28**	**527**
年末资产负债	**Year-end Assets-Liability**					
资产合计	Total Assets	4 450 244	61 551	16 741	732 888	3 639 065
流动资产小计	Sub-total of Current Assets	2 775 451	45 924	13 692	482 417	2 233 419
负债合计	Total Liabilities	3 303 743	48 415	16 281	511 667	2 727 380
所有者权益合计	Total Owners' Equities	1 146 501	13 136	459	221 221	911 685
损益及分配	**Loss, Profits and Distribution**					
主营业务收入	Revenue from Principal Business	7 214 127	111 366	32 331	1 141 522	5 928 908
主营业务成本	Cost of Principal Business	6 477 028	99 467	30 045	976 179	5 371 337
主营业务税金及附加	Taxes and Extra Charges on Principal Business	29 170	159	20	4 284	24 707
主营业务利润	Profits from Principal Business	707 929	11 740	2 266	161 059	532 864
其他业务利润	Profits from other Business	126 438	564	84	33 082	92 708
营业费用	Operating Costs	419 565	5 408	508	127 494	286 155
管理费用	Management Expenses	308 043	3 945	1 109	90 273	212 717
财务费用	Financial Expenses	69 555	152	172	2 845	66 385
利润总额	Total Profits	120 849	2 762	478	－29 909	147 518
经济效益	**Economic Benefit**					
商品经营费用率%	Ratio of Operating Costs to Revenue from Principal Business	5.82	4.86	1.57	11.17	4.83
商品销售利润率%	Ratio of Profit to Sales Revenue	9.81	10.54	7.01	14.11	8.99

15－7 分市、区城乡亿元商品交易市场分布情况(2012 年)

BASIC STATISTICS ON COMMODITY EXCHANGE MARKETS OF TRANSACTION VALUE OVER 100 MILLION YUAN BY REGION(2012)

市区名称	Region	亿元商品交易市场数量(个) Number of Commodity Exchange Markets of Transaction Value over 100 Million Yuan(unit)			亿元商品交易市场成交额(亿元) Turnover of Commodity Exchange Markets of Transaction Value over 100 Million Yuan (100 million yuan)		
		合计 Total	#综合市场 Integrated Markets	专业市场 Special Markets	合计 Total	#综合市场 Integrated Markets	专业市场 Special Markets
总计	**Total**	**69**	**9**	**60**	**1 217.7**	**195.4**	**1 022.3**
市区	Urban Area	30	2	28	516.8	48.2	468.6
#崂山区	Laoshan District	2	0	2	2.5	0.0	2.5
原黄岛区	Original Huangdao District	3	0	3	16.5	0.0	16.5
城阳区	Chengyang District	4	0	4	303.7	0.0	303.7
即墨市	Jimo	12	1	11	399.9	82.1	317.8
胶州市	Jiaozhou	8	2	6	148.9	42.7	106.2
原胶南市	Original Jiaonan	4	1	3	32.5	5.4	27.1
平度市	Pingdu	14	3	11	104.6	17.0	87.6
莱西市	Laixi	1	0	1	15.0	0.0	15.0

15-8 按经济类型分批发业企业网点数(2012年底)
OUTLETS OF WHOLESALE TRADES BY ECONOMIC TYPE(END OF 2012)

单位：个(unit)

市、区名称	Region	合计 Total	分经济类型 Grouped By Economic Type 国有及控股 State-owned and State-holding	私营 Private	其他 Others	外商投资 Foreign Funded
全市总计	**Total**	**24 105**	**247**	**21 937**	**1 450**	**471**
市区	Urban Area	18 797	182	17 110	1 060	445
市南区	Shinan District	5 577	61	4 790	561	165
原市北区	Original Shibei District	3 316	30	3 245	31	10
原四方区	Original Sifang District	2 745	36	2 685	12	12
李沧区	Licang District	1 456	25	1 397	13	21
崂山区	Laoshan District	1 403	9	1 210	142	42
原黄岛区	Original Huangdao District	2 613	20	2 363	181	49
城阳区	Chengyang District	1 687	1	1 420	120	146
即墨市	Jimo	1 509	6	1 433	61	9
胶州市	Jiaozhou	1 353	6	1 268	77	2
原胶南市	Original Jiaonan	693	23	469	197	4
平度市	Pingdu	860	25	785	45	5
莱西市	Laixi	893	5	872	10	6

15-9 按经济类型分批发业企业从业人员(2012年底)
EMPLOYMENT OF WHOLESALE TRADES BY ECONOMIC TYPE(END OF 2012)

单位：人(person)

市、区名称	Region	合计 Total Trades	分经济类型 Grouped By Economic Type 国有及控股 State-owned and State-holding	私营 Private	其他 Others	外商投资 Foreign Funded
全市总计	**Total**	**218 782**	**9 520**	**178 038**	**25 999**	**5 225**
市区	Urban Area	159 241	7 695	125 317	21 396	4 833
市南区	Shinan District	51 964	1 887	38 148	10 141	1 788
原市北区	Original Shibei District	27 935	2 380	25 125	342	88
原四方区	Original Sifang District	17 348	801	13 211	3 266	70
李沧区	Licang District	10 960	409	10 223	45	283
崂山区	Laoshan District	17 896	1 905	9 415	5 401	1 175
原黄岛区	Original Huangdao District	17 716	303	14 965	1 729	719
城阳区	Chengyang District	15 422	10	14 230	472	710
即墨市	Jimo	11 712	164	10 741	743	64
胶州市	Jiaozhou	15 782	226	14 523	1 011	22
原胶南市	Original Jiaonan	7 452	318	4 784	2 288	62
平度市	Pingdu	9 848	902	8 563	298	85
莱西市	Laixi	14 747	215	14 110	263	159

15－10 按经济类型分零售业企业网点数(2012年底)
OUTLETS OF RETAIL TRADES BY ECONOMIC TYPE(END OF 2012)

单位：个(unit)

市、区名称	Region	合计 Total	分经济类型 Grouped By Economic Type			
			国有及控股 State-owned and State-holding	私营 Private	其他 Others	外商投资 Foreign Funded
全市总计	**Total**	**12 127**	**242**	**10 201**	**1 498**	**186**
市 区	Urban Area	7 124	144	6 164	638	178
市南区	Shinan District	1 236	23	1 001	180	32
原市北区	Original Shibei District	2 363	26	2 241	80	16
原四方区	Original Sifang District	470	31	293	146	0
李沧区	Licang District	775	25	710	17	23
崂山区	Laoshan District	475	7	422	41	5
原黄岛区	Original Huangdao District	830	5	725	92	8
城阳区	Chengyang District	975	27	772	82	94
即墨市	Jimo	875	15	781	76	3
胶州市	Jiaozhou	1 004	11	947	45	1
原胶南市	Original Jiaonan	1 421	39	1 028	353	1
平度市	Pingdu	969	19	683	266	1
莱西市	Laixi	734	14	598	120	2

15－11 按经济类型分零售业企业从业人员(2012年底)
EMPLOYMENT OF RETAIL TRADES BY ECONOMIC TYPE(END OF 2012)

单位：人(person)

市、区名称	Region	合计 Total	分经济类型 Grouped By Economic Type			
			国有及控股 State-owned and State-holding	私营 Private	其他 Others	外商投资 Foreign Funded
全市总计	**Total**	**123 406**	**2 956**	**91 296**	**18 374**	**10 780**
市 区	Urban Area	74 272	1 762	53 976	8 771	9 763
市南区	Shinan District	17 091	781	7 180	3 248	5 882
原市北区	Original Shibei District	19 351	146	18 320	498	387
原四方区	Original Sifang District	6 267	178	2 977	3 112	0
李沧区	Licang District	9 160	141	8 601	272	146
崂山区	Laoshan District	5 012	92	3 853	16	1 051
原黄岛区	Original Huangdao District	6 138	18	4 795	1 290	35
城阳区	Chengyang District	11 253	406	8 250	335	2 262
即墨市	Jimo	7 902	146	5 513	1 525	718
胶州市	Jiaozhou	9 331	245	8 793	266	27
原胶南市	Original Jiaonan	12 629	280	9 471	2 869	9
平度市	Pingdu	10 641	323	6 823	3 342	153
莱西市	Laixi	8 631	200	6 720	1 601	110

15－12 批发和零售业个体网点数(2012 年底)

INDIVIDUAL OUTLETS OF WHOLESALE AND RETAIL TRADES(END OF 2012)

单位:个(unit)

市、区名称	Region	合计 Total	批发业 Wholesale Trade	零售业 Retail Trade
全市总计	**Total**	**369 015**	**73 803**	**295 212**
市　区	Urban Area	126 153	15 102	111 051
市南区	Shinan District	11 751	195	11 556
原市北区	Original Shibei District	21 426	1 302	20 124
原四方区	Original Sifang District	11 038	1 433	9 605
李沧区	Licang District	18 974	1 940	17 034
崂山区	Laoshan District	6 205	313	5 892
原黄岛区	Original Huangdao District	32 042	1 456	30 586
城阳区	Chengyang District	24 717	8 463	16 254
即墨市	Jimo	57 553	14 952	42 601
胶州市	Jiaozhou	48 434	13 001	35 433
原胶南市	Original Jiaonan	43 885	7 129	36 756
平度市	Pingdu	63 253	14 624	48 629
莱西市	Laixi	29 737	8 995	20 742

15－13 批发和零售业个体从业人员(2012 年底)

INDIVIDUAL EMPLOYMENT OF WHOLESALE AND RETAIL TRADES(END OF 2012)

单位:人(person)

市、区名称	Region	合计 Total	批发业 Wholesale Trade	零售业 Retail Trade
全市总计	**Total**	**841 350**	**189 884**	**651 466**
市　区	Urban Area	285 799	25 809	259 990
市南区	Shinan District	31 841	601	31 240
原市北区	Original Shibei District	68 729	4 914	63 815
原四方区	Original Sifang District	17 753	2 812	14 941
李沧区	Licang District	37 319	1 147	36 172
崂山区	Laoshan District	12 851	716	12 135
原黄岛区	Original Huangdao District	75 123	3 898	71 225
城阳区	Chengyang District	42 183	11 721	30 462
即墨市	Jimo	136 653	51 864	84 789
胶州市	Jiaozhou	113 922	31 011	82 911
原胶南市	Original Jiaonan	111 691	19 060	92 631
平度市	Pingdu	119 661	37 263	82 398
莱西市	Laixi	73 624	24 877	48 747

主要统计指标解释

社会消费品零售总额 指各种经济类型的批发和零售业、住宿和餐饮业以及其他行业对城乡居民和社会集团的消费品零售额总和。该指标从2003年开始不再包括制造业零售额和农民对非农居民的零售额。

商品购进总额 指从本企业(单位)以外的单位和个人购进(包括从国外直接进口)作为转卖或加工后转卖的商品。这个指标反映批发零售贸易业从国内、国外市场上购进商品的总量。商品购进总额包括:(1)从工农业生产者购进的商品;(2)从出版社、报社的出版发行部门购进的图书、杂志和报纸;(3)从各种类型的批发零售贸易企业(单位)购进的商品;(4)从其他单位购进的商品,如从机关、团体、企业、单位购进的剩余物资,从餐饮业、服务业购进的商品,从海关、市场管理部门购进的缉私和没收的商品,向居民收购的废旧商品等;(5)从国(境)外直接进口的商品,但不包括企业(单位)为自身经营用和未通过买卖行为而收入的商品以及销售退回、商品损益等。

商品销售总额 指对本企业(单位)以外的单位和个人出售(包括对国(境)外直接出口)的商品。这个指标反映批发零售贸易业在国内市场上销售商品以及出口商品的总量。商品销售总额包括:(1)售给城乡居民和社会集团消费用的商品;(2)售给工业、农业、建筑业、运输邮电业、批发零售贸易业、餐饮业、服务业等作为生产、经营使用的商品;(3)售给批发零售贸易业作为转卖或加工后转卖的商品;(4)对国(境)外直接出口的商品。不包括:出售本企业(单位)自用的废旧包装用品,未通过买卖行为付出的商品,经本单位介绍,由买卖双方直接结算,本单位只收取手续费的业务,购货退出的商品以及商品损耗和损失等。

Explanatory Notes on Main Statistical Indicators

Total Retail Sales of Consumer Goods refers to the sum of retail sales of consumer goods sold by all sectors of the national economy to urban and rural residents and social groups. Sectors of the national economy include wholesale and retail trade, accommodation and catering trade and others. Since 2003, retail sales of manufacture and retail sales of rural residents to urban residents are excluded in total retail sales.

Total Purchases of Commodities refer to the total value of purchases of commodities by the enterprises (establishments) from other establishments or individuals (including direct import from abroad) for the purpose of re-selling, either with or without further processing of the commodities purchased. This indicator is used to show the total value of purchases of commodities by wholesale and retail establishments from domestic and overseas markets. The total purchases include: (1) agricultural and industrial products purchased from producers; (2) books, magazines and newspapers purchased from distribution departments of the publishers; (3) commodities purchased from wholesale and retail establishments of different status of registration; (4) commodities purchased from other units, such as surplus materials purchased from government agencies, enterprises or institutions, commodities purchased from catering and service establishments, confiscated goods purchased from customs authorities or market management agencies, second-hand goods and wastes purchased from residents; and (5) commodities directly imported from abroad. Excluded are commodities purchased by enterprises (establishments) for use in their own business operation, commodities obtained without buying or selling procedures, rejected commodities, etc.

Total Sales of Commodities refer to value of commodities sold by the establishments to other establishments and individuals (including direct export). This indicator is used to show the total value of sales of commodities at domestic markets and export. The total sales include: (1) commodities sold to urban and rural residents and social groups for their consumption; (2) commodities sold to establishments in industry, agriculture, construction, transportation, post and telecommunications, wholesale and retail trades, hotels and catering services, and public utility for their production and operation; (3) commodities sold to wholesale and retail establishments for re-selling, with or without further processing; and (4) commodities for direct export to other countries. Excluded are selling of waste packaging materials used by the establishments (units) themselves, commodities transferred without buying or selling procedures, commission income from brokerage in transactions for which settlement is directly handled by buyers and sellers, rejected commodities in the purchase, loss in commodities, etc.

16 住宿、餐饮业和旅游
HOTELS, CATERING SERVICES AND TOURISM

简要说明

一、本篇资料的主要内容

本篇资料主要反映了全市住宿和餐饮业的经营情况和效益情况以及旅游的基本情况，主要包括住宿和餐饮业经营情况和财务情况、网点及从业人员、涉外以及国内旅游基本情况等方面的内容。

二、本篇资料的来源

本篇资料中住宿和餐饮业经营情况和财务情况资料来源于住宿和餐饮业统计年报和定期报表统计资料；网点资料依据市工商局提供的个体私营经济注册登记资料测算；旅游资料来源于市旅游局。由市统计局外经贸易统计处整理提供。

Brief Introduction

I. Main Content

Data in this chapter show the development of wholesale and retail trade and tourism of the whole city, mainly including the circulation and financial indices of hotels and catering services, outlets and employment, international and domestic tourism, etc.

II. Source of Data

Data on hotels and catering services are based on annual report and regular reports of hotels and catering services. Data on outlets are based on registration information of individual and private economy, and provided by Qingdao Municipal Bureau of Industry and Commerce. Data on international tourism are provided by Qingdao Tourism Bureau. The above data are prepared and compiled by the Division of Trade and External Economic Relations Statistics of Qingdao Municipal Bureau of Statistics.

16－1 限额以上住宿和餐饮业法人企业经营情况(2012年)

BUSINESS CONDITIONS OF ENTERPRISES OF HOTELS AND CATERING SERVICES ABOVE DESIGNATED SIZE(2012)

单位:万元(10 000 yuan)

项目	Item	营业额 Turnover	#客房收入 Income from Guest Rooms	餐费收入 Catering Income	商品销售收入 Income from Commodity Sales	其他收入 Other Income
总　计	**Total**	**996 652**	**223 364**	**696 422**	**31 779**	**45 087**
一、住宿业	**Hotels**	**435 735**	**204 205**	**175 643**	**14 709**	**41 178**
#国有企业	State-owned Enterprises	140 283	54 484	54 055	8 809	22 936
集体企业	Collective-owned Enterprises	2 995	1 107	1 657	16	216
其他企业	Other Enterprises	292 457	148 614	119 931	5 884	18 026
#独立门店	Freestanding Stores	402 096	192 354	162 770	11 292	35 680
连锁总店	General Chain Stores	486	427	34	8	17
连锁门店	Chain Stores	4 438	3 075	1 186	142	35
其他门店	Other Stores	28 715	8 349	11 653	3 267	5 446
#五星	Five Star Class	135 583	65 690	54 110	1 304	14 479
四星	Four Star Class	126 066	51 000	62 316	4 358	8 392
三星	Three Star Class	66 541	31 740	26 371	4 274	4 156
二星	Two Star Class	4 633	1 980	2 173	285	195
一星	One Star Class	1 326	1 156	170		
其他	Others	101 586	52 639	30 503	4 488	13 956
二、餐饮业	**Catering Services**	**560 917**	**19 159**	**520 779**	**17 070**	**3 909**
#国有企业	State-owned Enterprises	4 205	1 232	2 778	22	173
集体企业	Collective-owned Enterprises	1 052	80	972		
其他企业	Other Enterprises	555 660	17 847	517 029	17 048	3 736
#独立门店	Freestanding Stores	274 503	17 921	236 688	16 101	3 793
连锁总店	General Chain Stores	270 840		270 165	674	1
连锁门店	Chain Stores	2 618	627	1 965	14	12
其他门店	Other Stores	12 956	611	11 961	281	103

16-2 限额以上住宿业财务状况(2012 年)
FINANCIAL SITUATION OF HOTELS ABOVE DESIGNATED SIZE(2012)

单位:万元(10 000 yuan)

指标	Indicator	合计 Total	国有经济 State-owned Enterprises	集体经济 Collective-owned Enterprises	外商及港澳台经济 Foreign Funded Enterprises and Enterprises with Funds from Hong Kong, Macao and Taiwan	其它 Other Enterprises
单位数	**Number of Enterprises**	**162**	**35**	**4**	**13**	**110**
年末资产负债	**Year-end Assets-Liability**					
资产合计	Total Assets	1 107 415	415 064	4 887	253 888	433 576
流动资产小计	Sub-total of Current Assets	384 236	100 141	1 436	62 073	220 587
负债合计	Total Liabilities	757 068	220 690	5 334	188 842	342 202
所有者权益合计	Total Owners' Equities	350 347	194 374	-447	65 046	91 374
损益及分配	**Loss Profits and Distribution**					
主营业务收入	Revenue from Principal Business	421 287	136 591	2 956	95 695	186 046
主营业务成本	Cost of Principal Business	124 589	42 152	1 951	19 886	60 600
主营业务税金及附加	Taxes and Extra Charges on Principal Business	23 022	7 185	152	5 345	10 340
主营业务利润	Profits from Principal Business	273 677	87 255	853	70 464	115 106
其他业务利润	Profits from other Business	8 894	2 544	6	4 862	1 483
营业费用	Operating Costs	127 882	47 365	236	22 000	58 232
管理费用	Management Expenses	153 642	57 167	665	43 608	52 202
财务费用	Financial Expenses	17 078	1 958	15	6 430	8 676
利润总额	Total Profits	-7 942	-14 091	-69	5 277	941
其他	**Others**					
本年应付工资总额	Total Wages Payable in This Year	90 287	36 891	757	15 562	37 077
主营业务利润率	Profitability of Principal Business	64.96	63.88	28.84	73.63	61.87

16-3 限额以上餐饮业财务状况(2012年)

FINANCIAL SITUATION OF CATERING SERVICES ABOVE DESIGNATED SIZE(2012)

单位:万元(10 000 yuan)

指标	Indicator	合计 Total	国有经济 State-owned Enterprises	集体经济 Collective-owned Enterprises	外商及港澳台经济 Foreign Funded Enterprises and Enterprises with Funds from Hong Kong, Macao and Taiwan	其它 Other Enterprises
单位数	**Number of Enterprises**	**200**	**4**	**2**	**22**	**172**
年末资产负债	**Year-end Assets-Liability**					
资产合计	Total Assets	529 681	7 129	1 172	164 726	356 654
流动资产小计	Sub-total of Current Assets	217 016	1 412	235	48 489	166 880
负债合计	Total Liabilities	409 198	3 036	146	131 614	274 403
所有者权益合计	Total Owners' Equities	120 483	4 094	1 026	33 112	82 251
损益及分配	**Loss Profits and Distribution**					
主营业务收入	Revenue from Principal Business	551 168	3 978	889	272 733	273 568
主营业务成本	Cost of Principal Business	274 086	2 604	762	133 931	136 790
主营业务税金及附加	Taxes and Extra Charges on Principal Business	30 092	192	24	15 282	14 595
主营业务利润	Profits from Principal Business	246 990	1 183	103	123 520	122 184
其他业务利润	Profits from other Business	6 893	61		73	6 759
营业费用	Operating Costs	148 950	692	74	75 928	72 257
管理费用	Management Expenses	61 233	695	51	25 113	35 373
财务费用	Financial Expenses	13 377	54	9	3 367	9 947
利润总额	Total Profits	24 002	-177	-31	19 362	4 849
其它	**Others**					
本年应付工资总额	Total Wages Payable in This Year	86 441	914	58	41 126	44 344
主营业务利润率	Profitability of Principal Business	44.81	29.74	11.53	45.29	44.66

16－4 按经济类型分餐饮业企业网点数(2012 年底)

OUTLETS OF CATERING SERVICES BY ECONOMIC TYPE(END OF 2012)

单位:个(unit)

市、区名称	Region	餐饮业 Catering Services	分经济类型 Grouped by Economic Types			
			国有及控股 State-owned and State-holding	私营 Private	其他 Others	外商投资 Foreign Funded
全市总计	**Total**	**1 929**	**21**	**1557**	**174**	**177**
市　区	Urban Area	1 074	16	809	87	162
市南区	Shinan District	306	7	205	43	51
原市北区	Original Shibei District	175	1	157		17
原四方区	Original Sifang District	68		55		13
李沧区	Licang District	105	3	75	5	22
崂山区	Laoshan District	99	3	75		21
原黄岛区	Original Huangdao District	178	2	155	7	14
城阳区	Chengyang District	143		87	32	24
即墨市	Jimo	195		186	7	2
胶州市	Jiaozhou	143	2	124	11	6
原胶南市	Original Jiaonan	137	1	118	16	2
平度市	Pingdu	207	1	162	43	1
莱西市	Laixi	173	1	158	10	4

16－5 按经济类型分餐饮业企业从业人员(2012 年底)

EMPLOYMENT OF CATERING SERVICES BY ECONOMIC TYPE(END OF 2012)

单位:人(person)

市、区名称	Region	合计 Total	分经济类型 Grouped by Economic Types			
			国有及控股 State-owned and State-holding	私营 Private	其他 Others	外商投资 Foreign Funded
全市总计	**Total**	**46 193**	**1 696**	**34 248**	**4 365**	**5 884**
市　区	Urban Area	28 757	853	20 024	2 812	5 068
市南区	Shinan District	9 572	660	5 224	2 200	1 488
原市北区	Original Shibei District	5 254	18	4 112		1 124
原四方区	Original Sifang District	1 347		1 196		151
李沧区	Licang District	2 770	37	2 181	77	475
崂山区	Laoshan District	2 779	111	1 956		712
原黄岛区	Original Huangdao District	3 286	27	2 890	115	254
城阳区	Chengyang District	3 749		2 465	420	864
即墨市	Jimo	4 229		3 847	267	115
胶州市	Jiaozhou	3 335	511	2 297	321	206
原胶南市	Original Jiaonan	2 557	12	2 109	347	89
平度市	Pingdu	3 346	134	2 570	533	109
莱西市	Laixi	3 969	186	3 401	85	297

16－6 按经济类型分住宿业企业网点数(2012 年底)
OUTLETS OF HOTELS BY ECONOMIC TYPE(END OF 2012)

单位:个(unit)

市、区名称	Region	合 计 Total	分经济类型 Grouped by Economic Types 国有及控股 State-owned and State-holding	私营 Private	其他 Others	外商投资 Foreign Funded
合 计	**Total**	**804**	**83**	**604**	**94**	**23**
市 区	Urban Area	682	74	495	92	21
市南区	Shinan District	220	35	126	51	8
原市北区	Original Shibei District	168	12	143	4	9
原四方区	Original Sifang District	67	15	52		
李沧区	Licang District	60	2	58		
崂山区	Laoshan District	50	7	35	7	1
原黄岛区	Original Huangdao District	87	3	66	18	
城阳区	Chengyang District	30		15	12	3
即墨市	Jimo	28	4	22		2
胶州市	Jiaozhou	30	1	29		
原胶南市	Original Jiaonan	32	3	29		
平度市	Pingdu	22	1	21		
莱西市	Laixi	10		8	2	

16－7 按经济类型分住宿业企业从业人员(2012 年底)
EMPLOYMENT OF HOTELS BY ECONOMIC TYPE(END OF 2012)

单位:人(person)

市、区名称	Region	住宿业 Hotels	分经济类型 Grouped by Economic Types 国有及控股 State-owned and State-holding	私营 Private	其他 Others	外商投资 Foreign Funded
合 计	**Total**	**30 815**	**7 125**	**14 080**	**7 823**	**1 787**
市 区	Urban Area	26 171	6 053	10 771	7 823	1 524
市南区	Shinan District	14 275	4 780	2 897	5 210	1 388
原市北区	Original Shibei District	2 453	667	1 725	15	46
原四方区	Original Sifang District	859	153	706		
李沧区	Licang District	1 337	106	1 231		
崂山区	Laoshan District	2 335	175	1 432	728	
原黄岛区	Original Huangdao District	2 500	172	1 560	768	
城阳区	Chengyang District	2 412		1 220	1 102	90
即墨市	Jimo	1 259	463	533		263
胶州市	Jiaozhou	958	236	722		
原胶南市	Original Jiaonan	733	255	478		
平度市	Pingdu	982	118	864		
莱西市	Laixi	712		712		

16 –8 住宿和餐饮业个体网点数(2012 年底)

INDIVIDUAL OUTLETS OF HOTELS AND CATERING SERVICES(END OF 2012)

单位:个(unit)

市、区名称	Region	合 计 Total	住宿业 Hotels	餐饮业 Catering Services
合 计	**Total**	**48 013**	**9 717**	**38 296**
市 区	Urban Area	23 059	5 514	17 545
市南区	Shinan District	3 104	1 185	1 919
原市北区	Original Shibei District	3 185	820	2 365
原四方区	Original Sifang District	2 202	791	1 411
李沧区	Licang District	3 336	633	2 703
崂山区	Laoshan District	1 775	333	1 442
原黄岛区	Original Huangdao District	7 201	655	6 546
城阳区	Chengyang District	2 256	1 097	1 159
即墨市	Jimo	4 201	507	3 694
胶州市	Jiaozhou	7 782	1 271	6 511
原胶南市	Original Jiaonan	4 450	1 013	3 437
平度市	Pingdu	5 862	1 205	4 657
莱西市	Laixi	2 659	207	2 452

16 –9 住宿和餐饮业个体从业人员(2012 年底)

INDIVIDUAL EMPLOYMENT OF HOTELS AND CATERING SERVICES(END OF 2012)

单位:人(person)

市、区名称	Region	合 计 Total	住宿业 Hotels	餐饮业 Catering Services
合 计	**Total**	**199 311**	**39 323**	**159 988**
市 区	Urban Area	115 004	25 525	89 479
市南区	Shinan District	17 061	4 402	12 659
原市北区	Original Shibei District	17 736	3 154	14 582
原四方区	Original Sifang District	14 527	10 013	4 514
李沧区	Licang District	10 876	1 535	9 341
崂山区	Laoshan District	6 599	831	5 768
原黄岛区	Original Huangdao District	28 955	2 492	26 463
城阳区	Chengyang District	19 250	3 098	16 152
即墨市	Jimo	14 003	1 202	12 801
胶州市	Jiaozhou	24 059	4 023	20 036
原胶南市	Original Jiaonan	17 948	3 230	14 718
平度市	Pingdu	17 805	4 729	13 076
莱西市	Laixi	10 492	614	9 878

16－10 入境旅游人数(1990－2012年)

NUMBER OF OVERSEA VISITOR ARRIVALS (1990－2012)

单位:人次(person-time)

项目	Item	1990	1995	2000	2005	2006	2007	2008	2009	2010	2011	2012
总计	**Total**	**72 019**	**177 797**	**260 592**	**684 407**	**854 462**	**1 081 476**	**800 455**	**1 000 670**	**1 080 511**	**1 156 391**	**1 270 113**
一、外国人	**Foreigner**	**22 329**	**79 469**	**177 098**	**596 177**	**751 403**	**925 384**	**697 391**	**801 424**	**826 628**	**809 043**	**877 593**
韩国	Korea		20 330	69 878	295 111	373 712	509 369	340 648	363 181	382 225	298 096	338 383
日本	Japan	9 426	34 296	67 215	177 121	221 542	242 500	210 090	261 553	242 082	216 755	185 613
美国	United States	2 454	5 607	10 384	23 284	32 256	37 509	28 998	28 745	35 539	45 842	48 431
俄罗斯	Russia	163	449	4 820	12 062	17 457	10 949	3 774	9 525	15 793	15 750	26 432
德国	Germany	1 494	2 660	3 820	10 646	14 440	14 560	11 261	14 735	21 626	26 178	26 311
新加坡	Singapore	626	2 998	6 321	6 060	8 332	10 918	10 683	17 453	13 444	16 626	16 316
英国	United Kingdom	712	1 545	2 798	5 744	10 047	12 175	10 657	9 103	17 639	23 955	28 385
加拿大	Canada	556	930	1 865	4 397	5 727	7 095	5 467	7 741	9 279	12 007	11 678
法国	France	461	825	2 491	5 166	7 377	8 452	6 067	7 030	11 766	12 019	15 595
意大利	Italy	437	746	1 555	3 963	4 022	6 062	3 871	3 747	3 867	7 028	5 622
澳大利亚	Australia	351	1 009	1 817	4 257	7 106	8 505	7 940	6 641	8 223	15 465	16 644
菲律宾	Philippines	270	558	7 947	3 459	1 812	2 461	2 075	7 800	14 140	14 259	7 546
泰国	Thailand	406	299	780	3 261	2 464	2 682	2 236	3 685	2 572	3 271	2 369
印尼	Indonesia	237	670	1 241	2 349	2 301	3 127	1 589	4 221	7 863	8 128	4 571
新西兰	New Zealand	68	192	442	710	980	1 106	1 161	2 029	1 597	6 265	6 448
二、港澳和台湾同胞	**Chinese Compatriots from Hong Kong, Macao and Taiwan**	**29 276**	**39 223**	**60 367**	**88 230**	**103 059**	**156 092**	**103 064**	**199 246**	**253 883**	**347 348**	**392 520**

16－11 入境旅游收入(1990－2012年)

EARNINGS FROM INTERNATIONAL TOURISM (1990－2012)

单位:万元(10 000 yuan)

项目	Item	1990	1995	2000	2005	2006	2007	2008	2009	2010	2011	2012
总计	**Total**	**13 534**	**48 320**	**118 164**	**340 899**	**434 100**	**502 926**	**347 645**	**377 000**	**399 688**	**441 171**	**519 495**
旅游购物	Shopping	4 409	5 933	20 742	67 047	78 882	95 705	66 053	70 763	74 104	80 823	93 872
住宿费	Accommodation	3 267	18 509	17 443	37 277	44 011	53 662	37 198	41 093	43 933	59 823	59 378
餐饮费	Dining	1 160	5 361	11 223	33 557	39 611	48 182	33 374	36 569	38 747	40 191	51 378
交通费	Transportation	3 619	11 404	35 252	128 112	140 831	183 425	9 039	9 877	145 551	134 425	170 238
邮电费	Postal and Telecommunication Services	585	3 246	5 502	18 394	21 654	26 111	17 382	18 812	19 081	16 720	23 014
文化娱乐费	Culture and Entertainment	89	1 302	6 894	20 240	23 900	29 180	20 163	22 394	24 032	36 132	32 832
游览	Sightseeing						26 502	18 773	21 037	22 978	51 705	32 832
其他	Other Services				36 272	85 210	40 158	145 663	29 745	31 262	21 353	55 951

16 -12 国内旅游人数(2012 年)
NUMBER OF DOMESTIC TOURISTS(2012)

指　　标	Indicator	单位	Unit	2012
国内旅游人数	**Number of Domestic Tourists**	**万人次**	**10000 person-times**	**5 591**
1. 过夜旅游者人数	Number of Overnight Tourists	万人次	10000 person-times	3 711
(1)旅游住宿设施国内旅游人数	Domestic Tourists Staying Overnight at Hotels	万人次	10000 person-times	2 389
(2)住亲友家去景点的国内旅游人数	Domestic Tourists Staying Overnight at Relatives and Friends' s Home	万人次	10000 person-times	1 322
2. 不过夜旅游者(一日游人数)	Number of Same-day (One-day Sightseeing) Tourists	万人次	10000 person-times	1 880
旅游景点接待一日游人数	One-day Sightseeing Tourists Received by Tour Scenes	万人次	10000 person-times	1 880
(1)本地一日游人数	Number of Local One-day Sightseeing Tourists	万人次	10000 person-times	1 219
(2)外地一日游人数	Number of One-day Sightseeing Tourists from Outside Areas	万人次	10000 person-times	661
国内旅游人均花费	**Per Capita Expenditure of Domestic Tourist**	**元**	**yuan**	**1 351**
其中:旅游住宿设施国内旅游者人均花费	of which: Staying Overnight at Hotels	元	yuan	1 927
住亲友家去景点的国内旅游者人均花费	Staying Overnight at Relatives and Friends' s Home	元	yuan	1 378
一日游旅游者人均花费	Per Capita Expenditure of One-day Sightseeing Tourist	元	yuan	601
国内旅游收入	**Earings from Domestic Tourism**	**亿元**	**100 million yuan**	**756**
1. 接待过夜旅游者收入	Earings from Overnight Tourists	万元	10000 yuan	6 425 999
(1) 旅游住宿设施接待国内旅游者收入	of which: Staying Overnight at Hotels	万元	10000 yuan	4 604 096
(2)住亲友家去景点的国内旅游者旅游花费	Staying Overnight at Relatives and Friends' s Home	万元	10000 yuan	1 821 903
2. 接待不过夜旅游者 (一日游)收入	Earings from Same-day(One-day Sightseeing) Tourists	万元	10000 yuan	1 129 101

主要统计指标解释

住宿餐饮业营业额 指住宿和餐饮业法人企业、产业活动单位在经营活动中因提供服务或销售商品等取得的收入，包括客房收入、餐费收入、商品销售收入和其他收入。客房收入指住宿和餐饮业法人企业、产业活动单位在经营活动中因提供住宿服务取得的客房收入。餐费收入指住宿和餐饮业法人企业、产业活动单位因为顾客提供就餐服务取得的收入，包括经烹饪、调制加工后出售的各种食品，如主食、炒菜、凉拌菜等的收入。商品销售收入指住宿和餐饮业法人企业、产业活动单位伴随服务而出售商品所取得的收入。其他收入指营业收入中除客房收入、餐费收入、商品销售收入以外的其他收入，包括娱乐、健身和商务服务等。

国内旅游者 是指不以谋求职业、获取报酬为目的，离开惯常居住环境，到国内其它地方从事参观、游览、度假等旅游活动(包括外出探亲、疗养、考察、参加会议和从事商务、科技、文化、教育、宗教活动过程中的旅游活动)，出行距离超过10公里，出游时间超过6小时，但不超过12个月的我国大陆居民。

入境旅游者 指来我国参观、访问、旅行、探亲、访友、休养、考察、参加会议和从事经济、科技、文化、教育、体育、宗教等活动的外国人、华侨、港澳和台湾同胞的人数。不包括外国在我国的常驻机构，如领事馆、通讯社、企业办事处的工作人员；来我国常住的外国专家、留学生以及在岸逗留不过夜人员。

Explanatory Notes on Main Statistical Indicators

Business Revenue of Hotels and Catering Services refer to revenue received from providing services or selling commodities by corporate enterprises and establishments engaged in hotel and catering services, including income from hotel rooms, from catering services, from selling of commodities and from other services. Income from hotel rooms refers to income of corporate enterprises and establishments by providing lodging services. Income from catering services refers to income of corporate enterprises and establishments by providing catering services, including selling of cooked or prepared foods such as stable food, cooked dishes or cold dishes. Income from selling of commodities refers to income of corporate enterprises and establishments by selling commodities that accompany the services they provide. Income from other activities refers to income received other than income from hotel rooms, catering services or selling of commodities, such as income from providing recreation, fitness or business services.

Domestic Tourists refers to residents in mainland China who are not for the purpose of seeking employment, remuneration, and leaving the usual living environment, elsewhere to engage in domestic visitors, sightseeing, vacation travel (including to go out to visit relatives, infirmary, observing, participate in the meeting and engage in business, science and technology, culture, education, religious activities in the course of tourism activities), trip distance of more than 10 km, trips longer than six hours, but not more than 12 months.

Entrance Tourists refers to foreigners, overseas Chinese, Chinese compatriots from Hong Kong, Macao and Taiwan coming to China for sight-seeing, visits, tours, family reunions, vacations, study tours, conferences and other activities of a business, scientific and technological, cultural, educational and religious nature. It does not include representatives and employees of resident institutions of foreign countries in China such as embassies, consulates, news agencies and offices of foreign companies and organizations, nor does it include long-term foreign experts or students residing in China, or persons in transition without spending a night in China.

17 教育、科技和文化
EDUCATION ,SCIENCE & TECHNOLOY AND CULTURE

简要说明

一、本篇资料的主要内容

本篇资料主要反映了全市教育、科技和文化事业基本情况。教育部分主要包括高等教育、中等教育、初等教育、成人教育、职业教育、幼儿园等方面的基本情况。科技部分主要包括科研机构、科学技术奖励、大中型工业企业技术开发情况。文化部分主要包括文化、文物、广播、电视、报纸杂志出版、图书出版等方面的发展状况。

二、本篇资料的来源

1、教育部分，技工学校的资料来源于市人力资源和社会保障局，其他资料来源于市教育局。

2、科技部分，科研机构及科技奖励资料来源于市科技局，大中型工业企业科技活动资料来源于市统计局统计调查年报。

3、文化部分，图书、杂志、报纸出版有关资料来源于青岛出版集团、海大出版社其他资料来源于市文化广电新闻出版局。

本篇资料由市统计局人口和社会科技统计处整理提供。

Brief Introduction

I. Main Content

Data in this chapter show the basic conditions of education, science & technology and culture. Data on education show the development of higher education, secondary education, primary education, adult education, vocational education and kindergartens. Data on science & technology show the basic conditions of science research institutions, scientific and technological achievements and prizes, scientific & technological activities of large and medium-size industrial enterprises. Data on culture show the basic conditions of arts, cultural relics, broadcasting, television and publication of newspapers, magazines and books.

II. Source of Data

(1)In education component, data on the basic conditions of technical schools are provided by Qingdao Municipal Bureau of Human Resources and Social Security, and the other data on education are provided by Qingdao Municipal Bureau of Education.

(2)In science & technology component, data on science research institutions and scientific & technological achievements and prizes are provided by Qingdao Municipal Bureau of Science and Technology. Data on scientific and technological activities are from the annual report of scientific and technological activities, which is provided by Qingdao Municipal Bureau of Statistics.

(3)In culture component, data on publication of books, magazines and newspapers are provided by Qingdao Publishing Group and Ocean University Press. The other data are provided by Qingdao Municipal Bureau of Cluture, Broadcasting, Television, Press and Publication.

Data in this chapter are provided and compiled by the Division of Population and Science & Technology of Qingdao Municipal Bureau of Statistics.

17－1 各级各类学校基本情况(2012年)

BASIC STATISTICS ON SCHOOLS BY LEVEL AND TYPE OF SCHOOL(2012)

项目	Item	学校数(所) Schools (unit)	毕业生数(人) Graduates (person)	招生数(人) New Students Enrollment(person)	在校学生数(人) Students Enrollment(person)	教职工数(人) Teachers and Staff(person)	#专任教师 of which: Full-time Teachers
研究生	Postgraduates		8 006	9 984	27 647		6 410
普通高等学校	Regular Institutions of Higher Education	22	79 791	87 981	296 645	29 445	18 183
中等专业学校	Specialized Secondary Schools	8	7 113	9 278	27 005	1 273	872
技工学校	Technical Schools	24	8 186	8 559	27 099	1 858	1 287
职业学校	Vocational Schools	49	28 002	21 511	65 419	7 074	5 238
普通中学	Regular Secondary Schools	292	121 442	119 134	369 580	37 301	31 952
初中	Junior Secondary Schools	232	85 529	77 787	244 995	24 447	22 190
高中	Senior Secondary Schools	60	35 913	41 347	124 585	12 854	9 762
小学	Primary Schools	840	77 589	82 685	484 985	33 182	31 697
特殊教育学校	Special Education Schools	13	281	314	1 527	596	466
幼儿园	Kindergartens	2 475	76 873	72 017	232 403	21 812	14 669
成人高等学校	Adult Institutions of Higher Education	2	29 638	39 682	98 289	623	238
成人中等学校	Adult Secondary Education Schools	7	3 997	4 808	16 287	304	203
成人初等学校	Adult Primary Education Schools						

注:1. 研究生栏中专任教师指的是指导教师。
2. 成人中等学校仅包括成人中学和成人中专。

Note:1. Full-time teachers of postgraduates refer to instructors.
2. Adult secondary education schools refer to adult secondary schools and adult specialized secondary schools.

17 -2 主要年份各级各类学校在校学生数

MAJOR YEAR'S STUDENTS ENROLLMENT OF SCHOOLS BY LEVEL AND TYPE OF SCHOOL

单位：人（person）

年份 Year	普通高等学校 Regular Institutions of Higher Education	中等学校 Secondary Schools	中等专业学校 Specialized Secondary Schools	普通中学 Regular Secondary Schools	职业中学 Vocational Schools	技工学校 Technical Schools	小学 Primary Schools
1949	1 007	13 804	1 600	12 204			213 470
1952	2 761	27 951	3 770	24 181			413 286
1957	3 133	56 689	4 985	51 604	100		482 397
1962	4 381	62 646	2 791	58 639	243	973	522 921
1965	2 987	99 605	9 405	88 187	1 490	523	788 485
1970	320	222 521	105	220 262	2 154		723 433
1975	1 151	350 309	3 144	346 403		762	928 153
1978	3 465	464 584	4 269	457 460	2 000	865	634 905
1980	6 783	325 935	5 195	318 193	1 344	1 203	816 970
1985	10 631	327 446	11 475	279 915	33 945	2 111	691 341
1988	14 408	352 576	11 819	306 943	28 933	4 881	629 212
1989	15 183	348 367	14 401	296 318	32 283	5 365	634 794
1990	15 433	351 365	15 118	296 163	34 568	5 516	632 314
1991	15 491	353 410	14 618	298 568	34 421	5 803	612 772
1992	16 470	367 480	14 763	307 903	38 242	6 572	585 38[illegible]
1993	23 858	383 043	16 877	318 179	40 743	7 244	583 585
1994	25 018	420 077	20 582	347 667	43 734	8 094	593 419
1995	24 908	450 212	23 744	372 335	46 044	8 089	595 891
1996	26 076	468 561	26 951	382 760	50 131	8 719	607 284
1997	27 434	463 619	28 543	362 305	61 640	11 131	626 749
1998	29 507	442 525	28 757	336 918	65 989	10 861	625 308
1999	33 681	459 520	26 955	352 238	70 236	10 091	583 594
2000	46 131	497 391	25 192	398 458	63 894	9 847	534 922
2001	60 728	542 400	25 358	443 693	62 003	11 346	499 147
2002	82 539	575 599	27 421	467 628	67 085	13 465	478 634
2003	168 439	586 704	28 948	461 435	75 221	21 100	467 560
2004	201 739	598 804	30 881	436 117	101 553	30 253	476 897
2005	239 761	569 230	33 522	391 148	106 400	38 160	479 781
2006	260 339	554 308	32 051	365 192	116 487	40 578	483 892
2007	264 917	558 527	28 011	360 410	130 156	39 950	484 775
2008	269 314	582 932	25 330	373 884	143 126	40 592	477 230
2009	275 157	564 476	22 739	377 427	127 792	36 518	465 031
2010	284 788	535 079	24 014	380 025	98 560	32 480	462 722
2011	291 453	505 051	25 905	373 226	74 892	31 028	479 513
2012	296 645	489 103	27 005	369 580	65 419	27 099	484 985

17 –3 主要年份普通高等学校基本情况

MAJOR YEAR'S BASIC STATISTICS ON REGULAR INSTITUTIONS OF HIGHER EDUCATION

单位:人(person)

年份 Year	学校数(所) Schools (unit)	毕业生数 Graduates	招生数 New Students Enrollment	在校学生数 Students Enrollment	教职工数 Teachers and Staff	#专任教师 of which: Full-time Teachers
1949	1		250	1 007	779	226
1952	2	262	565	2 761	12 530	308
1957	2	356	755	3 133	1 308	622
1962	5	647	653	4 381	1 866	749
1965	3	741	529	2 987	1 539	623
1970	2	684		320	1 178	486
1975	2	460	473	1 151	1 353	582
1978	4	739	1 782	3 465	2 829	1 176
1980	6	431	1 717	6 783	4 182	1 606
1985	7	1 828	3 823	10 631	5 561	2 181
1988	7	3 496	4 687	14 408	6 875	2 499
1989	7	3 891	4 567	15 183	7 174	2 554
1990	7	4 495	4 745	15 433	7 305	2 624
1991	7	4 880	4 954	15 491	7 282	2 489
1992	7	4 458	5 428	16 470	7 344	2 523
1993	7	3 140	9 449	23 858	7 366	2 520
1994	4	7 059	8 042	25 018	7 466	2 650
1995	4	7 828	7 978	24 908	7 545	2 682
1996	4	6 691	7 956	26 076	7 606	2 745
1997	4	7 091	8 503	27 434	7 790	2 813
1998	4	6 912	8 849	29 507	7 662	2 907
1999	4	7 202	11 584	33 681	7 662	2 928
2000	6	7 128	18 427	46 131	8 030	3 278
2001	6	8 991	22 787	60 728	8 706	4 058
2002	7	13 053	29 731	82 539	9 517	4 723
2003	25	25 747	61 975	168 439	18 911	10 293
2004	25	34 860	70 022	201 739	21 437	12 347
2005	25	46 114	79 725	239 761	23 078	13 894
2006	25	55 931	79 094	260 339	24 881	15 195
2007	25	68 354	78 728	264 917	25 956	16 005
2008	25	75 198	86 878	269 314	26 654	16 805
2009	25	69 475	81 025	275 157	26 983	16 870
2010	25	70 450	82 220	284 788	28 145	16 996
2011	22	79 466	84 434	291 453	28 151	17 120
2012	22	79 791	87 981	296 645	29 445	18 183

17－4 各类成人教育基本情况(2012 年)

BASIC STATISTICS ON ADULT EDUCATION(2012)

单位:人(person)

各类学校	Schools by Type of School	学校数(所) Schools (unit)	毕业生数 Graduates	招生数 New Students Enrollment	在校学生数 Students Enrollment	教职工数 Teachers and Staff	#专任教师 of which: Full-time Teachers
总　计	**Total**	**9**	**33 635**	**44 490**	**114 576**	**927**	**441**
成人高等教育	Adult Higher Education	2	29 638	39 682	98 289	623	238
广播电视大学	Broadcasting and TV Universities	1	293	113	361	108	62
职工、农民大学	Universities of Vocational and Agricultural Education						
函授、夜大学	Correspondence and Evening College Education		29 258	39 569	97 840		
管理干部学校	Cadre Management Schools	1	87		88	515	176
成人中等教育	Adult Secondary Education	7	3 997	4 808	16 287	304	203
成人中等专业学校	Adult Specialized Secondary Schools	7	3 997	4 808	16 287	304	203

注:本年度成人高等自学考试毕业 3266 人;参加成人高等单科班、进修班、短训班、专业证书班学习毕业(结业)32036 人。

Note:3266 persons have been graduated from adult higher tech-oneself tests in the year, 32036 persons have been graduated from adult higher single subject courses, training courses, short-term training course and specialized diploma courses.

17－5 分市、区普通中学情况(2012 年)

BASIC STATISTICS ON REGULAR SECONDARY SCHOOLS BY REGION(2012)

单位:人(person)

市、区名称	Region	普通高中 Regular Senior Secondary Schools				普通初中 Regular Junior Secondary Schools			
		学校数(所) Schools (unit)	毕业生数 Graduates	招生数 New Students Enrollment	在校生数 Students Enrollment	学校数(所) Schools (unit)	毕业生数 Graduates	招生数 New Students Enrollment	在校生数 Students Enrollment
总　计	**Total**	**60**	**35 913**	**41 347**	**124 585**	**232**	**85 529**	**77 787**	**244 995**
市　区	Urban Area	34	13 465	14 381	42 549	76	26 517	28 286	82 993
#崂山区	Laoshan District	7	1 499	1 871	5 329	9	2 453	2 111	6 362
原黄岛区	Original Huangdao District	3	1 808	2 133	6 326	9	4 002	4 264	12 485
城阳区	Chengyang District	5	2 094	2 555	8 058	15	5 704	5 809	17 432
即墨市	Jimo	7	5 686	6 249	18 606	29	13 325	11 318	35 323
胶州市	Jiaozhou	5	3 536	4 998	14 180	22	10 926	9 062	28 351
原胶南市	Original Jiaonan	7	3 663	5 012	15 040	25	10 152	8 465	26 324
平度市	Pingdu	5	5 987	6 893	22 149	46	16 070	13 813	44 713
莱西市	Laixi	2	3 576	3 814	12 061	34	8 539	6 843	27 291

17－6 分市、区职业中学、小学情况(2012 年)

BASIC STATISTICS ON VOCATIONAL SECONDARY SCHOOLS AND PRIMARY SCHOOLS BY REGION(2012)

单位:人(person)

市、区名称	Region	职业中学 Vocational Secondary Schools				小学 Primary Schools			
		学校数(所) Schools (unit)	毕业生数 Graduates	招生数 New Students Enrollment	在校生数 Students Enrollment	学校数(所) Schools (unit)	毕业生数 Graduates	招生数 New Students Enrollment	在校生数 Students Enrollment
总　计	**Total**	**49**	**28 002**	**21 511**	**65 419**	**840**	**77 589**	**82 685**	**484 985**
市　区	Urban Area	30	11 473	7 192	22 357	243	28 184	31 729	179 968
#崂山区	Laoshan District	1	691	676	2 905	25	2 338	2 817	15 331
原黄岛区	Original Huangdao District	8	4 804	1 685	5 744	32	4 306	5 499	29 809
城阳区	Chengyang District	4	877	859	1 878	60	5 749	7 276	40 156
即墨市	Jimo	4	1 870	1 894	5 855	172	11 228	13 362	77 420
胶州市	Jiaozhou	1	1 805	2 603	7 842	87	8 842	9 607	59 213
原胶南市	Original Jiaonan	9	8 728	5 389	16 981	70	8 382	8 892	53 694
平度市	Pingdu	2	2 613	2 805	7 770	170	14 084	12 207	78 847
莱西市	Laixi	3	1 513	1 628	4 614	98	6 869	6 888	35 843

17－7 分市、区中小学教职工情况(2012 年)
BASIC STATISTICS ON TEACHERS AND STAFF IN SECONDARY AND PRIMARY SCHOOLS BY REGION(2012)

单位:人(person)

市、区名称	Region	普通中学 Regular Secondary Schools		职业中学 Vocational Secondary Schools		小学 Primary Schools	
		教职工数 Teachers and Staff	#专任教师 of which: Full-time Teachers	教职工数 Teachers and Staff	#专任教师 of which: Full-time Teachers	教职工数 Teachers and Staff	#专任教师 of which: Full-time Teachers
总　计	**Total**	**37 301**	**31 952**	**7 074**	**5 238**	**33 182**	**31 697**
市　区	Urban Area	12 685	10 201	3 592	2 474	11 912	11 343
#崂山区	Laoshan District	1 461	1 083	243	145	1 226	1 185
原黄岛区	Original Huangdao District	1 497	1 415	376	273	1 508	1 465
城阳区	Chengyang District	2 618	2 317	848	629	2 299	2 257
即墨市	Jimo	5 509	4 777	663	564	5 101	4 846
胶州市	Jiaozhou	3 963	3 322	682	459	3 990	3 860
原胶南市	Original Jiaonan	4 627	4 204	800	659	3 902	3 782
平度市	Pingdu	6 513	5 822	723	619	5 403	5 186
莱西市	Laixi	4 004	3 626	614	463	2 874	2 680

17－8 分市、区幼儿园基本情况(2012 年)
BASIC STATISTICS ON KINDERGARTENS BY REGION(2012)

单位:人(person)

市、区名称	Region	幼儿园(所) Kindergartens(unit)	幼儿数 Children	教职工数 Teachers and Staff	#专任教师 of which: Full-time Teachers
总　计	**Total**	**2 475**	**232 403**	**21 812**	**14 569**
市　区	Urban Area	581	93 378	11 376	6 361
#崂山区	Laoshan District	96	8 833	1 349	788
原黄岛区	Original Huangdao District	82	14 387	1 670	1 046
城阳区	Chengyang District	134	20 508	2 166	1 733
即墨市	Jimo	425	38 632	2 467	1 808
胶州市	Jiaozhou	464	27 334	2 299	1 605
原胶南市	Original Jiaonan	258	23 814	2 386	1 917
平度市	Pingdu	574	33 422	2 163	1 627
莱西市	Laixi	173	15 823	1 121	851

17－9 科研机构基本情况(1978－2012年)
BASIC STATISTICS ON SCIENTIFIC RESEARCH INSTITUTIONS(1978－2012)

年份 Year	独立自然科研机构(个) Independent Institutions of Natural Scientific Research(unit)	独立自然科研机构中科技人员(人) Personnel of Independent Institutions of Natural Scientific Research(person)	完成科研项目(项) Number of Scientific Research Projects Completed(item)	取得科技成果(项) Number of Achievements in S&T(item)
1978	31	2 701	306	306
1980			481	297
1982	41	2 345	451	451
1983	48	3 182	530	530
1984	53	3 312	507	507
1985	52	3 673	552	552
1986	63	3 998	577	577
1987	76	4 629	579	579
1988	101	5 199	544	510
1989	111	5 885	544	688
1990	141	6 046	414	931
1991	72	5 665	753	753
1992	71	5 726	659	659
1993	69	5 545	546	546
1994	69	5 540	467	467
1995	59	5 286	441	441
1996	58	4 738	613	613
1997	54	4 577	418	418
1998	52	4 142	517	517
1999	58	3 771	606	606
2000	54	3 637	621	621
2001	50	3 191	457	457
2002	52	3 248	406	406
2003	53	3 246	589	589
2004	50	3 226	506	506
2005	50	3 234	438	438
2006	50	3 291	548	548
2007	50	3 432	506	506
2008	42	3 709	416	416
2009	43	3 727	572	572
2010	44	4 088	472	472
2011	47	4 548	345	345
2012	48	4 967	304	304

注:1991年以后不包括民办科研机构。

Note: Since 1991, private institutions of scientific research are not included.

17－10 独立科学研究机构情况(2012 年)
BASIC STATISTICS ON INDEPENDENT INSTITUTIONS OF SCIENTIFIC RESEARCH(2012)

项　目	Item	计量单位	Unit	总　计 Total	中央属 Central	省属 Provincial	地市属 Local	县级市属 County
机构数	Number of Institutions	个	unit	48	11	11	24	2
职工人数	Staff and Workers	人	person	6 940	4 734	963	1 230	13
科技人员	Personnel Engaged in S&T	人	person	4 967	3 265	694	995	13
经费收入	Funding for S&T	万元	10000 yuan	244 077.6	23 448.2	29 029.3	191 523.1	77.0
经费支出	Expenditures for S&T	万元	10000 yuan	205 939.5	174 560.1	19 130.2	12 172.2	77.0

17－11 科学技术奖励情况(2012 年)
AWARD STATISTICS ON SCIENCE AND TECHNOLOGY(2012)

项　目	Item	单位	Unit	自然科学奖 Natural Science Prizes Awarded	技术发明奖 Invention Prizes Awarded	科技进步奖 Scientific And Technological Progress Prizes Awarded	科学技术功勋奖 Scientific And Technological Credit Prizes Awarded	国际科技合作奖 International S&T Cooperation Prizes Award	最高奖 Highest Prizes Award
国家级	**National Level**	**项**	**item**		**2**	**7**			
#一等	First Prize	项	item						
二等	Second Prize	项	item		2	7			
省级	**Provincial Level**	**项**	**item**	**7**	**5**	**93**			
#一等	First Prize	项	item			10			
二等	Second Prize	项	item	4	4	27			
三等	Third Prize	项	item	3	1	56			
市级	**Municipal Level**	**项**	**item**	**14**	**8**	**128**		**3**	**2**
#一等	First Prize	项	item	1	1	13			
二等	Second Prize	项	item	6	6	48			
三等	Third Prize	项	item	7	1	67			

注:国际科技合作奖、最高奖不分等级。

Note:There is no grade in international scientific and technological cooperation prizes award and highest prizes award.

17－12 大中型工业企业技术开发主要相对指标(1990－2012年)

MAJOR INDICATORS OF TECHNOLOGY DEVELOPMENT OF LARGE AND MEDIUM-SIZE INDUSTRIAL ENTERPRISES(1990－2012)

项　目	Item	单位	Unit	1990	1995	2000	2005	2006	2007	2008	2009	2010	2011	2012
企业技术开发人员占全部职工比重	Percentage of Technology Development Personnel to Staff and Workers	%	%	2.3	2.6	5.7	4.4	4.9	5.9	5.6	5.8	6.7	7.7	7.4
科学家工程师占技术开发人员比重	Percentage of Scientists and Engineers to Technology Development Personnel	%	%	32.4	39.0	62.3	66.1	63.1	62.4	63.0				
设有开发机构的企业占企业总数比重	Percentage of Enterprises Having Development Institutions to Total Number of Enterprises	%	%	59.5	59.3	29.7	20.8	21.8	26.1	24.6	24.0	26.2	28.1	26.7
科学家工程师占开发机构人员比重	Percentage of Scientists and Engineers to Personnel of Development Institutions	%	%	37.1	48.1	77.6								
平均每个企业技术开发经费筹集额	Average Funding for Technology Development of Each Enterprise	万元	10 000 yuan	144.0	118.2	873.0	1 535.8	1 577.0	1 805.0	1 815.6				
平均每个企业技术开发经费支出额	Average Expenditures for Technology Development of Each Enterprise	万元	10 000 yuan	125.0	114.5	812.0	1 626.0	1 716.0	1 931.0	1 894.9				
开发新产品用款占经费支出比重	Percentage of Expenditures on New Product Development to Total Expenditures	%	%	81.9	50.8	52.6	55.9	58.4	63.3	66.2				
技术开发经费支出占产品销售收入比重	Percentage of Expenditures on Technology Development to Revenue from Product Sales	%	%	2.1	1.0	3.1	2.7	2.7	2.6	2.3				
新产品产值比重	Percentage of Output Value of New Products	%	%	8.2		35.5	31.3	32.7	28.4	26.8	27.4	28.4	28.8	26.0
新产品销售额比重	Percentage of Sales Volume of New Products	%	%	8.0	12.2	32.7	32.5	32.4	30.5	28.7	28.8	28.9	29.3	27.0
新产品利税额比重	Percentage of Profits and Taxes of New Products	%	%	7.4	18.7	30.6								

17－13 主要年份文化机构数
MAJOR YEAR'S INSTITUTIONS OF CULTURE

单位：个(unit)

年份 Year	合计 Total	#影剧院 Cinemas	文化馆 Cultural Centers	艺术表演团体 Art Performance Troupes
1949	24	9	3	3
1952	50	11	15	8
1957	99	16	11	15
1962	103	17	12	13
1965	117	18	13	13
1970	121	20	12	13
1975	249	21	12	16
1978	402	24	13	15
1980	661	24	12	17
1985	1 290	81	12	11
1988	1 473	84	12	11
1989	1 308	106	12	11
1990	1 323	106	12	11
1991	1 185	108	12	11
1992	1 167	108	12	11
1993	1 079	103	12	11
1994	964	78	12	11
1995	767	61	13	11
1996	761	61	13	11
1997	634	61	12	11
1998	491	51	12	11
1999	638	43	12	11
2000	637	45	12	11
2001	614	44	12	11
2002	590	44	11	11
2003	492	50	11	11
2004	476	29	12	11
2005	478	39	12	12
2006	446	40	12	12
2007	451	40	12	12
2008	456	40	12	12
2009	459	40	12	12
2010	465	40	12	12
2011	470	40	12	10
2012	475	36	12	8

17-14 文化、文物事业机构、人员数(2012 年)

NUMBER OF INSTITUTIONS AND PERSONNEL IN CULTURE AND CULTURAL RELICS(2012)

项目	Item	文化机构数(个) Number of Cultural Institutions(unit)		文化人员数(人) Number of Cultural Personnel(person)	
		2012	2011	2012	2011
总计	**Total**	**250**	**259**	**2 393**	**2 406**
文化事业合计	**Culture**	**233**	**242**	**2 127**	**2 169**
一、艺术事业	Art	22	21	754	856
1. 艺术表演团体	Art Performance Troupes	8	10	620	732
2. 艺术表演场所	Art Centers	9	9	102	106
3. 艺术创作机构	Art Creation Institutions	3		13	
4. 艺术研究机构	Art Research Institutions	2	2	19	18
5. 艺术展览机构	Art Exhibition Institutions				
6. 其他	Others				
二、图书馆事业	Libraries	13	13	270	267
公共图书馆	Public Libraries	13	13	270	267
#县(区)级图书馆	County Libraries	12	12	165	158
三、群众文化事业	Mass Culture	177	186	677	688
1. 群众艺术馆	Mass Art Centers	1	1	52	55
2. 文化馆	Cultural Palaces	12	12	183	182
3. 文化站	Cultural Centers	164	173	442	451
4. 其他	Others				
四、其他文化事业	Other Cultural Units	21	22	426	358
文物事业合计	**Cultural Relics**	**17**	**17**	**266**	**237**
一、文物机构	Cultural Relics Institutions	5	5	38	16
二、博物馆纪念馆	Museums and Memorial Halls	10	10	205	202
三、文物商店	Cultural Relics Shops	1	1	10	8
四、文物科研机构	Scientific and Research Institutions of Cultural Relics	1	1	13	11

17－15 分市、区艺术表演、电影发行及放映机构数(2012 年)

NUMBER OF INSTITUTIONS OF ART PERFORMANCE,FILMS DISTRIBUTION AND PROJECTION BY REGION(2012)

单位:个(unit)

市、区名称	Region	合计 Total	影剧院 Cinemas	电影发行机构 Institutions of Films Distribution	流动放映单位 Travelling Projection Units
总　计	**Total**	**292**	**36**	**2**	**254**
市　区	Urban Area	53	27	2	24
#崂山区	Laoshan District	4	1		3
原黄岛区	Original Huangdao District	11	3		8
城阳区	Chengyang District	13	5		8
即墨市	Jimo	40	3		37
胶州市	Jiaozhou	32	1		31
原胶南市	Original Jiaonan	65	1		64
平度市	Pingdu	63	3		60
莱西市	Laixi	39	1		38

17－16 艺术表演、电影放映情况(2012 年)

STATISTICS ON ART PERFORMANCE AND FILMS PROJECTION(2012)

项　目	Item	机构数(个) Number of Institutions (unit)	座位数(个) Number of Seats (unit)	演出场次(场) Number of Performances (show)	观众人数(万人次) Number of Spectators (10 000 person-times)	票款收入(万元) Income from Ticket Sales (10 000 yuan)
艺术表演总计	Art Performance	9	2 346	116	11	201
电影放映总计	Films Projection	290	33 022	382 649	1 632	15 305
#影剧院	Cinemas	36	33 022	310 672	487	15 305
流动放映单位	Travelling Projection Units	254		71 977	1 145	

17 –17 文化部门艺术剧团情况(2012 年)
STATISTICS ON ART TROUPES OF CULTURAL DEPARTMENT(2012)

项目	Item	剧团数(个) Number of Troupes (unit)	职工人数(人) Staff and Workers (person)	演出场次(场) Number of Performances (show)	观众人数(万人次) Number of Spectators (10 000 person-times)	演出收入(万元) Income from Performance (10 000 yuan)	拨款经费(万元) Appropriation Funds (10 000 yuan)
总计	**Total**	**8**	**621**	**1 117**	**120.6**	**655.4**	**6 215.6**
一、按隶属关系分	**Grouped by Administrative Relationship**						
国营剧团	State-run Troupes	8	621	1 117	120.6	655.4	6 215.6
集体经营剧团	Collective-owned Troupes						
二、按剧种分	**Grouped by Type of Drama**						
1. 话剧团	Drama Troupes	1	95	159	9.5	147.2	964.5
2. 歌舞团	Song and Dance Troupes	1	202	142	13.5	239.1	2 428.1
3. 戏曲剧团	Local Opera Troupes	4	161	489	53.1	193.9	1 272.6
#京剧	of which:Beijing Opera	1	78	83	6.0	73.5	728.0
4. 曲艺团	Recitation and Ballad Troupes						
5. 文工团(艺术团)	Cultural and Performance Troupes	2	163	327	44.5	75.2	1 550.4

17 –18 图书馆、博物馆、文化馆情况
STATISTICS ON LIBRARIES,MUSEUMS AND CULTURAL CENTERS

项目	Item	单位	Unit	2012 全市合计 Total	2012 #市区 Urban Area	2010 全市合计 Total	2010 #市区 Urban Area
公共图书馆	**Public Libraries**	个	**unit**	**13**	**8**	**13**	**8**
工作人员	Staff and Workers	人	person	270	195	267	196
藏书册数	Collection Books	千册	1000 copies	5 304	3 929	4 709	3 506
阅览席位	Seating Capacity of Reading Rooms	张	seat	5 799	4 176	5 507	3 884
读者人数	Readers	万人次	10 000 person-times	408.4	289.5	326.7	233.7
博物馆、纪念馆	**Museums and Memorial Halls**	个	**unit**	**10**	**5**	**10**	**5**
工作人员	Staff and Workers	人	person	205	153	202	153
藏品数量	Collections	万件	10 000 copies	30	24	15.7	10.9
参观人数	Visitors	万人次	10 000 person-times	191	157	161.5	96.5
文化馆	**Cultural Centers**	个	**unit**	**12**	**7**	**12**	**7**

17－19 图书、杂志、报纸出版情况(1990－2012 年)
PUBLICATION OF BOOKS, MAGAZINES AND NEWSPAPERS(1990－2012)

项目	Item	单位	Unit	1990	1995	2000
图书出版	**Publication of Books**					
种数	Number of Publication	种	kind	292	530	572
总印数	Total Printed Copies	万册	10 000 copies	1 626	2 109	1 542
总印张数	Total Printed Sheets	千印张	1 000 sheets	40 358	75 242	71 826
杂志出版	**Publication of Magazines**					
种数	Number of Publication	种	kind	32	34	35
每期平均印数	Average Printed Copies per Issue	万册(份)	10 000 copies	41.71	37.42	75.41
总印数	Total Printed Copies	万册	10 000 copies	452	409	1 249
总印张数	Total Printed Sheets	千印张	1 000 sheets	6 422	5 630	31 946
报纸出版	**Publication of Newspapers**					
种数	Number of Publication	种	kind	4	8	14
每期平均印数	Average Printed Copies per Issue	万份	10 000 copies	64.25	81.51	84.74
总印数	Total Printed Copies	万份	10 000 copies	7 127	16 318	21 309
总印张数	Total Printed Sheets	千印张	1 000 sheets	56 670	231 642	555 503

注：自 2008 年图书出版种数改按种次统计，总印数，总印张数均按此口径进行统计。

Note: Number of book publication in 2008 are according to the type and times of statistical. The total printed copies and total printed sheets are the same calibre.

2005	2006	2007	2008	2009	2010	2011	2012
895	926	788	3 609	3 642	2 562	4 102	4 555
2 873	1 697	1 376	6 055	6 124	6 443	6 713	7 891.3
191 671	194 584	112 337	376 404	396 753	413 917	412 686	459 638.6
44	44	44	45	49	50	47	48
76.95	85.41	72.26	106.5	99.97	100.93	96.3	100
1 755	1 779	1 936	2 587	2 616	2 650	2 766	2 788
69 685	56 913	63 235	83 748	86 064	98 136	80 345	80 348
12	12	12	13	14	15	15	14
174.16	183.26	202.82	231.20	257.89	291.54	297.48	298.6
53 947	57 135	63 800	74 143	78 239	93 255	107 615	107 656
4 138 51	3 944 883	4 773 915	5 624 658	5 877 377	7 130 931	12 346 098	12 347 198

17－20 广播电视业基本情况(1990－2012 年)

BASIC STATISTICS ON RADIO AND TELEVISION STATIONS(1990－2012)

项　目	Item	单位	Unit	1990	1995	2000
一、广播基本情况	**Basic Statistics on Radio**					
电台个数	Number of Radio Stations	座	set	6	8	1
发射台个数	Number of Transmission Stations	座	set	7	9	9
节目套数	Number of Programs	套	set	7	10	10
平均日播音时间	Broadcasting Hours per Day	时:分	hour: minute	53:35	126:35	119:15
#自办节目	of which: Self-programs	时:分	hour: minute	41:15	117:05	107:50
#本年自制广播节目时间	Hours of Programs Making in the Year	小时	hour			
广播人口覆盖率	Radio Coverage of Population	%	%	94	94	96.0
二、电视基本情况	**Basic Statistics on Television**					
电视台个数	Number of Television Stations	座	set	4	8	1
发射台个数	Number of Transmission Stations	座	set	42	48	29
节目套数	Number of Programs	套	set	4	9	9
平均每周播出时间	Broadcasting Hour per Week	时:分	hour: minute	129:10	382:18	489:20
#自办节目	of which: Self-programs	时:分	hour: minute	38:25	327:35	410:54
#本年自制广播节目时间	Hours of Programs Making in the Year	小时	hour			
电视人口覆盖率	TV Coverage of Population	%	%	90.87	92.00	95.04
三、有线电视基本情况	**Basic Statistics on CATV**					
总用户数	Number of Users of CATV	万户	10 000 households			
有线电视入户率	CATV Coverage of Household	%	%			
网络总长	Length of the Network	公里	km			
广播电视卫星收转系统	Satellite Relaying Systems of Radio and Television	座	set			

200[illegible]	2006	2007	2008	2009	2010	2011	2012
[illegible]	1	1	1	1	1	1	1
1[illegible]	10	10	10	10	10	10	10
1[illegible]	12	12	12	12	12	12	12
17[illegible]:[illegible]	190:43	195:23	221:09	220:39	237:23	237:12	238:30
11[illegible]:[illegible]	139:25	137:48	163:49	174:44	183:40	182:48	182:18
3[illegible] 9[illegible]	48 604	50 853	60 892	61 642	64 146	66 075	65 767
[illegible]7[illegible]9	98.0	98.1	98.2	98.3	98.4	98.5	98.6
1	1	1	1	1	1	1	1
11	10	10	10	10	10	10	10
15	15	15	15	15	15	15	15
1 [illegible]2 38	1 653:25	1 659:37	1 618:56	1 640:32	1 771:36	1712:36	1766:27
[illegible]97[illegible]55	827:06	717:47	652:41	660:52	760:18	727:01	734:11
[illegible]11 [illegible]77	12 774	13 089	11 874	9 713	15 406	12 974	16 702
9[illegible] 70	97.80	97.90	98.00	98.10	98.20	98.30	98.41
17[illegible].60	201.60	218.48	218.57	241.55	253.83	268.2	
[illegible].05	84.96	91.29	90.48	93.79	103.72		
4[illegible] 827	46 479	49 303	50 871	51 297	52 617		
[illegible] 062	168	178	162	121	113		

主要统计指标解释

普通高等学校　指按照国家规定的设置标准和审批程序批准举办，通过国家统一招生考试，招收高中毕业生为主要培养对象，实施高等教育的全日制大学、独立设置的学院和高等专科学校、短期职业大学。

成人高等学校　指按照国家有关规定审批，招收通过全国成人高教统一招生考试的具有高中毕业或同等学历的在职从业人员，利用脱产、半脱产、业余或函授等多种形式对其实施高等学历教育，培养高等教育专科或本科毕业水平的专门人才，修业年限、课程设置和总学时数均按高等学历教育要求付诸实施的学校。包括广播电视大学、职工高等学校、农民高等学校、管理干部学院；教育学院、独立设置的函授学院等。

科技活动人员　指直接从事科技活动、以及专门从事科技活动管理和为科技活动提供直接服务，累计的实际工作时间占全年制度工作时间 10% 及以上的人员。

文化事业机构　指从事专业文化工作和为专业文化工作服务的独立建制的单独核算的单位。不包括这些单位另外举办独立核算的其他机构和各部门的业余文化组织。

Explanatory Notes on Main Statistical Indicators

Regular Institutions of Higher Education　refer to educational establishments set up according to the government evaluation and approval procedures, enrolling graduates from senior secondary schools and providing higher education courses and training for senior professionals. They include full-time universities, colleges, high professional schools, high professional vocational schools and others.

Adult Institutions of Higher Education　refer to educational establishments, set up in line with relevant rules approved by the government, enrolling staff and workers with senior secondary school or equivalent education, and providing higher education courses in many forms of correspondence, spare time, or full time for adults. Professionals thus trained receive a qualification equivalent to graduates studying regular courses at regular universities, colleges and professional colleges. Institutions of higher learning for adults include schools of high education for staff and workers, schools of high education for peasants, colleges for management cadres, pedagogical colleges, independent correspondence colleges, Radio and TV universities and other educational establishments.

Personnel Engaged in S&T Activities　refer to personnel directly engaged in S&T activities, in the management of S&T activities, and in providing direct service to S&T activities, who spend over 10% of the total working hours in a year in S&T activities.

Cultural Institutions　refer to units, which have their own organizational system and independent accounting system and specialize in or serve cultural development. They exclude other establishments run by these cultural institutions and amateur cultural groups established by various departments.

18 体育、卫生和民政、司法

SPORTS,PUBLIC HEALTH AND CIVIL AFFAIRS,JUDICIAL AFFAIRS

简 要 说 明

一、本篇资料的主要内容

本篇资料反映了全市体育、卫生、民政、司法等社会事业的基本情况。体育部分主要包括主要年份运动员、教练员、裁判员发展人数、体育运动破纪录、获奖情况。卫生部分主要包括各类卫生机构及其人员、床位数。民政部分主要包括婚姻登记、社会救济、社会福利事业基本情况、殡葬服务情况。司法部分主要包括律师、公证、调解、社会治安基本情况。

二、本篇资料的来源

1、体育部分来源于市体育局。

2、卫生部分来源于市卫生局。

3、民政部分来源于市民政局。

4、司法部分，社会治安资料来源于市公安局，其他资料来源于市司法局。

本篇资料由市统计局人口和社会科技统计处整理提供。

Brief Introduction

I. Main Content

Data in this chapter show the basic conditions of sports, public health, civil affairs and judicial affairs. Data on sports are mainly including the number of athletes, coaches and referees, conditions of record and awards. Data on public health are mainly including the number of health institutions, personnel and beds. Data on civil affairs are mainly including the conditions of marriage registration, social relief, social welfare and funeral services. Data on judicial affairs are mainly including the conditions of lawyers, notarization, mediation and social order.

II. Source of Data

(1)Data on sports are provided by Qingdao Municipal Bureau of Physical.

(2)Data on public health are provided by Qingdao Municipal Bureau of Health.

(3)Data on civil affairs are provided by Qingdao Municipal Bureau of Civil Affairs.

(4)In judicial affairs component, data on social order are provided by Qingdao Municipal Bureau of Public Security and the other data are provided by Qingdao Municipal Bureau of Justice.

Data in this chapter are provided and compiled by the Division of Population and Science & Technology of Qingdao Municipal Bureau of Statistics.

18－1 体育事业情况(1985－2012年)
STATISTICS ON SPORTS(1985－2012)

单位：人(person)

项目	Item	1985	1990	1995	2000	2005	2006	2007	2008	2009	2010	2011	2012
体育部门职工人数	**Staff and Workers in Sports Commissions**	**464**	**714**	**902**	**849**	**834**	**848**	**772**	**1210**	**910**	**1 015**		
#运动员	Athletes	31	88	121	90	87	81	55	452	512	287		
教练员	Coaches	129	166	175	174	235	221	211	173	106	170	136	
重点体校	Key Sports Schools	6	70	141	126	117	166	249	109	97	115	129	
业余体校	Sparetime Sports Schools	83	174	117	142	223	220	145		160			
体育专业队	Professional Sports Teams	31	120	158	135	132	154	121		144	192	87	84
优秀运动员	Excellent Athletes	31	82	121	90	87	81	55	71	72	146	57	
优秀运动队专职教练员	Full-time Coaches of Excellent Sports Teams	3	14	15	18	23	48	47	106	92	97	54	
等级裁判员发展人数	**Certified Referees**	**977**	**827**	**223**	**1 114**	**275**	**1 068**	**781**	**205**	**292**	**212**	**510**	**558**
#二级	Second Grades	381	402	50	451	275	1 068	781	181	252	169	510	484
三级	Third Grades	596	425	136	616								
等级运动员发展人数	**Certified Athletes**	**1 115**	**868**	**249**	**343**	**260**	**267**	**108**	**310**	**512**	**229**	**436**	**362**
#二级	Second Grades		7	135	209	260	267	108	281	448	229	436	256
三级	Third Grades	682	454	114	46								
少年级	Juvenile	433	395		88								

18－1 续表
continued

项目	Item	单位	Unit	1985	1990	1995	2000	2005	2006	2007	2008	2009	2010	2011	2012
全年获得奖牌数	**Number of Medals Won in the Year**	**枚**	**unit**	**184**	**281**	**278**	**347.5**	**669**	**829**	**481**	**494**	**602**	**754**	**829**	**746**
#国家级金牌	Golden Medals at National Level	枚	unit	28	20	34	45	62	71	61	26	30	14	105	88
国家级银牌	Silver Medal at National Level	枚	unit	36	23	18	28	48	54	38	21	23	7	49	100
省级金牌	Golden Medals at Provincial Level	枚	unit		83	94	116.5	187	363	116	168	207	459	225	193
省级银牌	Silver Medals at Provincial Level	枚	unit		79	47	62	174	144	93	122	149	116	155	110
体育运动破全国记录	**Records Broken the National Records**														
项目	Number of Events	项	item		5	2		2		1		1	1	2	1
人数	Number of Persons	人	person		8	2		2		1		1	1	2	1
次数	Number of Times	人次	person-time		7	2		4		1		1	1	2	1
体育运动破全省记录	**Records Broken the Provincial Records**														
项目	Number of Events	项	item		3	4	7	3	5		2		1		
人数	Number of Persons	人	person		3	5	7	1	3		2		1		
次数	Number of Times	人次	person-time		2	5	7	3	5		2		1		

18－2 主要年份卫生事业基本情况

MAJOR YEAR'S BASIC STATISTICS ON PUBLIC HEALTH

年份 Year	卫生机构数（个） Health Institutions (unit)	#医院 of which: Hospitals	医疗床位数（张） Beds in Health Institutions (bed)	#医院 of which: Hospitals	卫生技术人员（人） Medical and Technical Personnel (person)	#医生 of which: Doctors	每千人口拥有医生数（人） Number of Doctors per 1000 Population (person)	每千人口拥有床位数（张） Number of Hospital Beds per 1000 Population (bed)
1949	80	26	1 079	970	2 637	1 292	0.32	0.27
1952	260	34	2 943	1 691	3 748	1 559	0.37	0.70
1957	624	45	5 163	2 656	6 941	2 578	0.53	1.07
1962	849	149	7 167	4 526	8 279	2 972	0.64	1.55
1965	912	162	8 428	5 003	9 051	3 586	0.73	1.72
1970	712	170	8 613	6 603	9 591	3 761	0.70	1.60
1975	959	181	10 902	9 078	13 558	4 566	0.80	1.90
1978	1 192	212	13 084	10 709	16 921	5 893	1.01	2.24
1980	1 253	212	14 170	11 345	19 265	6 781	1.14	2.38
1985	1 517	219	18 469	13 214	23 413	9 694	1.55	2.95
1987	1 553	228	21 667	15 463	26 669	11 738	1.81	3.34
1989	1 566	232	22 668	15 670	27 195	13 555	2.06	3.46
1990	1 563	235	23 541	16 586	27 932	13 761	2.08	3.56
1991	1 579	235	23 727	16 796	27 772	13 227	1.98	3.54
1992	1 562	236	24 765	17 269	28 305	13 157	1.95	3.67
1993	1 540	237	24 885	17 469	28 705	13 312	1.97	3.68
1994	1 335	242	24 732	17 882	28 938	13 535	1.99	3.64
1995	1 347	228	25 282	18 126	29 816	13 840	2.02	3.69
1996	2 216	228	24 334	18 344	30 048	13 790	2.00	3.53
1997	2 193	239	25 201	19 046	31 121	14 400	2.07	3.62
1998	2 190	237	24 887	19 083	31 623	14 327	2.05	3.56
1999	2 185	235	25 481	19 798	31 965	14 453	2.06	3.62
2000	2 911	231	24 392	20 057	32 160	14 860	2.10	3.45
2001	3 199	217	24 755	20 313	32 765	15 772	2.22	3.48
2002	3 050	213	21 370	20 662	31 469	13 371	1.87	2.99
2003	3 111	213	23 980	21 605	32 337	13 452	1.87	3.33
2004	2 923	219	25 432	23 465	32 937	13 953	1.91	3.48
2005	2 609	235	30 627	28 564	33 942	15 008	2.03	4.13
2006	2 834	232	28 724	26 653	34 360	15 451	2.06	3.83
2007	2 116	251	30 062	28 107	33 807	15 018	1.98	3.97
2008	1 985	249	32 350	29 874	36 574	16 260	2.14	4.25
2009	2 017	252	32 803	30 527	40 217	16 734	2.19	4.30
2010	2 147	254	36 066	33 383	43 285	17 696	2.32	4.72
2011	2 549	280	39 980	35 600	47 347	18 310	2.39	5.22
2012	2 607	288	47 254	41 186	54 488	21 593	2.81	6.14

18－3 各类卫生机构、床位、人员数(2012 年底)

NUMBER OF HEALTH INSTITUTIONS, BEDS AND EMPLOYED PERSONS(END OF 2012)

项　　目	Item	机构数（个）Health Institutions (unit)	床位数（张）Beds in Health Institutions (bed)	人员数（人）Personnel (person)
总　　计		**2 607**	**47 254**	**64 181**
一、医院合计	**Sub-total of Hospitals**	**288**	**41 186**	**48 467**
1. 医院	Hospitals	179	33 493	40 792
综合医院	General Hospitals	103	23 139	29 283
中医医院	Hospitals Specialized in Traditional Chinese Medicine	16	3 029	3 415
中西医结合医院	Hospitals of Combination of Chinese and Western Medicine	3	595	514
专科医院	Specialized Hospitals	54	6 540	7 474
口腔医院	Stomatological Hospitals	2	42	201
眼科医院	Ophthalmology Hospitals	2	173	207
肿瘤医院	Tumor Hospitals	2	550	605
心血管病医院	Cardiovascular Diseases Hospitals	5	693	965
精神病医院	Mental Hospitals	6	1 470	382
传染病医院	Infectious Disease Hospitals	2	640	476
皮肤病医院		1	30	24
骨科医院	Orthopaedics Hospitals	5	736	540
其它专科医院	Other Specialized Hospitals	14	1 156	1 962
2. 卫生院	Sanitation Stations	109	7 693	7 675
二、社区卫生服务中心	**Neighborhood Service Centers**	**61**	**1 133**	**2 099**
三、门诊部	**Outpatient Service Stations**	**56**	**136**	**1 292**
四、诊所	**Clinics**	**1 627**	**0**	**4 910**
五、卫生所、医务室	**Medical Houses**	**265**	**0**	**747**
六、社区卫生服务站	**Neighborhood Service Stations**	**193**	**659**	**2 228**
七、急救中心	**First Aid Centers**	**2**	**0**	**147**
八、采供血机构	**Institutions of Blood Collection and Supply**	**1**	**0**	**235**
九、妇幼保健院(所、站)	**Maternity and Child Care Centers**	**13**	**400**	**1 016**
十、专科疾病防治院(所、站)	**Specialized Disease Prevention & Treatment Institutions**	**10**	**475**	**378**
十一、疾病预防控制中心(防疫站)	**Centers for Disease Control and Prevention (Epidemic Prevention Stations)**	**28**	**0**	**1 017**
十二、卫生监督所	**Sanitation Control Stations**	**14**	**0**	**377**
十三、卫生监督检验所(站)	**Sanitation Control and Test Stations**			
十四、医学科学研究机构	**Institutions of Medical Science**			
十五、医学在职培训机构	**Institutions of Medical Training for Working Personnel**			
十六、健康教育所(站、中心)	**Health Education Stations**	**1**	**0**	**4**
十七、其它卫生机构	**Other Health Institutions**	**34**	**0**	**307**
十八、疗养院	**Sanatoriums**	**14**	**3 265**	**957**

#卫生技术人员 Medical and Technical Personnel	#医生 Doctors	注册护士 Registered Nurses	药剂人员 Pharmacists	检验人员 Laboratory Technicians
54 488	**21 593**	**21 923**	**3 100**	**1 844**
41 104	**14 608**	**18 017**	**2 501**	**1 389**
34 134	12 072	15 976	1 912	1 120
24 835	8 737	11 903	1 359	755
2 973	1 209	1 180	214	92
398	134	160	48	19
5 839	1 971	2 702	287	251
167	103	52	4	1
154	64	77	5	5
487	136	266	27	25
750	211	332	30	25
676	181	422	26	15
365	118	179	27	28
21	10	5	2	1
530	283	180	22	15
1 614	510	708	90	81
6 970	2 536	2 041	589	269
1 762	**681**	**531**	**155**	**68**
1 023	**562**	**296**	**39**	**48**
4 829	**3 149**	**1 434**	**139**	**27**
722	**449**	**217**	**19**	**8**
1 854	**882**	**667**	**145**	**57**
78	**31**	**43**	**2**	**1**
161	**53**	**50**	**1**	**53**
818	**352**	**298**	**28**	**56**
311	**121**	**98**	**32**	**20**
793	**385**	**56**	**13**	**99**
330	**0**	**0**	**0**	**0**
3	**2**	**0**	**1**	**0**
267	**174**	**53**	**10**	**5**
433	**144**	**163**	**15**	**13**

18-4 分市、区各类卫生机构、床位、人员数(2012 年底)

NUMBER OF HEALTH INSTITUTIONS, BEDS AND EMPLOYED PERSONS BY REGION (END OF 2012)

市、区名称	Region	机构数(个) Institutions (unit)	医院小计 Sub-total of Hospitals	#医院 Hospitals	卫生院 Sanitation Stations	社区卫生服务中心 Neighborhood Service Centers
总　计	**Total**	**2 607**	**288**	**179**	**109**	**61**
市　区	Urban Area	1 783	131	119	12	54
#崂山区	Laoshan District	183	15	12	3	1
原黄岛区	Original Huangdao District	136	14	10	4	2
城阳区	Chengyang District	151	18	13	5	3
即墨市	Jimo	188	38	16	22	0
胶州市	Jiaozhou	154	26	12	14	4
原胶南市	Original Jiaonan	227	20	4	16	1
平度市	Pingdu	175	42	13	29	0
莱西市	Laixi	80	31	15	16	2

18-4 续表 1

continued

市、区名称	Region	采供血机构 Institutions of Blood Collection and Supply	妇幼保健院(所、站) Maternity and Child Care Centers	专科疾病防治院(所、站) Specialized Disease Prevention & Treatment Institutions
总　计	**Total**	**1**	**13**	**10**
市　区	Urban Area	1	8	2
#崂山区	Laoshan District		1	0
原黄岛区	Original Huangdao District		1	0
城阳区	Chengyang District		1	0
即墨市	Jimo		1	1
胶州市	Jiaozhou		1	0
原胶南市	Original Jiaonan		1	2
平度市	Pingdu		1	3
莱西市	Laixi		1	2

社区卫生服务站 Neighborhood Service Stations	门诊部 Outpatient Service Stations	诊所、卫生所、医务室 Clinics Medical Houses	急救中心 First Aid Centers
193	**56**	**1 892**	**2**
143	52	1 346	1
18	8	138	
0	16	94	
0	0	119	
36	0	84	
0	0	117	1
4	4	191	
0	0	125	
10	0	29	

疾病预防控制中心(防疫站) Centers for Disease Control and Prevention (Epidemic Prevention Stations)	卫生监督所 Sanitation Control Stations	卫生监督检疫所(站) Sanitation Control and Test stations	医学科学研究机构 Institutions of Medical Science	医学在职培训机构 Institutions of Medical Training for Working Personnel
28	**14**			
22	9			
1	1			
7	2			
9	1			
1	1			
1	1			
1	1			
1	1			
2	1			

18－4 续表 2
continued

市、区名称	Region	健康教育所（站、中心）Health Education Station	临床检验中心（所、站）	其他卫生机构 Other Health Institutions	疗养院 Sanatoriums	床位数（张）Beds in Health Institutions（bed）
总　计	**Total**	**1**		**34**	**14**	**47 254**
市　区	Urban Area			1	13	27 177
#崂山区	Laoshan District					1 022
原黄岛区	Original Huangdao District					2 465
城阳区	Chengyang District					3 044
即墨市	Jimo	1		24	1	5 382
胶州市	Jiaozhou			3		3 666
原胶南市	Original Jiaonan			2		2 799
平度市	Pingdu			2		4 101
莱西市	Laixi			2		4 129

18－4 续表 3
continued

市、区名称	Region	专科疾病防治院（所、站）Specialized Disease Centers	人员数（人）Personnel（person）	卫生技术人员 Medical and Technical Personnel
总　计	**Total**	**475**	**64 181**	**54 488**
市　区	Urban Area	35	41 747	34 744
#崂山区	Laoshan District		2 016	1 603
原黄岛区	Original Huangdao District		4 573	3 973
城阳区	Chengyang District		4 254	3 634
即墨市	Jimo		5 569	5 001
胶州市	Jiaozhou		4 506	3 942
原胶南市	Original Jiaonan	133	3 599	3 247
平度市	Pingdu	207	4 398	3 892
莱西市	Laixi	100	4 362	3 662

医院小计 Sub-total of Hospitals	#医院 Hospitals	卫生院 Sanitation Stations	门诊部 Outpatient Service Stations	妇幼保健院(所、站) Maternity and Child Care Centers
41 186	**33 493**	**7 693**	**136**	**400**
22 424	21 798	626	136	
886	801	85	18	
2 378	2 197	181	43	
2 928	2 568	360		
4 932	3 290	1 642		100
3 551	2 445	1 106		55
2 531	1 199	1 332		110
3 799	2 009	1 790		95
3 949	2 752	1 197		40

执业(助理)医师 Certified(Assistant) Doctors	注册护士 Registered Nurses	药剂人员 Pharmacists	检验人员 Laboratory Technicians	其他人员 Other Personnel
31 593	**21 923**	**3 100**	**1 844**	**3 255**
14 027	14 298	1 928	1 231	2 245
696	624	89	49	62
1 610	1 697	176	121	271
1 200	1 335	173	128	305
1 848	1 710	308	149	217
1 397	1 737	192	121	176
1 271	1 321	196	118	145
1 588	1 501	243	111	209
1 462	1 356	233	114	263

18－5 收养性社会福利单位情况(2012 年)
BASIC STATICTICS ON SOCIAL WELFARE INSTITUTIONS(2012)

市、区名称	Region	单位数(个) Number of Institutions (unit)	年末职工人数(人) Number of Staff and Workers at Year-end (person)	年末床位数(张) Number of Beds at Year-end (bed)
总　计	**Total**	**263**	**3 324**	**31 490**
市　区	Urban Area	157	2 592	20 155
#崂山区	Laoshan District	10	64	1 810
黄岛区	Huangdao District	36	320	3 258
城阳区	Chengyang District	11	120	1 622
即墨市	Jimo	33	244	3 951
胶州市	Jiaozhou	16	146	2 320
平度市	Pingdu	33	107	2 217
莱西市	Laixi	24	235	2 847

注:按新行政区划统计。
Note:The statistics data in this form are according to the new administrative division.

18－6 社会救济情况(2012 年)
BASIC STATISTICS ON SOCIAL RELIEF(2012)

市、区名称	Region	城镇居民最低生活保障人数(人) Number of Persons Receiving Minimum Living Allowance in Urban Area(person)	城镇居民最低生活保障家庭数(户) Number of Households Receiving Minimum Living Allowance in Urban Area(household)	城镇低保资金计划支出(万元) Planned Expense of Funds for Minimum Living Allowance in Urban Area (10 000 yuan)
总　计	**Total**	**38 492**	**19 641**	**10 098.9**
市　区	Urban Area	35 146	17 671	8 683.0
#崂山区	Laoshan District	466	249	175.8
黄岛区	Huangdao District	1 769	963	480.3
城阳区	Chengyang District	513	288	270.8
即墨市	Jimo	1 449	845	608.8
胶州市	Jiaozhou	693	398	316.0
平度市	Pingdu	650	403	258.6
莱西市	Laixi	554	324	232.5

注:农村低保含农村五保供养。
Note:Minimum living allowance in rural area contains rural households with livelihood guaranteed in five aspects.
注:按新行政区划统计。
Note:The statistics data in this form are according to the new administrative division.

年末在院人数(人) Residences at Year-end (person)	优抚对象 Disabled Military Servicemen and Family Members of War Heroes and Military Servicemen	"三无"对象 Senior Citizen, Disabled Persons, Minors Non-ability to Work, Non-source of income and Non-supports the human or the provider	自费人员 Self-supporting Persons
18 364	**501**	**5 965**	**11 898**
13 302	403	2 555	10 344
388	1	31	356
1 842	216	1 387	239
842	15	269	558
1 338	40	588	710
1 286	15	999	272
933	25	908	
1 505	18	915	572

农村居民最低生活保障人数(人) Number of Persons Receiving Minimum Living Allowance in Rural Area(person)	农村居民最低生活保障家庭数(户) Number of Households Receiving Minimum Living Allowance in Rural Area(household)	农村低保资金计划支出(万元) Planned Expense of Funds for Minimum Living Allowance in Rural Area(10 000 yuan)
97 597	**60 993**	**18 211.6**
26 890	15 413	3 904.2
3 770	1 812	567.0
17 710	10 740	1 681.6
5 410	2 861	1 655.6
19 953	12 276	5 151.3
16 166	9 194	3 787.7
17 751	11 487	2 769.2
16 837	12 623	2 599.2

18-7 分市、区婚姻登记情况(2012年)

BASIC STATISTICS ON MARRIAGE REGISTRATION BY REGION(2012)

市、区名称	Region	准予登记结婚 Registered Marriages					准予登记离婚(对) Registered Divorces (couple)	涉外婚姻登记(对) Registered Marriages with Foreigner(couple)
		合计(对) Total(couple)	初婚(人) First Marriages (person)	恢复结婚(对) Resumed Marriages (couple)	再婚(人) Remarriages(person) 男 Male	再婚(人) Remarriages(person) 女 Female		
总 计	**Total**	**78 041**	**130 547**	**1 051**	**12 906**	**12 629**	**16 259**	**346**
市 区	Urban Area	41 943	70 556	54	6 954	6 376	9 136	346
#崂山区	Laoshan District	3 636	6 526		409	337	377	
黄岛区	Huangdao District	12 131	19 976		2 142	2 144	2 714	
城阳区	Chengyang District	4 898	8 503	49	697	596	701	
即墨市	Jimo	9 522	15 559		1 748	1 737	2 243	
胶州市	Jiaozhou	7 653	12 632		1 354	1 320	1 451	
平度市	Pingdu	12 604	20 760	997	2 061	2 387	2 374	
莱西市	Laixi	6 319	11 040		789	809	1 055	

注:按新行政区划统计。

Note: The statistics data in this form are according to the new administrative division.

18-8 律师、公证、调解、社会治安基本情况(1985-2012年)

BASIC STATISTICS ON LAWYERS,NOTARIZATION,MEDIATION AND SOCIAL ORDER (1985-2012)

项目	Item	单位	Unit	1985	1990	1995	2000	2005	2006
一、律师工作	**Lawyers**								
律师事务所	Law Offices	个	unit	13	16	61	76	116	122
律师工作者	Lawyers	人	person	152	278	783	1 439	1 941	2 218
专职	Full-time Lawyers	人	person	68	111	458	971	1 542	1 616
兼职(含特邀)	Part-time Lawyers	人	person	84	167	325	150	73	75
聘请常年法律顾问单位	Units with Permanent Legal Advisors	个	unit	162	731	2 028	2 508	3 564	4 032
全年办理民事代理	Agent of Civil Cases	件	case	309	1 512	1 650	5 571	11 104	10 556
刑事辩护	Defender of Criminal Cases	件	case	275	1 172	1 009	1 755	3 003	2 917
非诉讼事件	Agent of Non-litigious Legal Affairs	件	case	128	252	3 885	5 251	6 501	10 049
解答法律询问	Agent of Legal Advisory Services	件	case	8 305	15 489	23 758	58 385	27 880	26 518
代写法律事务文书	Agent of Legal Documents Written on Behalf of Clients	件	case	1 460	2 237	4 635	9 335	8 595	8 171
二、公证工作	**Notarization**								
公证处	Notary Offices	个	unit	13	13	15	15	15	15
公证人员	Notarial Personnel	人	person	71	103	111	152	196	209
公证员	Notaries	人	person	46	56	89	106	112	117
办理公证文书	Notarized Documents	件	case	22 627	68 954	106 205	120 849	105 787	100 513
三、人民调解	**People's Mediation**								
人民调解委员会	People's Mediation Committees	个	unit	8 009	8 718	9 631	9 750	11 480	10 897
调解人员	Mediators	人	person	38 721	41 061	64 806	34 714	46 735	34 487
调解民间纠纷	Civil Disputes Mediated	件	case	22 409	21 175	17 552	18 501	13 658	14 094
四、社会治安	**Social Order**								
交通事故发生次数	Traffic Accidents	次	time	360	1 047	917	15 601	7 051	5 559
死亡人数	Deaths	人	person	90	345	600	1 371	776	689
受伤人数	Injuries	人	person	282	409	329	8 620	6 639	5 685
经济损失	Losses	万元	10 000 yuan	32.70	125.30	381.55	4 815.70	2 208.20	1 514.00
火灾发生次数	Fire Accidents	次	time	206	422	221	3 088	1 948	1 400
死亡人数	Deaths	人	person	18	12	18	10	3	8
受伤人数	Injuries	人	person	15	18	33	43	3	5
经济损失	Losses	万元	10 000 yuan	77.96	401.62	3 542.29	1 531.06	550.40	544.00

注:火灾发生次数自1997年统计方法及口径范围发生变化,与往年不可比。交通事故发生次数自1998年统计方法及口径范围发生变化,与往年不可比。

Note:The statistical method and coverage have been adopted in fire accidents since 1997 and in traffic accidents since 1998. The data are not comparable with those in preceding year.

18－8 续表
continued

项 目	Item	单位	Unit	2007	2008	2009	2010	2011	2012
一、律师工作	**Lawyers**								
律师事务所	Law Offices	个	unit	140	159	203	222	247	266
律师工作者	Lawyers	人	person	2 594	2 915	3 144	2 487	2 801	3 130
专职	Full-time Lawyers	人	person	1 738	1 855	1 934	2 377	2 643	2 944
兼职(含特邀)	Part-time Lawyers	人	person	79	90	86	94	105	107
聘请常年法律顾问单位	Units with Permanent Legal Advisors	个	unit	4 075	4 086	4 457	4 779	5 130	5 228
全年办理民事代理	Agent of Civil Cases	件	case	19 460	20 547	29 025	26 935	27 702	30 586
刑事辩护	Defender of Criminal Cases	件	case	3 311	3 655	3 758	3 964	4 535	4 935
非诉讼事件	Agent of Non-litigious Legal Affairs	件	case	7 710	5 467	5 897	4 274	3 576	4 251
解答法律询问	Agent of Legal Advisory Services	件	case	27 393	31 571	30 123	21 102	42 428	45 388
代写法律事务文书	Agent of Legal Documents Written on Behalf of Clients	件	case	8 012	9 077	6 015	6 210	6 762	6 388
二、公证工作	**Notarization**								
公证处	Notary Offices	个	unit	13	13	13	13	13	13
公证人员	Notarial Personnel	人	person	208	214	214	214	221	225
公证员	Notaries	人	person	116	117	118	117	119	118
办理公证文书	Notarized Documents	件	case	95 704	101 766	97 019	94 077	88 506	87 703
三、人民调解	**People's Mediation**								
人民调解委员会	People's Mediation Committees	个	unit	11 216	11 223	9 643	8 014	8 485	8 426
调解人员	Mediators	人	person	35 553	33 875	32 675	27 820	28 094	27 421
调解民间纠纷	Civil Disputes Mediated	件	case	16 586	12 803	14 660	20 550	22 882	23 999
四、社会治安	**Social Order**								
交通事故发生次数	Traffic Accidents	次	time	4 465	3 025	2 570	2 313	2 164	1 951
死亡人数	Deaths	人	person	556	489	402	393	374	343
受伤人数	Injuries	人	person	4 603	3 273	2 943	2 504	2 240	1 913
经济损失	Losses	万元	10 000 yuan	1 291.40	991.50	854.80	811.27	861.05	652.10
火灾发生次数	Fire Accidents	次	time	962	840	773	683	369	366
死亡人数	Deaths	人	person	9	16	5	9	1	6
受伤人数	Injuries	人	person		13		4	2	2
经济损失	Losses	万元	10 000 yuan	929.60	979.70	865.50	5 566.11	598.20	601.90

18-9 分区、市殡葬服务情况(2012年)
BASIC STATISTICS ON FUNERAL SERVICES(2012)

市、区名称	Region	单位数(个) Number of Institutions (unit)	年末职工人数(人) Number of Staff and Workers at Year-end (person)	火化炉数(台) Number of Cremators (unit)	处理遗体数(具) Number of Remains Cremated (body)
总计	**Total**	**9**	**201**	**43**	**60 161**
市区	Urban Area	4	107	22	26 215
#崂山区	Laoshan District				
黄岛区	Huangdao District	2	26	7	8 639
城阳区	Chengyang District	1	19	5	5 945
即墨市	Jimo	1	18	6	9 140
胶州市	Jiaozhou	1	10	4	6 610
平度市	Pingdu	1	20	5	11 975
莱西市	Laixi	2	46	6	6 221

注:按新行政区划统计。
Note: The statistics data in this form are according to the new administrative division.

18-9 续表
continued

市、区名称	Region	穴位数(个) Number of Graves (unit)	本年销售穴位数 Number of Graves Saled in the Year	安葬数(具) Number of Remains Buried(body)	本年安葬数 Number of Remains Buried in the Year
总计	**Total**	**21 383**	**492**	**19 694**	**509**
市区	Urban Area	19 197	401	18 439	433
#崂山区	Laoshan District				
黄岛区	Huangdao District				
城阳区	Chengyang District				
即墨市	Jimo				
胶州市	Jiaozhou				
平度市	Pingdu				
莱西市	Laixi	2 186	91	1 255	76

注:按新行政区划统计。
Note: The statistics data in this form are according to the new administrative division.

主要统计指标解释

卫生机构 包括医疗机构、疾病预防控制中心(防疫站)、采供血机构、卫生监督及监测(检验)机构、医学科研和在职培训机构、健康教育所等。

医疗机构 包括医院、社区卫生服务中心(站)、疗养院、卫生院、门诊部、诊所(卫生所、医务室)、妇幼保健院(所、站)、专科疾病防治院(所、站)、急救中心(站)和临床检验中心。医疗机构分为非赢利性医疗机构和赢利性医疗机构。

医院 包括综合医院、中医医院、中西医结合医院、民族医院、各类专科医院和护理院。

医生 指在医疗、预防保健机构工作且取得《执业医师证书》的执业医师和执业助理医师。

卫生技术人员 指卫生事业机构中现任职务为卫生技术工作的人员。包括中医师、西医师、中西医结合高级医师、护师、中药师、西药师、检验师、其他技师、中医士、西医士、护士、助产士、中药剂士、西药剂士、检验士、其他技士、其他中医、护理员、中药剂员、西药剂员、检验员、其他初级卫生技术人员。

社会福利事业单位 指集中收养社会孤老、残、幼的机构,包括由民政部门管理的社会福利院、儿童福利院、精神病人福利院和城镇集体举办的福利院及农村集体举办的敬老院以及优抚医院和具有收养能力的社区服务中心等。

Explanatory Notes on Main Statistical Indicators

Health Care Institutions include: medical institutions, disease prevention and control centers (epidemic prevention stations), blood gathering and supplying institutions, health supervision and inspection (check up) institutions, medicinal scientific research and on-job training institutions, health education and so on.

Medical Organizations include: hospitals, health service centers (stations) of communities, nursing homes, health centers, clinics, clinics (health stations and infirmaries), maternity and child care agencies (centers and stations), special disease prevention and curing agencies (centers and stations), first aid centers (stations) and clinical inspection centers. Medical organizations are grouped by two types: profit-making and non-profit-making medical organizations.

Hospitals include: polyclinics, traditional Chinese medical hospitals, hospitals integrated with traditional Chinese therapeutics and western therapeutics, ethical hospitals, various specialties hospitals and nursing hospitals.

Doctors refer to certified physicians and certified assistant physicians with certifications working in medical and health care and prevention agencies.

Medical Technical Personnel refers to those medical workers employed institutions, including doctors of Chinese and Western medicine, senior doctors of integrated Chinese-Western medicine, head nurses, pharmacists of Chinese and Western medicine, laboratory specialists, other specialists, junior doctors of Chinese and Western medicine, nurses, midwives, druggists of Chinese and Western medicine, laboratory technicians, other technicians, other practitioners of Chinese medicine, nursing attendants, pharmacological workers of Chinese and Western medicine, laboratory workers, and other primary medical personnel.

Social Welfare Institutions refer to institutions taking care of old people without children, handicapped people and orphans. They include social welfare institutions run by civil affairs departments, children welfare institutions, social welfare institutions for mental patients, collective-owned old people's homes in rural areas, convalescent homes and community service centers with the capacity of receiving those people.

附　录
APPENDIX

2012 年省内各市主要经济指标对比情况

MAJOR ECONOMIC INDICATORS ON CITIES OF THE PROVINCE(2012)

主要指标 Indicator	单位 Unit	青岛市 Qingdao	济南市 Jinan	淄博市 Zibo	枣庄市 Zaozhuang	东营市 Dongying	烟台市 Yantai
地区生产总值(GDP)	亿元 (100 million yuan)	7 302.11	4 812.68	3 557.21	1 702.92	3 000.66	5 281.38
比上年增长 YOY Growth	%	10.6	9.5	10.5	10.7	12.1	10.3
规模以上工业增加值比上年增长 YOY Growth of Industrial Added Value above Designated Size	%	11.61	10.11	11.43	11.47	12.71	11.43
固定资产投资 Investmentin Fixed Assets	亿元 (100 million yuan)	4 153.9	2 186.1	1 743.3	1 044.6	1 963.0	3 043.9
比上年增长 YOY Growth	%	22.3	20.4	20.5	22.7	23.4	20.5
进出口总额 Imports and Exports	亿美元 (100 million USD)	732.1	91.3	95.3	11.3	123.0	478.0
比上年增长 YOY Growth	%	4.2	-12.4	5.5	6.0	20.7	5.4
#出口 #Exports	亿美元 (100 million USD)	408.2	57.1	53.2	9.4	49.8	283.6
比上年增长 YOY Growth	%	3.6	-5.5	-0.1	11.3	14.3	6.2
社会消费品零售总额 Total Retail Sales of Consumer Goods	亿元 (100 million yuan)	2 564.5	2 323.6	1 363.64	552.4	516.08	1 859.80
比上年增长 YOY Growth	%	14.9	14.9	15.0	15.0	15.0	15.1
公共财政预算收入 Budgetary Revenue of Public Finance	亿元 (100 million yuan)	670.2	380.8	236.3	116.4	158.7	357.4
比上年增长 YOY Growth	%	18.4	17.2	16.1	16.2	17.3	17.9
城市居民人均可支配收入 Per Capita Disposable Income of Urban Households	元 (yuan)	32 145	32 570	28 189	22 960	30 953	30 045
比上年增长 YOY Growth	%	12.5	12.7	13.0	13.7	13.2	13.2
农民人均纯收入 Per Capital Net Income of Rural Households	元 (yuan)	13 990	11 786	12 379	9 606	11 489	13 298
比上年增长 YOY Growth	16	13.1	13.2	13.8	14.4	14.5	13.5

注:各市数据为快报数。

Note:The date are preliminary statistics

潍坊市 Weifang	济宁市 Jining	泰安市 Taian	威海市 Weihai	日照市 Rizhao	莱芜市 Laiwu	临沂市 Linyi	德州市 Dezhou	聊城市 Liaocheng	滨州市 Binzhou	菏泽市 Heze
4 012.43	3 18[illegible].37	2 547.00	2 337.86	1 352.57	631.41	3 012.80	2 230.56	2 145.65	1 987.73	1 787.36
10.6	11.0	10.7	9.4	11.8	11.1	11.8	12.1	12.7	10.8	13.0
13.49	1[illegible].49	12.70	10.50	12.68	13.11	19.02	19.12	19.39	13.11	20.78
3 012.9	1 8[illegible]9.7	1 774.5	1 595.5	922.4	441.1	2 016.7	1 401.6	1 260.7	1 262.7	687.1
22.3	[illegible]2.3	22.0	20.2	20.2	23.5	22.7	23.4	22.0	22.7	23.5
149.7	[illegible]51.2	21.3	171.3	252.9	21.6	78.9	27.2	55.9	62.8	31.8
6.3	-11.0	-40.8	1.6	21.3	18.5	15.5	1.4	0.3	-6.1	15.9
109.7	[illegible]2.0	7.3	106.6	38.8	12.2	39.0	18.7	18.5	28.3	15.3
5.8	4.1	-35.7	-0.2	-0.8	3.1	7.6	7.0	-1.4	-0.6	6.1
1 551.63	1 [illegible]00.1	928.3	923.1	420.1	228.1	1571.9	872.3	724.1	581.46	894.19
15.0	15.1	15.1	15.0	15.0	15.0	15.1	15.2	15.0	15.0	15.4
306.1	345.6	158.9	158.4	78.9	42.0	170.1	120.2	104.5	150.5	140.3
20.6	18.6	15.0	16.1	15.1	7.1	20.4	26.5	18.0	15.1	25.7
25 817	2[illegible] 454	25 659	28 630	22 817	26 589	24 452	22 440	23 685	25 810	19 140
14.7	13.6	13.1	13.2	13.5	13.1	14.1	13.5	14.7	14.5	15.0
11 797	[illegible] 002	10 194	13 962	10 026	10 887	9 149	9 602	8 872	10 017	8 187
13.3	14.8	13.6	13.2	14.5	13.1	14.1	15.0	14.7	14.9	15.0

2012 年十五个副省级城市主要经济指标对比资料

MAJOR ECONOMIC INDICATORS ON CITIES UNDER PROVINCIAL LEVELS(2012)

指标名称 Indicator	单位 Unit	青岛 Qingdao	沈阳 Shenyang	大连 Dalian	长春 Changchun	哈尔滨 Harbin
全市生产总值 GDP	亿元 (100 million yuan)	7 302.11	6 606.8	7 002.8	4 456.5	4 550.1
比上年增长 YOY Growth	%	10.6	10	10.3	12	10
第一产业 Primary Industry	亿元 (100 million yuan)	324.41	315.2	451.4	317.5	506.8
比上年增长 YOY Growth	%	3.2	5.1	5.1	4.3	9.2
第二产业 Secondary Industry	亿元 (100 million yuan)	3 402.2	3 389.1	3 634.8	2 291.5	1 638.9
比上年增长 YOY Growth	%	11.5	11.4	10.6	13.[illegible]	10.9
第三产业 Tertiary Industry	亿元 (100 million yuan)	3 575.5	2 902.5	2 916.7	1 847.6	2 404.4
比上年增长 YOY Growth	%	10.5	8.9	10.6	11.8	9.4
规模以上工业增加值比上年增长 YOY Growth of Industrial Added Value above Designated Size	%	11.6	11	11	1[illegible]	10
固定资产投资额 Investment in Fixed Assets	亿元 (100 million yuan)	4 153.9	5 625.4	5 624.4	3 172.9	3 950
比上年增长 YOY Growth	%	22.3	23.3	23.5	30.4	31.1
社会消费品零售总额 Total Retail Sales of Consumer Goods	亿元 (100 million yuan)	2 564.5	2 802.2	2 224	1 739.5	2 394.6
比上年增长 YOY Growth	%	14.9	15.5	15.5	13	15.7
进出口总额 Imports and Exports	亿美元 (100 million USD)	732.08	127.5	641.13	196.8	53.3
比上年增长 YOY Growth	%	4.2	20.1	6.8	13.5	4.2
其中:出口总额 of which:Exports	亿美元 (100 million USD)	408.2	59.7	346.82	29	18.6
比上年增长 YOY Growth	%	3.6	23.6	11.2	27.9	-17.8
实际使用外资金额 Foreign Investment Actually Utilized	亿美元 (100 million USD)	46.00	30.45	42.18	10.84	4.88
比上年增长 YOY Growth	%	27.8	-26.8	-31.6	103.3	9.6
公共财政预算收入 Budgetary Revenue of Public finance	亿元 (100 million yuan)	670.2	715	750.1	340.8	354.7
比上年增长 YOY Growth	%	18.4	15.3	15.2	18.1	18.1
城市居民人均可支配收入 Per Capita Disposable Income of Urban Households	元 (yuan)	32 145	26 430	27 539	22 969.7	22 498.6
比上年增长 YOY Growth	%	12.5	13.3	13.4	12.1	12.3
农民人均纯收入 Per Capita Net Income of Rural Households	元 (yuan)	13 990	13 259.7	15 990	8 570	11 443
比上年增长 YOY Growth	%	13.1	14.5	12.5	12.1	19.1
居民消费价格指数 Consumer Price Index	%	102.7	103	103.4	102.3	103.2

注:各市数据为快报数。

Note:The data are preliminary statistics.

南京 Nanjing	杭州 Hangzhou	宁波 Ningbo	厦门 Xiamen	济南 Jinan	武汉 Wuhan	广州 Guangzhou	深圳 Shenzhen	成都 Chengdu	西安 Xi'an
7 201.57	7 803.98	6 524.7	2 817.07	4 812.68	8 003.82	13 551.21	12 950.08	8 138.94	4 369.37
11.7	9	7.8	12.1	9.5	11.4	10.5	10	13	11.8
184.[illegible]4	255.93	269.97	25.21	252.92	301.21	220.72	5.56	348.07	195.59
4.9	2.5	1.6	0.4	4.7	4.5	3.3	-18.2	3.8	6
3 170.[illegible]8	3 626.88	3 516.73	1 374.01	1 938.14	3 869.56	4 713.16	5 737.64	3 790.62	1 893.79
11.9	8.5	6	12.6	9.2	13.2	9.9	7.3	15.6	11.8
3 845.[illegible]5	3 921.17	2 738	1 417.85	2 621.62	3 833.05	8 617.33	7 206.88	4 000.26	2 279.99
11.8	10.1	10.9	11.7	10.1	10	11.1	12.3	11.5	12.2
11.1	10.9	5	12.5	10.1	15.2	10.9	7.3	17.2	13
4 558.[illegible]9	3 722.75	2 901.43	1 332.64	2 186.08	5 031.25	3 758.39	2 314.43	5 890.1	4 243.43
21.3	20.1	21.6	18.1	20.4	20	10.1	12.3	17.7	26.6
3 080.[illegible]	2 944.63	2 329.3	882.11	2 323.6	3 432.43	5 977.27	4 008.78	3 317.67	2 236.06
15.4	15.5	15.4	10.2	14.9	16	15.2	16.5	16	15.5
55[illegible].35	616.8	965.7	744.91	91.47	203.54	1 171.31	4 667.85	475.39	130.14
-3.[illegible]	-3.6	-1.6	6.2	-12.1	-11	0.8	12.7	25.5	3.3
31[illegible].[illegible]	412.6	614.5	454.02	57.2	107.48	589.12	2 713.7	303.61	72.99
3.[illegible]	-0.6	1	6.5	-5.4	-8.3	4.3	10.5	32.4	25.3
29.9[illegible]	28.98	31.00	13.78	5.53	17.28	36.03	69.15	36.45	13.33
-18.[illegible]	29.4	4.4	-35.3	-35.7	10.9	-10.1	53.7	10.8	59.9
733.0[illegible]	859.99	725.5	422.91	380.82	828.58	1 102.25	1 482.08	781.02	396.96
15.[illegible]	9.5	10.3	14.1	17	23.1	12.5	10.6	18.9	24.6
35 32[illegible]	37 511	37 902	37 576	32 569.8	27 061	38 054	40 741.9	27 194	29 982
12.[illegible]	10.1	11.3	11.9	12.7	14	11.4	11.6	13.6	15.4
14 78[illegible]	17 017	18 475	13 455	11 786	11 190.4	16 898	–	11 301	11 442
12.[illegible]	11.6	11.8	12.8	13.2	14	14	–	14.2	16.9
102.[illegible]	102.5	101.7	102.1	102.4	102.8	103	102.8	103	102.8

中国统计出版社最新图书简目

(仅供参考,以最后出书为准)

统计资料

中国统计年鉴-2013
2013中国发展报告
中国劳动统计年鉴-2013
中国建筑业统计年鉴-2013
中国商品交易市场统计年鉴-2013
中国民政统计年鉴-2013
中国科技统计年鉴-2013
中国高技术产业统计年鉴-2013
全国农产品成本收益资料汇编-2013
大中型批发零售和住宿餐饮企业统计年鉴-2013
第二次全国R&D资源清查资料汇编－工业企业卷
第二次全国R&D资源清查资料汇编－综合卷

中国统计摘要-2013
中国第三产业统计年鉴-2013
中国社会统计年鉴-2013
中国人口和就业统计年鉴-2013
中国房地产统计年鉴-2013
中国贸易外经统计年鉴-2013
中国农村统计年鉴-2013
中国教育经费统计年鉴-2013
中国科学技术协会统计年鉴-2013
中国住户调查年鉴-2013
中国县域统计年鉴-2013
中国人才资源统计报告-2011
中国民族统计年鉴-2013

国际统计年鉴-2013
中国区域经济统计年鉴-2013
中国城市统计年鉴-2013
中国工业经济统计年鉴-2013
中国能源统计年鉴-2013
2013中国地区经济监测报告
中国农产品价格调查年鉴-2013
中国农村贫困监测报告-2013
工业企业科技活动资料-2013
中国价格统计年鉴-2013
中国农村全面建设小康监测报告-2013
中国零售和餐饮连锁企业统计年鉴-2013
2010年中国第六次人口普查公报

2013年省级综合统计年鉴系列

北京 天津 河北 山西 内蒙古
河南 湖北 湖南 广东 广西

辽宁 吉林 黑龙江 上海 江苏
海南 重庆 四川 贵州 云南

浙江 安徽 福建 江西 山东
西藏 陕西 甘肃 青海 宁夏
新疆 新疆生产建设兵团

2013年市(县)级综合统计年鉴系列

天津滨海新区
运城 忻州 临汾 呼和浩特 包头
上海浦东新区 南京 苏州 无锡
杭州 宁波 绍兴 台州 温州
厦门经济特区 宁德 南昌 上饶
十堰 荆州 咸宁 长沙 广州

石家庄 唐山 邯郸 太原 大同
通辽 沈阳 大连 长春 吉林市
常州 徐州 南通 盐城 镇江
金华 嘉兴 衢州 舟山
济南 青岛 潍坊 郑州
东莞 惠州 深圳 桂林 南宁
贵阳 昆明 庆阳 西安

长治 阳泉 晋城 朔州 晋中
四平 哈尔滨 黑龙江垦区
宿迁 泰州 连云港 江阴 丹阳
福州 福州经济技术开发区
洛阳 三门峡 南阳 武汉 宜昌
柳州 来宾 河池 海口 成都 绵阳
兰州 银川 乌鲁木齐

2010年人口普查资料系列

中国2010年人口普查资料
浙江 安徽 福建 江西 山东
西藏 陕西 甘肃 青海 宁夏
中国分县2010年人口普查资料

北京 天津 河北 山西 内蒙古
河南 湖北 湖南 广东 广西
新疆 新疆生产建设兵团
中国分乡镇、街道2010年人口普查资料

辽宁 吉林 黑龙江 上海 江苏
海南 重庆 四川 贵州 云南
河南省各市2010年人口普查资料丛书
中国分民族2010年人口普查资料

“十一五”规划教材

统计学（“十二五”规划，黄良文）
统计学（“十二五”规划，单微）
统计学：从数据到结论（十二五规划，吴喜之）
非参数统计（吴喜之）
多元统计分析（任雪松）
经济计量学教程（贺铿）
社会统计学（蒋萍）
国民经济核算教程(杨灿)

抽样调查理论与实践（“十二五”规划，冯士雍）
试验设计（“十二五”规划，茆诗松）
概率论与数理统计（茆诗松）
应用时间序列分析（王振龙）
质量管理统计方法（茆诗松）
市场调查与预测（蒋志华）
概率论与数理统计(经济、管理类专业使用，朱胜）

贝叶斯统计（“十二五”规划，茆诗松）
医学统计学（陆守曾）
现代金融投资统计分析（李腊生）
统计指数理论及应用（徐国祥）
统计实验系列教材（许涤龙）
统计学原理（非统计专业用，朱胜）

重点图书

挑大学选专业2013—高考志愿填报指南
挑大学选专业2013—考研择校指南

中国统计出版社发行部电话：（010）63376907,63376908 同榻行书店电话：68783171,68783172
通讯地址：北京市西城区三里河月坛南街57号 邮政编码：100826
网址：http://csp.stats.gov.cn